Praise for *The Mystery of Existence*

M000304843

"Recent discoveries in cosmology have led to a renewed surge of interest in ultimate questions of existence. What, if anything, came before the big bang? If the universe appeared from nothing in a law-like manner, then where did the laws come from, and why do they have the form that they do? Or is our universe but an infinitesimal fragment of an eternal, infinite sea of diverse laws and universes? This book provides a comprehensive review of attempts to grapple with such foundational questions, and skillfully charts the intersection of science, philosophy and theology. The authors have assembled an intellectual feast for all those who care about physical existence, the universe and our place within it."

Paul Davies, Director, BEYOND Center for Fundamental
Concepts in Science, Arizona State University
Author of *The Goldilocks Enigma: Why the Universe is Just Right for Life*

"This book gathers together some of the best that has been thought and written on what may be the most fundamental question of all: Why does anything exist? Readers won't find a definite answer – perhaps there isn't one that we're capable of understanding – but they will at least get a feel for the nature of the question. And in philosophy, understanding the question is in itself an important step forward."

Martin J. Rees, Astronomer Royal (UK)
Author of *Just Six Numbers: The Deep Forces that Shape the Universe*

"A very useful collection containing many of the most prominent responses to the question why there is something rather than nothing, with helpful introductions by the editors."

Richard Swinburne, University of Oxford
Author of *The Existence of God*

"This book will be an indispensable resource for anyone who wants to think seriously about the questions, 'Why is there something – and not rather nothing?' and 'Why is there *this* something – and not rather some entirely different "something"?'"

Peter van Inwagen, the University of Notre Dame
Author of *Existence: Essays in Ontology*

The Mystery of Existence

Why Is There Anything At All?

Edited by

John Leslie
Robert Lawrence Kuhn

A John Wiley & Sons, Inc., Publication

This edition first published 2013
© 2013 John Wiley & Sons, Inc

Wiley-Blackwell is an imprint of John Wiley & Sons, formed by the merger of Wiley's global Scientific, Technical and Medical business with Blackwell Publishing.

Registered Office
John Wiley & Sons, Ltd, The Atrium, Southern Gate, Chichester, West Sussex, PO19 8SQ, UK

Editorial Offices
350 Main Street, Malden, MA 02148-5020, USA
9600 Garsington Road, Oxford, OX4 2DQ, UK
The Atrium, Southern Gate, Chichester, West Sussex, PO19 8SQ, UK

For details of our global editorial offices, for customer services, and for information about how to apply for permission to reuse the copyright material in this book please see our website at www.wiley.com/wiley-blackwell.

The right of John Leslie and Robert Lawrence Kuhn to be identified as the authors of the editorial material in this work has been asserted in accordance with the UK Copyright, Designs and Patents Act 1988.

Wiley also publishes its books in a variety of electronic formats. Some content that appears in print may not be available in electronic books.

Designations used by companies to distinguish their products are often claimed as trademarks. All brand names and product names used in this book are trade names, service marks, trademarks or registered trademarks of their respective owners. The publisher is not associated with any product or vendor mentioned in this book. This publication is designed to provide accurate and authoritative information in regard to the subject matter covered. It is sold on the understanding that the publisher is not engaged in rendering professional services. If professional advice or other expert assistance is required, the services of a competent professional should be sought.

Library of Congress Cataloging-in-Publication Data applied for

Hardback ISBN: 9780470673546
Paperback ISBN: 9780470673553

A catalogue record for this book is available from the British Library.

Cover image: Space background with blue light © avian/Shutterstock.
Cover design by Cyan Design.

Set in 11/13pt Dante by SPi Publisher Services, Pondicherry, India
Printed in Singapore by Ho Printing Singapore Pte Ltd

1   2013

Contents

About the Editors

John Leslie is University Professor Emeritus of Philosophy at the University of Guelph, Canada, and Fellow of the Royal Society of Canada. Well known in the philosophy of cosmology and religion, he has held visiting professorships at institutions including the Australian National University (Research Department of Philosophy) and the University of Liège (Institute of Astrophysics). He is the author of numerous publications, including *Value and Existence* (Blackwell, 1979), *Universes* (1989), *The End of the World: The Science and Ethics of Human Extinction* (1996), *Infinite Minds* (2001), and *Immortality Defended* (Blackwell, 2007).

Robert Lawrence Kuhn is a public intellectual and the creator and host of *Closer To Truth*, the long-running PBS / public television series on science and philosophy. With a doctorate in brain research (UCLA), he is the author or editor of more than 30 books, including *Closer To Truth: Challenging Current Belief* (2000) and *Closer To Truth: Science, Meaning, and the Future* (2007). A recognized expert on Chinese politics and economics, he is the author of *The Man Who Changed China: The Life and Legacy of Jiang Zemin* (2005), China's best-selling book of 2005, and *How China's Leaders Think* (Wiley, 2011). He is a frequent commentator on the BBC, Bloomberg, CNBC, China Central Television (CCTV), and Euronews.

Acknowledgments

Plans for this volume were formed during filming for Episode 305, "Why Is There Something Rather Than Nothing?", of Robert's *Closer to Truth* TV series. John mentioned that he was obsessed, and had been ever since age seventeen, with the puzzle of why there is a universe instead of utter emptiness. Robert commented that he had his own obsession with this puzzle, beginning at age twelve. Could the two of us join, then, in editing a volume about it? A volume trying to cover all of the many ways in which philosophers, physicists, and theologians had reacted to it?

It was clear that a volume of any reasonable size could reprint only a few examples of the most important ways of reacting. A very extensive set of Suggestions for Further Reading would therefore be needed. For help with compiling these suggestions, and also for ideas about what writings should be reprinted plus a few comments on the Editorial Introductions, we editors are grateful to many people. They include David Buchanan, Paul Davies, Tyron Goldschmidt, Friedrich Hermanni, Larry Hitterdale, Jim Holt, Brian Leftow, Tim Mawson, Don Page, Derek Parfit, John Roberts, Eric Steinhardt, Richard Swinburne, Michael Walsh, and the anonymous referees consulted by Wiley-Blackwell before the volume was commissioned.

Thanks are due as well to many at Wiley-Blackwell including Nick Bellorini, Jeff Dean, Jen Bray, and Janet Moth for their enthusiasm and professionalism. Also to Jill Leslie and Dora Serviarian-Kuhn for constant support.

1

General Introduction

Why Any World At All?

Why does there exist *anything*? Why a world with its stars, its planets, its humans, its atoms – why these or any other such items? Why couldn't they all vanish, one after another, and why have there ever been any of them instead of utter emptiness? The puzzle can make our minds dizzy, can fill us with awe. Suppose, for example, that God explains everything else. Could God be *self-explaining*? And if God could be self-explaining then why not the entire cosmos, the sum total of all existing things? Might the cosmos be self-explaining, self-creating, completely inevitably and for reasons that quantum theory has revealed, as some physicists now suggest? Or could it "just exist" for no reason whatever? Would reasonless existence be no mystery, or less of a mystery, if there always had existed at least one thing, throughout infinite time?

Such questions interact with ones about what the world is really like. Might it consist of many huge regions each worth calling "a universe"? Perhaps it might, for many physicists offer to explain why many such regions could have come to exist. Again, people have argued that we, together with all the other things in what we call "our universe," could be patterns of activity inside one of the gigantic computers that a technologically advanced civilization might be expected to use for "simulating" universes. Well, might it be better to picture our universe in the way suggested by Hindu and Islamic writings, as a structure or pattern of activity inside an infinite divine being? Might existence inside such a being be easier to explain than existence outside it? Or would even the gigantic computer be a reality more plausible than any infinite being? Many atheists have argued that *being infinite* would make a divine being *infinitely implausible*.

The Mystery of Existence: Why Is There Anything At All?, First Edition. Edited by
John Leslie and Robert Lawrence Kuhn.
© 2013 John Wiley & Sons, Inc. Published 2013 by John Wiley & Sons, Inc.

A volume about these matters might feature as few as a dozen writings by ancient authors, or else by contemporary writers discussing medieval ideas, or by philosophers with newly coined ideas, or by religious leaders, theologians, or physicists. The present volume instead reprints some fifty authors from Plato onwards. They were chosen not because they fitted any particular label such as "philosopher" or "physicist," but because they discuss "*Why the World?*" intriguingly. Not all of them think it a sensible question. Several insist that the sole possible answer is "That's just how matters are – the world exists, and that's that."

It could seem that no other answer would make sense. For a start, it is hard to see how a thing could be self-explaining. Couldn't this be like lifting yourself by tugging on your own hair? So when trying to explain any one thing, aren't we forced to point to another that we think explains it, and doesn't this mean we could never explain why there hadn't been an absence, always, of all things? Sure enough, some realities can be called too abstract to be *things*. It can be a reality that there are at least two people in a room, and another slightly less abstract reality that between sixty and seventy people are crammed into it. These two realities are not *things* unless in the very wide sense that makes even round squares and married bachelors into "*things* we can discuss," but don't they depend on the existence of the room and the people? Realities like those might explain various affairs – the reason, for instance, why John left the room is that it was so crowded – but not why there exists even a single thing. And what realities could there possibly be except ones which were *either* existing things *or else* abstractions which depended on existing things for their reality?

Well, the right answer to that last question might be that all sorts of realities, infinitely many realities, are not existing things or dependent on existing things – the reality, for instance, that two and two make four. Absolute Nothingness, the absence not just of existing things but of absolutely all realities, could be absolutely impossible. And if so, then one or more of the realities that made it impossible could perhaps explain the world of existing things.

What might any world-explaining realities be? We need to look hard at whether Absolute Nothingness truly is impossible, and if so, then at just what makes it impossible.

Why Not Absolute Nothingness?

Like infinitely many other mathematical affairs, the fact that two and two make four could surely be called something *real*, but must it therefore *exist*? Couldn't it be an eternal reality, showing that Absolute Nothingness will forever be impossible, while not being an existent of any sort?

You might use those words the other way round. You might say that two and two making four "*exists*, yet isn't anything *real*." [Sherlock Holmes: "My dear

Watson, you see everything that I see, but you *observe* nothing." Why not instead "You observe everything that I observe, but you *see* nothing"? It's the distinction that is important, not the language!] Let us just agree that there seem to be many facts, for instance the fact about two and two, which in no way depend on anything existing in the way that stars, planets, and humans do. The reality of such facts – or, if that's your preferred word, their "existence," or their "subsistence" as some prefer to say – could be in some need of explanation. Believe it or not, a truly firm proof of Two And Two Make Four can fill several pages. Nevertheless, two and two making four may quickly convince you that Absolute Nothingness is impossible. If all *things* were absent, would Two And Two Make Four be *a non-reality*, remaining like that until at least four things had come to exist? Presumably the answer must be No.

Again, in the absence of all existing things – *a blank*, let us call it – might it not be *a fortunate reality* that a cosmos consisting only of people in agony *didn't* exist? And couldn't it be a pity, *an unfortunate reality*, that the blank hadn't been replaced by a good cosmos?

In the blank, wouldn't it at least be a reality that there might have existed a cosmos instead, since this would have involved no logical absurdity? It can seem clear enough that our cosmos couldn't have existed unless it had *first* been real that no absurdity was involved. Not first through being earlier in time, but first as a prerequisite, and as a prerequisite which wouldn't have depended on the actual existence of any thing or things – on the actual existence of experts on Logic, for instance. What is more, there are presumably countless distinct ways in which, instead of our cosmos, there could have been a different one that wasn't logically absurd – as absurd as a round square, a husband without a wife, a lion with three heads but only two heads. Now, this appears to give us a very crowded field of realities. Ways of being a cosmos that are available logically – ways not condemned to unavailability of the kind to which being a round square is condemned – presumably form vastly many distinct realities, none of them depending on the actual existence of any thing or group of things. Simply having no properties that conflict with their other properties seems enough to make these cases of *what's logically possible* into items that are *real*, even if not in quite the way in which stars, planets, and humans are real.

People would sometimes reject some of those points. They are philosophical points, and in philosophy conclusive arguments are very rare. What strike some people as ridiculous positions are fully defensible in the eyes of other people. Trying to base all facts on existing things, one very clever philosopher wrote that all facts about the past, such as that Napoleon reached Moscow, are facts only about what we call memories, records, and traces. Other philosophers of equal brainpower have reasoned that Einstein must certainly have been right in believing (as he emphasized when writing to the relatives of his dead friend Michele Besso) that the dead are not absent from the cosmos. Einstein's cosmos has what he described as "a four-dimensional existence." The dead do not live in the cosmos *of today*, but the cosmos that we of today call "the cosmos of today" is only a slice of Einstein's four-dimensionally existing whole, just as what you yourself call "here" is only the region of the world that is near you. In agreeing with Einstein, the philosophers reason that if past events weren't in existence "back there along the fourth dimension" there would be *no facts* about them. Most folk, however, would say that if the entire cosmos vanished – "cosmos" meaning the sum total, four-dimensional or otherwise, of all existing things, so that absolutely nothing existed to show that things had once been there – then it would still be a fact that Napoleon had reached Moscow and that they themselves had existed. They reject the idea that every fact, every reality, must depend on some existing thing or group of things.

It may, though, come as a surprise that Time of one type might be real when no cosmos existed, Time of a kind that flowed because of *the mere possibility of alterations*, the sheer fact that changes might in theory be taking place. Time of that type could be important when a physicist suggested that universes "quantum-fluctuate" into existence out of nothing, then picturing the "nothing" as obeying laws of quantum physics that make things spring into being by chance and from time to time. Could such Time indeed be real? Imagine a cosmos initially composed of many billion motionless particles and nothing else. It is changeless except that the particles start fading away at random moments. The period that each takes to fade away is brief compared with the "half-life" of the particles, the period it is most likely to take for half of them to have faded away. The particles are at first so numerous that many thousand are fading at any one moment. Eventually, however, so few remain that there are short periods, and then longer periods, during which no particles are fading. Short and longer stretches of time, that is to say, during which nothing alters. Time that really passes because changes really could be happening. Time of that variety could continue to flow even after all the particles had vanished, for the coming to exist of new particles, one after another, would at least be logically possible, unlike the arrival of more and more round squares. It would be a species of Time in which even a four-dimensionally existing cosmos – a sum total of all existing things, with a time dimension and clocks which measured distances along that dimension – might suddenly come into existence.

In short, it does seem that not every reality depends on the existence of things. When we try to explain why there is a cosmos, it is something to bear in mind. Existing things might be born not from absolutely nothing but from "nearly nothing" – from one or more factors abstract enough to be beyond all existing things. From Time of a sort that did not itself depend on the existence of things; from laws of quantum physics that managed to be real beyond all actual events; from the sheer need for a good cosmos to exist, which is what Plato thought; from some other abstract requirement that made the existence of the cosmos as a whole, or of a divine being in particular, into something that was absolutely necessary; from the mathematical fact of there being *only one possible way* of there existing nothing, *infinitely many possible ways* of there existing something. And so on.

A Genuine Problem?

"Even if there were nothing, you'd still be complaining!" – It's a joke, attributed to a philosopher reacting to the alleged puzzle of existence. Yet what is the actual point of the joke? Is the philosopher laughing at Leibniz's idea that the absence of all existing things would have been "simpler and easier"? [Simpler for sure, and maybe easier since the situation would then have contained no item whose creation might have been difficult.] Or was the point of the joke that something has to exist – *your own self, for a start* – for you to be able to "complain" about anything, to wonder why, and that this makes it silly to ask why the cosmos isn't empty of all things? That point could be an interesting mistake. If a nuclear bomb had exploded near your parents when they met for the first time, you'd have every cause to wonder *why you existed* so as to be able to wonder why about anything.

Trying to imagine a blank – defined, remember, as an absence of all existing things – would you succeed only in imagining yourself looking at empty space? The right reaction to this might be *"Yes; but so what?"*. It wouldn't at once prove that a blank would be logically impossible – that like a spherical cube or a bachelor with seven wives it would contain a contradiction. Still, clever people have argued that it would in fact contain one. The idea of any situation, some folk declare, assumes that there somewhere exists some conscious experience of that situation, or some act of thinking about it. This shows, they say, that there cannot fail to be at least one mind or at least one case of free-floating consciousness. Other folk say "at least one thing," claiming that thing-hood is so fundamental to reality that things could not vanish one by one until at last there *really was* a situation empty of all things. Might they be right? It would have strange implications for cosmology. Cosmologists sometimes think that the cosmos contains many completely independent universes, and that each came to exist in a chance-governed way. There is no conflict with mass-energy conservation, they maintain, because the gravitational energy that holds each universe together must be counted as *negative energy* which balances all the energy tied up in the universe's material particles. Having quantum-fluctuated into existence, each universe might at any moment vanish, much as in the case of the particles that are for ever fluctuating into existence and vanishing throughout what we call "empty space." If, however, the absence of all existing things would be an actual contradiction, then at least one of those universes would have to continue to exist! Yet how would any last remaining universe know it no longer had a right to vanish? How could its physics suddenly have changed? It can certainly seem that the vanishing of even a very last atom would involve no contradiction, and that therefore the existence of the cosmos could present a puzzle.

Could we argue, though, that we ought to be puzzled only by matters that are in conflict with past experience? Obviously we have never experienced an absence of all things.

Some people have given precisely that argument. A variant is that the world's existence must be "natural" because, after all, that is what we find in Nature. And a popular theme among philosophers of recent times, and among many scientists as well, is that things can be explained only by earlier things plus the laws of nature governing how each existing group of things leads to the next. When this is challenged, its supporters ask in disgust whether we should instead explain things by pointing to *fictions*: to imps and dragons, for example. But remember, pointing to affairs which aren't fictions might not mean pointing to any existing thing or group of things. It looks altogether questionable to assume that realities, if they are not themselves existing things, must at least be somehow dependent on existing things and hence Couldn't possibly explain why there isn't a blank. For how about *abstract facts* of various types, such as the fact that a blank can be a blank in only one way whereas there are infinitely many possible ways of being a cosmos, and how about *requirements* based on the natures of various possible things, and how about *physical laws* that made emptiness somehow impossible or at least "unstable"? All of these might be items that did not owe their reality to any existing thing, and that might perhaps have acted as Explainers. Admittedly, things never come with labels saying "Needs explanation." We lack evidence against the idea, even, that for an infinitely long period there was a blank, and then a cosmos started to exist for no reason at all. But it is today widely recognized that we cannot begin to make sense of the world – to experience it as more than buzzing confusion – unless we use principles whose correctness cannot be shown by any evidence. Without such principles, nothing could even look like evidence. The whole idea of one fact as evidence of another would be meaningless. Now, one such principle could be that existing things always need to be accounted for. Or at least, that we shouldn't quickly give up on trying to account for them.

Ways of Explaining Existence

Attempts to answer *"Why Existence?"* overlap in many intricate ways. They strongly resist being forced into tidy little boxes. We editors have provided boxes of a sort, grouping various writers into separate sections. Every section has a heading – *Chance*, for example – that tries to give some rough idea of what will be found in it. At the start of each section, one or two sentences try to make that rough idea just a little less rough. Yet the process of picking the correct section for a particular writer was often little better than tossing a coin, so please attach no great importance to the section headings.

In this General Introduction there is no room for summarizing the contents of the various sections. You might, though, like to hear something about some of the arguments scattered through the volume. Here, for a start, is one way of trying to make existence unproblematic. Simply deny the distinction between *being a mere logical possibility*, something involving no contradiction, and *existing in point of fact*. The suggestion is that every single logical possibility exists somewhere. There are infinitely many separately existing "worlds," all equally real. If a thing's existence is logically possible then it exists in at least one of the worlds. This theory, known as Modal Realism, was developed by David Lewis, perhaps the most formidably intelligent philosopher of recent times.

Modal Realism could be judged a particularly grotesque product of the idea that there are no facts without existing things – that only existing things can be "truthmakers." The existence of unicorns is said to be logically possible; can that really be true? "Indeed it can," may come the reply, "yet only because there are, *as truthmakers for it*, all the worlds where unicorns exist." Still, advocates of Modal Realism are not forced to talk of truthmaking. A more attractive way of presenting their position could be as follows. The distinction between *really being possible* and *really existing* can be surprisingly hard to make. Now, if all logically possible things really exist somewhere then there is no need to make it – except, that is, by saying that many of the things fail to exist in *our* world. "What, no unicorns?" is then like "What, no beer?" – meaning that there is none in the house.

In addition, the real existence of all logically possible worlds, though it could seem a fantastically complex situation, would be in a way simplest and least arbitrary. It could be very simply described, in very few words. ["The real existence of all logically possible worlds" is eight words only.] It would avoid such questions as "Why only one world?" or "Why exactly forty-two?".

All the same, Modal Realism has few supporters. More widespread is this theory: that the existence of the cosmos is no problem because it has been a fact for infinitely many years. True, our universe can appear to have started off in a Big Bang about 13.7 billion years ago. Yet maybe the cosmos contains countless Big Bang universes and has never been empty throughout past eternity. Or maybe the Bang only reversed an earlier Big Crunch that was preceded by another Bang, and so on backwards forever. The idea that each situation was preceded by an earlier situation, in an infinite chain, is occasionally viewed as *providing an explanation* for the chain as a whole. Each situation is explained by the one before, so the chain in its entirety is explained! Often, though, people think that's nonsense, and that they can do better. To their way of thinking, the fact that each link in the chain has its explanation in the link that preceded it *removes all need to explain* the chain as a whole: "The infinite chain is simply there, and that is all" strikes them as an adequate answer to why the cosmos exists. Among those who accept this answer, however, a few think that it is adequate only because thoughts or conscious experiences are cosmically fundamental. The eternal existence of Mind or of Consciousness seems to them less of a problem than the eternal existence of protons and electrons.

Occasionally, wanting to avoid an endless regress of situations explained by earlier situations, people have made a *finite* chain go round and join up with itself. It involves a circular kind of Time, but this perhaps isn't absurd. Yet could there truly be *an explanation* here? Imagine a time machine which nobody invented. It existed in the year 2012 because it had remained in existence since the year 1950. And why did it exist in the year 1950? Answer: It had traveled back from the year 2012. A preposterous answer, we might well feel, no matter how we felt about time machines.

An eternal chain might feature a law that material particles, hydrogen atoms for example, come into existence entirely reasonlessly, at an extremely slow rate. This could look quite as sensible as having everything spring into existence in a Big Bang. But some physicists urge us to see a Bang as particularly unproblematic. They say there was no Time before it, this making it wrong to seek earlier events by which it could be explained.

Alternatively, any need to explain might perhaps be reduced or removed by making everything start off featureless or almost featureless, perhaps as a "dust" of mere points. One philosophical theory makes the original featureless situation into an utterly simple Ocean of Being, *infinite* in the strong sense of having no limitations whatever. Some of it then splits off to form a cosmos which, even if infinitely large, is limited in all sorts of ways. But sometimes it is suggested that words like "infinite," "featureless," "Being" themselves do too much to limit the ultimate source of everything. Sometimes this starting point, this Ultimate Beyond, is called "God."

Then there is belief in God in any of several other forms. Some have argued that God is a Person whose perfection includes the property of *existing*, which means God must exist. A currently more fashionable idea is that God's perfection is crowned by the property of *existing necessarily*. The necessity is sometimes viewed as *logical*: a situation without God would be somehow self-contradictory, even though every proof of God that human logicians could construct would have at least one controversial premise. At other times the talk is of a requirement not of Logic but of Value, *a need* for God to exist – a ground or reason for God to exist, lying in the infinite worth of any situation that included God. Whether this was responsible for God's existence might be utterly unknowable. If, however, it was responsible, then God could never have failed to exist. The contents of God's mind being supremely wonderful in a way that God could eternally experience and enjoy, the need for God's existence would be eternal. Aristotle apparently thought this was why God always had existed and always would exist, and people have thought it ever since.

There might be an interesting alternative. God, instead of being an existing thing, a divine mind, a Supreme Being, could be the Principle suggested by Plato, that the sheer need for a good cosmos can exert creative power without the aid of anybody or anything. Would this truly be *an alternative*, though? Couldn't it take us straight back to belief in *God as a Being*? For the very first thing the Platonic Principle generated might be God as a Being, a Being ruling supreme over any other things that the Principle generated. Note that the Being might be thought to have created all other things, or else all so-called other things could be pictured as numerous pantheists picture them, as elements in the Being's own existence. In Islamic thought it is standard to view Allah as containing all lesser things.

Then again, God might perhaps be Pure Being, the mysteriously simple unity described by Aquinas in which God's goodness *just is* God's knowledge, which *just is* God's power, which *just is* God Himself. [Aquinas believed that this made God's reality absolutely inevitable, but that humans could not prove it.] Or possibly God's infinitude would make God's existence more plausible even though it remained a brute fact, totally without an explanation. For God's infinitude, some have argued, would make God's existence simple, and therefore easy to believe in, since infinitude is particularly easy to describe. [What, for instance, does God know? Short and simple answer: All the infinitely many facts that are knowable.] Or finally there is this. God might be easier to believe in because nothing outside God could possibly have created God, or could have stood the slightest chance of preventing God's existence.

Once God had been reached, any things that existed outside God might be readily explained.

In this edited volume you will find details of such answers to why there isn't a blank. There are more answers out there in the world's libraries, in the spoken words of mystics, in vague ideas running through the heads of all the millions who find the world's existence puzzling. Focusing on various answers that seem to us outstandingly interesting, we editors might never have heard of others which we could have found equally intriguing – for the field is enormous. Probing it to any great depth would have required several fat volumes. Even with only fifty or so authors to be reprinted, it has been necessary to cut many words which were not central to their arguments. In several instances reprinting hundreds more words would in any case only have made the waters muddier. Hegel provides a prime example. Hegel struggled to express ideas so difficult that he never claimed to have understood them fully. In the volume he is represented by mere snippets – but snippets that people knowing little about Kant, his predecessor, might hope to understand.

The volume's Suggestions for Further Reading are extremely wide-ranging. Although you can sometimes guess what various authors discuss when you see the titles they gave to their articles and books, the survey article "Why Not Nothing?", reprinted near the end of the volume, will give you further guidance. It introduces numerous writings, many of them recent. Thanks largely to the physicists, the topic is starting to attract much new attention.

Why Ask Why?

The right answer to *"Why Existence?"* could be that things exist for no reason whatever. After all, a situation containing one or more things must have been every bit as possible as a situation empty of all things, and Logic required that either the one situation or the other would be real, these being the sole alternatives. Hence there can be no entirely clear need for any factor that selected what there would be, a non-empty world or an empty one. Even if selected by nobody and nothing, one of the alternatives would be the winner.

All the same, there could be some factor that made the world non-empty. While we may perhaps have little chance of finding it, searching for it could be worthwhile. It might show something very sad about the human race if none of its members could be bothered with this. And although science can discover a great deal about the world without answering why it is there at all, most of us have some preferred answer and can reasonably let it influence our ideas about what science has discovered. It can be schizoid thinking, "doublethink" as in George Orwell's *Nineteen Eighty-Four*, to imagine that a preference for such and such an answer *hasn't* influenced your own ideas about what the world is like. Here are just a few examples of how they could be influenced:

(a)   If you think some physical mechanism brought our universe into existence, then you could well conclude that the cosmos contains infinitely many universes which came to exist through that same mechanism. It could be odd to think the mechanism operated only once, or only thirty million times.

(b)   If thinking that everything "just exists," you are unlikely to accept that we have immortal souls and that there is such a place as Heaven. And if you instead think that our universe was created by God then, whether or not you have hopes of a heavenly afterlife, this may well affect whether you believe that some situations *are really better than others* in basically the same way as Africa is really larger than India. You will be virtually certain to believe it, even if rejecting the idea that God's arbitrary choice made some situations really better. Of course atheists, too, do very frequently believe it. When, though, they are professional philosophers, crowds of them *don't*. They instead teach that when you call situations of one type better than those of another type, you are just issuing to everybody, yourself included, instructions to favor those situations, and that calling those instructions better than other possible instructions is issuing yet another instruction, an instruction to follow the instructions.

(c)   How about Plato's suggestion that the cosmos exists *simply because this is good*? Influential for well over two thousand years, the suggestion still has its defenders today among theologians and philosophers. [Of us two editors, one finds it remarkably attractive: in this volume, see the section "Value/Perfection as Ultimate."] If accepting the suggestion, you might theorize that Reality consists of infinitely many minds each fully aware of everything worth knowing or experiencing; for wouldn't this be *best*? The patterns of infinitely many universes could be among the things experienced. They could exist in the experiences of them and nowhere else. Now, it might be impossible for us to refute this startling world-picture. It might be as much immune to evidence as the theory that our universe is simply a pattern inside a gigantic computer, very expertly programmed by members of an advanced civilization. But if requirements of Value Couldn't possibly explain the existence of anything, then the chance that the world-picture was right would presumably have to be called zero or almost zero. Some world-pictures can be outrageously weird until placed against the background of *"Why Does Any World Exist?"*.

(d)   Treatments of Fine-Tuning can reasonably be influenced by ideas about why there is a cosmos. Physicists are now often convinced that our universe is "fine-tuned for life" in the following sense: that very minor changes to its physics – for instance to the strength of forces such as electromagnetism and gravity – would have made it a lifeless universe. This was at first resisted by many physicists. Seeing a divine Fine-Tuner as the sole possible explanation of the alleged tuning, they treated it as illusory. But it subsequently became clear that plausible physical mechanisms could generate many huge cosmic regions, "universes" largely or entirely separate from one another, which differed in their physics. The strength of electromagnetism, the mass difference between the proton and the neutron, whether there were even any particles recognizable as protons and neutrons, and numerous other factors *might vary* from universe to universe. It could then be likely that at least a few universes would have life-permitting properties. Obviously living beings would find themselves only in such universes. Problem Solved, without bringing in God? Perhaps yes, if the number of variations was sufficiently high.

String Theory, now our main hope for a Final Theory or "Theory of Everything," at first seemed to predict only about a million variations. Leonard Susskind (a leading string theorist) judged this far from sufficient for explaining the fine-tuning of even just one factor, the one called "the cosmological constant," for this appears to have needed tuning with awe-inspiring accuracy, equivalent to throwing a dart to hit a microscopically tiny target positioned at the far edge of the observable universe. Yet it was later found that the true number of variations predicted by String Theory could be ten followed by four hundred and ninety-nine zeros. When universes existed in that gigantic number of varieties, this could render it probable that a universe or two would be life-permitting.

The disappointing side to any solution along those lines was that it would mean abandoning the search for the Holy Grail of physics, the ability to derive everything from fundamental theoretical principles. Force strengths, particle masses, the cosmological constant, etcetera would not be predicted by the Final Theory. They would instead be like the mass of our planet, the atmospheric pressure at its surface, the strength of its magnetic field. But it would now be reasonable for atheists to accept Fine-Tuning as a reality.

However, what about the physicists who believe that God created all other things? Well, they also could accept the existence of multiple universes. But they might picture God as choosing physical principles that made all of the universes life-permitting. They could therefore retain high hopes of finding the Grail.

2

Some Quotations

Here is how some famous figures have reacted to the fact that there's anything in existence:

"[N]othing takes place without sufficient reason, that is, [...] nothing happens without it being possible for someone who knows enough things to give a reason sufficient to determine why it is so and not otherwise. Assuming this principle, the first question we have the right to ask will be, *why is there something rather than nothing?* For nothing is simpler and easier than something. Furthermore, assuming that things must exist, we must be able to give a reason for *why they must exist in this way*, and not otherwise."

G.W. Leibniz, in section 7 of *Principles of Nature and Grace*, from G. W. Leibniz, *Philosophical Essays*, trans. R. Ariew and D. Garber (Indianapolis: Hackett Publishing, 1989)

"Unconditioned necessity, which we so indispensably require as the last bearer of all things, is for human reason the veritable abyss. Eternity itself, in all its terrible sublimity, as depicted by a Haller, is far from making the same overwhelming impression on the mind; for it only *measures* the duration of things, it does not *support* them. We cannot put aside, and yet also cannot endure the thought, that a being, which we represent to ourselves as supreme amongst all possible beings, should, as it were, says to itself: 'I am from eternity to eternity, and outside me there is nothing save what is through my will, *but whence then am I?*'"

Immanuel Kant, at A613 of *Critique of Pure Reason*, trans. Norman Kemp Smith (London: Macmillan, 1933)

The Mystery of Existence: Why Is There Anything At All?, First Edition. Edited by John Leslie and Robert Lawrence Kuhn.
© 2013 John Wiley & Sons, Inc. Published 2013 by John Wiley & Sons, Inc.

"Only to the brutes, who are without thought, does the world and existence appear as a matter of course; to man, on the contrary, it is a problem, of which even the most uneducated and narrow-minded becomes vividly conscious in certain brighter moments […] In fact, the pendulum which keeps in motion the clock of metaphysics, that never runs down, is the consciousness that the non-existence of this world is just as possible as its existence."

> Arthur Schopenhauer, in volume 3, chapter 17 of *The World as Will and Idea*,
> trans. R.B. Haldane and J. Kemp (London: Routledge & Kegan Paul, 1883)

"How comes the world to be here at all instead of the nonentity which might be imagined in its place? […] One need only shut oneself in a closet and begin to think of the fact of one's being there, of one's queer bodily shape in the darkness (a thing to make children scream at, as Stevenson says), of one's fantastic character and all, to have the wonder steal over the detail as much as over the general fact of being, and to see that it is only familiarity that blunts it. Not only that *anything* should be, but that *this* very thing should be, is mysterious! Philosophy stares, but brings no reasoned solution, for from nothing to being there is no logical bridge. […] All of us are beggars here, and no school can speak disdainfully of another or give itself superior airs."

> William James, from chapter 3 of *Some Problems of Philosophy*
> (New York: Longmans, Green & Co., 1911)

"Existence is […] odious to the logician. To him it seems a truly monstrous excrescence and superfluity in being, since anything existent is more than the description of it, having suffered an unintelligible emphasis or materialisation to fall upon it, which is logically inane and morally comic."

> George Santayana, in chapter 7 of *Scepticism and Animal Faith*
> (New York: Dover Publications, 1923)

"It is nonsense to say that I wonder at the existence of the world, because I cannot imagine it not existing."

> Ludwig Wittgenstein, "Lecture on Ethics," delivered at Cambridge in
> 1929 or 1930

"I should say that the universe is just there, and that is all."

> Bertrand Russell, during the Russell–Copleston debate, BBC Radio,
> January 28, 1948

"That anything should exist at all does seem to me a matter for the deepest awe."

> J.J.C. Smart, in "The Existence of God," a lecture delivered in Adelaide in 1951

"I ask myself: How come the quantum? How come the universe? How come existence?"

John A. Wheeler, in chapter 12 of *Geons, Black Holes and Quantum Foam*
(New York: W.W. Norton, 1998)

"What it is that breathes fire into the equations and makes a universe for them to govern? Although science may solve the problem of how the universe began, it cannot answer the question: Why does the universe bother to exist?"

Stephen Hawking, in chapter 9 of *Black Holes and Baby Universes*
(New York: Bantam Books, 1993)

"Whatever our final theory of physics, we will be left facing an irreducible mystery. For perhaps there could have been nothing at all. Not even empty space, but just absolutely nothing [...] If you believe God is the creator, well, why is God that way? The religious person is left with a mystery which is no less than the mystery with which science leaves us."

Steven Weinberg, in *Closer to Truth: Cosmos, Consciousness, God* (PBS/Public television episodes "Why is there Something Rather than Nothing?" and "Arguing God's Existence," first broadcast 2008 and 2009)

3

Possible Responses to "Why Anything?"*

Here are various ways of reacting to the mystery of existence, tidily classified by one of America's most influential philosophers:

NICHOLAS RESCHER

An inventory of possible responses to the question: "Why is there anything at all?"

I. The question is illegitimate and improper. [*Rejectionism*]
II. The question is legitimate
    (1) but unanswerable: it represents a *mystery*. [*Mystificationism*]
    (2) and answerable
        (a) though only by the *via negativa* of an insistence that there really is no "answer" in the ordinary sense—no sort of explanatory rationale at all. The existence of things in the world is simply a brute fact. [The *no-reason* approach.]
        (b) via a *substantival* route of roughly the following sort: "There is a substance [viz. God] whose position in the scheme of things is one that lies outside the world, and whose activity explains the existence of things in the world." [The *theological* approach.]

* From chapter 1 of *The Riddle of Existence* (Lanham, MD, and London: University Press of America, 1984). Reprinted with permission of University Press of America, a member of the Rowman & Littlefield Publishing Group.

The Mystery of Existence: Why Is There Anything At All?, First Edition. Edited by John Leslie and Robert Lawrence Kuhn.
© 2013 John Wiley & Sons, Inc. Published 2013 by John Wiley & Sons, Inc.

(c) via a *nonsubstantival* route of roughly the following sort: "There is a principle of creativity that obtains *in abstracto* (i.e., without being embedded in the characteristics of any substance and thus without a basis in any preexisting thing), and the operation of this principle accounts for the existence of things." [The *nomological* approach.]

(d) via the quasi-logical route of considerations of absolute necessity. [The *necessitarian* approach.]

4

First Solution
A Blank is Absurd

Editorial Introduction

Did there have to exist *at least one thing*, even if no specific thing, not even God, had the property of existing necessarily? Or could it be that all conceivable things exist? Might the existence of all of them be unavoidable, so that each existed somewhere even if not in our universe, perhaps because *being genuinely conceivable* cannot be truly different from *existing in point of fact*? Or if not unavoidable, might it at least be an outstandingly simple state of affairs, this supplying good grounds for believing in it? Or again, might the existence of the cosmos have been forced in a way that physicists are now starting to understand? Forced, perhaps, so firmly that utter emptiness would be seen as an absurdity if we knew enough physics?

An infinitely large field of logical possibilities could seem bound to be real – real in a way that not even divine power could have prevented. That's because, on a view fairly standard nowadays, being logically possible means nothing more dramatic than *not being self-contradictory* like a spherical cube or a vegetarian cannibal. In contrast, our world's galaxies, its mountains, its humans, items with a reality that is "concrete" instead of "abstract," all look as if they hadn't been inevitable. The absence of all humans can appear easy to imagine. Similarly with the absence of the cosmos in its entirety – of every single existing thing, including any divine being.

Unfortunately, asking what we can or cannot "imagine" may not settle anything. A mathematician might imagine discovering a highest prime number. Would this prove there really was a highest prime number? Of course not. Ludwig Wittgenstein couldn't imagine the nonexistence of the world, he said. Did this give him a right

The Mystery of Existence: Why Is There Anything At All?, First Edition. Edited by John Leslie and Robert Lawrence Kuhn.
© 2013 John Wiley & Sons, Inc. Published 2013 by John Wiley & Sons, Inc.

to the conclusion he drew, that wondering why the world exists "is nonsense"? Not unless he could give some argument showing that the world's nonexistence would be a contradiction. Yet he offered no such argument.

Others have attempted to do better. The affair can quickly get difficult. Even making the distinction between being a mere logical possibility (something "abstract") and existing in actual fact ("concretely") can be surprisingly tricky. Also, what can look logically possible to most of us might not look the same way to the physicists. As we'll see, Stephen Hawking may go so far as to think that Logic forces the existence of our universe.

Our reprinted material begins with a passage from Francis Herbert BRADLEY, who once ruled supreme in British philosophy. Much influenced by Hegel, he admired the Hegelian idea that conflicting theories often need to be fused "dialectically" for us to understand the world. Ultimate Reality ("the Absolute") could only be glimpsed, but we could at least know, Bradley argued, that it was a single, fully unified existent, and that it was mental through and through. Everything real had the nature of Thought. The reprinted material shows him reaching what he sees as the obvious conclusion. Nothingness would not be an instance of thought, and therefore it could never be real. There could not have failed to be a world.

It might be unfair to reject this without bothering to study Bradley's philosophical system. However, that system has few supporters nowadays. In most quarters, Bradley's proof of the world's necessity would be called even weaker than Wittgenstein's.

Henri BERGSON tells us there could never be an absence of all things. The absence of one thing is always, he writes, the presence of another thing instead. But where does he give us any supporting argument? And would he seriously say that if (as cosmologists sometimes suggest) there exist many universes entirely disconnected from one another, and all are mere "quantum fluctuations" so that each at every moment has some slight chance of vanishing, then the vanishing of all but one universe would suddenly mean that this last remaining universe could not vanish? Bergson can seem to show only that his own mind refuses to stop thinking about one thing after another.

Bede RUNDLE tries to improve on this. Could things vanish one by one until there remained nothing whatever? Rundle cannot understand such a suggestion. In trying to conceive the remaining nothingness, don't we succeed only in picturing a space that has been emptied? Yet such a space would itself be an existing something, wouldn't it? Even if no particular thing were blessed with necessary existence, couldn't it still be necessary that something or other existed? The words "There might have been nothing" do not describe anything at all, Rundle protests, so how on earth could they express a truth?

More support for There Must Exist Something comes from David LEWIS, famous for his "Modal Realist" theory that all logically possible things exist somewhere. Just so long, he has written, as they can be described without self-contradiction, all the Greek gods – Zeus for instance – do really exist, but of course not locally; they cannot be found in our world. Instead they inhabit other worlds. There are infinitely many worlds, each fully isolated from the rest. Try imagining a world of absolutely any kind. If it contains no wifeless husbands or other actual contradictions, then the world that you've imagined is no mere fiction. All of its things are genuinely existing things.

Why ever should we accept this? Look again at Rundle's central notion that "There might have been nothing" fails to describe anything *that could make it true.* Why not tell Rundle that there certainly is something to make it true, namely, the possible absence of all existing things? Well the trouble is that, for many philosophers nowadays, "truthmakers" must always be existing things – not "possible absences." Lewis takes a large step towards that philosophical camp. Refusing to make logical possibilities into useful fictions, or mere truths about consistent language, he instead insists that they must truly *be.* Yet what two varieties of being could they choose between? How could other logically possible worlds differ in their manner of existing from our own world, which of course is itself logically possible instead of impossible? "I do not have the slightest idea," Lewis writes, "what a difference in manner of existing is supposed to be." But this becomes a non-problem if all the infinitely many logical possibilities exist in one and the same fashion.

Lewis gets many incredulous stares. By writing that there are "uncountable infinities of donkeys and protons and puddles and stars, and of planets very like Earth, and of cities very like Melbourne, and of people very like yourself," he has abandoned common sense, as he freely admits. Common sense is simply how people commonly think, and he sees many philosophical advantages in thinking differently, for instance when dealing with events which *really could have happened.* [Would a window really have broken if hit by a brick? He can treat this as asking what *did* happen in a world very like ours, when such a brick actually hit such a window.] And he has escaped any need to say what could be meant by *purely possible existence*: possible existence which isn't, as in the case of our world, a case of real existence *as well.*

Some folk think they detect a fatal flaw. If real existence extends to all logically possible worlds then there exist countless worlds in which people just like us, our counterparts or duplicates, are surrounded by much more chaos than they believe. For example there will be ever so many worlds whose histories, right up to the present moment, are precisely the same as our world's history, but which then develop in utterly disorderly ways. Worlds in which all humans vanish, perhaps, or change into swirling dust, jelly, cabbages, palm trees, elephants. Well, why remain confident that our world won't turn out to be one of those?

Lewis replies that of course there are ever so many ways in which chaos could overwhelm us. In thinking that the future will resemble the past, we run a risk. Sudden chaos is always *possible.* But, he says, *no more likely* on his world-view than on the normal world-view. This, though, has been widely doubted. In trying to get a handle on the distinction between really existing and being purely possible, it can help to say that pure possibilities *don't matter*. Innumerable logically possible beings undergo tortures far more frightful than all tortures ever inflicted in our world. It doesn't matter, does it? Not because we can't do anything about it, but instead because there's nothing awful to do anything about. Those tortured beings are nothing more than possible. They don't suffer real pain – not unless Lewis is right. But if Lewis is right then the tortures really are happening somewhere: indeed, in infinitely many somewheres. Although we couldn't do anything about it, this ought to fill us with horror. It would matter. Now, likewise with suddenly turning into elephants. There's no logically firm guarantee we won't, but the possibility of our doing so doesn't matter, we can tell ourselves, because it will never happen anywhere. The innumerable ways in which Logic would allow it (big elephants? small ones? gray ones? pink?) can be disregarded because, we can tell ourselves, they will none of them be real in any world, let alone in our world. Lewis, however, cannot tell himself this. Instead of just recognizing that our future *conceivably might* be very different from what past experience would lead us to expect, his theory could seem to say that it almost surely will be very different – if not elephantine then cabbage-like or swirling-dust-like or whatever.

The affair is controversial, though. Peter UNGER, for one, thinks Lewis has no problem here. Unger defends "a suitably enormous infinite variety of independent domains, of mutually isolated worlds," a Plenitude in which "every way that a world could possibly be is a way that some world is." Unsure whether to join Lewis in accepting a world for every single consistent set of logical possibilities, affairs involving no actual contradiction, he wants at least "a very liberal conception of possibility" so that the range of worlds will be "enormously abundant." He reasons that this would reduce *the arbitrariness* of Real Existence As A Whole.

Ask yourself why physicists find electromagnetism acting on protons and electrons. Unger can answer that in his Plenitude of all possible worlds there had to be worlds with electromagnetism, protons, electrons, and it's in one such world that you and I, folk in great part made up of protons and electrons interacting electromagnetically, actually find ourselves. Since he pictures the various worlds as totally isolated from one another, he can explain why people typically believe that ours is the sole world in existence. Yet the fact that our world's properties so often look arbitrary – instead of forming a system so tight-knit and elegant that physicists might say it "just had to be right" – can suggest the existence of a greater, simpler whole of which our world is just a complex fragment. If there existed only a single world then the question "Why electromagnetism and protons and electrons?" could need answering. To comment, "The world had to be *somehow*, so why not like this?", might well be thought inadequate. A large fragment of an eggshell, complexly and "arbitrarily" shaped, could suggest the earlier simple, complete eggshell to a visiting extraterrestrial who had never seen eggs, and it's this way of minimizing arbitrariness that Unger has in mind. Yes, he is uncertain whether a blank was flatly impossible. But he certainly thinks that the cosmos would be far too near to being a blank if it contained our world and nothing else. It would include far too little, making it disturbingly arbitrary – or, to put the point in another way, disturbingly *complicated*. Think of how "1, 3, 4, 7, 10" can be considered much more complicated than "1, 2, 3, 4, 5, 6, 7, 8, 9, 10."

Notice an advantage Unger might have over Lewis. Is Lewis in true difficulties through his confidence that we won't turn into elephants or swirling dust? If so, then Unger could avoid the difficulties – for remember, while wanting "a very liberal conception of possibility" he is unsure whether to join Lewis in believing in every single world that involves no actual contradictions. Even if he decided that things like our turning into elephants, although not self-contradictory, *weren't genuinely possible*, his cosmos could be rich enough to be praised for how little arbitrariness it contained.

Stephen HAWKING and Leonard MLODINOW have a very different approach. That the laws of physics "just had to be these ones" can seem a main conclusion to their *The Grand Design* – the other chief conclusion being, so it can seem, that the laws themselves guaranteed the actual existence of a universe. A startling change, we might think, from Hawking's earlier position! Hawking had long defended the idea that our universe must have zero total energy, given the actual laws of physics. There was therefore no need for a deity to *breathe energy into* its earliest moments. But, his view had been, there would be a need for something or other to make those particular laws of physics govern a real world, something to "breathe fire into the equations" expressing the laws instead of into other equations, or instead of leaving an empty situation – a situation in which no equations applied to anything actually in existence. Yet in *The Grand Design* Hawking and Mlodinow could well appear to suggest, first, that the laws of "M-theory" (which they call "the most general supersymmetric theory of gravity," the sole theory of gravity that could "predict finite results for quantities that we can measure") are dictated simply by Logic, and next that these laws themselves generated a universe for them to govern. "Because there is a law like gravity," they say, "the universe can and will create itself from nothing."

Zero total energy is widely accepted by cosmologists. One counts the gravitational energy of the cosmos as *negative*, this allowing it to cancel the positive energy of everything else. Gravitational energy is "binding energy" – it holds things together – and it is standard physics to treat binding energies as negative. This is crucial, for instance, to understanding how our sun burns. But why must there be a law of gravity combined with Conservation of Energy? Because otherwise, Hawking and Mlodinow can seem to say, the universe couldn't create itself from nothing; yet who on earth said that it did? And because there would otherwise be "no reason that bodies could not appear anywhere and everywhere"; yet how could it be Logic that told bodies not to? No mere need to avoid logical contradiction could stop diamonds, pumpkins, and gorillas jumping into existence all over the place! Also, why would the universe in fact create itself from nothing just because the laws of M-theory permitted it? Is it that Everything Not Forbidden Is Compulsory? If so, then what breathed fire into *that*?

It might be, though, that such protests put too much weight on words these authors wrote rather too hurriedly. "Abstract considerations of logic," Hawking and Mlodinow suggest, "lead to a unique theory that predicts and describes a vast universe." They could certainly seem to be suggesting that a blank would be seen as an absurdity of the worst sort, a logical absurdity, if only our powers of reasoning were sufficiently developed. But what they really mean might be no more than this, that perhaps only a single theory could consistently describe any universe at all like ours. Anything marginally different, although it might seem a good candidate for describing our universe, would then in fact be as self-contradictory as an elliptical triangle or a daughter without a parent. Like eggshell china, the theory would shatter if you tried bending it even slightly. Look, too, at the statement that "the universe can and will create itself from nothing." The move from "can" to "and will" might be nothing more than enthusiasm bursting into unfortunate words. The idea could simply be that we need not invoke a deity who breathed fire into mathematical equations. After all, many a philosopher has held that there is no need to explain why there is a universe, not a blank – that this is just how matters happen to be. Hawking and Mlodinow might simply be insisting that, even without a deity "to light the blue touch paper," the origin of our universe can be described without getting into trouble with Conservation of Energy.

Perhaps, though, they are making a more controversial point. Imagine a law stating that nine yellow devils have to exist. If the law applied to Reality then there really would exist nine yellow devils, but why ever should it apply? Logic could not guarantee that it applied, not even when the law itself said that there had to be real devils for it to apply to! The case would be quite unlike that of the "law" that husbands always have wives. However, Hawking and Mlodinow may be imagining physical laws that guaranteed that there would be a universe to which they applied, but *not* through Logic and nothing else. Logic itself would state only that the laws were like eggshell china. The laws would have to be more than just mathematical equations since those couldn't themselves create anything; "they would have to be laws breathing creative fire", we might say. Now, if Hawking and Mlodinow were in fact thinking along those lines then it could be hard to prove them wrong. Just so long as it wasn't a claim about what might be dictated simply by Logic, the suggestion that physical laws were universe-creating might make sense. Note that many people already think that *once a universe existed* its physical laws could "breathe fire", forcing it to evolve in particular ways instead of merely describing its evolution. There might therefore be nothing too odd in the theory that physical laws could *also* force a universe to exist. And this might be exciting even if we saw no answer to *"Why those laws instead of others, and why any laws at all?"*.

Still, one matter looks certain. Scientific collection of evidence could never prove that physical laws created our universe. There never could be evidence distinguishing physical laws which were mere equations describing the structure and evolution of a universe from "fire-breathing" physical laws which had compelled that universe to exist.

The Negative Judgment*

F.H. BRADLEY

The contradictory idea, if we take it in a merely negative form, must be banished from logic. If Not-A were solely the negation of A, it would be an assertion without a quality, and would be a denial without anything positive to serve as its ground. A something that is only not something else, is a relation that terminates in an impalpable void, a reflection thrown upon empty space. It is a mere nonentity which can not be real. And, if such were the sense of the dialectical method (as it must be confessed its detractors have had much cause to suppose), that sense would, strictly speaking, be nonsense. It is impossible for anything to be *only* Not-A. It is impossible to realize Not-A in thought. It is less than nothing, for nothing itself is not wholly negative. Nothing at least is empty thought, and that means at least my thinking emptily. Nothing means nothing else but failure. And failure is impossible unless something fails [...]

Abolition of Everything is Self-Destructive†

HENRI BERGSON

[...][P]art of metaphysics moves, consciously or not, around the question of knowing why anything exists – why matter, or spirit, or God, rather than nothing at all? But the question presupposes that reality fills a void, that underneath Being lies nothingness, that de *jure* there should be nothing, that we must therefore explain why there is *de facto* something. And this presupposition is pure illusion, for the idea of absolute nothingness has not one jot more meaning than a square circle. The absence of one thing being always the presence of another – which we prefer to leave aside because it is not the thing that interests us or the thing we were expecting – suppression is never anything more than substitution, a two-sided operation which we agree to look at from one side only: so that the idea of the abolition of everything is self-destructive, inconceivable; it is a pseudo-idea, a mirage conjured up by our imagination.

---

* From book 1, chapter 3, section 16 of *The Principles of Logic*, 2nd edn., revised (London: Oxford University Press, 1928).

† From chapter 3 of *The Two Sources of Morality and Religion*, trans. from the French by R. Ashley Audra and Cloudesley Brereton (New York: Henry Holt, 1935).

Why There Is Something Rather Than Nothing*

BEDE RUNDLE

[...] [I]t could be that no being can be held to exist of necessity, and yet it was a necessary truth that something existed. [...] We might insist that it is not possible that there should be, or have been, nothing at all; whether animate or inanimate, material or immaterial, there had to be *something*. On the other hand, it may well be that of no particular thing can one say that it is inconceivable that it should not have existed; our galaxy did not have to exist, nor did galaxies quite generally. [...] [G]iven the lack of transparency in the notion of an individual [God] whose existence is logically necessary, or of a being which somehow has its existence through itself, it is prima facie more likely that we could sustain an argument for the claim that there has to be something without having to demonstrate that there is something that has to be.

How might this weaker claim be supported? Our first thought may well be that it, too, is unsustainable: there is an essential contingency about affirmations of existence, both particular and general, which means that there might indeed have been nothing whatsoever. However, I suspect that our attempts at conceiving of total non-existence are irredeemably partial. We are always left with something, if only a setting from which we envisage everything having departed, a void which we confront and find empty, but something which it makes sense to speak of as having once been home to bodies, radiation, or whatever.

'There might have been nothing" need not, of course, be the same as 'Nothing might have existed', an evident falsehood contradicted by the many things which could – indeed do – exist. Likewise, imagining (conceiving, supposing) nothing is not what we are being called upon to do. That is not imagining anything, which is simply failing to imagine, not imagining at all. None the less, talk of imagining there was nothing – which is what is called for – does run the risk of being treated as if a matter of imagining nothing, and that is refraining from imagining anything. Either that, or, I suggest, it is to imagine things lacking where there might have been something: we suppose we can imagine the stars ceasing to exist one by one – like so many lights going out – but we still look to where they were. [...] To have literally nothing, rather than a domain we might meaningfully speak of as becoming progressively re- or de-populated, seems not to make sense. Consider 'There was nothing, and then the universe spontaneously sprang into being.' Here it is as though 'There was nothing' sets the scene for this cosmic event: there was nothing *where* the universe came to be; 'There might have been nothing' is a matter of: "There might have been nothing *there*." We can envisage all manner of thing *in*

---

* From chapter 5, section 5.2, of *Why There Is Something Rather Than Nothing* (Oxford: Clarendon Press, 2004), pp. 109–113, 117 Reprinted with permission of Oxford University Press.

place of what we have, but "There might have been nothing" is not a truth about anywhere, is not about the way things might have been, does not describe anything at all. [...] [T]he proposition that nothing exists comes out as [...] incoherent when formulated as "Nothing is anything", and at least highly dubious when taken as positing some kind of domain, as with "Nowhere is (there) anything" or "Nothing is anywhere."

On the Plurality of Worlds*

DAVID LEWIS

The world we live in is a very inclusive thing. Every stick and every stone you have ever seen is part of it. And so are you and I. And so are the planet Earth, the solar system, the entire Milky Way, the remote galaxies we see through telescopes, and (if there are such things) all the bits of empty space between the stars and galaxies. There is nothing so far away from us as not to be part of our world. Anything at any distance at all is to be included. Likewise the world is inclusive in time. No long-gone ancient Romans, no long-gone pterodactyls, no long-gone primordial clouds of plasma are too far in the past, nor are the dead dark stars too far in the future, to be part of this same world. Maybe, as I myself think, the world is a big physical object; or maybe some parts of it are entelechies or spirits or auras or deities or other things unknown to physics. But nothing is so alien in kind as not to be part of our world, provided only that it does exist at some distance and direction from here, or at some time before or after or simultaneous with now.

The way things are, at its most inclusive, means the way this entire world is. But things might have been different, in ever so many ways. This book of mine might have been finished on schedule. Or, had I not been such a commonsensical chap, I might be defending not only a plurality of possible worlds, but also a plurality of impossible worlds, whereof you speak truly by contradicting yourself. Or I might not have existed at all – neither I myself, nor any counterpart of me. Or there might never have been any people. Or the physical constants might have had some-what different values, incompatible with the emergence of life. Or there might have been altogether different laws of nature; and instead of electrons and quarks, there might have been alien particles, without charge or mass or spin but with alien physical properties that nothing in this world shares. There are ever so many ways that a world might be; and one of these many ways is the way that this world is.

Are there other worlds that are other ways? I say there are. I advocate a thesis of plurality of worlds, or *modal realism*, which holds that our world is but one world among many. There are countless other worlds, other very inclusive things. Our

*   From sections 1.1, 1.9, 2.5, and 2.8 of *On the Plurality of Worlds* (Oxford and New York: Basil Blackwell, 1986), pp. 1–3, 92–93, 116–117, 133–135. Reprinted with permission of John Wiley & Sons, Ltd.

world consists of us and all our surroundings, however remote in time and space; just as it is one big thing having lesser things as parts, so likewise do other worlds have lesser otherworldly things as parts. The worlds are something like remote planets; except that most of them are much bigger than mere planets, and they are not remote. Neither are they nearby. They are not at any spatial distance whatever from here. They are not far in the past or future, nor for that matter near; they are not at any temporal distance whatever from now. They are isolated: there are no spatiotemporal relations at all between things that belong to different worlds. Nor does anything that happens at one world cause anything to happen at another. Nor do they overlap; they have no parts in common, with the exception, perhaps, of immanent universals exercising their characteristic privilege of repeated occurrence.

The worlds are many and varied. There are enough of them to afford worlds where (roughly speaking) I finish on schedule, or I write on behalf of *impossibilia*, or I do not exist, or there are no people at all, or the physical constants do not permit life, or totally different laws govern the doings of alien particles with alien properties. There are so many other worlds, in fact, that absolutely *every* way that a world could possibly be is a way that some world *is*. And as with worlds, so it is with parts of worlds. There are ever so many ways that a part of a world could be; and so many and so varied are the other worlds that absolutely every way that a part of a world could possibly be is a way that some part of some world is.

The other worlds are of a kind with this world of ours. To be sure, there are differences of kind between things that are parts of different worlds – one world has electrons and another has none, one has spirits and another has none – but these differences of kind are no more than sometimes arise between things that are parts of one single world, for instance in a world where electrons coexist with spirits. The difference between this and the other worlds is not a categorial difference.

Nor does this world differ from the others in its manner of existing. I do not have the slightest idea what a difference in manner of existing is supposed to be. Some things exist here on earth, other things exist extraterrestrially, perhaps some exist no place in particular; but that is no difference in manner of existing, merely a difference in location or lack of it between things that exist. Likewise some things exist here at our world, other exist at other worlds; again, I take this to be a difference between things that exist, not a difference in their existing. You might say that strictly speaking, only this-worldly things *really* exist; and I am ready enough to agree; but on my view this "strict" speaking is *restricted* speaking, on a par with saying that all the beer is in the fridge and ignoring most of all the beer there is [...]

The worlds are not of our own making. It may happen that one part of a world makes other parts, as we do; and as other-worldly gods and demiurges do on a grander scale. But if worlds are causally isolated, nothing outside a world ever makes a world; and nothing inside makes the whole of a world, for that would be an impossible kind of self-causation. We make languages and concepts and descriptions and imaginary representations that apply to worlds. We make stipulations that select some worlds rather than others for our attention. Some of us even make assertions to the effect that other worlds exist. But none of these things we make are the worlds themselves.

Why believe in a plurality of worlds? – Because the hypothesis is serviceable, and that is a reason to think that it is true. The familiar analysis of necessity as truth at all possible worlds was only the beginning. In the last two decades, philosophers have offered a great many more analyses that make reference to possible worlds, or to possible individuals that inhabit possible worlds. I find that record most impressive. I think it is clear that talk of *possibilia* has clarified questions in many parts of the philosophy of logic, of mind, of language, and of science – not to mention metaphysics itself. Even those who officially scoff often cannot resist the temptation to help themselves abashedly to this useful way of speaking [...]

I say that ours is one of many worlds. Ours is the actual world; the rest are not actual. Why so? – I take it to be a trivial matter of meaning. I use the word "actual" to mean the same as "this-worldly". When I use it, it applies to my world and my worldmates; to this world we are part of, and to all parts of this world [...] This makes actuality a relative matter: every world is *actual at* itself, and thereby all worlds are on a par [...]

Given my acceptance of the plurality of worlds, the relativity is unavoidable. I have no tenable alternative. For suppose instead that one world alone is *absolutely* actual [...] What a remarkable bit of luck for us if the very world we are part of is the one that is absolutely actual! Out of all the people there are in all the worlds, the great majority are doomed to live in worlds that lack absolute actuality, but we are the select few. What reason could we ever have to think it was so? [...]

[An objection] has been raised by Peter Forrest, in "Occam's Razor and Possible Worlds"; by George Schlesinger; and (in discussion) by Robert M. Adams and J. J. C. Smart. They say that a modal realist ought to be a sceptic; because there are ever so many deceptive worlds, full of people very like us – counterparts or duplicates of us – who learn from experience in exactly the same way that we do, but who learn falsehoods.

Some of our deceived counterparts expect the future to resemble the past in the appropriate ways; but they live in worlds where the future does not at all resemble the past. Such worlds exist by recombination: graft any future onto any past. For some of the deceived, things will go wrong in a subtle and insidious way: new observations will tend to confirm the ether drift after all. Those are the lucky ones. For others, things will degenerate into utter chaos all around them. Others will never learn of their errors, for one reason or another. They will never be disappointed, but they will have been no less deceived.

Some are deceived not about the future but about the past: they live in brand-new worlds full of false traces and records of a past that never was. There might have been a Falsifier to make the false traces. But there needn't have been – for any possible state, there are worlds that begin in just that state.

Some are deceived even about their present. Some wield Occam's razor just as we do; they favour the most parsimonious theory that fits their observations, but unfortunately their worlds are full of epiphenomenal rubbish that does not interact in any way with them or with anything they can observe. Some are the playthings of powerful field linguists, who irradiate their surfaces so as to prompt assent to falsehoods. Some are brains in vats. However reasonably they theorise, their theories are almost entirely wrong.

Shouldn't the sad fate of all these counterparts and duplicates of ours be a warning to us? What business have we to trust what we call "reasonable" methods of forming beliefs and expectations, if we know how those methods betray so many others so like ourselves? Why should we expect better luck than theirs? A modal realist has no right to trust induction – he should turn sceptic forthwith.

(I shall use the word "induction" broadly, to cover all the methods we deem reasonable for forming beliefs about the unobserved parts of our world on the basis of experience with the observed parts. Induction narrowly speaking – the extrapolation of frequencies from samples to the populations sampled – is, of course, an important part of induction. But what I mean in general is a complicated matter of inheriting, devising, testing, revising, and applying hypotheses; of judging the *a priori* credibility of alternative possibilities, and of continually reapportioning our credence among them under the impact of new evidence; done sometimes thoughtfully, more often by habit, sometimes betwixt and between.)

I have no intention of becoming a sceptic. What we call "inductive reason" is rightly so called; and I, as a modal realist, have no more reason to foresake inductive reason than anyone else has. I *do* have the reason that everyone has; and I agree with common opinion that this reason is insufficient.

The reason that everyone has is that induction is fallible. It is possible, and it is possible in very many ways, that by being reasonable we shall be led into error. By trusting induction we run a risk, and we proceed in the confident hope that the genuine possibilities of error will seldom be realised. All that, I say, is quite independent of any theory of the nature of possibilities. I recognise the possibilities of error that everyone else recognises; they are no more and no less possibilities of error for being understood as other worlds of a kind with our own. They give me no more and no less reason to forsake inductive reason than they give to someone who holds a rival metaphysical view of their nature, or to someone who holds no particular view. Even if someone says there are no such entities as possibilities at all, but still he says it is possible in very many ways that we might be deceived (I have no idea what he thinks there are many of!), I think that he and I have equal reason, and equally insufficient reason, to distrust induction.

I once complained that my modal realism met with many incredulous stares, but few argued objections […] The arguments were soon forthcoming. They lead at worst to standoffs. The incredulous stares remain. They remain unanswerable. But they remain inconclusive.

Modal realism *does* disagree, to an extreme extent, with firm common sense opinion about what there is. (Or, in the case of some among the incredulous, it disagrees rather with firmly held agnosticism about what there is.) When modal realism tells you – as it does – that there are uncountable infinities of donkeys and protons and puddles and stars, and of planets very like Earth, and of cities very like Melbourne, and of people very like yourself, … small wonder if you are reluctant to believe it. And if entry into philosophers' paradise requires that you do believe it, small wonder if you find the price too high.

I might ask, of course, just what common sense opinion it is with which my modal realism disagrees. Is it the opinion that there do not *actually* exist an uncountable infinity of donkeys? I don't disagree at all with *that* – to actually exist is to be part of this world, and I dare say that there are only finitely many donkeys among our worldmates […]

Common sense has no absolute authority in philosophy. It's not that the folk know in their blood what the highfalutin' philosophers may forget. And it's not that common sense speaks with the voice of some infallible faculty of "intuition". It's just that theoretical conservatism is the only sensible policy for theorists of limited powers, who are duly modest about what they could accomplish after a fresh start. Part of this conservatism is reluctance to accept theories that fly in the face of common sense. But it's a matter of balance and judgement. Some common sense opinions are firmer than others, so the cost of denying common sense opinion differs from one case to the next. And the costs must be set against the gains […] The proper test, I suggest, is a simple maxim of honesty: never put forward a philosophical theory that you yourself cannot believe in your least philosophical and most commonsensical moments.

The incredulous stare is a gesture meant to say that modal realism fails the test. That is a matter of judgement and, with respect, I disagree. I acknowledge that my denial of common sense opinion is severe, and I think it is entirely right and proper to count that as a serious cost. How serious is serious enough to be decisive? – That is our central question, yet I don't see how anything can be said about it. *I* still think the price is right, high as it is. Modal realism ought to be accepted as true. The theoretical benefits are worth it.

Provided, of course, that they cannot be had for less.

Minimizing Arbitrariness*

PETER UNGER

A particular fact or event often appears arbitrary and puzzling, until it is exhibited as the outcome of certain and causal processes. Usually, though not always, such a causal explanation helps to relieve the feeling of arbitrariness, at least for a while.

*   From "Minimizing Arbitrariness: Toward a Metaphysics of Infinitely Many Concrete Worlds," *Midwest Studies in Philosophy*, 9, pp. 29–51, ed. P.A. French, T.E. Uehling, and H.K. Wettstein (Minneapolis: University of Minnesota Press, 1984), pp. 29–34, 40–41, 43–45, 48–49. Reprinted with permission of John Wiley & Sons, Inc.

But it is easy and natural for our feeling of reassert itself: We are moved to ask why just *those* causal processes governed the situation of that fact or event, rather than some others. To deal with this further, larger question, often we can exhibit those causal processes as being, themselves, the results of, or certain specific instances of, prior or more general causalities. Or, much the same, we can redescribe the initial particular fact, and perhaps the cited cause as well, and display the items thus described as an instance of some very general, fundamental law or phenomenon. But any of this will only push the question back one step more. For we can always press on and ask: Why is it that just *that* very general phenomenon, or law, should be so fundamental, or indeed obtain at all, in the world in which we have our being? Within the usual framework of explanation, law and causation, there seems no place for such curiosity to come to rest. There seems no way for us to deal adequately with the brute and ultimate *specificity* of the ways in which almost everything appears to happen. And what seems worse, the specific character of certain of these laws or ways, even of quite fundamental ones, often seems so quirky, the very height of arbitrariness.

For an example of what I mean, why is it that, as science says, there is a certain particular upper limit on velocities for all (ordinary) forms of physical objects (which is, in familiar conventional units, very nearly 186,000 miles per second)? Why does just *this* limit obtain and not some other one, or better, some *range of variation* of uppermost speeds? Why must causal processes involving motion all conform to *this particular* restriction, rather than to some other, or to no such restriction at all?

For another example, why is it that almost all of the matter that there is comes in just *three* (rather small) sorts of "parcels" (protons, electrons, and neutrons)? Why not so much matter coming in just *two* sorts of parcels, at the level now in question, or better, just *one* sort?

For a third example, we may consider what current science takes to be the basic (types of) physical forces of nature: As of this writing, scientists recognize exactly four of these forces. At the same time, physicists are hard at work seeking to unify matters at least somewhat, so that there will be recognized no more than three such basic forces, possibly fewer. Certain deep intellectual feelings, feelings that are, I believe, shared by many scientists, philosophers, and others, motivate this reduction. Along such reductionist, unifying lines, these *rationalist feelings* will not be much satisfied until we think of our world as having, at base, only one sort of basic physical force (or alternatively, having none at all, forces then giving way to some more elegant principle of operation).

Two Forms of Rationalism

How far can these rationalist feelings be followed? Unless his world is so chaotic as to be beyond any apparent cooperation, for a scientist it will almost always be rational to follow them as far as he can: Reduce the specificities of one's world to a very few principles, maybe one, operating with respect to a very few (kinds of) substances, maybe one; further, have the ultimate quantitative values occurring in the principles be as simple and unquirky as possible.

If scientists are *extremely* successful in satisfying these feelings, a philosopher (who may of course also be a scientist) might rest content with just those findings. Such a philosopher will hold a unique and beautifully simple principle to hold sway over *all* of (concrete) reality. Let me call this philosopher a *moderate rationalist*.

Another sort of philosopher will press on with these feelings, even in the face of the enormous scientific success just imaginatively envisioned. He is an *extreme rationalist*, and even in that happy situation, he will say this: Though the working of *our world* is as elegant as might be, why should *everything* there is behave in accord with just *this* specific principle? Why should *any* specific way, even a most metaphysically elegant, be preferred to any *other* specific way for a world to be? Why shouldn't there be *somewhere*, indeed be *many domains*, where things are less beautifully behaved? If so, then, *over all*, everything there is will be metaphysically most elegant, the *universe as a whole* preferring *no specific* way to any other, but, rather, giving each and every way its place and due. With a suitably enormous infinite variety of independent domains, of mutually isolated concrete worlds, we will have, over all, *the least arbitrary universe entire*; otherwise we will not, over all, have so little arbitrariness.

Both of these forms of rationalism are appealing to our deep rationalistic feelings (even while we have other feelings that go against them both). In this paper, I will not substantially favor either form over the other. Nor will I argue that it is most rational for us to adopt either of the rationalisms. My aim will be avowedly rationalist, but it will also be modest: I will be arguing that, at least in the evidential situation in which we do find ourselves, the metaphysics proposed by an extreme-rationalist (for any evidential situation) should be taken very seriously. In other words, at least in our actual evidential situation, we should take very seriously a metaphysics of infinitely many mutually isolated concrete worlds.

Now, though it is not quite so dominant as it was some years ago, a heavily empiricist approach to concrete reality is, still, much more fashionable than a more rationalist approach. Accordingly, many philosophers will tell us not to worry about any apparent brute and fundamental arbitrariness in nature, which we seem to see and are, in fact, at least somewhat troubled by. Taken altogether, they will say, things just are the specific way that they are or, if one insists in putting it so, the specific way they happen to be.

Perhaps this basic empiricist attitude is unobjectionable; I do not know. Although I find it somewhat unappealing, perhaps there is no way it can be faulted. At the same time, there seems nothing that requires us to prefer this fashionable approach and to reject a more rationalist approach to all of concrete reality.

A Rationalist Motivation for Concrete Possible Worlds

In our physical science, I am told, certain magnitudes are taken as fundamental and universal. For instance, an example already cited, there is a fundamental upper limit on the velocity of any (normal) particle or signal. But, why just *that* upper limit, for *all* such speeds, everywhere and always? Why not just a bit more speed allowed or alternatively, not even that much, if not around here and now, then many, many galaxies away, or many, many eons from now?

Consider a physical theory according to which there was a limit on speeds, but one that varied with the place of the mover in question. This might be due to, as the theory says, the mover's place being under an influence that varies with respect to place – for example, the influence of vast structures of intergalactic structures of matter, which surround any given place in all, or many, directions. On such a theory there would be no universality to, and thus no universal preference for, just the limit in our (only pretty big) neighborhood. Far away enough over there, the limit would be higher; and far enough away over *there*, it would be lower. Because it would not be universal, our neighborhood speed limit would not seem, or be, so arbitrary. By localizing our specificity, we minimize the arbitrariness that is associated with it.

A strategy of localization, it seems to me, does have its merits. But the present attempt at applying the strategy has at least two difficulties. First of all, according to what science seems to tell us, there is little or no evidence for thinking that our world conforms to the sort of theory just considered. Rather, available evidence seems to indicate the opposite; (Even if given infinite space) we'll get the same speed limit for *every* (big) neighborhood, no matter how remote from ours it may be. (Morever, there seems to be a lot of evidence that we don't have infinite space, or infinite time.) So an attempt at spatial localization does not in fact seem feasible.

Second, and perhaps more important, any imagined law of variation of speeds would *itself* have some numbers constant for it. And then we might ask: Why should velocities vary with surrounding spaces in just *that* way, with just *those* constants constraining variation? Why shouldn't the regularities of varying speeds be otherwise, other than they happen to be in our whole physical world?

To remove or to minimize this remaining arbitrariness, we might try to "localize" the mode of spatial variation, too, staying with our general strategy. But how are we to do so? We might stretch things out over time: Different variation factors for different vast epochs. But the same problems arise here, too. First, what evidence there is about physical time is not so congenial. And, more fundamentally, there will be left as universal (and unexplained) some factors for variation over time of the space-variation constant(s). Why should just *those* temporal factors hold, and hold universally? Why not some others? Either we must admit defeat or we must reach out further, in order to achieve a *new form of localizing*.

Having used up all of space and time, even assuming both are infinite in all their directions, where do we go? We must expand our idea of the "entire universe," of all that there is. But in what why? A certain philosophical conception of *possible worlds* might provide the best route for our rationalistic localizing strategy. Indeed, it might provide the only route. It is my rationalist suggestion, then, to try to make more sense of concrete reality by adopting a metaphysics of many concrete worlds.

Two Approaches to a Metaphysics of Isolated Concrete Worlds: The Rationalist and the Analytic

It will be in tentative and an exploratory spirit that I will advocate a metaphysics of many concrete words. The view I will favor is at least very similar to, and is perhaps the very same as, the view of such worlds developed by David Lewis. My present motivation for taking such a view seriously, however, is quite different from his (main) motivation. The differences are such, it will emerge, that my approach is aptly called *rationalist*, or rationalistic, whereas his approach might better be called *analytic*, or analytical. It seems true however, that, at least in their main elements, the rationalist approach and the analytic approach are entirely compatible with each other.

Let us suppose the two approaches are indeed compatible. Then whatever motivation each yields can add to that from the other, so as to make more acceptable their shared metaphysical position. It is my hope that this is so.

At the same time, there are those philosophers unfriendly to this metaphysics for whom, I suppose, Lewis's analyses themselves are entirely unhelpful and implausible. Now, insofar as my rationalistic approach can be made appealing, such thinkers will have, perhaps for the first time, at least some motivation for accepting a metaphysics of many concrete worlds.

Possible Worlds as Concrete Entities

It is fashionable for philosophers to talk of possible worlds. But much of this talk seems metaphorical, or heuristic, at best. This observation has moved several philosophers, J. L. Mackie being notable among them, to question the (significance of) this fashion. In his *Truth, Probability and Paradox*, Mackie writes "[...] talk of possible worlds [...] cries out for further analysis. There are no possible worlds except the actual one; so what are we up to when we talk about them?" In my opinion, these words express a dilemma felt by many philosophers, though Mackie expresses it in a somewhat oblique and indirect way.

More directly put, the dilemma is this: Philosophical accounts of possible worlds fall into either of just two baskets. In the first basket are accounts where "possible world" is to denote some "abstract entity," such as a set of mutually consistent propositions that, together, purport to describe comprehensively the world in which we live. Presumably, just one of these sets yields a completely successful description, all the others then failing.

Whatever their philosophical value, such accounts use the expression "possible world", and even the word "world", in a way that is bound to mislead. For such accounts, the world in which we live is *not* a possible world at all, let alone the most vivid and accessible example of one. For we live in a world consisting, directly and in the main, of stones, animals, people, and suchlike, not of sentences or propositions (however numerous and well behaved). We live in a world that is, at least in the main, *concrete*. So it is most unclear how any other candidate worlds, on the one hand, and the world we live in, on the other, might be suitably related so that *all* of them are *worlds*. Such accounts, then, tend to collapse into mere heuristic devices, even if some may be very helpful heuristically.

In the second basket, we find the story told by David Lewis and variants upon it. On such accounts, possible worlds are concrete entities, generally constituted of smaller concrete things that are at them, or in them. In this central respect, all of the (other) possible worlds are just like the actual world, the world in which *we* live. On this sort of account, the relations between worlds are just those of qualitative similarity and difference, as regards the various respects in which these concrete entities may be compared. These relations are of the same sort as some of those that obtain between "lesser" objects, e.g., between individual inhabitants, whether of the same world or of different ones.

On Lewis's treatment of worlds and their parts, no object can be at, or be a part of, more than one world, while every concrete object is at, or is a part of, at least one world. So each concrete entity that is itself not a world, but is only a world-part, is a part of exactly one of the infinity of concrete worlds. I shall assume this treatment it what follows. I will advocate a many worlds metaphysics where each chair and each person, for examples, are at one and only one concrete possible world: A given chair, or a given person, is just at its own world and, thus, is *not identical* with *any* chair, or *any* person, that is at *any other* world. At most, the others are (mere) *counterparts* of the concrete objects first considered.

How does such a story go as regards relations of space, time and causality? First, there are some tiny worlds; the whole world here is, say, a single space-time point. Beyond those, the concrete inhabitants of a given world are related spatially and/or temporally and/or causally to at least some other inhabitants of that same world, so the world forms a spatial and/or temporal and/or causal system. But inhabitants of *different* worlds do *not* bear any of these relations to each other, nor does any complete world bear any to any other complete world. Causally, spatially, and temporally *isolated* from each other are the infinity of worlds.

In this second sort of account, it seems to me, it is clear enough, and not misleading, how the others, like the actual world, should *all* be *worlds*. But there is another sort of trouble with this account: It seems incredible, crazy, way beyond the reach of any even halfway reasonable belief.

So this is, in brief, our dilemma of possible worlds. On any account where matters are not incredible, things seem badly obscure or misleading. On any where things seem much less misleading, we face a "universe" that seems utterly incredible. What are we to do?

Formally, at least, there are three alternative: First, we just don't take talk of possible worlds to be literal or serious; we treat it as *at best* a helpful heuristic. Second, we work out some way in which it's clear how both some abstract structures, on the one hand, and our actual concrete selves and surroundings, on the other, can all be worlds. Finally, we try to make a story of isolated concrete realms somewhat more credible, or less incredible […]

On the Resistance to the Idea of Infinitely many Isolated Concrete Worlds

Let us confront the great resistance people feel toward the view of many mutually isolated concrete worlds. For unless we unearth implicit factors of resistance and promise to do something to disarm them, any more positive steps toward greater credibility are likely to fall on deaf ears. Why, then, are so very many philosophers, as indeed they are, so terribly resistant to such a view? Why do people think it so crazy to consider such a view a serious candidate for acceptability?

The metaphysics we propose to take seriously posits a group of concrete worlds with two salient features. First, *infinite diversity*: every way for anything to be, or behave, is a way that (some) things are, or do behave, if not in a particular given world (say, the actual world), then in some other one. Second, *total isolation*: each world is totally isolated from every other world. Each of these two features does, as a matter of psychological fact, promote much resistance to our metaphysical view.

The matter of infinite diversity has been rather extensively discussed in the literature. For example, this diversity has been thought to undermine the rationality of predictions about the actual world, and it has been thought to foster an attitude of indifference toward our own future actions and their consequences. Does the infinite diversity implicit in our metaphysics have such dire implications, otherwise avoidable? If so, then that would be reason, even if not conclusive reason, to reject the metaphysics.

Especially in his most recent writings, Lewis has argued, convincingly to my mind, that there are no such problems stemming from a metaphysics of infinitely many concrete worlds, but only various confusions to such a threatening effect. Although it would be useful for still more to be said to counter this source of resistance, there is not now an acute need to do so.

I turn, then, to spend some energy meeting resistance stemming from the other main feature of our metaphysic, total isolation. The total isolation of each world promotes two main sorts of worry. One of them is more blatant and obvious; the other, I think, is more profound. Both merit some discussion in the present essay.

The more obvious worry is this: in that there is total isolation of worlds, there is, in particular, complete causal isolation among them. So nothing in our world, ourselves included, will ever interact with any other world, or anything in any other world. Accordingly, the metaphysics in question posits all sorts of things that none of us ever will, or ever can, connect with any experience or observation. Worlds there are with cows that fly, and with particles generally like our electrons but a hundred times as massive. As we are causally isolated from these worlds, cows, and heavy electrons, we can never perceive them, nor any of their causes or effects. So it seems that we can never have any experiential reason for thinking there to be such things. But if no experiential reason for such a thought as to such contingent existents, then no reason is possible for us at all. Such a rarified metaphysics is difficult even to tolerate, let alone to find at all acceptable.

This worry can be met in either of two main ways. As I understand him, Lewis would meet it by arguing that we need not have *experiential* reason to believe in such otherworldly things to accept them with reason. Rather, adequately searching ratiocination about contingency and necessity, conducted (largely) a priori, will give us reason enough for our metaphysical view. This is, or is very close to, a position of extreme rationalism. Now, whatever the strengths and the weaknesses of this sort of answer, there is another way to meet the worry in question.

From a position of moderate rationalism, we can argue that there can be some *very indirect experiential* evidence for the idea of such outlandish, isolated entities. Near this paper's end [...] I will attempt such an argument. Moreover, I will there argue that we *now do have* some such indirect experiential reason, or evidence [...]

A Sort of Unity for a Universe of many Isolated Concrete Worlds

[...] When will there be a universe that is a unity? When the worlds altogether exhibit completeness, but do not exhibit redundancy. Well, when will *that* be?

The universe will be complete providing that every way that a world could possibly be is a way that some world is. What are the possibilities here? As far as the details go, I have no way of knowing. But we need not say what they are. To help ensure the wanted completeness, though, we should have a *very liberal* conception of possibility at work. We need not, I think, allow "situations that are to make true statements that are contradictory." But our range of possibilities, our range of various worlds, must be enormously abundant; in an old-fashioned word, we need a *plenitude*. So our range of metaphysical possibilities must include, I imagine, many that are quite beyond our own abilities to conceive of in any illuminating way or detail, as well as many that may at times seen mere fabrications of mind-spinning: As a (self-styled) rationalist, I need unity for the universe entire. For this unity, I need an *extremely great infinite variety* of worlds; without so very many qualitatively different worlds, we'll lack completeness and, thus, lack unity.

[…] [H]ow many worlds are there of each character? The rationalist aspects of my mind find two answers that seem at least somewhat more appealing than any others: one and, at the other extreme, an *infinite* number of each character. The latter answer, infinity, itself raises questions as to what *size* of infinity we have at hand. As this further question appears to find no motivated answer, there seems to be a preference, generated thereby, for the former. In addition, the former answer – no duplicate for any world – might find some adequate indiscernibility argument in its favor, though really good indiscernibility arguments are, I think, very hard to come by. At any rate, all things considered, I hesitantly advocate the answer, *one*. So, I thus advocate a metaphysics of an *extremely* great infinity of mutually isolated concrete worlds, not even one of which is duplicated even once in the universe entire.

Empirical Science and Metaphysics

[…] As empirical science presents it to us, is the world we live in, the world of which we are a part, is this a world notable for its lack of natural arbitrariness? Far from it, the actual world, our evidence seems to indicate, is full of all sorts of fundamental arbitrary features, quirks that seem both universal for the world and absolutely brute. The particular universal limit on velocities in our world is just one conspicuous example. Another is the apparent ultimate, universal validity of quantum physics. A third is the tripartite division of most matter. And so on, and so forth.

According to available evidence, and to such a theory of our actual world as the evidence encourages, the actual world has nowhere near the lack of arbitrariness that rationalist intuitions find most tolerable. To satisfy the rationalist approach, our evidence tells us, we must look beyond the reaches of our actual space and time, beyond our actual causal network. For there to be a minimum of arbitrariness in the universe entire, indeed anything anywhere near a minimum, we might best understand the universe as including, not only the actual world, but infinitely many other concrete worlds as well.

The Grand Design*

STEPHEN HAWKING AND LEONARD MLODINOW

[...] Any set of laws that describes a continuous world such as our own will have a concept of energy, which is a conserved quantity, meaning it doesn't change in time. The energy of empty space will be a constant, independent of both time and position. One can subtract out this constant vacuum energy by measuring the energy of any volume of space relative to that of the same volume of empty space, so we may as well call the constant zero. One requirement any law of nature must satisfy is that it dictates that the energy of an isolated body surrounded by empty space is positive, which means that one has to do work to assemble the body. That's because if the energy of an isolated body were negative, it could be created in a state of motion so that its negative energy was exactly balanced by the positive energy due to its motion. If that were true, there would be no reason that bodies could not appear anywhere and everywhere. Empty space would therefore be unstable. But if it costs energy to create an isolated body, such instability cannot happen, because, as we've said, the energy of the universe must remain constant. That is what it takes to make the universe locally stable – to make it so that things don't just appear everywhere from nothing.

If the total energy of the universe must always remain zero, and it costs energy to create a body, how can a whole universe be created from nothing? That is why there must be a law like gravity. Because gravity is attractive, gravitational energy is negative: One has to do work to separate a gravitationally bound system, such as the earth and moon. This negative energy can balance the positive energy needed to create matter, but it's not quite that simple. The negative gravitational energy of the earth, for example, is less than a billionth of the positive energy of the matter particles the earth is made of. A body such as a star will have more negative gravitational energy, and the smaller it is (the closer the different parts of it are to each other), the greater this negative gravitational energy will be. But before it can become greater than the positive energy of the matter, the star will collapse to a black hole, and black holes have positive energy. That's why empty space is stable. Bodies such as stars or black holes cannot just appear out of nothing. But a whole universe can.

Because gravity shapes space and time, it allows space-time to be locally stable but globally unstable. On the scale of the entire universe, the positive energy of the matter *can* be balanced by the negative gravitational energy, and so there is no

---

restriction on the creation of whole universes. Because there is a law like gravity, the universe can and will create itself from nothing […] Spontaneous creation is the reason there is something rather than nothing, why the universe exists, why we exist. It is not necessary to invoke God to light the blue touch paper and set the universe going.

Why are the fundamental laws as we have described them? The ultimate theory must be consistent and must predict finite results for quantities that we can measure. We've seen that there must be a law like gravity, and […] for a theory of gravity to predict finite quantities, the theory must have what is called supersymmetry between the forces of nature and the matter on which they act. M-theory is the most general supersymmetric theory of gravity. For these reasons M-theory is the *only* candidate for a complete theory of the universe. If it is finite – and this has yet to be proved – it will be a model of a universe that creates itself. We must be part of this universe, because there is no other consistent model.

M-theory is the unified theory Einstein was hoping to find. The fact that we human beings – who are ourselves mere collections of fundamental particles of nature – have been able to come this close to an understanding of the laws governing us and our universe is a great triumph. But perhaps the true miracle is that abstract considerations of logic lead to a unique theory that predicts and describes a vast universe full of the amazing variety that we see. If the theory is confirmed by observation, it will be the successful conclusion of a search going back more than 3,000 years. We will have found the grand design.

5

Second Solution
No Explanation Needed

Editorial Introduction

Is no explanation needed for the existence of Something instead of Nothing? Or at least, is none needed if things have existed throughout infinite ages? Here discussions are scenes of tumultuous disagreement over what facts need to be explained, with still more heated disputes about what explanations have even the slightest chance of being correct, or whether the word "explanation" could meaningfully be applied to various candidates. Could a deity, for instance, have created all other things? If a deity, or things in general, could somehow possess *necessary existence*, existence that was utterly inevitable, might not a world which just happened to exist be equally satisfactory?

EPICURUS declares that "nothing can be created from the non-existent." If this means that nothing could be created by remolding non-existent stuff, then that's obviously right. If, in contrast, Epicurus is saying that nothingness could never have been replaced by somethingness, so that the universe must have been around for infinitely many years, then this can be challenged. Still, many admire his claim that the universe always has existed and cannot meaningfully be said to have an external cause.

In his *Treatise*, David HUME finds no contradiction in a thing that begins to exist without a cause. It is easy, he writes, "to conceive any object to be non-existent this moment, and existent the next, without conjoining to it the distinct idea of a cause or productive principle." Would a cause be needed in order to fix the time of the object's coming into existence? Hume comments that there is no contradiction, either, in supposing that nothing fixed the time. If the coming into existence could be causeless, why not also the time? Yet he nowhere claims that our universe did

The Mystery of Existence: Why Is There Anything At All?, First Edition. Edited by John Leslie and Robert Lawrence Kuhn.
© 2013 John Wiley & Sons, Inc. Published 2013 by John Wiley & Sons, Inc.

suddenly and inexplicably leap into being, and in his *Dialogues Concerning Natural Religion* he suggests that it has instead existed for ever. A system that exists from eternity, the argument runs, must necessarily lack a cause, since causes exist *before* their effects. Each element in an eternal chain of things would, however, have its cause in some earlier part of the chain, so that nothing would be left unexplained. Suppose you had been shown causes for each of twenty particles. It would, says Cleanthes in the *Dialogues*, be "very unreasonable, should you afterwards ask me, what was the cause of the whole twenty."

What ought we to think of such reasoning today? Discussing atoms that suddenly decay radioactively, or particles that suddenly "quantum-fluctuate" into existence, writers often say physics has shown that matters are here settled causelessly and by chance. Yet some eminent physicists think otherwise, and it is hard to see how we could ever refute all possible variants of their position. As for infinite chains of explanation, well, some people think Hume has a strong point. Yes, in an infinite chain each explanation simply raises a new problem – but each new problem in turn has its own solution! Others protest that when each so-called explanation always depends on another that is earlier in the chain, nothing ever gets explained.

Fred Hoyle's "Steady State" universe was once extremely popular. Our universe is in constant expansion but, Hoyle reasoned, it could have kept the same density throughout an infinite past if new matter perpetually appears at a very slow rate, "about one atom every century in a volume equal to the Empire State Building." In *Frontiers of Astronomy* he talks of a "creation field" generating the new matter. This, though, might seem little advance on saying that new atoms *just do* come into existence as already existing atoms drift apart. Later, the idea of a creation field became very speculatively linked to other ideas in physics: see Inflationary Cosmology as discussed in the sixth section of this volume, and then think of Hoyle's Steady State as reincarnated in Eternal Inflation which now attracts many cosmologists, where the cosmos is a scene of perpetually expanding turmoil and Big Bang "universes" are mere patches in which things become calmer. Yet the later speculations might be wrong, and Hoyle's original approach was not in the least unreasonable. After all, some laws of nature must presumably be ultimate instead of derived from other laws. Why shouldn't it be an ultimate law that new atoms arrive as old ones drift apart? How could a continual tiny trickle of new matter, far too slow to be easily detected, be absurd by comparison with a Bang in which an entire universe sprang into existence? Philosophers, at any rate, often praised Hoyle's approach, viewing the Big Bang with considerable suspicion until the astronomers began saying that it had been confirmed.

William Bonnor's universe instead oscillates eternally. Big Bangs are forever succeeded by Big Squeezes in which everything is pulled together by gravity. Each Squeeze ends in a Big Crunch which gives rise to a new Bang. Like Hoyle's picture, Bonnor's is now known to be wrong in its details, but new oscillating-universe models are still being developed today: see, for instance, Steinhardt 2011 in the Suggestions for Further Reading at the end of this volume.

Has Bonnor too strong a dislike for a Bang that started off infinitely dense, a Bang that was the very beginning of the universe rather than just reversing an earlier contraction? When he calls it "highly improper" to bring in God to explain the Bang, couldn't he be going much too far? "There is no place in science," he writes, "for miraculous interventions of this sort." Yet many would protest that *miracles* can only be breakdowns in *already existing* law-controlled systems, and that science can at most describe such systems instead of dealing with why they exist. All the same, Bonnor might be right in his view that an infinite series of oscillations would be better than "handing over to God 8,000 million [or, as we'd say now, 13,700 million] years ago."

The historic debate between Bertrand Russell and Father Frederick Copleston features intricate fighting over Hume's idea that being infinitely old could make a universe unmysterious. Copleston believes in a divine person, God. God possesses necessary existence, he says, because God's essence and existence are identical. God's nature *actually is* "to exist." However we don't have "any clear intuition of God's essence as yet" so we cannot, just by contemplating this extraordinary essence, have our proof that God exists. Instead we deduce God's necessary existence from the fact that the universe would otherwise have to be "its own cause," which Copleston views as an absurd idea. Even if successive stages of the universe formed an infinite chain, each link caused by an earlier one, this could not remove the need for God. Without God, there would be nothing to give existence to the chain as a whole.

Russell buys none of this. He views necessity as a property that cannot be had by any existing thing. He could accept that everything in an infinite chain needed a cause without accepting any cause of the chain in its entirety: "I see no reason to suppose that the total has any cause whatsoever. [...] I should say that the universe is just there, and that is all. [...] Every man who exists has a mother, and it seems to me your argument is that therefore the human race must have a mother." To which Copleston replies that the cause of the entire universe would be "a transcendent cause" rather than just one more mother among others. Yet, to Russell's way of thinking, asking for such a cause is not merely unnecessary; it is utterly meaningless.

Comments:

(1)   It can well seem that an infinite chain of explanations would not really explain anything. Some Muslims view the Quran as co-eternal with Allah. Would they, would anybody, accept the following explanation for its eternal existence: that it exists now because it existed a second ago, its existence at that earlier second being due to its having existed a second before *that*, and so on ad infinitum? Surely not.

(2)   On the other hand, Copleston would seem to have given no actual argument against Russell's idea that the universe "is just there," for absolutely no reason.

What a pity that Russell tied this to an aggressive claim that asking why there is a universe makes no sense whatever!

(3)   On God's necessary existence, Russell might again appear too aggressive, this time through insisting that nothing of the kind can fit inside his own brand of Logic. But equally, Copleston could appear to have done little to throw light on the notion of necessary existence. "A being which cannot not-exist," while not sounding as meaningless as "A slithy tove which gimbles" or as ridiculous as "a mathematical equation suffering from a headache," still might not describe anything *really possible*: possible as a matter of reality, in other words, rather than simply as being something that we cannot rule out. Furthermore, Copleston's assumption that a divine being can supply a reason for its own existence only if its essence *is* "to exist" might look rather too hasty (people following in Plato's footsteps have seen an alternative) and also very hard to make sense of.

In "Creation in Cosmology" and "Why Is There a Universe AT ALL, Rather Than Just Nothing?" Adolf GRÜNBAUM makes many complex points. However, all of them center on the idea that the universe, whatever its details, ought to be viewed as "natural". Pope Pius XII welcomed the Big Bang as proof of a Creator, yet how, Grünbaum asks, could we possibly show that the Bang was "unnatural" and thus in need of an external cause? Suppose, controversially, that no universe had existed before the Bang. The Bang still wouldn't have been "a sudden and fantastic violation of the law of conservation of matter and energy" for there would have been no already flowing time inside which it was "sudden," no earlier situation whose matter and energy needed to be conserved. Besides, Steady State theorists made no obvious mistake when they treated a perpetual, very slow appearance of new material as itself fully natural. The hypothesis of creation by God culpably fails to specify a "causal *process* that would *link* the presence of the supposed divine (causal) agency to the effects that are attributed to it." The "divine word-magic" of "Let there be light" is nowise made intelligible through talk of divine omnipotence. The idea of the universe as existing at every instant thanks to God's "timeless causation" is "obscure if not incoherent." Descartes was *"empirically* wrong" in supposing that all material objects would vanish immediately unless God maintained them in their existence, for the chemist Lavoisier showed that matter or matter-energy conservation is *"spontaneous, natural, unperturbed* behavior" in "a closed, finite system on the medium-sized macroscopic scale." Many do find the existence of a universe very puzzling, strongly wish to have it explained, desire this all the more when physicists describe an eternal trickle of new atoms or a Big Bang that was preceded by no earlier states, yet "a question cannot be regarded as a well-posed challenge merely because the questioner finds it psychologically insistent."

The psychological itch might go away, Grünbaum tells us, when the questioner was shown some model of a universe which had existed for infinitely many years, or a model in which the distinction between space and time breaks down completely in the very early Big Bang which might therefore be viewed as a space-time "bowl" – asking what happened *before* the Bang, to cause it, then being like asking about events on Earth's surface to the north of the North Pole. But, he insists, the itch would have been wrong in principle, rather than giving us a right to demand such models. Even assuming that a Null World, utter emptiness, would have been simplest, Simplicity fails to guarantee anything, he declares. Empirically based scientific theories are *"our sole epistemic avenue to the 'natural' behavior of the universe at large,"* and no empirical evidence supports the claim that it is natural "for our universe *not* to exist, rather than to exist." Nobody would ask why a person didn't "metamorphose spontaneously into an elephant" when this was logically possible, describable without self-contradiction. Why, then, feel astonished "that the Null Possibility, if genuine, has remained a *mere* logical possibility, and that something does exist *instead*"?

Powerful though these points no doubt are, there are possible ways of countering them. Just how far can we push the principle, "This is Nature, so there could be nothing more natural"? If Bibles were known to have appeared early in the Big Bang, if cherubs constantly materialized out of thin air, wouldn't the principle look rather inadequate? Yes, things come with no labels stating their degrees of "naturalness" and you might argue that the need to explain the Bibles and the cherubs was based on wide experience of how the world works – but if all our interpretative principles had to be derived from experience then we never could make sense of how the world works, as was recognized by Hume, Kant, and William James. Now, one such principle is *"Expect Simplicity."* Psychologists find it hard to say why the world isn't perceived as what James called "blooming, buzzing confusion." Mathematicians know that the world's actual events up to the present moment, even when describable by equations simple enough for us to discover, *can alternatively* be described by equations of fantastic complexity, equations predicting that future events will take the weirdest forms (the case is like that of a line which is at first simple, completely straight, but could begin wriggling wildly when extended – for there are equations to fit lines that start straight yet wriggle later). Yet physicists do look for simple equations to fit events, equations that predict that the world will continue to develop in what humans in physics departments would classify as orderly ways, ways that they would call "regularities," and even young children perceive the world as having considerable simplicity instead of confusion, this allowing them to exert some control over it. *"Expect Simplicity"* serves us well. Now, a blank could seem far simpler than our universe – and therefore, we might well think, there would have been a blank, were it not for some overriding reason for there to be a universe. Searching for some such reason can be thought very different from wanting to know why, when it was logically possible, Mr. Jones hasn't turned into an elephant.

Again, just how did Lavoisier show that Descartes was *"empirically* wrong" in supposing that stones, for instance, would disappear at once in the absence of continued divine support? Wouldn't that have meant placing magical screens around stones to ensure that God couldn't act on them, thus proving experimentally that their existence needed no such support? In asking for empirical evidence that the universe has a natural tendency not to exist, Grünbaum could well be setting an impossible task. Imagine, even, that the universe keeps vanishing after every fifty years, its reappearance being always only 36 percent probable so that we are very, very lucky that it has in fact always reappeared. We'd not even detect the flipping between existence and nonexistence. Whenever the universe wasn't there, we'd not be there to know it. But if empirical evidence could not possibly be supplied, then how could it be fair to ask anyone to supply it? Why does Grünbaum consider people foolish when, making no attempt to supply it, they instead point to how a blank would be simpler than a universe?

Note, though, that asking *"Why a Universe?"* need not assume firmly that a blank would be "natural" in the absence of God or of some other such Creative Factor. We might just be wondering *what might have settled it* that there was a universe, not a blank. Even if a need to explain the universe could never be proved, let alone proved empirically, might it not still *have* an explanation? Could its existence have been settled by chance, perhaps quantum-physical chance? Was the existence of a universe virtually certain because there were infinitely many possible ways of there being a universe, whereas a blank could be a blank in only a single way? Grünbaum writes "the Null Possibility, if genuine," as if thinking it altogether doubtful that a blank was possible; well, might a blank be logically impossible for the sorts of reason given (see earlier pages) by Bradley or by Rundle? Or are better suggestions provided by some of the other authors appearing in this volume?

Letter to Herodotus*

EPICURUS

The first principle is that nothing can be created from the non-existent: for otherwise any thing would be formed from any thing without the need of seed. If all that disappears were destroyed into the non-existent, all matter would be destroyed, since that into which it would be dissolved has no existence. Truly this universe has always been such as it now is, and so it shall always be; for there is nothing into which it can change, and there is nothing outside the universe that can enter into it and bring about a change. [...]

---

* From *Epicurus' Letters, Principal Doctrines and Vatican Sayings*, trans. R.M. Geer (Indianapolis: Bobbs-Merrill, 1964).

Moreover, the universe consists of material bodies and void. That the bodies exist is made clear to all by sensation itself, on which reason must base its judgment in regard to what is imperceptible. […] If that which we call "void" and "space" and "the untouchable" did not exist, the particles of matter would have no place in which to exist or through which to move, as it is clear they do move.

In addition to these two, there is nothing that we can grasp in the mind, either through concepts or through analogy with concepts, that has real existence and is not referred to merely as a property or an accident of material things or of the void.

Of material things, some are compounds, others are the simple particles from which the compounds are formed. The particles are indivisible and unchangeable, as is necessary if all is not to be dissolved to nothing, but something strong is to remain after the dissolution of the compounds, something solid, which cannot be destroyed in any way. Therefore, it is necessary that the first beginnings be indivisible particles of matter.

Causeless Beginning or Eternal Chain?*

DAVID HUME

From *A Treatise of Human Nature*

[…]

'Tis a general maxim in philosophy, that *whatever begins to exist, must have a cause of existence*. This is commonly taken for granted in all reasonings, without any proof given or demanded. 'Tis suppos'd to be founded on intuition, and to be one of those maxims, which tho' they may be deny'd with the lips, 'tis impossible for men in their hearts really to doubt of. But if we examine this maxim by the idea of knowledge above-explain'd, we shall discover in it no mark of any such intuitive certainty; but on the contrary shall find, that 'tis of a nature quite foreign to that species of conviction.

All certainty arises from the comparison of ideas, and from the discovery of such relations as are unalterable, so long as the ideas continue the same. These relations are *resemblance, proportions in quantity and number, degrees of any quality, and contrariety*; none of which are imply'd in this proposition, *Whatever has a beginning has also a cause of existence*. That proposition therefore is not intuitively certain. At least any one, who wou'd assert it to be intuitively certain, must deny these to be the only infallible

* From book 1, part 3, section 3, of *A Treatise of Human Nature*, ed. L.A. Selby-Bigge (Oxford: Clarendon Press, 1888), pp. 72–82. Reprinted with permission of Oxford University Press, and from part 9 of *Dialogues concerning Natural Religion*, ed. Norman Kemp Smith (New York: Social Science Publishers, 1948).

relations, and must find some other relation of that kind to be imply'd in it; which it will then be time enough to examine.

But here is an argument, which proves at once, that the foregoing proposition is neither intuitively nor demonstrably certain. We can never demonstrate the necessity of a cause to every new existence, or new modification of existence, without shewing at the same time the impossibility there is, that any thing can ever begin to exist without some productive principle; and where the latter proposition cannot be prov'd, we must despair of ever being able to prove the former. Now that the latter proposition is utterly incapable of a demonstrative proof, we may satisfy ourselves by considering, that as all distinct ideas are separable from each other, and as the ideas of cause and effect are evidently distinct, 'twill be easy for us to conceive any object to be non-existent this moment, and existent the next, without conjoining to it the distinct idea of a cause or productive principle. The separation, therefore, of the idea of a cause from that of a beginning of existence, is plainly possible for the imagination; and consequently the actual separation of these objects is so far possible, that it implies no contradiction nor absurdity; and is therefore incapable of being refuted by any reasoning from mere ideas; without which 'tis impossible to demonstrate the necessity of a cause.

Accordingly we shall find upon examination, that every demonstration, which has been produc'd for the necessity of a cause, is fallacious and sophistical. All the points of time and place, say some philosophers, in which we can suppose any object to begin to exist, are in themselves equal; and unless there be some cause, which is peculiar to one time and to one place, and which by that means determines and fixes the existence, it must remain in eternal suspence; and the object can never begin to be, for want of something to fix its beginning. But I ask; Is there any more difficulty in supposing the time and place to be fix'd without a cause, than to suppose the existence to be determin'd in that manner? [...]

The second argument, which I find us'd on this head, labours under an equal difficulty. Every thing, 'tis said, must have a cause; for if any thing wanted a cause, *it* wou'd produce *itself*; that is, exist before it existed; which is impossible. But this reasoning is plainly unconclusive; because it supposes, that in our denial of a cause we still grant what we expressly deny, *viz.* that there must be a cause; which therefore is taken to be the object itself [...]

'Tis exactly the same case with the third argument, which has been employ'd to demonstrate the necessity of a cause. Whatever is produc'd without any cause, is produc'd by *nothing*; or in other words, has nothing for its cause. But nothing can never be a cause, no more than it can be something, or equal to two right angles. By the same intuition, that we perceive nothing not to be equal to two right angles, or not to be something, we perceive, that it can never be a cause; and consequently must perceive, that every object has a real cause of its existence.

I believe it will not be necessary to employ many words in shewing the weakness of this argument, after what I have said of the foregoing. They are all of them founded on the same fallacy, and are deriv'd from the same turn of thought. 'Tis sufficient only to observe, that when we exclude all causes we really do exclude them, and neither suppose nothing nor the object itself to be the causes of the existence; and consequently can draw no argument from the absurdity of these suppositions to prove the absurdity of that exclusion. If every thing must have a cause, it follows, that upon the exclusion of other causes we must accept of the object itself or of nothing as causes. But 'tis the very point in question, whether every thing must have a cause or not; and therefore, according to all just reasoning, it ought never to be taken for granted.

From *Dialogues concerning Natural Religion*

[...]

[I]n tracing an eternal succession of objects, it seems absurd to inquire for a general cause or first Author. How can any thing, that exists from eternity, have a cause, since that relation implies a priority in time and a beginning of existence?

In such a chain too, or succession of objects, each part is caused by that which preceded it, and causes that which succeeds it. Where then is the difficulty? But the WHOLE, you say, wants a cause. I answer, that the uniting of these parts into a whole, like the uniting of several distinct counties into one kingdom, or several distinct members into one body, is performed merely by an arbitrary act of the mind, and has no influence on the nature of things. Did I show you the particular causes of each individual in a collection of twenty particles of matter, I should think it very unreasonable, should you afterwards ask me, what was the cause of the whole twenty. This is sufficiently explained in explaining the cause of the parts.

The Continuous Origin of Matter*

FRED HOYLE

There is an impulse to ask where originated material comes from. But such a question is entirely meaningless within the terms of reference of science. Why is there gravitation? Why do electric fields exist? Why is the Universe? These queries are on a par with asking where newly originated matter comes from, and they are just as meaningless and unprofitable. The dividing line between what can validly

---

* From chapter 20 of *Frontiers of Astronomy* (New York: Harper & Brothers, 1955), pp. 302–303. Reprinted with kind permission of the Estate of Fred Hoyle, Hoyle Productions Limited.

be asked and what cannot depends on the organisation of science, in particular on the role played by the laws of physics. We can ask questions quite freely about the consequences of the laws of physics. But if we ask why the laws of physics are as they are, we shall receive only the answer that the laws of physics have consequences that agree with observation. If further we ask why this agreement exists, we enter into the territory of metaphysics – the scientist at all events will not attempt any answer. Newton's law of gravitation can be used to predict when and where the next total eclipse of the Sun is going to occur, and you may depend on it that events will fall pat in accordance with prediction. But we must then be satisfied. We must not go on to ask why.

It follows that when the origin of matter becomes a law of physics it is completely protected from such prying questions as: where does matter come from? An impregnable shield against such questions is provided by law, scientific law, the *modus operandi* of science. This does not of course mean that the continuous origin of matter is protected from all attack. It means that the attack must come from a different quarter. It must come from a comparison of the consequences of the law with observation [...]

The present situation is not new. When a neutron changes to a proton by a β-process an electron is disgorged. The electron originates. It did not exist before the process, after the process it does. Yet no one ever seems to have been worried by the question of where the electron comes from. We say that it originates in accordance with the laws of β-disintegration.

It is time now that we came to the law of the continuous origin of matter itself. Matter is capable of exerting several types of influence – or fields as they are usually called. There is the nuclear field that binds together the atomic nuclei. There is the electro-magnetic field that enables atoms to absorb light. There is the gravitational field that holds the stars and galaxies together. And according to the new theory there is also a creation field that causes matter to originate. Matter originates in response to the influence of other matter. It is this latter field that causes the expansion of the Universe. The distances over which the several fields operate are in an ascending scale – the nuclear field has the smallest range, although within this range it is easily the most powerful; next come the electromagnetic influences which have their main importance over the range of size from atoms up to stars (the range in which we humans lie); then the gravitational field is dominant over all sizes from planets and stars up to the clusters of galaxies; and lastly comes the universal field, the creation field, dominant in the largest aspects of the Universe.

We can pull off an important stroke at this stage. Because the creation influence is mainly determined by very distant material it cannot vary much from point to point. The proximity of the Sun does not produce any enhanced influence here on the Earth, nor does the fact that we happen to lie in the Galaxy. It may well be this smooth distribution of the creation influence that is responsible for the large scale spatial uniformity of the Universe.

Unending Oscillations*

W.B. BONNOR

[...] [T]he more plausible models are of two types. The first type predicts that the expansion will continue for ever: the nebulae which we see will get fainter and fainter, and the average density of matter in the universe will continually diminish. According to the second type of model, the expansion is slowing down fairly rapidly, and will eventually change to a contraction. If this is correct, the distant nebulae will one day approach the Earth instead of receding from it, and to observers of that time the light from them will appear more violet than the corresponding terrestrial light, instead of redder. The prospect of this contraction need cause no anxiety, as it would not begin to happen for many thousands of millions of years.

According to the models of either type, the expansion started about 8,000 million years ago. We can, from the models, estimate the average density of matter in the universe at any given time. We find that this density becomes greater and greater as we go backwards in time towards the moment the expansion started. At that moment itself, the density is infinite. The models suggest no way in which this infinite density could have come about; they give no information about what the universe was like before the expansion started. The trail we have been following seems to come to a dead end.

It is for this reason that the start of the expansion is sometimes called the creation of the universe. The conclusion to be drawn from the failure of the models is, it is argued, that all matter, compressed to an enormous density, was created at this time. At the same moment some sort of explosion took place, and the expansion started.

This view I regard as highly misleading and unscientific. The difficulty to be faced is that at the start of the expansion certain quantities in our differential equations become infinite. This frequently happens with differential equations, and when it does the equation is said to contain a mathematical singularity. A singularity in the mathematics describing a physical problem is usually an indication of the breakdown of the theory, and the physicist's normal response is to try to get a better one.

This procedure has not generally been followed in cosmology, and some scientists have identified the singularity at the start of the expansion with God, and thought that at this moment he created the universe. It seems to me highly improper to introduce God to solve our scientific problems. There is no place in

*   From "Relativistic Theories of the Universe," in H. Bondi, W.B. Bonnor, R.A. Lyttleton, and G.J. Whitrow, *Rival Theories of Cosmology* (London: Oxford University Press, 1960), pp. 4–8, 10. Reprinted with permission of Oxford University Press.

science for miraculous interventions of this sort; and there is a danger, for those who believe in God, in identifying him with singularities in differential equations, lest the need for him disappear with improved mathematics.

To me the correct approach seems to be to admit that the present cosmological models become unsatisfactory if one extrapolates them back the 8,000 million years or so to the start of the expansion. This is not to say that they are inadequate to describe the present, and the immediate past and future; this they are probably capable of doing. But they have to be altered so that they no longer become singular in the distant past.

The first obvious difficulty here is that 8,000 million years is a very long time, and anything we say about what the universe was like then is bound to be tentative, to say the least of it. Cosmology here meets the usual problems of any historical research concerned with the remote past. Some physicists think that the extrapolations involved are so enormous and the conclusions therefore so uncertain that the entire activity is a waste of time. There is something to be said for this view, but my argument against it is that to most people the past history of the universe is such an exciting matter that it is worth speculating about.

Secondly, even if we suppose that the infinite density given by our equations is a mathematical fiction with no physical meaning, it is probable that there *was* a period of very high density and temperature about 8,000 million years ago. This would be consistent with observed facts, which suggest that the age of our own nebula is somewhere about this figure. It is reasonable to suppose that after the period of intense heat, the nebulae, including our own, formed as the universe cooled. The effect of this period would be to obliterate evidence of what the universe was like before the expansion started. Any relics of a previous epoch would have been reduced to the uniformity of a gas, or even a fluid of atomic particles. For this reason there is little hope of obtaining by direct observations any information about the epochs before the expansion. We have to proceed by more indirect inference. Here the situation is more hopeful. I will describe some possible lines of attack, with special reference to models of the second type. According to these models the contraction, when it sets in, will eventually gather speed, bringing the nebulae closer and closer together; and if we follow the models to their end they reach a condition of infinite density – in fact, a singular state like the one in which they began. If one is prepared to regard the first singularity as the creation, the second presumably represents the annihilation of the universe.

In my opinion it is more satisfactory to suppose that as the singular state is approached some mechanism starts to operate which slows down the contraction and ultimately reverses it. The universe is thus launched on an expanding phase again, and starts a new cycle of existence. According to this picture, the history of the universe is an unending series of oscillations. [...] There is no reason whatever for downing tools and handing over to God 8,000 million years ago.

God's Existence: A Debate*

BERTRAND RUSSELL AND F.C. COPLESTON

COPLESTON: As we are going to discuss the existence of God, it might perhaps be as well to come to some provisional agreement as to what we understand by the term "God". I presume that we mean a supreme personal being, distinct from the world, and creator of the world. Would you agree – provisionally at least – to accept this statement as the meaning of the term "God"?

RUSSELL: Yes, I accept this definition.

COPLESTON: My position is the affirmative position that such a being actually exists, and that his existence can be proved philosophically. […] For clarity's sake, I will divide the argument into distinct stages. First of all, I should say, we know that there are at least some beings in the world who do not contain in themselves the reason for their existence. For example, I depend on my parents, and now on the air, and on food, and so on. Secondly, the world is simply the real or imagined totality or aggregate of individual objects, none of which contain in themselves alone the reason for their existence. There isn't any world distinct from the objects which form it, any more than the human race is something apart from the members of it. Therefore, I should say, since objects or events exist, and since no object of experience contains within itself the reason of its existence, […] the totality of objects must have a reason external to itself. That reason must be an existent being, and this being is either itself the reason for its own existence, or it is not. If it is, well and good. If it is not, then we must proceed further. But if we proceed to infinity in that sense, then there is no explanation of existence at all. So, I should say, in order to explain existence, we must come to a being which contains within itself the reason for its own existence – that is to say, which cannot not-exist.

RUSSELL: This raises a great many points and it is not altogether easy to know where to begin, but I think that perhaps in answering your argument, the best point at which to begin is the question of a necessary being. The word "necessary", I should maintain, can only be applied significantly to propositions. And, in fact, only to such as are analytic, that is to say such as it is self-contradictory to deny. […] I don't admit the idea of a necessary being, and I don't admit that there is any particular meaning in calling other beings "contingent". These phrases don't for me have a significance except within a logic that

* From "The Existence of God," debate on BBC Radio broadcast in 1948. As printed in *The Collected Papers of Bertrand Russell*, volume 11, ed. John G. Slater (London and New York: Routledge, 1997), pp. 524–530, 532, 540–541. Reprinted with permission of Taylor & Francis Books, UK, and the BBC.

I reject. [...] A being that must exist and cannot not-exist, would surely, according to you, be a being whose essence involves existence.

COPLESTON: Yes, a being the essence of which is to exist. But I should not be willing to argue the existence of God simply from the idea of His essence, because I don't think we have any clear intuition of God's essence as yet. I think we have to argue from the world of experience to God. [...] [A]re you going to say that we can't, or we shouldn't, even raise the question of the existence of the whole of this sorry scheme of things, of the whole universe?

RUSSELL: Yes. I don't think there is any meaning in it at all [...]

COPLESTON: My belief is that what we call the world is intrinsically unintelligible, apart from the existence of God. You see I can't believe that the infinity of the series of events [...] would be in the slightest degree relevant to the situation. If you add up chocolates you still get chocolates after all and not a sheep. If you add up chocolates to infinity, you presumably get an infinite number of chocolates. So if you add up contingent beings to infinity, you still get contingent beings, not a necessary being. An infinite series of contingent beings will be, to my way of thinking, as unable to cause itself as one contingent being. However, you say, I think, that it is illegitimate to raise the question of what will explain the existence of any particular object.

RUSSELL: It is quite all right if you mean by explaining it simply finding a cause for it.

COPLESTON: Why stop at one particular object? Why shouldn't one raise the question of the cause of the existence of all particular objects?

RUSSELL: Because I see no reason to think there is any. The whole concept of cause is one we derive from our observation of particular things. I see no reason to suppose that the total has any cause whatsoever.

COPLESTON: To say that there isn't any cause is not the same thing as saying that we shouldn't look for a cause. The statement that there isn't any cause should come, if it comes at all, at the end of the enquiry, not the beginning. In any case, if the total has no cause, then to my way of thinking it must be its own cause, which seems to me impossible. Moreover, the statement that the world is simply there, if in answer to a question, presupposes that the question has meaning.

RUSSELL: No, it doesn't need to be its own cause; what I am saying is that the concept of cause is not applicable to the total.

COPLESTON: Then you would agree with Sartre that the universe is what he calls "gratuitous"?

RUSSELL: The word "gratuitous" suggests that it might be something else. I should say that the universe is just there, and that is all.

COPLESTON: I can't see how you can rule out the legitimacy of asking the question how the total, or anything at all, comes to be there. Why something rather than nothing? That is the question. The fact that we gain our knowledge of causality empirically, from particular causes, does not rule out the possibility of asking what the cause of the series is [...]

RUSSELL: I can illustrate what seems to me your fallacy. Every man who exists has a mother, and it seems to me your argument is that therefore the human race must have a mother, but obviously the human race hasn't a mother; that is a different logical sphere.

COPLESTON: I can't really see any parity. If I were saying "every object has a phenomenal cause therefore the whole series has a phenomenal cause" there would be a parity, but I am not saying that; I am saying every object has a phenomenal cause if you insist on the infinity of the series; but the series of phenomenal causes is an insufficient explanation of the series. Therefore, the series has not a phenomenal cause but a transcendent cause.

RUSSELL: That is always assuming that not only every particular thing in the world, but the world as a whole must have a cause. For that assumption I see no ground whatever. [...]

COPLESTON: [Y]our general point then, Lord Russell, is that it is illegitimate even to ask the question of the cause of the world?

RUSSELL: Yes, that is my position.

COPLESTON: If it is a question that for you has no meaning, it is of course very difficult to discuss it, isn't it?

RUSSELL: Yes, it is very difficult. [...]

COPLESTON: Perhaps it is time I summed up my position. I have argued two things. First, that the existence of God can be philosophically proved by a metaphysical argument. Secondly, that it is only the existence of God that will make sense of man's moral experience and of religious experience. [...] As regards the metaphysical argument, we are apparently in agreement that what we call the world consists simply of contingent beings. That is, of beings no one of which can account for its own existence. You say that the series of events needs no explanation: I say that if there were no necessary being, no being which must exist and cannot not-exist, nothing would exist. The infinity of the series of contingent beings, even if proved, would be irrelevant. Something does exist; therefore, there must be something which accounts for this fact, a being which is outside the series of contingent beings. If you had admitted this, we could then have discussed whether that being is personal, good, and so on; on the actual point discussed, whether there is or is not a necessary being, I find myself, I think, in agreement with the great majority of classical philosophers.

You maintain, I think that existing beings are simply there, and that I have no justification for raising the question of the explanation of their existence. But I would like to point out that this position cannot be substantiated by logical analysis; it expresses a philosophy which itself stands in need of proof. I think we have reached an impasse because our ideas of philosophy are radically different; it seems to me that what I call a part of philosophy, that you call the whole, in so far at least as philosophy is rational. It seems to me, if you will pardon my saying so, that besides your own logical system – which you call "modern" in opposition to antiquated logic (a tendentious adjective) – you maintain a philosophy which cannot be substantiated by logical analysis. After all, the problem of God's existence is an existential problem, whereas logical analysis does not deal directly with problems of existence. So it seems to me, to declare that the terms involved in one set of problems are meaningless because they are not required in dealing with another set of problems, is to settle from the beginning the nature and extent of philosophy, and that is itself a philosophical act which stands in need of justification.

RUSSELL: I should like to say just a few words by way of summary on my side. First, as to the metaphysical argument: I don't admit the connotations of such a term as "contingent" or the possibility of explanation in your sense. I think the word "contingent" inevitably suggests the possibility of something that wouldn't have this, what you might call, accidental character of just being there, and that I don't think it is true except in the purely causal sense. You can sometimes give a causal explanation of one thing as being the effect of something else, but that is merely referring one thing to another thing and there is no – to my mind – explanation in your sense of anything at all; nor is there any meaning in calling things "contingent" because there isn't anything else they could be.

The Cosmos Needs No Explanation*

ADOLF GRÜNBAUM

From *Encyclopedia of Cosmology*

The existence of matter-energy allegedly poses for cosmology a problem of creation that many cosmologists consider scientifically insoluble. There is a genuine question whether the world or the matter-energy in it had a temporal origin, but this problem is often fallaciously transmuted into a pseudo problem of creation by a cause *external* to the physical world.

The idea of creation is laden with the notion of a creating *agency* or *cause* external to the created objects, and the presumed beginning of the universe a finite time ago tends to suggest, in some quarters, the operation of a creator. This view was endorsed by Pope Pius XII in a famous address in 1951 to the Pontifical Academy of Sciences. The English astronomer Sir Bernard Lovell has given an

*   From "Creation in Cosmology," in Norris S. Hetherington, ed., *Encyclopedia of Cosmology* (New York and London: Garland Publishing Inc., 1993), pp. 126–135. Reprinted with permission of Taylor & Francis LLC; and from "Why Is There a Universe AT ALL Rather Than Just Nothing?", in C. Glymour et al., eds., *Logic, Methodology and Philosophy of Science: Proceedings of the Thirteenth International Congress* (London: King's College London Publications, 2009), pp. 7, 9, 10, 15. Reprinted with kind permission of the author.

explicitly theological twist to the most fundamental cosmological question by making two major claims: (1) there is an inescapable problem of creation in both the steady state and big bang cosmologies, but neither of them is capable of offering a scientific solution to it; and (2) a satisfactory explanatory solution "must eventually move over into metaphysics" by postulating *divine* creation. Claiming that one can meaningfully speak of "the time before the [big bang]," Lovell reasons that "one must still inquire [...] how the primeval gas [of the big bang] originated. Science has nothing to say on this issue."

Elaborating on Pope Pius XII's creationist gloss on big bang cosmology, the English physicist C.J. Isham wrote: "Perhaps the best argument in favour of the thesis that the Big Bang supports theism is the obvious unease with which it is greeted by some atheist physicists. At times this has led to scientific ideas, such as continuous creation or an oscillating universe, being advanced with a tenacity which so exceeds their intrinsic worth that one can only suspect the operation of psychological forces lying very much deeper than the usual academic desire of a theorist to support his/her theory." The advocacy of an oscillating universe by the atheistic British physicist W. Bonnor is a case in point, since Bonnor rejected a big bang model featuring a finite past in the belief that it lends support to divine creation, a belief that will be seen to be mistaken.

John Maddox, the editor of *Nature*, also judged the big bang cosmogony "philosophically unacceptable," claiming that "creationists [...] have ample justification in the doctrine of the Big Bang," because it is vitiated by "the philosophical difficulty that an important issue, that of the ultimate origin of our world, cannot be discussed." In due course, I shall challenge Maddox's assertions fundamentally, but it behooves me to register a twofold caveat at the outset: First, suppose that – contrary to actual fact – the best model of recent physical cosmogony *were* evidentially supportive of divine creation *ex nihilo* à la Augustine. In that counterfactual eventuality, it would be an impermissible apriorism to reject the model for that particular reason, as some atheists have done. Second, on the other hand, posit that in the context of the big bang model, Maddox's construal of the question of "the ultimate origin of the world" turns out to be a pseudo problem, as indeed it will. Then this unfavorable verdict on his question shows it to be a pointless query. But this pointlessness surely does not license his conclusion that "creationists ... have ample justification in the doctrine of the Big Bang."

Before I enter into the cosmological particulars, let me note that the invocation of a divine creator to provide *causal* explanations in cosmology suffers from a fundamental defect vis-à-vis scientific explanations: As we know from 2,000 years of theology, the hypothesis of divine creation does not even envision, let alone specify, an appropriate *intermediate* causal *process* that would *link* the presence of the supposed divine (causal) agency to the effects that are attributed to it. Nor, it seems, is there any prospect at all that the chronic inscrutability of the putative causal linkage will be removed by new theoretical developments. In sharp contrast, the discovery that "an aspirin a day keeps many a heart attack away" has been quickly followed by the quest for a specification of the mode of action that mediates the prophylaxis afforded by this drug against coronary infarcts – similarly for therapeutic benefits from placebos wrought by the mediation of endorphin release in the brain and by the secretions of interferon and steroids. In physics, there is either an actual specification or at least a quest for the *mediating causal dynamics* linking presumed causes to their effects. In the case of laws of coexistence or action at a distance, there is a specification of concomitant variations in the sense of John Stuart Mill. Yet, despite the failure of theology to provide just such a dynamic linkage, Newton invoked divine intervention in the belief that it could plug explanatory lacunae that his physics had left unfilled.

In the face of the inherently irremediable dynamic inscrutability of divine causation, the resort to God as creator, ontological conserver of matter, or intervener in the course of nature is precisely a *deus ex machina* that lacks a vital feature of causal explanations in the sciences. The Book of Genesis tells us about the divine word-magic of creating photons by *saying* "Let there be light," but we aren't even told whether God said it in Hebrew. As far as causation goes, we are being told, to all intents and purposes, that an intrinsically elusive, mysterious agency X inscrutably produces the effect, and the appeal to the supposed divine attributes of omnipotence, omniscience, and omnibenevolence merely baptizes this cardinal explanatory lacuna.

Thomas Aquinas recognized, to his credit, that divine causal explanations are problematic by being global, although he thought he could neutralize his own initial objection to them by his famous "Five Ways." As he put the explanatory challenge: "[I]t seems that everything we see in the world can be accounted for by other principles, supposing God did not exist" (*Summa Theologica* I.1.6, third article, objection 2).

Indeed, atheists have nothing to fear from any of the twentieth-century physical cosmologies. None of these theories support the hypothesis that divine creation *ex nihilo* produced the big bang or is operative at other times.

Much of contemporary scientific and philosophical literature on cosmology is rife with a confusion of two quite different questions. The first of these queries is, Does the physical universe have a temporal *origin*, and, if so, what does physical cosmology tell us about it? The second question is, What was the external cause of the big bang at the beginning of time, and what light, if any, can science throw on it? Within the framework of the now largely defunct steady state cosmology of Hermann Bondi and Thomas Gold, Lovell asks relatedly: "What is the cause of the new hydrogen atoms that come into being in violation of matter-energy conservation?"

Those who insist on asking for the external or supernatural cause of the big bang by reference to prequantum cosmogony, steady state cosmology, or quantum cosmogony overlook that their questions are hardly mere requests for information. Instead, such requests are laden with very questionable underlying assumptions that the interlocutors simply take for granted rather than justify by pertinent evidence. In fact, precisely these underlying assumptions are denied respectively by just the physical theories to which the interlocutors are addressing their question. Thus, their creation question contains a *petitio principii* by assuming, rather than showing, that any good theory needs to answer it. After all, a question cannot be regarded as a well-posed challenge merely because the questioner finds it psychologically insistent, experiences a strong feeling of puzzlement, and desires an answer to it.

The question of creation – as distinct from origination – is just as ill-posed in the context of contemporary rival physical cosmologies as was the following sort of problem, which agitated philosophers until the middle of the eighteenth century: Why do ordinary material objects not simply vanish into nothingness? René Descartes in his Meditation III simply assumed, at least tacitly, that when a physical system is closed, it will simply *not* obey matter conservation spontaneously and, quite naturally, *without* external causal intervention. Having made that assumption, he was driven to suppose that an *external cause* supplied by God's activity was required at every instant of time to prevent matter from *lapsing into nothingness*. Ironically, whereas Lovell calls God to the rescue as the cause of the continual nonconservative hydrogen production in the steady state universe, Descartes had assigned that same indispensable causal role to the deity just to keep contingently existing material objects from vanishing into thin air: "It is a matter of fact perfectly clear and evident to all who consider with attention the nature of time, that, in order to be conserved in each moment in which it endures, a substance has need of the same power and action as would be necessary to produce and create it anew, supposing it did not yet exist, so that the light of nature shows us clearly that the distinction between creation and conservation is solely a [conceptual] distinction of the reason [rather than of ontological causation]."

But the eighteenth-century French chemist Lavoisier showed there is, indeed, matter conservation (or matter-energy conservation) in a closed finite system on the medium-sized macroscopic scale *qua spontaneous, natural, unperturbed behavior of the system*. And, if so, Descartes was *empirically* wrong to have assumed that such conservation requires the intervention of an external cause. Therefore, if he was thus wrong, his claim that external divine intervention in particular is needed to keep an object from disappearing into nothingness was based on a false presupposition. More generally, if the presupposition of a philosophical or scientific question is false, the question is at best misleading and at least ill-posed or pointless.

False or unwarranted underlying assumptions can vitiate not only questions, but also characterizations, of cosmological models that employ at best inappropriate or misleading vocabulary. Thus, when speaking of a prequantum big bang model of the expanding universe featuring an initial radius of zero, Isham says, "This is essentially the sense in which space and time can be said to 'come into being' at the point of creation." And Alexander Vilenkin speaks of a quantum model featuring an initial minimum radius as having been "created from nothing" at the minimum radius. But the British cosmologist Stephen Hawking rightly exposes the dubious underlying assumption: "However, the use of the word 'create' would seem to imply that there was some concept of time in which the universe did not exist before a certain instant and then came into being. But time is defined only within the universe, and does not exist outside it."

Surprisingly, Hawking even credits St. Augustine with the recognition of just this restriction by quoting Augustine's assertion that "time itself was made by God." Augustine made this claim to undercut the premise of a challenger who had asked him, "What did God do before He made Heaven and Earth?" Isham sees Augustine's notion of the divine creation of *both* time *and* matter as a "profound" answer to the challenger's question, but when Augustine tells us that "time itself was made by God," the location "was made" is subject to precisely the objection that Hawking justly raised against the word "created." This Augustinian assertion therefore seems incoherent and, moreover, unhelpful to Hawking's well-taken caveat against Vilenkin.

Yet some Catholic theologians, including Aquinas, have interpreted Book XI of Augustine's *Confessions* as enunciating the doctrine of *timeless* causation as follows: At any time whatever, the existence of time itself and of the world are entirely dependent on God for their very being. However, since this *atemporal* metaphysical version of Augustine's creation ex nihilo is not relevant to current physics, and is quite obscure if not incoherent, we need not be concerned with it here.

At present, the big bang theory is in vogue, whereas the Bondi and Gold steady state theory is largely defunct on empirical grounds. Indeed, the so-called inflationary early expansion and quantum cosmology have modified these earlier twentieth-century cosmologies. Yet it is instructive to examine first a typical argument for divine creation in the context of the earlier two rival theories, despite their replacement by newer models. The philosophical issues have remained essentially the same, although the technical details have changed considerably.

More recently, the plasma cosmology originally developed by Hannes Alfvén – which assigns a critical cosmic role to hot, electrically charged gases – has posed a major challenge to the gravity-dominated big bang cosmology. By featuring a universe that has *existed forever*, without any beginning, plasma cosmology altogether obviates even the temptation to invoke divine creation ex nihilo. Such preclusion of creation would become important if plasma cosmology were to supplant the big bang theory in response to observational findings contradicting some of the latter's evolutionary tenets.

The Pseudo Problem of Creation in
Prequantum Twentieth-Century Cosmologies

Alleged philosophical defects of the Bondi and
Gold steady state theory

In the Bondi and Gold theory, the formation of new hydrogen atoms violates matter conservation because they assume that the *density* of matter is constant over time even as the universe is *expanding*. Thus, their theory features the conservation of density but *not* of matter. Yet this violation of matter-energy conservation should be described by means of such words as "accession or accretion of matter" rather than by the term "creation." By the same token, the use of the term "creation" throughout Isham's paper "Creation of the Universe as a Quantum Process" is to be deplored. Unfortunately, Bondi himself uses the term *creation* misleadingly to describe this denial of energy conservation in cosmology: "It should be clearly understood that the creation here discussed [in the context of the steady state theory] is the formation of matter not out of radiation but out of nothing." Alas, the term *creation* suggests misleadingly that Bondi was postulating the operation of a creator or creating *agency*. Fortunately, however, he goes on to use the much better term *formation*.

More recently, the cosmologist J. Narlikar has claimed that the currently popular so-called inflationary model of the universe is an updated form of Fred Hoyle's version of the steady state theory, as distinct from the Bondi and Gold original. The affinity between the new inflationary and the old steady state theories derives from the fact that the new theory features the conservation of *energy density* as the universe inflates very rapidly. This feature is the counterpart of the conservation of *matter density* in the old steady state versions.

To gain perspective on Lovell's philosophical complaint that the "steady-state theory has no solution to the problem of the creation of [new] matter," let us first look at the lesson that can be learned from the history of science in regard to the evidential warrant for postulating external causes for the behavior of physical and biological systems. According to Aristotle, an external force is needed as the cause of a sublunar body's nonvertical motion. In his physics, the demand for such a disturbing external cause to explain such motion arises from the following assumption: When a sublunar body is not acted on by an external force, its *natural*, spontaneous unperturbed behavior is to be at rest at its "proper place" or, if it is not already there, to move vertically toward it. Yet, as we know, Galileo's analysis of the motions of spheres on inclined planes led him to conclude that the empirical evidence speaks against just this Aristotelian assumption. As Newton's first law of motion tells us, uniform motion never requires any external force as its cause; only accelerated motion does. But if that is so, the Aristotelian demand for an *explanation* of *any* nonvertical sublunar motion by reference to an *external*, perturbing force begs the explanatory question by means of a false underlying assumption, rather than asks a well-posed legitimate question as to the "why" of uniform nonvertical motion. By the same token, Galileo and Newton could only shrug their shoulders or throw up their hands in despair if an Aristotelian told them that he had a solution to the "problem" of the *external* cause of such uniform motion whereas they did not. It would, of course, be legitimate for the Aristotelian to try to offer empirical evidence that Newton's first law was false despite Galileo's observations on an inclined plane. But begging the question hardly constitutes such evidence.

An Aristotelian who would reason like Lovell could just as well say the following: If a sublunar body moves nonvertically while *not* being subjected to an external physical force, then we must explain this motion – even if it is uniform – as the result of external supernatural divine intervention. Just as Galileo and Newton rejected, on empirical grounds, the Aristotelian idea of rest or vertical motion as the naturally inevitable, unperturbed state of sublunar bodies, so also Bondi and Gold rejected matter conservation on the huge cosmological scale as the inevitable natural career of externally undisturbed physical systems. Instead, they postulated *density* conservation in an expanding universe, which requires nonconservative matter accretion. And just as it is a matter of *empirical* fact whether uniform motion requires a force as its external cause, so also is the question whether the natural, spontaneous, unperturbed behavior of physical systems conserves the quantity of matter *or* rather its density in an expanding universe. After all, our scientific conceptions of which state of affairs is the spontaneous, natural, and unperturbed one are no better than the scope of their supporting evidence, and as the history of science shows all too clearly, as our evidence grows, these conceptions need to be changed by stretching our intellectual horizons.

If matter conservation is indeed the natural, unperturbed course of things, even on a cosmological scale, then the steady state theory is physically false. On the other hand, if large-scale *density* conservation in an expanding universe is the spontaneous, *unperturbed*, natural state as a matter of empirical fact, Lovell is not entitled to his insistence that *in every theory*, matter conservation *must* be held to be the natural state. Yet just that insistence is the basis for his demand for an external supernatural cause to explain the matter increase required by density conservation in an expanding universe. Thus, Lovell complains that the steady state theory makes no provision for "the energy input which gave rise to the created [hydrogen] atom." No wonder, therefore, that in his view, the *nonconservative* matter production postulated by Bondi and Gold poses a "problem of creation" so acute that it "can tear the individual's mind asunder." To prevent such mental disintegration, he urges that "we move over into metaphysics" and characterizes the matter increase causally as a miracle by saying that "the creation process is a divine act which is proceeding continuously." Thus, in that sense, Lovell is prepared to accept the steady state cosmology if observation were to confirm it empirically. Ironically, Lovell seems to have overlooked that Descartes had claimed divine intervention to explain ordinary matter *conservation*, after assuming a state of nothingness to be the unperturbed natural state of the world. In a steady state world containing humanoids who live long enough to observe its formation of matter many, many times, it would seem quite natural to them.

We see that the hypothesized increase of matter in a steady state universe is turned into a divine miracle only by the gratuitous insistence on matter conservation as the natural cosmic state, no matter what the empirical evidence. But those who share Lovell's view of miraculousness cannot justify a criterion of "naturalness" that would turn the continual accretion of new matter into something "outside the natural order" instead of just being itself a part of that very order. Thus, the astronomer Herbert Dingle's rejection of matter accretion as supernaturally miraculous was ill-founded. It emerges that Lovell, the theist, and Dingle, the atheist, made the identical conservation assumption in thinking that a matter increase would be miraculous, although they made opposite uses of that hypothesis in their attitude toward the steady state theory. Philosophically, they are brothers under the skin in this context. The key point that should not be overlooked is: Just as a theory postulating matter conservation does not require God to prevent the conserved matter from being annihilated, so also the steady state theory has no need at all for a divine agency to cause its new hydrogen to come into being.

The foregoing argument, as developed from the history of physics from Aristotle to Bondi and Gold, could likewise be articulated from the history of inquiry into the natural possibility of the spontaneous generation of living substances from inorganic materials. After Pasteur's work led to the denial of that possibility in an oxidizing atmosphere, Oparin and Urey asserted it for a reducing atmosphere over much longer time periods.

Alleged philosophical defects of the prequantum big bang cosmogony

When the prequantum version of the big bang theory is contrasted with its steady state rival, it is often called "evolutionary." It tells us that before the chemical elements were formed, an explosion of primeval matter resulted in the present expansion of the universe. That explosion is called the big bang.

It may perhaps still be an open question whether the big bang might be somehow accommodated in a mathematically meaningful fashion in an Einsteinian universe such that the big bang is not a singular boundary of space-time. In one such sketchily envisioned model, the big bang would have been preceded by an infinite sequence of prior contractions and expansions, like those of an accordion. But quite apart from current technical doubts about the eternally oscillating model of the universe, it does not even provide a point of departure for the argument from creation ex nihilo, and such models will therefore be ignored in the following discussion.

Big bang models *prima facie* allow two cases, but only one of these is a bona fide model within general relativity theory. Nonetheless, we will deal here with the other model as well, because Narlikar and others have invoked it to claim that t (time)$=0$ is a bona fide instant at which "the primary creation event" actually occurred.

Narlikar is instructively articulate in confusing the question of the origin of the universe with the purported problem of its creation. Having conflated these two different questions, he then complains, "The most fundamental question in cosmology is, 'Where did the matter we see around us originate in the first place?'

This point has never been dealt with in the big bang cosmologies in which, at $t=0$, there occurs a sudden and fantastic violation of the law of conservation of matter and energy. After $t=0$ there is no such violation. By ignoring the primary creation event most cosmologists turn a blind eye to the above question."

Narlikar had set the stage for the formulation of his question: "So we have the following description of a big bang universe. At an epoch, which we may denote by $t=0$, the Universe explodes into existence. [...] the epoch $t=0$ is taken as the event of 'creation.' Prior to this there existed no Universe, no observers, no physical laws. Everything suddenly appeared at $t=0$. The 'age' of the Universe is defined as the cosmic time which has elapsed since this event. [...] Although scientists are not in the habit of discussing the creation event or the situation prior to it, a lot of research has gone into the discussion of what the Universe was like immediately after its creation."

Two sorts of big bang models have been invoked by creationists. One, which figured in Narlikar's complaint, features a cosmic time interval that is closed at the big bang instant $t=0$, and furthermore, this instant had *no temporal predecessor*. In this case, $t=0$ was a singular, temporally first event of the physical space-time to which all of the worldlines of the universe converge backward. This means that there simply did not exist any instants of time before $t=0$. But it would be (potentially) misleading to describe this state of affairs by saying that "time began" at $t=0$. This description makes it sound as if time began in the same sense in which, say, a musical concert begins. And that is misleading precisely because a concert is actually preceded by actual instants of time when it has not yet begun. But in the big bang model under consideration, there were no such earlier instants before $t=0$ and hence no instants when the big bang had not yet occurred. Yet Narlikar deplored the fact that "scientists are not in the habit of discussing [...] the situation prior to [the big bang]."

To suggest or assume tacitly that such prior instants existed after all is simply incompatible with the physical correctness of the big bang model, and thus implicitly denies its soundness. Since Aristotle believed that a first instant of time is *inconceivable* (*Physics* 8.25 lb), he implicitly denied even the logical possibility of the model and, therefore, also its physical possibility. It is now clear that the physical correctness of this model is also implicitly denied by anyone who addresses any of the following questions to it: What happened *before* $t=0$? What prior events *caused* matter to come into existence at $t=0$? or What *caused* the big bang to occur at $t=0$? In just this vein, Lovell asks "how the primeval gas originated" and then complains that "science has nothing to say on this issue." As Barrow and Tipler point out, the question What happened before $t=0$? makes just as little sense as to ask, in the case of a universe featuring an *infinite* past, What happened before the Universe began?

Of course, Narlikar and Lovell are entitled to reject the given big bang model by trying to give cogent reasons for postulating the existence of times *before* $t=0$. But failing that, it is altogether wrongheaded to complain that, even when taken to be physically adequate, this model fails to answer questions based on assumptions that it denies as false.

The question-begging presupposition of instants before $t=0$ is also made in another form by asking in the context of the *pre*-quantum models: How did the matter existing at $t=0$ come *into* being? The model to which this question is addressed features the *conservation* of matter-energy. Thus, the model requires that at all existing instants of time, the total matter-energy content of the universe be the same. To ask how this matter came into existence in the first place is to presuppose not only earlier moments of time, but also the *non*-existence of any matter at those supposed earlier times. *Yet precisely these presuppositions are denied by the matter-conservation that is asserted by the model.* Therefore, Narlikar was wrong when he wrote that "in big bang cosmologies ... at $t=0$, there occurs a sudden and fantastic violation of the law of conservation of matter and energy." Such illegitimate ways of begging the question generate the so-called problem of creation.

More generally, the terms *creation* and *annihilation* can each be especially misleading in descriptions of processes that conform to energy-conservation laws. Take, for example, the phrases "pair creation" and "pair annihilation," which are familiar from the theory of particle reactions. In that theory, these phrases are employed to describe energy-conserving processes featuring the intertransformation between radiation and a particle pair consisting of one kind of particle and its antiparticle. Thus, when an electron and a positron collide, their rest-mass is *converted* into two photons of gamma radiation emitted in two opposite directions. Although the rest-mass of these photons may well be zero, this gamma radiation is obviously much more than just "nothing." Nevertheless, even the distinguished philosopher of physics Hans Reichenbach wrote that the particle and its antiparticle disappear "into nothing." Evidently, the phrase "pair annihilation" obscures the fact that the energy of the original positive rest-mass of the particles reappears in the resulting gamma radiation, although the term "annihilation-radiation" is not similarly misleading. Corresponding remarks apply to the transformation of gamma radiation into an electron-positron pair: such pair production is certainly not a case of pair "creation" *out of nothing*.

If, as in one of the versions of quantum cosmology to be discussed below, the "big bang" is no longer held to comprise *all* early past time ($t \geq 0$) but to start later, then it may well no longer be misguided to ask what caused the big bang, as Paul Davies has noted. But in that quantum version, general relativity turns out to tell us *why* there is an "inflationary" expansion, thereby obviating any explanatory resort to an external divine cause.

The second class of general relativistic big bang models that have been claimed to warrant the sort of questions asked by Narlikar and Lovell differs from the first. The first featured a cosmic time interval closed at the big bang instant $t=0$, which has no temporal predecessor. The second excludes the mathematical singularity at $t=0$ as not being an actual moment of time. Thus, their cosmic time interval is *open* in the past by lacking the instant $t=0$, although the duration of that past interval in years is finite, say, 15 billion years or so. But just as for the first class, no instants of time exist *before* t=0 for the second. And despite the equality of finite duration of the time intervals in the two classes of models, the crucial difference between them is the following: For the second class of models, there is no first instant of time at all, just as there is no leftmost point of an infinite Euclidean line that extends in both directions. And in both cases, the nonexistence of time *before* t=0 allows that matter has *always* existed, although the age of the universe is finite in either case. This assertion is true because, here as elsewhere, the term *always* refers to all actual (past) instants of time.

Nevertheless, even in the second class, the finite age of the universe has tempted some people to make the tacit false assumption that there were moments of time after all before the big bang, an assumption incompatible with both models. And once this question-begging assumption is made, the door is open for all the same illegitimate, ill-posed creation questions. Hawking expresses a cognate view: "In general relativity, time [...] does not have any meaning outside the spacetime manifold. To ask what happened before the universe began is like asking for a point on the Earth at 91 degrees north latitude; it just is not defined. Instead of talking about the universe being created, and maybe coming to an end, one should just say: The universe is."

The Pseudo Problem of Creation in Quantum Cosmology

Despite the replacement of the classical big bang theory by quantum cosmology, the philosophical issues with which we have been concerned, as well as their resolution, remain essentially the same.

In quantum cosmology there are two sorts of so-called vacuum: the "true" and "false" ones. The true vacuum is constituted by space that differs from being totally devoid of matter and energy only to the extent of allowing energy fluctuations. The false vacuum, on the other hand, contains energy without matter. Referring to the initial true vacuum state, Victor Weisskopf recalls the biblical statement "The world was without form and void, and darkness was upon the face of the deep." But the affinity between that vague biblical statement and the assertion of an initial true vacuum in the technical sense of particle physics turns out to be altogether unavailing to the proponent of divine creation out of nothing.

The initial true vacuum state does not last. There is a transition from it to the false vacuum, as Weisskopf tells us: "Everything, including the true vacuum, is subject to fluctuations – in particular to energy fluctuations. The field that provides energy to the false vacuum is absent in the true vacuum, but not completely. There must be fluctuations in the field. Thus, at one moment a small region somewhere in space may have fluctuated into a false vacuum."

To the question of how energy fluctuations can occur in a true vacuum that is supposed to be free of energy and matter, Weisskopf replies, "I did not explain this because it would have been difficult to do so in ordinary language. [...] No doubt the statement I made, if applied to the true vacuum, contradicts the idea of total emptiness. In this sense the common concept of a vacuum is not valid. The recognition of fundamental fluctuations in empty space is one of the great achievements of quantum mechanics. In some special cases the existence of such fluctuations has been established by experiment. And that is the basis of the idea that indeed something can come out of nothing." More emphatically, Barrow and Tipler issue the following salutary caveat: "[T]he modern picture of the quantum vacuum differs radically from the classical and everyday meaning of a vacuum – nothing."

Thus, according to quantum theory, the emergence of energy by fluctuation is ex nihilo only in a rather metaphorical sense, and proceeds in accord with pertinent physical principles, rather than as a matter of inscrutable external divine causation.

As is known from Einstein's general theory of relativity, a false vacuum "is bound to expand suddenly and explosively, filling more and more space with false vacuum." Just this "inflationary" expansion, which is far more rapid than the rates familiar from the classical conceptions of the expanding universe, "is supposed to be the Big Bang!" according to Weisskopf.

For precisely the same reasons that were developed above with regard to the classical big bang at $t=0$, there is no warrant for invoking an external cause – let alone a divine one – for the initial true vacuum. *A fortiori*, there is no warrant for seeking an external cause of any sort for effecting the various successive transitions from the true vacuum to the false one, then to the "inflationary expansion," and finally to the more familiar slow expansion that features the formations outlined previously. These transitions are, after all, matters of natural physical laws. Hawking reaches the conclusion that there is no problem of creation, because at that stage, the very distinction between space and time becomes mushy, as does the notion of an initial singular instant of time.

In his 1986 paper, Lovell referred to an updated big bang model that features an initial quantum vacuum state, followed by the expansion. And he said in effect that if we call the vacuum state a state of "nothing," this model provides a scientific justification of Augustine's theory of creation out of nothing. But in the discussion after his oral delivery of the paper at a 1986 Locarno congress, Lovell agreed with Adolf Grünbaum that the transition from the vacuum state to the expansion need not require any external cause at all, let alone a divine one.

We may conclude here by taking issue with Isham's gloss on the Hartle and Hawking account of quantum cosmology. Isham considers a space-time different from the prequantum conical one of classical general relativity "because the classical solution to Einstein's equations [...] is itself singular and ill-defined" at the vertex of the cone. And he explains the motivation for the choice of an alternative space-time: "Had this [classical] procedure worked it would have described the creation of the universe from an initial 'point.' However, we are interested in creation from 'nothing,' which suggests [...] a spacetime [...] whose boundary is just a single three-dimensional space." His accompanying figure representing the latter is a bowl whose rim stands for the single three-dimensional space that is avowedly the only boundary of the space-time.

How, then, does Isham manage to have the bowl space-time originate "from nothing"? It would appear that he does so by sheer verbal fiat: "The initial space from which the universe 'emerged' can be defined to be that part of the boundary of the four-dimensional space which is *not* part of the (later) three-surface [boundary]. But this is the empty set, which gives a precise mathematical definition of the concept of nothing!" Then Isham adds pointedly: "The creation from nothing is precisely that."

But note that, as Isham himself has told us, the bowl space-time is one "whose boundary is just a single three-dimensional space," (i.e., the rim of the bowl). What then is temporally "initial" about an empty set, generated by the following stipulative definition: The "initial" space is that portion, if any, of the space-time boundary that is definitionally excluded from the only boundary possessed by the space-time? Apparently, the empty set in question is verbally labeled to be "initial" by mere definitional fiat.

Besides, such physicists as Hartle and Hawking, and Vilenkin speak misleadingly of certain primordial physical states as "nothing" even though these states are avowedly only "a realm of unrestrained quantum gravity," which is "a state with no classical spacetime." As Barrow and Tipler rightly point out, "It is, of course, somewhat inappropriate to call the origin of a bubble universe in a fluctuation of the vacuum 'creation *ex nihilo*,' for the quantum mechanical vacuum is not truly 'nothing'; rather, the vacuum state has a rich structure which resides in a previously existing substratum of space-time, either Minkowski or de Sitter space-time." And if the very notion of physical time becomes problematic in fundamental physics, as urged by John Wheeler, even the *temptation* to misinvoke divine creation ex nihilo is altogether undercut.

But let us suppose, just for the sake of argument, that there is an initial state that qualifies as "nothing" in virtue of being the empty set. In that putative case, the bowl universe described by Isham could in fact be said to have *originated* from nothing. That is still a very far cry from having been *created* out of nothing, since the purported creation has hardly been shown to be creation *by an agency* or *external cause*. Yet Isham insists on saying, "The creation from nothing is precisely that." By the same token, one should deplore the following assertion by Barrow and Tipler: "Clearly, a true 'creation ex nihilo' would be the spontaneous generation of everything – space-time, the quantum mechanical vacuum, matter – at some time in the past." Having adopted this misleading usage of the term *creation*, Barrow and Tipler claim entitlement to say that if the second class of general relativistic big bang models – those excluding the mathematical singularity at $t = 0$ as not being an actual moment of time – were correct, "we could truly have a creation *ex nihilo*."

It would appear that, more appropriately, Isham recognizes the slide to a Creator as being psychologically motivated: [O]ne might consider [...] the eradication of the conical singularity in the [prequantum] conventional Big Bang picture. [...] There is no doubt that psychologically speaking, the existence of this initial singular point is prone to generate the idea of a Creator who sets the whole show rolling. The new theories would appear to plug this gap rather neatly."

Isham's professed rejection of the philosophical or theological misappropriation or twisting of scientific results is to be applauded when he says that "there is a regrettable, but recurrent, tendency for the results of science to be mis-stated and mis-used in the propagation of world views that are not in themselves scientific." Isham's own gloss on the Hartle and Hawking space-time as featuring "creation from nothing" is, however, a case in point, even though he presumably does not want it to be.

After all is said and done, the notion of temporal creation ex nihilo dies hard.

From *Logic, Methodology and Philosophy of Science*

[...]

If some of us were to consider the logical possibility that a person we see might conceivably metamorphose spontaneously into an elephant, for example, I doubt strongly that we would feel even the *slightest* temptation to ask why that *mere logical possibility is not realized*. Why then, I ask Parfit, should anyone reasonably feel astonished at all that the Null Possibility, if genuine, has remained a *mere* logical possibility, and that something does exist *instead? In short, why **should** there be just nothing, merely because it is **logically possible?** This *mere* logical possibility of the Null World, I claim, does *not suffice* to legitimate Parfit's demand for an **explanation** of why the Null World does *not* obtain, an explanation he seeks as a philosophical anodyne for his misguided astonishment that anything at all exists. [...]

[...] Some philosophers, notably Leibniz and Richard Swinburne, have appealed to the presumed *a priori* simplicity of the Null World. [...] *Even if the supposed maximum ontological simplicity of the Null World is warranted a priori, that presumed simplicity would **not** mandate the claim* [...] *that de jure **the thus simplest world must be spontaneously realized ontologically** in the absence of an overriding cause.* After all, having the simplest ontological constitution does not itself make for the actualization or instantiation of the world featuring that constitution! Yet, to my knowledge, neither Leibniz nor Swinburne nor any other author has offered any cogent reason at all to posit such an ontological imperative. [...]

[E]mpirically-based scientific theories are our sole epistemic avenue to the "'natural'"
behavior of the universe at large, though of course only fallibly so.

What then is the *empirical cosmological verdict on the corollary* […] which asserts
that "It is natural for our universe *not* to exist, rather than to exist"? Apparently,
there is no empirical evidence for this corollary from cosmology.

6

Third Solution
Chance

Editorial Introduction

Might all things exist through chance, though perhaps in a way on which quantum theory could throw light? Physicists have suggested that a gigantic universe could develop from a few grams of material or from a very tiny amount of "space-time foam," or maybe from a single point or nothing at all, but always in a way governed by probabilities. And from Philosophy comes the suggestion that the existence of a universe, although not guaranteed, was overwhelmingly probable because, while there are countless possible ways of being a universe, there is only a single way of being utter emptiness.

Alan GUTH sees a Big Bang as firmly established yet as needing a theory for describing the universe's earliest moments. The Bang could seemingly have expanded much too fast for all of its regions to interact in ways leading to the large-scale uniformities that we see when our telescopes scan the sky – similarities everywhere in density, in temperature, and in other factors. Again, the expanding universe could appear to have been almost certain to recollapse almost at once, pulled together by gravity, or else to fly apart rapidly, soon becoming nothing but very cold, very dilute gas and very weak radiation. In actual fact the expansion speed was such that it managed to avoid both those life-excluding results. The uniformity and the speed could look very improbably "fine-tuned" in ways leading to stars, planets, and living beings. Guth proposes the following explanation. Very early in the history of the universe, a tiny region doubled in volume repeatedly and very quickly, each doubling taking the same brief amount of time as the previous one. At the end of this "inflationary" period, "a hot, uniform soup of particles"

The Mystery of Existence: Why Is There Anything At All?, First Edition. Edited by John Leslie and Robert Lawrence Kuhn.
© 2013 John Wiley & Sons, Inc. Published 2013 by John Wiley & Sons, Inc.

was generated. Expansion then continued at a much slower rate. Irregularities in the soup, caused by quantum fluctuations, were the seeds from which galaxies would grow. Small areas on the surface of an immensely inflated balloon would be very close to being flat. Analogously, the space in the inflated region would be almost exactly flat (it would obey the laws of Euclidean geometry almost exactly) over a distance that would by now have expanded right out to as far as our telescopes can probe. And Einstein tells us that such near-flatness would automatically have meant an expansion speed in the extremely narrow range needed for collapse to be avoided and for galaxies to form.

Why the inflation? Maybe merely because regions in the very early universe varied randomly in their energies. A minuscule patch, initially perhaps "a hundred billion times smaller than a proton," could have chanced to get into a "false vacuum" state, words meaning that its energy density was high and could not rapidly be lowered. It would then have expanded immensely thanks to its intense gravitational field, gravity here acting repulsively. Now, the energy density would have remained virtually constant despite huge growth in the volume of the patch. More and more could seem to have come into existence by magic. In fact, however, there would have been absolutely no increase in the total mass-energy. The energy of the gravitational field, repeatedly increasing, would have entered the equations as *negative energy* able to balance the positive mass-energy of everything that had been created. When the inflation had ended the "soup" could therefore have contained all the mass necessary for forming the many galaxies we see today. "The entire universe can develop," Guth writes, "from just a few ounces of primordial matter"; "*everything* can be created from nothing, or at least from very little." It is "the ultimate free lunch."

Inflation provides so apparently powerful a mechanism for getting the right expansion speed and degree of uniformity (think of how wrinkles on a balloon vanish when it inflates) that it is very much the standard scenario among cosmologists. Nevertheless it has its difficulties. Recent studies suggest that the conditions necessary for Inflation to start, for it to continue appropriately, for it to end in the right way, may all have needed to be extremely special, "fine-tuned" in a manner ruining any claim that Inflation removes the need for fine-tuning. Roger Penrose has argued, even, that getting an almost flat universe would be vastly more likely *without* Inflation.

Note, too, that Guth's claim that Inflation permits "the entire universe" to be created from "just a few ounces" comes with an important caveat. The patch that supposedly inflated to give rise to all the galaxies seen by astronomers was "incredibly small," he writes, when it started to inflate, but "I am *not* saying that the universe as a whole was very small. The inflationary model makes no statement about the size of the universe as a whole, which might in fact be infinite." Hence by that "entire universe" coming from those "few ounces" he means only the entire visible universe, the situation right out to our present horizon, plus anything else – it might be much more, but still far from the entire cosmos – to which the patch gave rise.

Stephen HAWKING's universe also features Inflation and a Big Bang. Had the Bang started with "a singularity," a situation infinitely dense, then this would be "a disaster for science," Hawking tells us. Science alone could never say what would come out of the singularity since all known laws would break down there. Hoping to do better, he and Jim Hartle considered "only nonsingular curved spaces" and used a "sum over histories" approach to quantum theory. Considering the universe as a sum of the possible histories of nonsingular curved spaces, "one would not have to appeal to some agency external to the universe to determine how it began." Hartle and Hawking proposed that the laws of nature allowed only curved spaces that were, like Earth's surface, "without boundaries or edges." Only then would the laws on their own dictate how the universe developed, up to the limits set by quantum theory's Uncertainty Principle.

Hartle and Hawking made use of "imaginary time," meaning that their calculations used numbers like the square root of minus one. Hawking writes: "The beginning in real time will be the big bang singularity. However, the beginning in imaginary time will not be a singularity. Instead, it will be a bit like the North Pole of the earth." These ideas involve mathematical complexities very hard to express in ordinary English. Still, you can get the strong impression that the universe really does start off singularity-free. As times get ever earlier, quantum uncertainties render it ever harder to say what's earlier than what, and space-time becomes closer and closer to being merely spatial like the surface of our planet. The North Pole would be "a perfectly ordinary point on the earth," Hawking points out, and similarly "the event that we might choose to label as 'the beginning of the universe in imaginary time' would be an ordinary point in space-time much like any other." But, his readers might well think, this could be so only if the situation contained many points that truly were much alike, quantum fuzziness making it utterly arbitrary or downright wrong to "choose to label" any one point as the point out of which everything else came. Besides, the suggestion that the points would be much alike "only in imaginary time" seems to make nonsense of Hawking's talk about removing the "disaster for science" that any singularity must involve.

Hawking's idea that Inflation starting at time zero produced the universe "literally out of nothing," because when the universe "was a single point, like the North Pole, it contained nothing," could thus seem altogether questionable. A region in which quantum uncertainties had so messed up space-time that you could not say which events were earlier than which, let alone that some particular event was definitely the very earliest, might be a region with a very small radius. It could never be *a single point* from which everything else was born, a point which might perhaps be called "nothing." But in any case Hawking's message isn't that the mystery of existence would vanish, had the universe been born from a single point. He is instead saying that the universe can be a self-contained whole with no need for an external event to set it going. It could not have been created by any event before it because there was no "before," just as nothing on Earth's surface is north of the North Pole. Yet, he comments, whatever laws the universe obeyed would be "only a set of equations. What is it that breathes fire into the equations and makes a universe for them to govern?" At the time when he wrote these words, he could see no way of answering the question. He was irritated, however, when believers in God then kept quoting him.

Alex VILENKIN is completely serious about origination from nothing, at least so long as the "nothing" obeys the laws of quantum physics. Accepting cosmic Inflation, he at first felt forced to postulate "a strong initial blast of expansion" before it could begin. Suddenly he realized that quantum theory allows a universe to have "tunneled" through an energy barrier so as to be expanding very fast when it first appeared. There could be "loads of failed universes" that existed only fleetingly before collapsing, yet Chance rules the realm of the quantum and, thanks to tunneling, some universes start off expanding so quickly that they "will make it big." How small could be the size of any initial situation from which tunneling could occur? To his surprise, "the tunneling probability did not vanish as the initial size approached zero." A universe could even have tunneled "from a zero size – from nothing!" Further, for the tunneling "no cause is required." Some quantum processes "have no cause at all," Vilenkin confidently asserts; they only have probabilities of occurring; and the energy of a universe which is "closed" like Earth's surface (which curves around and joins up with itself) is always zero so that even something as large and long-lived as our universe could be a product of quantum chance. "The energy of matter is positive, the gravitational energy is negative," and in a closed universe "the two contributions exactly cancel each other." Appreciating this point, Edward Tryon proposed that our entire universe was "a vacuum fluctuation," not caused but "simply one of those things which happen from time to time" inside some pre-existing space. Tryon, though, couldn't actually explain why there existed anything at all. So-called "empty space," "vacuum," has energy and tension, can bend and warp, and is therefore "unquestionably different from nothing," Vilenkin points out. With his tunneling not from space but from nothing, he views himself as getting round the difficulty.

Vilenkin discusses the Hartle-Hawking picture which required that space-time be closed, having "no boundary, or edge, in the past direction of time." "The only problem," he comments, "was that spacetimes closed to the past do not exist" because they cannot fail to have "some pathological points with more than one timelike direction." The switch from real to imaginary time, otherwise known as "Euclidean time" because the time direction becomes "no different from another spatial direction," solved nothing. It involved considering universe-histories "that are certainly impossible, because we do not live in Euclidean time." Moreover the Hartle-Hawking approach would appear to make infinite space the most probable thing "to pop out of nothing," which he finds "very hard to believe."

Vilenkin's scheme of things will inflate eternally, but having tunneled from nothing gives it a beginning. It contains countless "island universes" where

Inflation has given way to slower expansion, universes where "constants of nature that shape the character of our world take different values" so that conditions hospitable to life are found in only a tiny fraction of the universes. However, the whole fails to include all conceivable mathematical structures as proposed by Max Tegmark, since typical mathematical structures would presumably be "horrendously large and cumbersome." Everything instead obeys simple, beautiful equations. The "nothing" from which it tunneled could still be in an important respect "something" because it obeyed those equations, the fundamental laws of physics. And although Vilenkin may find no need for fire to be breathed into the equations so that they can act creatively – the equations would themselves give a probability to a universe beginning to exist, and that could be that! – he certainly sees a need to answer "*Why those equations and not others?*" and "*How are they 'there' prior to the universe itself?*". "In the absence of space, time, and matter, what tablets could they be written upon?" They are in the language of mathematics. May this mean, he asks, that Mind comes first?

Martin Rees emphasizes that physicists who claim that our universe "evolved essentially from nothing" may forget that latent in the physicist's vacuum "are all the particles and fields described by the equations of physics." He does see a need for fire to be breathed into those equations – a need for an answer to "the philosophical question of why there *is* a universe." Now, he could well be right. Imagine an equation specifying that the number of dragons increases at seventy dragons per second. If applying to reality, the equation would guarantee the existence of numerous dragons. Still, why would it apply to reality? And similarly if another equation said that the existence of at least one dragon was 15 percent probable. Why would even this more humble equation apply?

Peter van Inwagen suspects he might have an answer to why there isn't a blank, an absence of all existing things. Once again a probability is involved, although he thinks it an overwhelmingly large probability. There are infinitely many possible worlds that are not empty. Each includes at least one existing thing. In contrast, there is at most one possible empty world, for there is only a single way of being a blank. Now, he argues, each of the possible worlds would be neither more nor less probable than any other. A blank was therefore infinitely improbable.

Leibniz wrote that Nothing (meaning an absence of all existing things, rather than a situation empty even of possibilities) would have been "simpler and easier." Van Inwagen is unimpressed. *In what way* simpler? Simpler, no doubt, in the sense of being easier to describe, yet why would this be relevant? Thinking it relevant appears, he says, to involve the idea that some kind of thing existing outside all the worlds that are possible could select the simplest among them, a world that was entirely empty. Yet such an idea, he argues, could never be correct because no "pre-cosmic selection machine" could be beyond every possible world. If existing so as to be able to do the selecting, it would be inside a world, wouldn't it? And likewise with "being easier," he reasons.

Would machinery find cosmos-creation easy or difficult? That's irrelevant, for mechanisms *operating beyond all possible worlds* are nonsense.

However, this reasoning might be too quick. Why assume that worlds could be rendered probable or improbable, easy or difficult to get, only by mechanisms and suchlike? When we think there would have been a blank, had it not been for some cosmos-creating factor, why can't we treat a blank, Nothing, as "Nothing to be explained"? The Fundamental Conviction that existing things cry out for explanation, whereas a blank wouldn't, might of course be mistaken. Yet it surely isn't foolish, for why must the presence or absence of various things be made easy or difficult *always by other things* such as machines? Why not instead by abstract requirements? If anything abstract would be "too unlike a machine" to have any importance, then wouldn't van Inwagen's own theory be in trouble? For when he points out that a blank was just one possibility among infinitely many, doesn't he give importance to mere possibilities and to the relative sizes of two fields of possibility, a first field that contains just a single possibility and a second field that is infinitely large, and aren't these clear instances of *abstractions*?

There is nothing wrong with having fundamental convictions, absolutely basic convictions, the sorts of conviction (often inborn, instinctive) whose rightness really isn't provable. Think of the philosophical baby, repeatedly crawling into the fire. The baby lacks the Fundamental Conviction that the past is a guide to the future. *In the past* it would have done better if convinced that the past was a guide to the future. It would not have kept getting burned. Yet, says the baby, this doesn't logically imply that in *the future* the past will be a guide to the future. There's no contradiction in supposing that the future will be different. The baby is a fine logician – the point is due to that philosophical giant, David Hume – but it will continue getting burned.

There is a second potential weakness of van Inwagen's position. Had the world been selected randomly from among all *logically possible* worlds, all worlds not containing items such as married bachelors and round squares, then wouldn't it be overwhelmingly likely to be a scene of utter chaos, there being so many logically possible ways in which disorder could break out at any instant? If so, then van Inwagen will need to put severe restrictions on what worlds are "fully possible." He will need to deny that the sheer logical possibility of various situations gives them a right to be considered when we ask what kind of cosmos had been probable – an orderly cosmos or a chaotic one, an empty cosmos or one that wasn't empty. His argument will become far less straightforward.

Here there is something we need to be clear about. If an utterly chaotic cosmos were sufficiently enormous then somebody such as you, surrounded by things such as those you are now experiencing, would occasionally come to exist by chance like the encyclopedia that an immortal monkey at a typewriter would type from time to time. This, though, is a poor reason for admiring the suggestion that the cosmos truly is utterly chaotic. If accepting the suggestion then you ought to expect to die – to be replaced by chaos – at the very next moment. Each time the monkey has finished typing the encyclopedia, his next output will almost always be rubbish.

Cosmic Inflation*

ALAN H. GUTH

The big bang theory traces its roots to the calculations of Alexander Friedmann, who showed in 1922 that the equations of general relativity allow an expanding solution that starts from a singularity. The evidence for the big bang is now over-whelming. The expansion of the universe was first observed in the early 1920s by Vesto Melvin Slipher, and in 1929 was codified by Edwin Hubble into what we now know as "Hubble's Law": on average, each distant galaxy is receding from us with a velocity that is proportional to its distance. In 1965 Arno Penzias and Robert Wilson detected a background of microwave radiation arriving at Earth from all directions – radiation believed to be the afterglow of the primordial hot dense fireball. Today we know, based on data from the *Cosmic Background Explorer* (COBE) satellite, that the spectrum of this background radiation agrees with exquisite precision – to 50 parts per million – with the thermal spectrum expected for the glow of hot matter in the early universe. In addition, calculations of nucleosynthesis in the early universe show that the big bang theory can correctly account for the cosmic abundances of the light nuclear isotopes: hydrogen, deuterium, helium-3, helium-4, and lithium-7. (Heavier elements, we believe, were synthesized much later, in the interior of stars, and were then explosively ejected into interstellar space.)

Despite the striking successes of the big bang theory, there is good reason to believe that the theory in its traditional form is incomplete. Although it is called the "big bang theory," it is not really the theory of a bang at all. It is only the theory of the *aftermath* of a bang. It elegantly describes how the early universe expanded and cooled, and how matter clumped to form galaxies and stars. But the theory says nothing about the underlying physics of the primordial bang. It gives not even a clue about what banged, what caused it to bang, or what happened before it banged. The inflationary universe theory, on the other hand, is a description of the bang itself, and provides plausible answers to these questions and more. Inflation does not do away with the big bang theory, but instead adds a brief prehistory that joins smoothly to the traditional description.

* From "Inflation and the New Era of High-Precision Cosmology," in *MIT Physics Annual 2002* (Cambridge, MA: Massachusetts Institute of Technology), pp. 30–35 © Alan H. Guth 2002. Reprinted with kind permission of the author.

A Very Special Bang

Could the big bang have been caused by a colossal stick of TNT, or perhaps a thermonuclear explosion? Or maybe a gigantic ball of matter collided with a gigantic ball of antimatter, releasing an untold amount of energy in a powerful cosmic blast.

In fact, none of these scenarios can plausibly account for the big bang that started our universe, which had two very special features which distinguish it from any typical explosion.

First, the big bang was far more homogeneous, on large scales, than can be explained by an ordinary explosion. If we imagine dividing space into cubes of 300 million light-years or more on a side, we would find that each such cube closely resembles the others in all its average properties, such as mass density, galaxy density, light output, etc. This large-scale uniformity can be seen in galaxy surveys, but the most dramatic evidence comes from the cosmic background radiation. Data from the COBE satellite, confirmed by subsequent ground-based observations, show that this radiation has the same temperature in all directions (after correcting for the motion of the Earth) to an accuracy of one part in 100,000.

To see how difficult it is to account for this uniformity in the context of an ordinary explosion, we need to know a little about the history of the cosmic background radiation. The early universe was so hot that the gas would have been ionized, filling space with a plasma so opaque that photons could not travel. After about 300,000 years, however, the universe cooled enough for the plasma to form a highly transparent gas of neutral atoms. The photons of the cosmic background radiation have traveled on straight lines ever since, so they provide today an image of the universe at an age of 300,000 years, just as the photons reaching your eye at this moment provide an image of the page in front of you. Thus, the observations of the cosmic background radiation show that the universe was uniform in temperature, to one part in 100,000, at an age of several hundred thousand years.

Under many circumstances such uniformity would be easy to understand, since anything will come to a uniform temperature if left undisturbed for a long enough time. In the traditional form of the big bang theory, however, the universe evolves so quickly that there is no time for the uniformity to be established. Calculations show that energy and information would have to be transported at about 100 times the speed of light in order to achieve uniformity by 300,000 years after the big bang. Thus, the traditional big bang theory requires us to postulate, without explanation, that the primordial fireball filled space from the beginning. The temperature was the same everywhere by *assumption*, but not as a consequence of any physical process. This shortcoming is known as the *horizon problem*, since cosmologists use the word "horizon" to indicate the largest distance that information or energy could have traversed, since the instant of the big bang, given the restriction of the speed of light.

The second special feature of the big bang is a remarkable coincidence called the *flatness problem*. This problem concerns the pinpoint precision with which the mass density of the early universe must be specified for the big bang theory to agree with reality.

To understand the problem, we must bear in mind that general relativity implies that 3-dimensional space can be curved, and that the curvature is determined by the mass density. If we adopt the idealization that our universe is homogeneous (the same at all places) and isotropic (looks the same in all directions), then there are exactly three cases. If the total mass density exceeds a value called the *critical density*, which is determined by the expansion rate, then the universe curves back on itself to form a space of finite volume but without boundary. In such a space, called a *closed universe*, a starship traveling on what appears to be a straight line would eventually return to its point of origin. The sum of the angles in a triangle would exceed 180°, and lines which appear to be parallel would eventually meet if they are extended. If the average mass density is less than the critical density, then the space curves in the opposite way, forming an infinite space called an *open universe*, in which triangles contain less than 180° and lines that appear to be parallel would diverge if they are extended. If the mass density is exactly equal to the critical density, then the space is a *flat universe*, obeying the rules of Euclidean geometry that we all learned in high school.

The ratio of the actual mass density to the critical value is known to cosmologists by the Greek letter Ω (Omega). Ω is very difficult to determine. Five years ago the observationally preferred value was 0.2–0.3, but the new observations suggest that to within 5% it is equal to 1. For either range, however, one finds a very surprising situation when one extrapolates backwards to ask about the early universe. $\Omega = 1$ is an *unstable equilibrium point* of cosmological evolution, which means that it resembles the situation of a pencil balancing on its sharpened tip. The phrase *equilibrium point* implies that if Ω is ever exactly equal to one, it will remain exactly equal to one forever – just as a pencil balanced precisely on end will, according to the laws of classical physics, remain forever vertical. The word *unstable* means that any deviation from the equilibrium point, in either direction, will rapidly grow. If the value of Ω in the early universe was just a little above one, it would have rapidly risen toward infinity; if it was just a smidgen below one, it would have rapidly fallen toward zero. For Ω to be anywhere near one today, it must have been extraordinarily close to one at early times. For example, consider one second after the big bang, the time at which the processes related to big bang nucleosynthesis were just beginning. Even if Ω differed from unity today by a factor of 10, at one second after the big bang it must have equalled one to an accuracy of 15 decimal places!

A simple explosion gives no explanation for this razor-sharp fine-tuning, and indeed no explanation can be found in the traditional version of the big bang theory. The initial values of the mass density and expansion rate are not predicted by the theory, but must be postulated. Unless, however, we postulate that the mass density at one second just happened to have a value between 0.999999999999999 and 1.000000000000001 times the critical density, the theory will not describe a universe that resembles the one in which we live.

The Inflationary Universe

Although the properties of the big bang are very special, we now know that the laws of physics provide a mechanism that produces exactly this sort of a bang. The mechanism is known as cosmic inflation.

The crucial property of physical law that makes inflation possible is the existence of states of matter which have a high energy density that cannot be rapidly lowered. Such a state is called a *false vacuum*, where the word *vacuum* indicates a state of lowest possible energy density, and the word *false* is used to mean *temporary*. For a period that can be long by the standards of the early universe, the false vacuum acts as if the energy density cannot be lowered, since the lowering of the energy is a slow process.

The peculiar properties of the false vacuum stem from its pressure, which is large and *negative*. Mechanically such a negative pressure corresponds to a suction, which does not sound like something that would drive the universe into a period of rapid expansion. The mechanical effects of pressure, however, depend on pressure differences, so they are unimportant if the pressure is reasonably uniform. According to general relativity, however, there is a gravitational effect which is very important under these circumstances. Pressures, like energy densities, create gravitational fields, and in particular a positive pressure creates an attractive gravitational field. The negative pressure of the false vacuum, therefore, creates a repulsive gravitational field, which is the driving force behind inflation.

There are many versions of inflationary theories, but generically they assume that a small patch of the early universe somehow came to be in a false vacuum state. Various possibilities have been discussed, including supercooling during a phase transition in the early universe, or a purely random fluctuation of the fields. A chance fluctuation seems reasonable even if the probability is low, since the inflating region will enlarge by many orders of magnitude, while the non-inflating regions will remain microscopic. Inflation is a wildfire that will inevitably take over the forest, as long as there is some chance that it will start.

Once a patch of the early universe is in the false vacuum state, the repulsive gravitational effect drives the patch into an inflationary period of exponential expansion. To produce a universe with the special features of the big bang discussed above, the universe must expand during the inflationary period by at least a factor of 10^{25}. There is no upper limit to the amount of expansion. [...] Eventually the false vacuum decays, and the energy that had been locked in the false vacuum is released. This energy produces a hot, uniform soup of particles, which is exactly the assumed starting point of the traditional big bang theory. At this point the inflationary theory joins onto the older theory, maintaining all of its successes.

In the inflationary theory the universe begins incredibly small, perhaps as small as 10^{-24} cm, a hundred billion times smaller than a proton. The expansion takes place while the false vacuum maintains a nearly constant energy density, which means that the total energy increases by the cube of the linear expansion factor, or at least a factor of 10^{75}. Although this sounds like a blatant violation of energy conservation, it is in fact consistent with physics as we know it.

The resolution to the energy paradox lies in the subtle behavior of gravity. Although it has not been widely appreciated, Newtonian physics unambiguously implies that the energy of a gravitational field is always negative, a fact which holds also in general relativity. [...] The possibility that the negative energy of gravity could supply the positive energy for the matter of the universe was suggested as early as 1932 by Richard Tolman, although a viable mechanism for the energy transfer was not known.

During inflation, while the energy of matter increases by a factor of 10^{75} or more, the energy of the gravitational field becomes more and more negative to compensate. The total energy – matter plus gravitational – remains constant and very small, and could even be exactly zero. Conservation of energy places no limit on how much the universe can inflate, as there is no limit to the amount of negative energy that can be stored in the gravitational field.

This borrowing of energy from the gravitational field gives the inflationary paradigm an entirely different perspective from the classical big bang theory, in which all the particles in the universe (or at least their precursors) were assumed to be in place from the start. Inflation provides a mechanism by which the entire universe can develop from just a few ounces of primordial matter. Inflation is radically at odds with the old dictum of Democritus and Lucretius, "Nothing can be created from nothing." If inflation is right, *everything* can be created from nothing, or at least from very little. If inflation is right, the universe can properly be called the ultimate free lunch.

Inflation and the Very Special Bang

Once inflation is described, it is not hard to see how it produces just the special kind of bang that was discussed earlier.

Consider first the horizon problem, the difficulty of understanding the large-scale homogeneity of the universe in the context of the traditional big bang theory. Suppose we trace back through time the observed region of the universe, which has a radius today of about 10 billion light-years. As we trace the history back to the end of the inflationary period, our description is identical to what it would be in the traditional big bang theory, since the two theories agree exactly for all times after the end of inflation. In the inflationary theory, however, the region undergoes a tremendous spurt of expansion during the inflationary era. It follows that the region was incredibly small before the spurt of expansion began – 10^{25} or more times smaller in radius than in the traditional theory. (Note that I am *not* saying that that universe as a whole was very small. The inflationary model makes no statement about the size of the universe as a whole, which might in fact be infinite.)

While the region was this small, there was plenty of time for it to have come to a uniform temperature, by the same mundane processes by which a cup of hot coffee cools to room temperature as it sits on a table. So in the inflationary model, the uniform temperature was established before inflation took place, in an extremely small region. The process of inflation then stretched this region to become large enough to encompass the entire observed universe. The uniformity is preserved by this expansion, because the laws of physics are (we assume) the same everywhere.

The inflationary model also provides a simple resolution for the flatness problem, the fine-tuning required of the mass density of the early universe. Recall that the ratio of the actual mass density to the critical density is called Ω, and that the problem arose because the condition $\Omega = 1$ is unstable: Ω is always driven away from one as the universe evolves, making it difficult to understand how its value today can be in the vicinity of one. [...] During the inflationary era, however, [...] the universe is driven very quickly and very powerfully *towards* a critical mass density. This effect can be understood if one accepts from general relativity the fact that Ω must equal one if the space of the universe is geometrically flat. The huge expansion factor of inflation drives the universe toward flatness for the same reason that the Earth appears flat, even though it is really round. A small piece of any curved space, if magnified sufficiently, will appear flat.

Thus, a short period of inflation can drive the value of Ω very accurately to one, no matter where it starts out. There is no longer any need to assume that the initial value of Ω was incredibly close to one.

The Origin of the Universe*

STEPHEN HAWKING

The problem of the origin of the universe is a bit like the old question: Which came first, the chicken or the egg? In other words, what agency created the universe, and what created that agency? Or perhaps the universe, or the agency that created it, existed forever and didn't need to be created. Up to recently, scientists have tended to shy away from such questions, feeling that they belong to metaphysics or religion rather than to science. In the last few years, however, it has emerged that the laws of science may hold even at the beginning of the universe. In that case the universe could be self-contained and determined completely by the laws of science.

The debate about whether and how the universe began has been going on throughout recorded history. Basically, there were two schools of thought. Many early traditions, and the Jewish, Christian, and Islamic religions, held that the universe was created in the fairly recent past. (In the seventeenth century Bishop Ussher calculated a date of 4004 b.c. for the creation of the universe, a figure he arrived at by adding up the ages of people in the Old Testament.) One fact that was used to support the idea of a recent origin was the recognition that the human race is obviously evolving in culture and technology. We remember who first performed that deed or developed this technique. Thus, the argument runs, we cannot have been around all that long; otherwise, we would have already progressed more than we have. In fact, the biblical date for the creation is not that far off the date of the end of the last ice age, which is when modern humans seem first to have appeared.

On the other hand, there were people such as the Greek philosopher Aristotle who did not like the idea that the universe had a beginning. They felt that would imply divine intervention. They preferred to believe that the universe had existed and would exist forever. Something that was eternal was more perfect than something that had to be created. They had an answer to the argument about human progress described above: Periodic floods or other natural disasters had repeatedly set the human race right back to the beginning.

Both schools of thought held that the universe was essentially unchanging with time. Either it was created in its present form, or it has endured forever as it is today. This was a natural belief, because human life – indeed, the whole of recorded history – is so brief that during it the universe has not changed significantly. In a static, unchanging universe, the question of whether it has existed forever or whether it was created at a finite time in the past is really a matter for metaphysics or religion: Either theory could account for such a universe. Indeed, in 1781 the philosopher Immanuel Kant wrote a monumental and very obscure work, *The Critique of Pure Reason*, in which he concluded that there were equally valid arguments both for believing that the universe had a beginning and for believing that it did not. As his title suggests, his conclusions were based simply on reason; in other words, they did not take any account of observations of the universe. After all, in an unchanging universe, what was there to observe?

In the nineteenth century, however, evidence began to accumulate that the earth and the rest of the universe were in fact changing with time. Geologists realized that the formation of the rocks and the fossils in them would have taken hundreds or thousands of millions of years. This was far longer than the age of the earth as calculated by the creationists. Further evidence was provided by the so-called second law of thermodynamics, formulated by the German physicist Ludwig Boltzmann. It states that the total amount of disorder in the universe (which is measured by a quantity called entropy) always increases with time. This, like the argument about human progress, suggests that the universe can have been going only for a finite time. Otherwise, it would by now have degenerated into a state of complete disorder, in which everything would be at the same temperature.

Another difficulty with the idea of a static universe was that according to Newton's law of gravity, each star in the universe ought to be attracted toward every other star. If so, how could they stay motionless, at a constant distance from each other? Wouldn't they all fall together?

Newton was aware of this problem. In a letter to Richard Bentley, a leading philosopher of the time, he agreed that a *finite* collection of stars could not remain motionless; they would all fall together to some central point. However, he argued, an infinite collection of stars would not fall together, for there would not be any central point for them to fall to. This argument is an example of the pitfalls that one can encounter when one talks about infinite systems. By using different ways to add up the forces on each star from the infinite number of other stars in the universe, one can get different answers to the question of whether the stars can remain at constant distances from each other. We now know that the correct procedure is to consider the case of a *finite* region of stars, and then to add more stars, distributed roughly uniformly outside the region. A finite collection of stars will fall together, and according to Newton's law, adding more stars outside the region will not stop the collapse. Thus, an infinite collection of stars cannot remain in a motionless state. If they are not moving relative to each other at one time, the attraction between them will cause them to start falling toward each other. Alternatively, they can be moving away from each other, with gravity slowing down the velocity of the recession.

Despite these difficulties with the idea of a static and unchanging universe, no one in the seventeenth, eighteenth, nineteenth, or early twentieth century suggested that the universe might be evolving with time. Newton and Einstein both missed the chance of predicting that the universe should be either contracting or expanding. One cannot really hold it against Newton, because he lived two hundred and fifty years before the observational discovery of the expansion of the universe. But Einstein should have known better. The theory of general relativity he formulated in 1915 predicted that the universe was expanding. But he remained so convinced of a static universe that he added an element to his theory to reconcile it with Newton's theory and balance gravity.

The discovery of the expansion of the universe by Edwin Hubble in 1929 completely changed the discussion about its origin. If you take the present motion of the galaxies and run it back in time, it would seem that they should all have been on top of each other at some moment between ten and twenty thousand million years ago. At this time, a singularity called the big bang, the density of the universe and the curvature of space-time would have been infinite. Under such conditions, all the known laws of science would break down. This is a disaster for science. It would mean that science alone could not predict how the universe began. All that science could say is: The universe is as it is now because it was as it was then. But science could not explain why it was as it was just after the big bang.

Not surprisingly, many scientists were unhappy with this conclusion. There were thus several attempts to avoid the conclusion that there must have been a big bang singularity and hence a beginning of time. One was the so-called steady state theory. The idea was that, as the galaxies moved apart from each other, new galaxies would form in the spaces in between from matter that was continually being created. The universe existed and would continue to exist forever in more or less the same state as it is today.

For the universe to continue to expand and new matter be created, the steady state model required a modification of general relativity, but the rate of creation needed was very low: about one particle per cubic kilometer per year, which would not conflict with observation. The theory also predicted that the average density of galaxies and similar objects should be constant both in space and time. However, a survey of sources of radio waves outside our galaxy, carried out by Martin Ryle and his group at Cambridge, showed that there were many more faint sources than strong ones. On average, one would expect the faint sources to be the more distant ones. There were thus two possibilities: Either we are in a region of the universe in which strong sources are less frequent than the average; or the density of sources was higher in the past, when the light left the more distant sources on its journey toward us. Neither of these possibilities was compatible with the prediction of the steady state theory that the density of radio sources should be constant in space and time. The final blow to the theory was the discovery in 1964 by Arno Penzias and Robert Wilson of a background of microwave radiation from far beyond our galaxy. This had the characteristic spectrum of radiation emitted by a hot body, though in this case the term *hot* is hardly appropriate, since the temperature was only 2.7 degrees above absolute zero. The universe is a cold, dark place! There was no reasonable mechanism in the steady state theory to generate microwaves with such a spectrum. The theory therefore had to be abandoned.

Another idea that would avoid a big bang singularity was suggested by two Russian scientists, Evgenii Lifshitz and Isaac Khalatnikov, in 1963. They said that a state of infinite density might occur only if the galaxies were moving directly toward or away from each other; only then would they all have met up at a single point in the past. However, the galaxies would also have had some small sideways velocities, and this might have made it possible for there to have been an earlier contracting phase of the universe, in which the galaxies might have come very close together but somehow managed to avoid hitting each other. The universe might then have re-expanded without going through a state of infinite density.

When Lifshitz and Khalatnikov made their suggestion, I was a research student looking for a problem with which to complete my Ph.D. thesis. I was interested in the question of whether there had been a big bang singularity, because that was crucial to an understanding of the origin of the universe. Together with Roger Penrose, I developed a new set of mathematical techniques for dealing with this and similar problems. We showed that if general relativity is correct, any reasonable model of the universe must start with a singularity. This would mean that science could predict that the universe must have had a beginning, but that it could not predict how the universe *should* begin: For that, one would have to appeal to God.

It has been interesting to watch the change in the climate of opinion on singularities. When I was a graduate student, almost no one took them seriously. Now, as a result of the singularity theorems, nearly everyone believes that the universe began with a singularity, at which the laws of physics broke down. However, I now think that although there is a singularity, the laws of physics can still determine how the universe began.

The general theory of relativity is what is called a classical theory. That is, it does not take into account the fact that particles do not have precisely defined positions and velocities but are "smeared out" over a small region by the uncertainty principle of quantum mechanics that does not allow us to measure simultaneously both the position and the velocity. This does not matter in normal situations, because the radius of curvature of space-time is very large compared to the uncertainty in the position of a particle. However, the singularity theorems indicate that space-time will be highly distorted, with a small radius of curvature at the beginning of the present expansion phase of the universe. In this situation, the uncertainty principle will be very important. Thus, general relativity brings about its own downfall by predicting singularities. In order to discuss the beginning of the universe, we need a theory that combines general relativity with quantum mechanics.

That theory is quantum gravity. We do not yet know the exact form the correct theory of quantum gravity will take. The best candidate we have at the moment is the theory of superstrings, but there are still a number of unresolved difficulties. However, certain features can be expected to be present in any viable theory. One is Einstein's idea that the effects of gravity can be represented by a space-time that is curved or distorted – warped – by the matter and energy in it. Objects try to follow the nearest thing to a straight line in this curved space. However, because it is curved their paths appear to be bent, as if by a gravitational field.

Another element that we expect to be present in the ultimate theory is Richard Feynman's proposal that quantum theory can be formulated as a "sum over histories." In its simplest form, the idea is that every particle has every possible path, or history, in space-time. Each path or history has a probability that depends on its shape. For this idea to work, one has to consider histories that take place in imaginary time, rather than in the real time in which we perceive ourselves as living. Imaginary time may sound like something out of science fiction, but it is a well-defined mathematical concept. In a sense it can be thought of as a direction of time that is at right angles to real time. One adds up the probabilities for all the particle histories with certain properties, such as passing through certain points at certain times. One then has to extrapolate the result back to the real space-time in which we live. This is not the most familiar approach to quantum theory, but it gives the same results as other methods.

In the case of quantum gravity, Feynman's idea of a sum over histories would involve summing over different possible histories for the universe: that is, different curved space-times. These would represent the history of the universe and everything in it. One has to specify what class of possible curved spaces should be included in the sum over histories. The choice of this class of spaces determines what state the universe is in. If the class of curved spaces that defines the state of the universe included spaces with singularities, the probabilities of such spaces would not be determined by the theory. Instead, the probabilities would have to be assigned in some arbitrary way. What this means is that science could not predict the probabilities of such singular histories for space-time. Thus, it could not predict how the universe should behave. It is possible, however, that the universe is in a state defined by a sum that includes only nonsingular curved spaces. In this case, the laws of science would determine the universe completely; one would not have to appeal to some agency external to the universe to determine how it began. In a way the proposal that the state of the universe is determined by a sum over only nonsingular histories is like the drunk looking for his key under the lamp-post: It may not be where he lost it, but it is the only place where he might find it. Similarly, the universe may not be in the state defined by a sum over nonsingular histories, but it is the only state in which science could predict how the universe should be.

In 1983, Jim Hartle and I proposed that the state of the universe should be given by a sum over a certain class of histories. This class consisted of curved spaces without singularities, which were of finite size but which did not have boundaries or edges. They would be like the surface of the earth but with two more dimensions. The surface of the earth has a finite area, but it doesn't have any singularities, boundaries, or edges. I have tested this by experiment. I went around the world, and I didn't fall off.

The proposal that Hartle and I made can be paraphrased as: The boundary condition of the universe is that it has no boundary. It is only if the universe is in this no-boundary state that the laws of science, on their own, determine the probabilities of each possible history. Thus, it is only in this case that the known laws would determine how the universe should behave. If the universe is in any other state, the class of curved spaces in the sum over histories will include spaces with singularities. In order to determine the probabilities of such singular histories, one would have to invoke some principle other than the known laws of science. This principle would be something external to our universe. We could not deduce it from within our universe. On the other hand, if the universe is in the no-boundary state, we could, in principle, determine completely how the universe should behave, up to the limits of the uncertainty principle.

It would clearly be nice for science if the universe were in the no-boundary state, but how can we tell whether it is? The answer is that the no-boundary proposal makes definite predictions for how the universe should behave. If these predictions were not to agree with observation, we could conclude that the universe is not in the no-boundary state. Thus, the no-boundary proposal is a good scientific theory in the sense defined by the philosopher Karl Popper: It can be disproved or falsified by observation.

If the observations do not agree with the predictions, we will know that there must be singularities in the class of possible histories. However, that is about all we would know. We would not be able to calculate the probabilities of the singular histories; thus, we would not be able to predict how the universe should behave. One might think that this unpredictability wouldn't matter too much if it occurred only at the big bang; after all, that was ten or twenty billion years ago. But if predictability broke down in the very strong gravitational fields in the big bang, it could also break down whenever a star collapsed. This could happen several times a week in our galaxy alone. Our power of prediction would be poor even by the standards of weather forecasts.

Of course, one could say one need not care about the breakdown in predictability that occurred in a distant star. However, in quantum theory, anything that is not actually forbidden can and will happen. Thus, if the class of possible histories includes spaces with singularities, these singularities could occur anywhere, not just at the big bang and in collapsing stars. This would mean that we couldn't predict anything. Conversely, the fact that we are able to predict events is experimental evidence against singularities and for the no-boundary proposal.

So what does the no-boundary proposal predict for the universe? The first point to make is that because all the possible histories for the universe are finite in extent, any quantity that one uses as a measure of time will have a greatest and a least value. Thus, the universe will have a beginning and an end. The beginning in real time will be the big bang singularity. However, the beginning in imaginary time will not be a singularity. Instead, it will be a bit like the North Pole of the earth. If one takes degrees of latitude on the surface of the earth to be the analogue of time, one could say that the surface of the earth begins at the North Pole. Yet the North Pole is a perfectly ordinary point on the earth. There's nothing special about it, and the same laws hold at the North Pole as at other places on the earth. Similarly, the event that we might choose to label as "the beginning of the universe in imaginary time" would be an ordinary point of space-time, much like any other. The laws of science would hold at the beginning, as elsewhere.

From the analogy with the surface of the earth, one might expect that the end of the universe would be similar to the beginning, just as the North Pole is much like the South Pole. However, the North and South poles correspond to the beginning and end of the history of the universe in imaginary time, not in the real time that we experience. If one extrapolates the results of the sum over histories from imaginary time to real time, one finds that the beginning of the universe in real time can be very different from its end.

Jonathan Halliwell and I have made an approximate calculation of what the no-boundary condition would imply. We treated the universe as a perfectly smooth and uniform background, on which there were small perturbations of density. In real time, the universe would appear to begin its expansion at a very small radius. At first, the expansion would be what is called inflationary: that is, the universe would double in size every tiny fraction of a second, just as prices double every year in certain countries. The world record for economic inflation was probably Germany after the First World War, where the price of a loaf of bread went from under a mark to millions of marks in a few months. But that is nothing compared to the inflation that seems to have occurred in the early universe: an increase in size by a factor of at least a million million million million million times in a tiny fraction of a second. Of course, that was before the present government.

The inflation was a good thing in that it produced a universe that was smooth and uniform on a large scale and was expanding at just the critical rate to avoid recollapse. The inflation was also a good thing in that it produced all the contents of the universe quite literally out of nothing. When the universe was a single point, like the North Pole, it contained nothing. Yet there are now at least ten-to-the-eightieth particles in the part of the universe that we can observe. Where did all these particles come from? The answer is that relativity and quantum mechanics allow matter to be created out of energy in the form of particle/antiparticle pairs. And where did the energy come from to create this matter? The answer is that it was borrowed from the gravitational energy of the universe. The universe has an enormous debt of negative gravitational energy, which exactly balances the positive energy of the matter. During the inflationary period the universe borrowed heavily from its gravitational energy to finance the creation of more matter. The result was a triumph for Keynesian economics: a vigorous and expanding universe, filled with material objects. The debt of gravitational energy will not have to be paid until the end of the universe.

The early universe could not have been completely homogeneous and uniform because that would violate the uncertainty principle of quantum mechanics. Instead, there must have been departures from uniform density. The no-boundary proposal implies that these differences in density would start off in their ground state; that is, they would be as small as possible, consistent with the uncertainty principle. During the inflationary expansion, however, the differences would be amplified. After the period of inflationary expansion was over, one would be left with a universe that was expanding slightly faster in some places than in others. In regions of slower expansion, the gravitational attraction of the matter would slow down the expansion still further. Eventually, the region would stop expanding and would contract to form galaxies and stars. Thus, the no-boundary proposal can account for all the complicated structure that we see around us. However, it does not make just a single prediction for the universe. Instead, it predicts a whole family of possible histories, each with its own probability. There might be a possible history in which the Labour party won the last election in Britain, though maybe the probability is low.

The no-boundary proposal has profound implications for the role of God in the affairs of the universe. It is now generally accepted that the universe evolves according to well-defined laws. These laws may have been ordained by God, but it seems that He does not intervene in the universe to break the laws. Until recently, however, it was thought that these laws did not apply to the beginning of the universe. It would be up to God to wind up the clockwork and set the universe going in any way He wanted. Thus, the present state of the universe would be the result of God's choice of the initial conditions.

The situation would be very different, however, if something like the no-boundary proposal were correct. In that case the laws of physics would hold even at the beginning of the universe, so God would not have had the freedom to choose the initial conditions. Of course, He would still have been free to choose the laws that the universe obeyed. However, this may not have been much of a choice. There may only be a small number of laws, which are self-consistent and which lead to complicated beings like ourselves who can ask the question: What is the nature of God?

And even if there is only one unique set of possible laws, it is only a set of equations. What is it that breathes fire into the equations and makes a universe for them to govern? Is the ultimate unified theory so compelling that it brings about its own existence? Although science may solve the problem of how the universe began, it cannot answer the question: Why does the universe bother to exist? I don't know the answer to that.

Creation from Nothing*

ALEX VILENKIN

Inflation at the End of the Tunnel

Back in 1982, inflation was still a very new field, full of unexplored ideas and challenging problems – a gold mine for an aspiring young cosmologist. The most intriguing of these problems, and perhaps the least relevant for the present state of the universe, was the question of how inflation could have started. An inflating universe quickly "forgets" its initial conditions, so the state at the onset of inflation has little effect on what happens afterward. Thus, if you want to find ways of testing inflation observationally, you should not waste your time worrying about how it began. But the puzzle of the beginning was still there and could not be avoided. It drew me like a magnet.

*   Slightly adapted from chapters 17 and 19 of *Many Worlds in One: The Search for Other Universes* (New York: Hill & Wang, 2006), pp. 178–191 and 203–205. Reprinted with permission of Farrar, Straus & Giroux LLC, Brockman Inc., and the author.

At first sight, the problem looked relatively simple. We know that a small region of space filled with false vacuum is enough to drive inflation. So, all I had to figure out was how such a region could have arisen from some earlier state of the universe.

The prevailing view at the time was based on the Friedmann model, where the universe expanded from a singular state of infinite curvature and infinite matter density. Assuming that the universe is filled with a high-energy false vacuum, any matter that was initially present is diluted, and the vacuum energy eventually dominates. At that point, the repulsive gravity of the vacuum takes over, and inflation begins.

This would be fine, except, Why was the universe expanding to begin with? One of the achievements of inflation was to explain the expansion of the universe. Yet, it looked as if we needed to have expansion before inflation even started. The attractive gravity of matter is initially much stronger than the gravitational repulsion of the vacuum, so if we don't postulate a strong initial blast of expansion, the universe would simply collapse and inflation would never begin.

I pondered this argument for a while, but the logic was very simple and there seemed to be no escape. Then, suddenly, I realized that instead of collapsing, the universe could do something much more interesting and dramatic …

Suppose we have a closed spherical universe, filled with a false vacuum and containing a certain amount of ordinary matter. Suppose also that this universe is momentarily at rest, neither expanding nor contracting. Its future will depend on its radius. If the radius is small, the matter is compressed to a high density and the universe will collapse to a point. If the radius is large, the vacuum energy dominates and the universe will inflate. Small and large radii are separated by an energy barrier, which cannot be crossed unless the universe is given a large expansion velocity.

What I suddenly realized was that the collapse of a small universe was inevitable only in classical physics. In quantum theory, the universe could *tunnel* through the energy barrier and emerge on the other side – like a nuclear particle in Gamow's theory of radioactive decay.

This looked like a neat solution to the problem. The universe starts out extremely small and is most likely to collapse to a singularity. But there is a small chance that instead of collapsing, it will tunnel through the barrier to a bigger radius and start inflating. So, in the grander scheme of things, there will be loads of failed universes that will exist only for a fleeting moment, but there will also be some that will make it big.

I felt that I was making progress, so I pressed on. Is there any bound to how small the initial universe could be? What happens if we allow it to get smaller and smaller? To my surprise, I found that the tunneling probability did not vanish as the initial size approached zero. I also noticed that my calculations were greatly simplified when I allowed the initial radius of the universe to vanish. This was really crazy: what I had was a mathematical description of a universe tunneling from a zero size – from nothing! – to a finite radius and beginning to inflate. It looked as though there was no need for the initial universe!

Tunneling from Nothing

The concept of a universe materializing out of nothing boggles the mind. What exactly is meant by "nothing"? If this "nothing" could tunnel into something, what could have caused the primary tunneling event? And what about energy conservation? But as I kept thinking about it, the idea appeared to make more and more sense.

The initial state prior to the tunneling is a universe of vanishing radius, that is, no universe at all. There is no matter and no space in this very peculiar state. Also, there is no time. Time has meaning only if something is happening in the universe. We measure time using periodic processes, like the rotation of the Earth about its axis, or its motion around the Sun. In the absence of space and matter, time is impossible to define.

And yet, the state of "nothing" cannot be identified with *absolute* nothingness. The tunneling is described by the laws of quantum mechanics, and thus "nothing" should be subjected to these laws. The laws of physics must have existed, even though there was no universe [...]

As a result of the tunneling event, a finite-sized universe, filled with a false vacuum, pops out of nowhere ("nucleates") and immediately starts to inflate. The radius of the newborn universe is determined by the vacuum energy density: the higher the density, the smaller the radius. For a grand-unified vacuum, it is one hundred-trillionth of a centimeter. Because of inflation, this tiny universe grows at a staggering rate, and in a small fraction of a second it becomes much greater than the size of our observable region.

If there was nothing before the universe popped out, then what could have caused the tunneling? Remarkably, the answer is that no cause is required. In classical physics, causality dictates what happens from one moment to the next, but in quantum mechanics the behavior of physical objects is inherently unpredictable and some quantum processes have no cause at all. Take, for example, a radioactive atom. It has some probability of decaying, which is the same from this minute to the next. Eventually, it will decay, but there will be nothing that causes it to decay at that particular moment. Nucleation of the universe is also a quantum process and does not require a cause.

Most of our concepts are rooted in space and time, and it is not easy to create a mental picture of a universe popping out of nothing. You cannot imagine that you are sitting in "nothing" and waiting for a universe to materialize – because there is no space to sit in and there is no time.

In some recently proposed models based on string theory, our space is a three-dimensional membrane (brane) floating in a higher-dimensional space. In such models, we can imagine a higher-dimensional observer watching small bubble universes – braneworlds – pop out here and there, like bubbles of vapor in a boiling pot of water. We live on one of the bubbles, which is an expanding three-dimensional spherical brane. For us, this brane is the only space there is. We cannot get out of it and are unaware of the extra dimensions. As we follow the history of our bubble universe back in time, we come to the moment of nucleation. Beyond that, our space and time disappear.

From this picture, there is only a small step to the one that I originally proposed. Simply remove the higher-dimensional space. From our internal point of view, nothing will change. We live in a closed, three-dimensional space, but this space is not floating anywhere. As we go back in time, we discover that our universe had a beginning. There is no spacetime beyond that.

An elegant mathematical description of quantum tunneling can be obtained using the so-called *Euclidean time*. This is not the kind of time you measure with your watch. It is expressed using imaginary numbers, like the square root of -1, and is introduced only for computational convenience. Making the time Euclidean has a peculiar effect on the character of spacetime: the distinction between time and the three spatial dimensions completely disappears, so instead of spacetime we have a four-dimensional space. If we could live in Euclidean time, we would measure it with a ruler, just as we measure length. Although it may appear rather odd, the Euclidean-time description is very useful: it provides a convenient way to determine the tunneling probability and the initial state of the universe as it emerges into existence […]

I wrote all this up in a short paper entitled "Creation of Universes from Nothing." Before submitting it to a journal, I made a day trip to Princeton University, to discuss these ideas with Malcolm Perry, a well-known expert on the quantum theory of gravitation. After an hour at the blackboard, Malcolm said, "Well, maybe this is not so crazy […] How come I have not thought of it myself?" What better compliment can you get from a fellow physicist!

The Universe as a Quantum Fluctuation

My model of the universe tunneling out of nothing did not appear from nothing – I had some predecessors. The first suggestion of this sort came from Edward Tryon of Hunter College, City University of New York. He proposed the idea that the universe was created out of vacuum as a result of a quantum fluctuation.

The thought first occurred to him in 1970, during a physics seminar. Tryon says that it struck him like a flash of light, as if some profound truth had suddenly been revealed to him. When the speaker paused to collect his thoughts, Tryon blurted out, "Maybe the universe is a vacuum fluctuation!" The room roared with laughter. […]

[T]he vacuum is anything but dull or static; it is a site of frantic activity. Electric, magnetic, and other fields are constantly fluctuating on subatomic scales because of unpredictable quantum jerks. The spacetime geometry is also fluctuating, resulting in a frenzy of spacetime foam at the Planck distance scale. In addition, the space is full of *virtual* particles, which spontaneously pop out here and there and instantly disappear. The virtual particles are very short-lived, because they live on borrowed energy. The energy loan needs to be paid off, and according to Heisenberg's uncertainty principle, the larger the energy borrowed from the vacuum, the faster it has to be repaid. Virtual electrons and positrons typically disappear in about one-trillionth of a nanosecond. Heavier particles last even less than that, as they require more energy to materialize. Now, what Tryon was suggesting was that our entire universe, with its vast amount of matter, was a huge quantum fluctuation, which somehow failed to disappear for more than 10 billion years. Everybody thought that was a very funny joke.

But Tryon was not joking. He was devastated by the reaction of his colleagues, to the extent that he forgot his idea and suppressed the memory of the whole incident. But the idea continued brewing at the back of his mind and resurfaced three years later. At that time, Tryon decided to publish it. His paper appeared in 1973 in the British science journal *Nature*, under the title "Is the Universe a Vacuum Fluctuation?"

Tryon's proposal relied upon a well-known mathematical fact – that the energy of a closed universe is always equal to zero. The energy of matter is positive, the gravitational energy is negative, and it turns out that in a closed universe the two contributions exactly cancel each other. Thus, if a closed universe were to arise as a quantum fluctuation, there would be no need to borrow energy from the vacuum and the lifetime of the fluctuation could be arbitrarily long.

[In] the creation of a closed universe out of the vacuum a region of flat space begins to swell, taking the shape of a balloon. At the same time, a colossal number of particles are spontaneously created in that region. The balloon eventually pinches off, and – voilà – we have a closed universe, filled with matter, that is completely disconnected from the original space. Tryon suggested that our universe could have originated in this way and emphasized that such a creation event would not require a cause. "In answer to the question of why it happened," he wrote, "I offer the modest proposal that our universe is simply one of those things which happen from time to time."

The main problem with Tryon's idea is that it does not explain why the universe is so large. Closed baby universes are constantly pinched off any large region of space, but all this activity occurs at the Planck distance scale. Formation of a large closed universe is possible in principle, but the probability for this to happen is much smaller than that for a monkey to randomly type the full text of Shakespeare's *Hamlet*.

In his paper Tryon argued that even if most of the universes are tiny, observers can only evolve in a large universe and therefore we should not be surprised that we live in one. But this falls short of resolving the difficulty, because our universe is much larger than necessary for the evolution of life.

A more fundamental problem is that Tryon's scenario does not really explain the origin of the universe. A quantum fluctuation of the vacuum assumes that there was a vacuum of some pre-existing space. And we now know that "vacuum" is very different from "nothing." Vacuum, or empty space, has energy and tension, it can bend and warp, so it is unquestionably *something*. As Alan Guth wrote, "In this context, a proposal that the universe was created from empty space is no more fundamental than a proposal that the universe was spawned by a piece of rubber. It might be true, but one would still want to ask where the piece of rubber came from."

The picture of quantum tunneling from nothing has none of these problems. The universe is tiny right after tunneling, but it is filled with a false vacuum and immediately starts to inflate. In a fraction of a second, it blows up to a gigantic size.

Prior to the tunneling, no space or time exists, so the question of what happened *before* is meaningless. *Nothing* – a state with no matter, no space, and no time – appears to be the only satisfactory starting point for the creation. [...]

The Hawking Factor

In July 1983 several hundred physicists from all over the world gathered in the Italian city of Padova for the tenth International Conference on General Relativity and Gravitation. [...] The highlight of the program was the talk by Stephen Hawking, entitled "The Quantum State of the Universe." [...]

In his talk Hawking unveiled a new vision for the quantum origin of the universe, based on the work he had done with James Hartle of the University of California at Santa Barbara. Instead of focusing on the early moments of creation, he asked a more general question: How can we calculate the quantum probability for the universe to be in a certain state? The universe could follow a large number of possible histories before it got to that state, and the rules of quantum mechanics can be used to determine how much each particular history contributes to the probability. The final result for the probability depends on what class of histories is included in the calculation. The proposal of Hartle and Hawking was to include only histories represented by spacetimes that have no boundaries in the past.

A space without boundaries is easy to understand: it simply means a closed universe. But Hartle and Hawking required that the spacetime should also have no boundary, or edge, in the past direction of time. It should be closed in all four dimensions, except for the boundary corresponding to the present moment.

A boundary in space would mean that there is something beyond the universe, so that things can come in and go out through the boundary. A boundary in time would correspond to the beginning of the universe, where some initial conditions would have to be specified. The proposal of Hartle and Hawking asserts that the universe has no such boundary; it is "completely self-contained and not affected by anything outside itself." That sounded like a very simple and attractive idea. The only problem was that spacetimes closed to the past do not exist. There should be three spacelike and one timelike direction at every spacetime point, but a closed spacetime necessarily has some pathological points with more than one timelike direction.

To resolve this difficulty, Hartle and Hawking suggested that we switch from real time to Euclidean time. Euclidean time is no different from another spatial direction; so the spacetime simply becomes a four-dimensional space, and there is no problem making it closed. Thus, the proposal was that we calculate probabilities by adding up contributions from all Euclidean spacetimes without boundaries. Hawking emphasized that this was only a proposal. He had no proof that it was correct, and the only way to find out was to check whether or not it makes reasonable predictions.

The Hartle-Hawking proposal has a certain mathematical beauty about it, but I thought that after switching to Euclidean time it lost much of its intuitive appeal. Instead of summing over possible histories of the universe, it instructs us to sum over histories that are certainly impossible, because we do not live in Euclidean time [...]

Much Ado about Nothing

An important difference between the "tunneling from nothing" and "no boundary" proposals is that they give very different, and in some sense opposite, predictions for the probabilities. The tunneling proposal favors nucleation with the highest vacuum energy and the smallest size of the universe. The no-boundary prescription, on the contrary, suggests that the most likely starting point is a universe of the smallest vacuum energy and largest possible size. The most probable thing to pop out of nothing is then an infinite, empty, flat space. I find this very hard to believe! [...]

Mathematical Democracy

If we ever discover the final theory of nature, the question will still remain: Why this theory? Mathematical beauty may be useful as a guide, but it is hard to imagine that it will suffice to select a unique theory out of the infinite number of possibilities. As the physicist Max Tegmark put it, "Why should one mathematical structure, and only one, out of all the countless mathematical structures, be endowed with physical existence?" Tegmark, now at Massachusetts Institute of Technology, suggested a possible way out of this impasse.

His proposal is as simple as it is radical: he argues that there should be a universe corresponding to each and every mathematical structure [...]

If successful, this line of reasoning would drive the Creator entirely out of the picture. Inflation relieved him of the job of setting up the initial conditions of the big bang, quantum cosmology unburdened him of the task of creating space and time and starting up inflation, and now he is being evicted from his last refuge – the choice of the fundamental theory of nature.

Tegmark's proposal, however, faces a formidable problem. The number of mathematical structures increases with increasing complexity, suggesting that "typical" structures should be horrendously large and cumbersome. This seems to be in conflict with the simplicity and beauty of the theories describing our world. It thus appears that the Creator's job security is in no immediate danger.

Many Worlds in One

[...]

At the heart of the new worldview is the picture of an eternally inflating universe. It consists of isolated "island universes," where inflation has ended, immersed in the inflating sea of false vacuum. The boundaries of these postinflationary islands are rapidly expanding, but the gaps that separate them are widening even faster. Thus there is always room for more island universes to form, and their number increases without bound.

Viewed from the inside, each island is a self-contained infinite universe. We live in one of these island universes [...]

The entire eternally inflating spacetime originated as a minuscule closed universe. It tunneled, quantum-mechanically, out of nothing and immediately plunged into the never-ending fury of inflation. Thus the universe is eternal, but it did have a beginning.

Inflation rapidly blows the universe up to an enormous size, but from a global viewpoint it always remains closed and finite. And yet, due to the peculiar structure of inflationary spacetime, it contains an unlimited number of infinite island universes.

Constants of nature that shape the character of our world take different values in other island universes. Most of these universes are drastically different from ours, and only a tiny fraction of them are hospitable to life. [...]

The picture of quantum tunneling from nothing raises another intriguing question. The tunneling process is governed by the same fundamental laws that describe the subsequent evolution of the universe. It follows that the laws should be "there" even prior to the universe itself. Does this mean that the laws are not mere descriptions of reality and can have an independent existence of their own? In the absence of space, time, and matter, what tablets could they be written upon? The laws are expressed in the form of mathematical equations. If the medium of mathematics is the mind, does this mean that mind should predate the universe?

This takes us far into the unknown, all the way to the abyss of great mystery.

Essentially from Nothing?*

MARTIN REES

The ultraearly universe may one day be triumphantly subsumed into some overarching theory that applies from the Planck time (10^{-43} seconds) onward. Indeed some physicists already claim that our universe evolved essentially from nothing. But they should watch their language, especially when talking to philosophers. The physicist's vacuum is a far richer construct than the philosopher's "nothing": latent in it are all the particles and fields described by the equations of physics. In any case, such a claim doesn't bypass the philosophical question of why there *is* a universe. To quote Stephen Hawking, "What is it that breathes fire into the equations? [...] Why does the Universe go to all the bother of existing?"

Why Is There Anything At All?†

PETER VAN INWAGEN

[...] I will not try to show that it is impossible for there to be nothing. Rather I will argue that if there being nothing is not impossible, it is at any rate *improbable* – as improbable as anything can be. If something is as improbable as anything can be, its probability is, of course, 0: I am going to argue that the probability of there being nothing is 0.

I confess I am unhappy about the argument I am going to present. Like Descartes's ontological argument, with which it shares the virtue of simplicity, it seems a bit *too* simple. No doubt there is something wrong with it – it may share that defect with Descartes's argument – but I should like to be told what it is.

The argument has four premises:

(1) There are some beings;
(2) If there is more than one possible world, there are infinitely many;
(3) There is at most one possible world in which there are no beings;
(4) For any two possible worlds, the probability of their being actual is equal.

---

*   From chapter 9 of *Before the Beginning* (Reading, MA: Addison-Wesley, 1997).
†   From "Why Is There Anything At All?", *Aristotelian Society*, supplementary volume 70 (1996), pp. 99–101 and 104–109. Reprinted with permission of The Aristotelian Society.

Now let *Spinozism* be the thesis that there is just one possible world. We proceed by cases.

If Spinozism is true, then, by premise (1), it is a necessary truth that there are some beings, and the probability of there being no beings is 0.

If Spinozism is false, then, by premise (2), logical space comprises infinitely many possible worlds. If logical space comprises infinitely many possible worlds, and if any two worlds are equiprobable – premise (4) – then the probability of every world is 0. If a proposition is true in at most one world, and if the probability of every world is 0, then the probability of that proposition is 0. But then, by premise (3), the probability of there being no beings is 0.

Hence, the probability of there being no beings is 0. [...]

[...] Premise (4) is the one that people are going to want to dispute. Why should the probability of any given world's being actual be equal to the probability of any other given world's being actual?

Well, this seems very plausible to me. [...] Let us say that a system of objects is *isolated* if no facts about objects external to the system could in any way influence the system. More exactly, a system is isolated *with respect to a certain set of its states* if no facts about objects external to the system could in any way have any influence on which of those states the system was in. In the sequel, I will mostly ignore this bit of fine-tuning and will speak of a system's being isolated *simpliciter*.

I propose: for any system of objects (that has maximal states) the maximal states of the system should be regarded as equally probable, provided that the system is isolated. [...] But then we have an argument for the conclusion that any two possible worlds are of equal probability: "Reality" is an isolated system, and possible worlds are maximal states of Reality.

There are, however, intuitions that oppose the thesis that the "empty world" is no more probable than any other world, and we must examine them. Consider, for example, the famous passage in *Principles of Nature and Grace* in which Leibniz argues that it is necessary to search for an explanation of there being something rather than nothing, since "nothing is simpler and more easy [*facile*] than something". If "nothing" is indeed simpler than "something", might not the simplicity of "nothing" at least suggest that "nothing" is *more probable* than "something" – or at least more probable than any *given* arrangement of "somethings"?

In what sense is "nothing" *simpler* than "something"? [...] Would the fact that the empty world is vastly, even infinitely, easier to describe than our world give us any reason to prefer the first probability assignment to the second? I have a hard time seeing why anyone should think that it did. It seems to me that one can find this plausible only if one is covertly thinking that there is something that is outside the "Reality" of which possible worlds are maximal states, something by whose operations actuality is conferred on whatever world it is that enjoys that status. One might, for example believe that the greater simplicity of the empty world made it more probable than ours if one believed that there was a "pre-cosmic selection machine", not a part of Reality, the operations of which select a maximal state for Reality to be in, and that something about the not-fully-deterministic workings of this machine made it more probable that it would select a state that could be simply described than one that required a very complicated description.

Leibniz believed something like this, although his selector was God, not a machine. But only something *like* this. Leibniz's "possible worlds" are not possible worlds in the current sense of the term. They are rather possible Creations. They are not therefore maximal states of Reality but only of the created part of it. And, of course, simplicity might well be a factor that would recommend a particular possible Creation to a potential Creator contemplating the question, "Which possible Creation shall I cause to be actual?"

Something very similar can be said about ease. Suppose, for example, that it is *easier* for God to bring about the actuality of the state of affairs *There being nothing besides God* than the state of affairs *There being something besides God* – perhaps He has to do nothing to produce the former and something rather difficult to produce the latter; something that would require, say, six days of work and a day of recuperation afterwards – and if God, like most of us, preferred not to expend effort without good reason, then it might be more probable that there not be any created beings than that there be any.

Whatever merit these speculations may have, they are of no use to someone who wants to know about the probability of there being nothing at all: they are relevant only to a question of conditional probability: What is the probability of there being nothing created, given that there is an uncreated being capable of creation? [...]

I conclude – tentatively – that the simplicity of the empty world provides us with no reason to regard it as more probable than any other possible world.

7

Fourth Solution
Value/Perfection as Ultimate

Editorial Introduction

Suppose that good and bad are not always simply matters of individual taste, like the goodness or badness of mustard in a sandwich. Suppose that a thing, if it were to exist all by itself, could in some cases be *absolutely better than a blank*: than an absence of all things, that's to say. Whether or not anything in fact existed, the need for one or more good things – the need for a divine mind, perhaps, or the need for a good cosmos – might then always be "there," eternally and unconditionally real. Now, could such a reality *itself have acted creatively*, ensuring that there wasn't a blank? Or could Perfection, maybe of a kind having nothing particularly to do with goodness, be somehow responsible for the existence of a divine mind or of the entire cosmos?

PLATO suggests in his *Republic* that The Good, a factor which "is not existence, but lies far beyond it in dignity and power," is what "bestows existence on all known things." It can certainly sound as if he is suggesting that ethical needs – needs for good things to exist, realities which are themselves too abstract to be "things that exist" – directly account for why there is a cosmos, not a blank. This way of interpreting him can look still more clearly correct when you find his *Phaedo* presenting "the good and the right" as what "holds and binds things together," arranging them "for the best."

Ethical needs that themselves create a cosmos? Nowadays folk often think this ridiculous. They may protest that – despite how Ethics deals with goodness of all types, not just good actions – ethical needs are always just needs for people to act in particular ways. And they may not be satisfied on finding the word

The Mystery of Existence: Why Is There Anything At All?, First Edition. Edited by John Leslie and Robert Lawrence Kuhn.

"ethical" replaced by the word "axiological" (from the Greek *axios*, worth) when Nicholas Rescher defends a Platonic explanation of the cosmos in such books as *Axiogenesis*. Perhaps they will even insist that no thing could be the slightest bit good or bad unless some already existing person could do deeds to support or to oppose its existence. They may then use a Principle of Charity to interpret Plato's words so as to make more sense to their ears. Might he not mean that we ought to look always on the bright side, *seeing* things *as* good? Or perhaps that The Good is Top Dog since other inhabitants of Plato's realm of abstract realities, "the Forms," inhabit it only because they organize our mental processes *well*?

It can be hard to know what philosophers of past centuries meant, and there might be excuses for interpreting Plato in those or other "charitable" ways. His words have, however, led hundreds of philosophers to think the sorts of thing that they certainly sound as if suggesting. For surely a need – an ethical (or, if you prefer that word, "axiological") *reason for this or that to exist* – could be a reality even when there existed nobody who could do anything about it. Well, *just why* couldn't such a reason be responsible for the actual existence of something, without help from anybody? The goodness of God's existence, for example, could be a factor that itself explained why God exists. It is what ARISTOTLE's words seem to say.

To Aristotle it is unlikely to be through Chance alone that things "manifest goodness and beauty both in their being and in their coming to be." Better to believe in a principle "which is at the same time the cause of beauty, and that sort of cause from which things acquire movement"; "the cause of all goods is the good itself." God is the First Mover that "exists of necessity; and in so far as it exists by necessity, its mode of being is good." God's "self-dependent actuality" is "life most good and eternal," a life of contemplation which is "what is most pleasant and best." All this is no mere repetition of Plato. Whereas Plato's cosmic principle was too abstract to be an existent, Aristotle's God is a divine mind. Still, there are strong echoes of Plato here, in particular in the idea of an ethical aspect to God's necessary existence.

In PLOTINUS the echoes are stronger still. "The Good is that on which all else depends," yet it itself "does not possess Being"; "the Supreme has no need of Being." The cosmos therefore came to exist "not as the result of a judgement establishing its desirability, but by sheer necessity." Yet the necessity acted as if it involved a good Maker's intelligent planning, for the world "stands a stately whole, serving at once its own purpose and that of all its parts."

AQUINAS has the puzzling theory that God "is absolutely simple." "Goodness and being are really the same, and differ only in idea," and "for God to be good is identical with God. He is, therefore, His goodness." And similarly with God's "understanding, willing, producing things, and the like." Those "are not diverse realities, since each of these actions in God is His very being." Might this supply a proof of God's existence, then? Aquinas views us as having little insight into God's absolute simplicity, so that we could not know such a proof's correctness; we could not announce that since all God's so-called "other qualities" were really no different from God's existence, only fools could deny that God existed. And philosophers would now tend to protest that, even were God defined as "having no properties except that of existing," this still could show only that *if* God were a reality *then* God would definitely be an existing thing – unlike, say, the reality that four and four make eight, which would be an abstraction.

However, would the God of Aquinas truly be an existing thing in any straightforward sense? Aquinas is eager to distinguish God, alias Being, from all mere beings. Trying to understand him, we could point to such statements as "Goodness, as a cause, is prior to being," or "God's very essence is His active power," or – from his commentary *On Interpretation*, a work of his hero Aristotle – "The divine will must be understood as existing outside the order of beings, as a cause producing the whole of being and all its differences." Could these statements express a Platonic theory that God is an ethical requirement that a good world exist, a requirement which is itself creatively effective instead of needing to be put into effect by a genuine person who straightforwardly knows things, straight-forwardly wills things, and possesses creative power? Such a theory might shed light on God's absolute simplicity, for *a creatively effective requirement* wouldn't be *a complicated reality* like somebody who judged that something was good and then decided to bring it about with the help of a powerful right arm. Talk of the requirement as *eternally real* could also seem none too odd; the need for a good cosmos could well be considered eternal. The creative aspect of the requirement might still strike us as mysterious, but isn't God mysterious in virtually all religious thought? We could want to see a Platonic way of thinking developed in detail before deciding whether it involved more of a mystery than a theory that pictured God as "a Being," not as an abstract Creative Force of the type that Plato seems to have had in mind.

True, various passages in Aquinas suggest that he is no follower of Plato. It is hard, though, to name any philosopher who manages to be totally consistent. Besides, hasn't total consistency been called "the virtue of trains and of small minds"?

ANSELM develops what became known as Ontological Arguments for God's existence, lines of reasoning based on defining God as the greatest conceivable being. Maximal greatness is typically taken to include not just supreme goodness but also omniscience, omnipotence, and so forth. Anselm's first argument is that a being would be greater if it existed not "in the understanding alone" (we'd nowadays say "as a logical possibility only") but in reality as well. Such reasoning has few fans today. Even if we accept – which Kant didn't – that existence is one of God's properties, this would seem to show only that *if* God were real *then* God would be an existent, unlike the reality that every cube must have six faces, or the reality that an apple a day is good for you.

Anselm's second argument, in contrast, has influential supporters. Here, God "cannot be conceived not to exist" and this is judged essential to maximal greatness. In modern terms, God's definition includes not mere existence, but

Necessary Existence. It could look like a useful property to have. If God had it, God would exist eternally. No demon could hope to destroy a Necessary Being. Still, this second argument faces a new difficulty. Even if – which many deny – necessary existence is a possible property, could we compel something to have it by definition? Could a Maximally Dreadful Demon be *defined into* having it, on the excuse that he'd then exist eternally and couldn't without contradiction be killed? No, for surely the demon would be exactly as dreadful if existing eternally, unkillably, just as a brute fact. Now, similarly with a deity who existed eternally just as a brute fact, there being nothing able to destroy him.

DESCARTES can seem to run something much like the second of Anselm's arguments. By definition, God is "supremely perfect"; hence the idea of God "contains not only possible but wholly necessary existence"; therefore God exists. But why, then, does Descartes ask us to "spend a great deal of time and effort on contemplating the nature of a supremely perfect being" so as to see God's existence "without a formal argument"?

The answer is that he appreciates that, if considered only as manipulating words, his argument fails. "A word's implying something is no reason for that thing's truth," he had written. "Perfect" is just a word. He relies instead on an idea of God's nature that God himself inserted into our minds, the mark of the workman impressed on his work. Contemplated with much time and effort, it compensates for the defects of a formal proof.

Using the heavy machinery of contemporary philosophical analysis, Alvin PLANTINGA constructs an Ontological Argument he thinks sound. Still, he points out, this does not make it *a proof*. By "sound" he means only that it is logically valid – "God exists" follows logically from its premises – and that the premises are, he thinks, correct. As premises he gives: (1) "There is a possible world in which maximal greatness is instantiated." (2) "Necessarily, a being is maximally great only if it has maximal excellence in every world": every possible world, that is to say. Now, a being can of course have maximal excellence (or, indeed, any other quality) in any particular possible world only if it *exists in* that world. And if it exists in *every* possible world, then it exists necessarily – because existing in every possible world is what "existing necessarily" means. But as Plantinga says, it is not clear that maximal greatness, as he defines it, is even possible.

We could add that it isn't clear, either, that God's greatness would have to involve existing necessarily. In a being possessing *every other* wonderful property – total inability to be destroyed, infinite power over all further matters, infinite knowledge, infinite goodness, and so on – that could be had by a necessarily existing deity, couldn't existence in the actual world as an eternal brute fact be *equally great*? For just why should supreme greatness be thought to depend on being present, as well, in other worlds when those were nothing more than possible? Does Richard Swinburne's omnipotent, omniscient, infinitely good Divine Person (discussed on later pages) lack something that's self-evidently essential to supreme greatness because, while the actual world always has contained this Person and always will contain him since he cannot be expelled from it by anybody or anything, some *possible but non-existent worlds* do not? Bear in mind that in Plantinga's language only a single world can be actual – actually existing – in addition to being possible. When he calls the other worlds *possible*, he's not saying that we can't be sure whether they exist.

SPINOZA is famous mainly for his *Ethics*. His *Short Treatise* – far easier to understand, far less eager to establish things through mere Logic – is in some respects the better book. God's infinite perfection, it tells us, makes God "a cause of himself." Talk of God's self-causation might seem much less preposterous when you remembered Spinoza's earlier statement that the one and only Infinite Reality must exist unchangingly: "it cannot change into anything better, because it is perfect." If God exists because his own infinite nature sets up an unbeatable ethical need for this, then God could indeed be "self-causing" in rather an odd sense. Notice that the "perfection" which could not change *into anything better* clearly isn't something merely on the lines of "having maximal quantity or degree of being" without any genuine *goodness* – although some commentators on the *Ethics* have interpreted "perfection" on precisely those lines, as if they had forgotten the book's title.

Besides being unchanging, the *Short Treatise* declares, God "has all things perfectly in himself"; "there is nothing outside him." You and your cat and all the stars must therefore in a sense be unchanging as well. The world forms what today would be called an Einsteinian four-dimensional block-universe.

By striving for logical proofs everywhere, the *Ethics* tries to make these waters clearer. It may only cloud them. We learn that God "has from Himself an absolutely infinite power of existence." For what reason? Spinoza answers that "perfection does not prevent the existence of a thing but establishes it; imperfection, on the other hand, prevents existence; and so of no existence can we be more sure than of the existence of the Being absolutely infinite." This risks looking like a particularly wretched Ontological Proof.

In trying to account for existence, LEIBNIZ rejects an infinite chain of explanations. The reason why a book discusses geometry cannot, he writes, be given by pointing to an infinite sequence of such books, each copied from the one before. Yet "from the very fact that there exists something rather than nothing, it follows that in possible things, or in possibility or essence itself, there is a certain need of existence or, so to speak, a claim to exist, in a word, that essence of itself tends to existence." Although the world "is not metaphysically necessary, so that its opposite involves a contradiction or logical absurdity, it is nevertheless so determined that its opposite involves imperfection or moral absurdity."

Leibniz pictures possible things as struggling for existence. The better they are, the stronger their tendencies to exist. The best possible combination of them is then generated, somewhat as the greatest possible descent of weight is produced when heavy bodies linked by pulleys compete to move downward. God could of course never be defeated in such a struggle between possibilities since God's infinite goodness would make God's claim to existence infinitely strong, and you might perhaps expect Leibniz to tell us that God's existence is due to this. For suppose he instead thought that God – *God at the very least, God even if nothing else* – existed without this being due to the success of a claim to existence. It would immediately destroy his theory that *nothing whatever* would have existed, were it not for the reality of such claims. [Look again at those words "from the very fact that there exists something rather than nothing it follows that in possible things, or in possibility or essence itself, there is […] a claim to exist."] But remember, Leibniz is writing in an age of very strong pressure – getting classified as a heretic can still have very serious consequences – to make God the ultimate foundation of all explanations and to deny all limits to God's power. Just a little earlier, Descartes has written that God's power extends to whether four and four make eight! It is therefore no surprise that Leibniz hurries to assure us that the struggle between possible things really took place only in God's mind when God considered what best to create – instead of saying that God Himself, even when infinitely sure to succeed in any struggle between possibilities, had actually been compelled to take part in such a struggle, a creative process occurring independently of His will.

Don't our eyes see something very unlike a best possible combination of goods? Leibniz comments that we know only "a very small part of eternity." If we covered all but a tiny fraction of a beautiful picture, what would we see except "a confused mass of colours"? He also has his theory that there exists "the greatest amount of reality," but unfortunately he and his predecessors never really explained what "amount of reality" (at other times Leibniz says "amount of essence" and "degree of essence") could mean. Apart, that is, from insisting that amount or degree of reality or of essence was *greater* in things that were *better*.

In HEGEL the concept of degrees of reality which are also degrees of goodness gets an interpretation going far beyond anything Leibniz had in mind. As in the case of Spinoza's system, all the world's things are present inside a single, fully unified existent which can be called God. All are mere aspects of its unsurpassable excellence, somewhat as the roughness of a rock is just an aspect of the rock. What we see as their separateness is therefore in part illusory. Similarly with all their qualities; the ordinary picture of these involves contradictions. All illusoriness disappears with the passage of time, yet Time itself is in part illusory. Time's final state, supremely good and absolutely real, is already in some sense "radically and really achieved" (as Hegel puts it) since Absolute Reality eternally underlies all the illusions; it is the thing into which all the apparent contradictions flow.

God alias Absolute Reality is fully mental, "the Idea that thinks itself." It "embraces all characteristics in its unity." Its supreme goodness ensures its existence since "the Idea is not so impotent as merely to have a right or an obligation to exist without actually existing."

The idea that God's goodness is the reason why God is more than a mere possibility – the idea that God has a claim to existence, a "requiredness," which is not only ethical or "axiological" but actually explains why God exists – appears in many philosophers in addition to such figures as Aristotle, Descartes, Spinoza, Leibniz, Hegel. And although numerous writers prefer to use "God" as the name not for a Being but for a force with an ethical side to it, a force creating the cosmos, they themselves then sometimes describe the cosmos in ways making it a candidate for Godhood: for instance as perfectly good, as fully unified, and as mental throughout. Others, however, picture God as a deity who creates things that exist outside himself, a Person whose own existence is due solely to the ethical need for it, whereas other things exist thanks to that Person's decision to bring a good world into existence. Alfred Cyril EWING is a recent philosopher in this tradition.

Ewing cannot understand why people treat God as *logically necessary* – necessary to avoid contradiction. "You must," he protests, "ascribe conflicting attributes to something if you are to contradict yourself, but if you merely deny the existence of something you are not ascribing any attributes to anything." "But," he asks, "need the necessity be logical necessity?" The sole alternative he can see is to make God's existence "necessary not because there would be any internal contradiction in denying it but because it was supremely good that God should exist"; "the hypothesis that complete perfection does constitute an adequate ground for existence does seem to be the only one which could make the universe intelligible and give an ultimate explanation of anything."

Ewing accepts that God's omnipotence is important to "a fully satisfying religious view," for it means God is not fighting a war "in which he might well be defeated." But, he writes, "the worship of power as such is not good but evil." Only supreme goodness "could give a title to worship."

Writing as Oxford's Regius Professor of Divinity, Keith WARD agrees with Ewing on how God's existence could be explained. "Nothing other than God can account for God. Either God cannot be accounted for – which makes the divine existence and nature something which just happens to be the case – or the divine nature accounts for its own existence." Which it might indeed do, for God eternally knows his own being and "it is good in itself that there should be a state which consists in the contemplation of supreme beauty and goodness. This is the best of reasons for the existence of a being of supreme goodness, namely, that its existence is supremely desirable, not least to itself."

Similar ideas attract John POLKINGHORNE. Polkinghorne suspects that the theologically traditional "equation of divine essence and divine existence" amounts to viewing God as "self-subsistent perfection, identifying within himself not only cause and effect but also supreme goodness and its instantiation." He comments that John Leslie's talk of "the creative effectiveness of supreme ethical required-ness" could thus "properly be understood, purely and simply, as an insight into the divine nature itself."

LESLIE theorizes that Value explains why there exists Something, not a blank. The entire cosmos, or perhaps a divine mind in particular, exists just because this is good. He thinks it a thoroughly unoriginal theory. It has had crowds of supporters ever since the days of Plato. When an ethical need is pictured as standing outside the cosmos and creating it, the theory might be named Neoplatonism. When it is instead said that a divine mind owes its existence to its own ethical requiredness, it might be called Platonic Theology. However, any distinction here could be purely verbal. Believing that a cosmos or a divine mind "owed its existence to the ethical need for it" could be no different from believing that the cosmos or the divine mind "owed its existence to its own ethical requiredness, a property tied to its other properties." Instead of being *moral* requiredness, the requiredness would of course have to be *ethical* requiredness (or "axiological" requiredness, as Nicholas Rescher prefers to say). Moral requiredness, obligatoriness, being a duty, the requiredness of actions by which people bring about what is needed, cannot possibly explain why there isn't a blank.

It would be foolish to view this Platonic theory as correct because of mere Logic. The concept of *being ethically required* is not the same as that of *being required ethically and with creative success*, any more than the concept of a cow is the same as that of a brown cow, or of a cow that gives milk. All that we could hope to show, Leslie writes, is that an ethical requirement would be "in the right ballpark" for acting creatively, and that its creative effectiveness would be *just as simple* as its creative *in*effectiveness. It would be just as simple because nothing would "make" an ethical requirement creatively powerful. Either it would be creatively powerful or else it wouldn't – in each case necessarily rather than through chance, but in neither case with logical necessity or thanks to intricate machinery or complex magic spells. Compare how, necessarily but without logical necessity, some things really are good or else, once again necessarily but without logical necessity, goodness is a fiction. No machinery or magic spells there!

Leslie thinks it odd to complain that we *never see* things that were created by ethical requirements. Don't we see a universe instead of emptiness, and isn't the universe in many ways strikingly good? Isn't it orderly, not a chaos? Aren't its laws impressive in how they allow intelligent life to evolve? And aren't these affairs often treated – sometimes by the very folk who do the complaining – as *visible signs* of a divine person's creative goodness? Why not instead treat them as signs of ethical requirements that acted without anybody's aid? True enough, we never see meals appearing out of thin air to feed the hungry. The world contains many evils. But we might account for evils in a very standard way, saying that possible goods could not all be present simultaneously – the good of freedom, for instance, combined with the good of decisions that are guaranteed never to be wicked or misguided.

Would that very standard maneuver be sufficient, though? Why, after calling a divine mind omnipotent and supremely good, do people think it created hugely many beings all infinitely inferior to itself? Why, if Value is in control, does there exist *anything except* divine thinking? The right answer, Leslie suggests, is that *there doesn't*. Spinoza was correct; our minds and all other things in our universe are structures inside an infinite mind which we might want to call "divine." Eternally, the mind in question thinks about everything worth thinking about, including the structures of infinitely many universes in addition to ours. All the universes exist just as patterns in its eternal thought. Our universe might be far from the best of them, but it merits its inclusion in that mind. Its annihilation would be a calamity.

Also included, presumably, would be the patterns of countless things – dreamlike situations and immortal afterlives could be among them – *not* organized into law-controlled universes. And if Value truly were in control, then there would exist innumerable further minds of the same supremely good type. Might the entire infinite ocean of those minds be named "God"?

The Good Creates an Orderly Cosmos*

PLATO

From the *Republic*

You would say, would you not, that the sun is not only the author of visibility in all visible things, but of generation and nourishment and growth, though he himself is not generation?

Certainly.

In like manner you must say that the good not only infuses the power of being known into all things known, but also bestows upon them their being and existence, and yet the good is not existence, but lies far beyond it in dignity and power.

From the *Phaedo*

Then I heard someone reading, as he said, from a book of Anaxagoras, that mind was the disposer and cause of all, and I was delighted at this notion, which appeared quite admirable, and I said to myself: If mind is the disposer, mind will dispose all for the best, and put each particular in the best place; and I argued that if anyone desired to find out the cause of the generation or destruction or existence of anything, he must find out what state of being or doing or suffering was best for that thing, and therefore a man had only to consider what was best and most desirable both for the thing itself and for other things, and then he must necessarily also know the worse, since the same science comprehended both. Arguing in this way, I rejoiced to think that I had found in Anaxagoras a teacher of the causes of existence such as I desired, and I imagined that he would tell me first whether the earth is flat or round; and after telling me this, he would proceed to explain the cause and the necessity of this being so, starting from the greater good, and demonstrating that it is better for the earth to be such as it is; and if he said that the earth was in the centre, he would further explain that this position was the better,

---

* From book 6 of the *Republic* and from the *Phaedo*, in *The Dialogues of Plato*, trans B. Jowett, 4th edn., revised (Oxford: Clarendon Press, 1953), vol. 2, pp. 372; vol. 1, pp. 454–456.

and I should be satisfied with the explanation given, and not want any other sort of cause. And I thought I would then go on and ask him about the sun and moon and stars, and that he would explain to me their comparative swiftness, and their returnings and various states, active and passive, and in what way all of them were for the best. For I could not imagine that when he spoke of mind as the disposer of them, he would give any other account of their being as they are, except that this was best; and I thought that while explaining to me in detail the cause of each and the cause of all, he would also explain to me what was best for each and what was good for all. These hopes I would not have sold for a large sum of money, and I seized the books and started to read them as fast as I could in my eagerness to know the best and the worse.

How high were my hopes, and how quickly they were lost to me! As I proceeded, I found my philosopher altogether forsaking mind and making no appeal to any other principle of order, but having recourse to air, and ether, and water, and many other eccentricities. […] I wonder that they cannot distinguish the cause from the condition without which the cause would never be the cause; it is the latter, I think, which the many, feeling about in the dark, are always mistaking and misnaming "cause". And thus one man sets the earth within a cosmic whirling, and steadies it by the heaven; another gives the air as a support to the earth, which is a sort of broad trough. They never look for the power which in arranging them as they are arranges them for the best; and instead of ascribing it to any super-human strength, they rather expect to discover another Atlas who is stronger and more everlasting than this earthly Atlas, and better able to hold things together. That it is really the good and the right which holds and binds things together, they never reflect.

The Necessarily Existing First Mover*

ARISTOTLE

From *Alpha*

[I]t is not likely either that fire or earth or any such element should be the reason why things manifest goodness and beauty both in their being and in their coming to be, […] nor again could it be right to entrust so great a matter to spontaneity and chance. When one man said, then, that reason was present – as in animals, so throughout nature – as the cause of order and of all arrangement, he seemed like a sober man in contrast with the random talk of his predecessors. We know

*   From books *Alpha* and *Lambda* of *Metaphysica*, in *The Works of Aristotle: The Oxford Translation of Aristotle*, vol. 8, trans. W.D. Ross, 2nd edn. (Oxford: Clarendon Press, 1928), pp. 989, 1071. Published by Oxford University Press. Reprinted with permission of Oxford University Press.

that Anaxagoras certainly adopted these views, but Hermotinus of Clazomenae is credited with expressing them earlier. Those who thought thus stated that there is a principle of things which is at the same time the cause of beauty, and that sort of cause from which things acquire movement. [...] [I]f we said that Empedocles in a sense both mentions, and is the first to mention, the bad and the good as principles, we should perhaps be right, since the cause of all goods is the good itself.

From *Lambda*

The first mover [...] exists of necessity; and in so far as it exists by necessity, its mode of being is good, and it is in this sense a first principle. For the necessary has all these senses – that which is necessary perforce because it is contrary to the natural impulse, that without which the good is impossible, and that which cannot be otherwise but can exist only in a single way.

On such a principle, then, depend the heavens and the world of nature. And it is a life such as the best which we enjoy, and enjoy for but a short time (for it is ever in this state, which we cannot be), since its actuality is also pleasure. [...] [T]he act of contemplation is what is most pleasant and best. If, then, God is always in that good state in which we sometimes are, this compels our wonder; and if in a better this compels it yet more. And God *is* in a better state. And life belongs to God; for the actuality of thought is life, and God is that actuality; and God's self-dependent actuality is life most good and eternal.

The Good, Creative, Itself Transcends Being*

PLOTINUS

[...] The Good is that on which all else depends, towards which all Existences aspire as to their source and their need, while Itself is without need, sufficient to Itself, aspiring to no other, the measure and Term of all, giving out from itself the Intellectual-Principle and Existence and Soul and Life and all Intellective-Act. [...] [It is] That which transcends all the realm of Being.

This Cosmos of parts has come into being not as the result of a judgement establishing its desirability, but by [...] sheer necessity. [...] The world, we must reflect, is a product of Necessity, not of deliberate purpose. [...] And

---

* From First Ennead, eighth tractate; Third Ennead, second tractate; and Sixth Ennead, seventh tractate, in *Plotinus: The Enneads*, trans. Stephen MacKenna, 4th edn., revised by B.S. Page (London: Faber & Faber, 1956).

none the less, a second consideration, if a considered plan [had] brought it into being it would still be no disgrace to its maker – for it stands a stately whole, complete within itself, serving at once its own purpose and that of all its parts which, leading and lesser alike, are of such a nature as to further the interests of the total.

"He is" does not truly apply: the Supreme has no need of Being: [...] he does not possess Being.

The Divine Simplicity*

ST. THOMAS AQUINAS

From *Summa Theologica*

Goodness and being are really the same, and differ only in idea; which is clear from the following argument. The essence of goodness consists in this, that it is in some way desirable. Hence the Philosopher says: *Goodness is what all desire.* Now it is clear that a thing is desirable only in so far as it is perfect, for all desire their own perfection. But everything is perfect so far as it is actual. Therefore it is clear that a thing is perfect so far as it is being; for being is the actuality of everything, as is clear from the foregoing. Hence it is clear that goodness and being are the same really. But goodness expresses the aspect of desirableness, which being does not express. [...]

[G]oodness, as a cause, is prior to being [...] [G]oodness has the aspect of the end in which not only actual things find their completion, but also towards which tend even those things which are not actual, but merely potential. [...]

From *Contra Gentiles*

God is absolutely simple. Therefore, for God to be good is identical with God. He is, therefore, His goodness.

[...] God's very essence is His active power. [...] God's power is His substance. [...] [I]n God power and action are not distinct. [...]

---

* From part 1, question 5, articles 1 and 2, of *Summa Theologica* in *Basic Writings of Saint Thomas Aquinas*, vol. 1, ed. A.C. Pegis (New York: Random House, 1945), and from chapter 38 of book 1, trans. A.C. Pegis, and chapters 8, 9, and 10 of book 2, trans. J.F. Anderson, of *On the Truth of the Catholic Faith: Summa contra Gentiles* (New York: Image Books, 1955). Also a sentence from book 1, lesson 14 (entirely by Aquinas) in *Aristotle On Interpretation: Commentary by St. Thomas and Cajetan*, trans. J.T. Oesterle (Milwaukee: Marquette University Press, 1962).

[T]he multifarious actions attributed to God, as understanding, willing, producing things, and the like are not diverse realities, since each of these actions in God is His very being, which is one and the same.

From *Commentary on Aristotle*

[T]he divine will must be understood as existing outside of the order of beings, as a cause producing the whole of being and all its differences.

God's Necessary Existence*

ST. ANSELM

And so, Lord, do thou, who dost give understanding to faith, give me, so far as thou knowest it to be profitable, to understand that thou art as we believe; and that thou art that which we believe. And, indeed, we believe that thou art a being than which nothing greater can be conceived. Or is there no such nature, since the fool hath said in his heart, there is no God? (Psalms xiv. 1). But, at any rate, this very fool, when he hears of this being of which I speak – a being than which nothing greater can be conceived – understands what he hears, and what he understands is in his understanding; although he does not understand it to exist.

For, it is one thing for an object to be in the understanding, and another to understand that the object exists. When a painter first conceives of what he will afterwards perform, he has it in his understanding, but he does not yet understand it to be, because he has not yet performed it. But after he has made the painting, he both has it in his understanding, and he understands that it exists, because he has made it.

Hence, even the fool is convinced that something exists in the understanding, at least, than which nothing greater can be conceived. For, when he hears of this, he understands it. And whatever is understood, exists in the understanding. And assuredly that, than which nothing greater can be conceived, cannot exist in the understanding alone. For, suppose it exists in the understanding alone: then it can be conceived to exist in reality; which is greater.

Therefore, if that, than which nothing greater can be conceived, exists in the understanding alone, the very being, than which nothing greater can be conceived, is one, than which a greater can be conceived. But obviously this is impossible.

---

* Chapters 2 and 3 of *Proslogium* in *Saint Anselm: Basic Writings*, trans. S.N. Deane (La Salle: Open Court, 1903), pp. 7–9.

Hence, there is no doubt that there exists a being, than which nothing greater can be conceived, and it exists both in the understanding and in reality.

And it assuredly exists so truly, that it cannot be conceived not to exist. For, it is possible to conceive of a being which cannot be conceived not to exist; and this is greater than one which can be conceived not to exist. Hence, if that, than which nothing greater can be conceived, can be conceived not to exist, it is not that, than which nothing greater can be conceived. But this is an irreconcilable contradiction. There is, then, so truly a being than which nothing greater can be conceived to exist, that it cannot even be conceived not to exist; and this being thou art, O Lord, our God.

So truly, therefore, dost thou exist, O Lord, my God, that thou canst not be conceived not to exist; and rightly. For, if a mind could conceive of a being better than thee, the creature would rise above the Creator; and this is most absurd. And, indeed, whatever else there is, except thee alone, can be conceived not to exist. To thee alone, therefore, it belongs to exist more truly than all other beings, and hence in a higher degree than all others. For, whatever else exists does not exist so truly, and hence in a less degree it belongs to it to exist. Why, then, has the fool said in his heart, there is no God (Psalms xiv. 1), since it is so evident, to a rational mind, that thou dost exist in the highest degree of all? Why, except that he is dull and a fool?

Supreme Perfection Necessarily Exists*

RENÉ DESCARTES

Arguments
proving the existence of God and the distinction
between the soul and the body
arranged in geometrical fashion

Definitions

[...]

VIII. The substance which we understand to be supremely perfect, and in which we conceive absolutely nothing that implies any defect or limitation in that perfection, is called *God*. [...]

---

* From the end of his Replies to the Second Set of Objections to the *Meditations on First Philosophy*, in *The Philosophical Writings of Descartes*, volume 2, trans. J. Cottingham et al. (Cambridge: Cambridge University Press, 1984).

Postulates

[...]

Fifthly, I ask my readers to spend a great deal of time and effort on contemplating the nature of the supremely perfect being. Above all they should reflect on the fact that the ideas of all other natures contain possible existence, whereas the idea of God contains not only possible but wholly necessary existence. This alone, without a formal argument, will make them realize that God exists; and this will eventually be just as self-evident to them as the fact that the number two is even or that three is odd, and so on.

The Ontological Argument*

ALVIN PLANTINGA

I wish to discuss the famous "ontological argument" first formulated by Anselm of Canterbury in the eleventh century. This argument for the existence of God has fascinated philosophers ever since Anselm first stated it. Few people, I should think, have been brought to belief in God by means of this argument; nor has it played much of a role in strengthening and confirming religious faith. At first sight Anselm's argument is remarkably unconvincing if not downright irritating; it looks too much like a parlor puzzle or word magic. And yet nearly every major philosopher from the time of Anselm to the present has had something to say about it; this argument has a long and illustrious line of defenders extending to the present. Indeed, the last few years have seen a remarkable flurry of interest in it among philosophers. What accounts for its fascination? Not, I think, its religious significance, although that can be under-rated. Perhaps there are two reasons for it. First, many of the most knotty and difficult problems in philosophy meet in this argument. Is existence a property? Are existential propositions – propositions of the form *x exists* – ever neces-sarily true? Are existential propositions about what they seem to be about? Are there, in any respectable sense of "are," some objects that do not exist? If so, do they have any properties? Can they be compared with things that do exist? These issues and a hundred others arise in connection with Anselm's argument. And second, although the argument certainly looks at first sight as if it ought to be unsound, it is profoundly difficult to say what, exactly, is wrong with it. [...]

* From part 2, section c, of *God, Freedom, and Evil* (Grand Rapids, MI: William B. Eerdmans, 1977), pp. 85, 108–112. © 1977 Wm. B. Eerdmans Publishing Company, Grand Rapids, MI. Reprinted with permission of the publisher. All rights reserved. Points in numbered lists have been renumbered from the original to begin at 1.

The Argument Restated

[...] [W]e can restate the present version of the argument in the following more explicit way.

(1)   It is possible that there be a being that has maximal greatness.
(2)   So there is a possible being that in some world *W* has maximal greatness.
(3)   A Being has maximal greatness in a given world only if it has maximal excellence in every world.
(4)   A being has maximal excellence in a given world only if it has omniscience, omnipotence, and moral perfection in that world.

And now we no longer need the supposition that necessary existence is a perfection; for obviously a being can't be omnipotent (or for that matter omniscient or morally perfect) in a given world unless it *exists* in that world. From (1), (3), and (4) it follows that there actually exists a being that is omnipotent, omniscient, and morally perfect; this being, furthermore, exists and has these qualities in every other world as well. For (2), which follows from (1), tells us that there is a possible world *W'*, let's say, in which there exists a being with maximal greatness. That is, had *W'* been actual, there would have been a being with maximal greatness. But then according to (3) this being has maximal excellence in every world. What this means, according to (4), is that in *W'* this being has omniscience, omnipotence, and moral perfection *in every world*. That is to say, if *W'* had been actual, there would have existed a being who was omniscient and omnipotent and morally perfect and who would have had these properties in every possible world. [...] Accordingly these premises, (1), (3), and (4), entail that God, so thought of, exists. Indeed, if we regard (3) and (4) as consequences of a *definition* – a definition of maximal greatness – then the only premise of the argument is (1).

But now for a last objection. What about (2)? It says that there is a *possible being* having such and such characteristics. But what *are* possible beings? We know what *actual* beings are – the Taj Mahal, Socrates, you and I, the Grand Teton – these are among the more impressive examples of actually existing beings. But what is a *possible* being? Is there a possible mountain just like Mt. Rainier two miles directly south of the Grand Teton? If so, it is located at the same place as the Middle Teton. Does that matter? Is there another such possible mountain three miles east of the Grand Teton, where Jenny Lake is? Are there possible mountains like this all over the world? Are there also possible oceans at all the places where there are possible mountains? For any place you mention, of course, it is *possible* that there be a mountain there; does it follow that in fact *there is* a possible mountain there?

These are some questions that arise when we ask ourselves whether there are merely possible beings that don't in fact exist. And the version of the ontological argument we've been considering seems to make sense only on the assumption that there are such things. [...]

The Argument Triumphant

[W]e can restate this last version of the ontological argument in such a way that it no longer matters whether there are any merely possible beings that do not exist. Instead of speaking of the possible being that has, in some world or other, a maximal degree of greatness, we may speak of *the property of being maximally great* or *maximal greatness*. The premise corresponding to (1) then says simply that maximal greatness is possibly instantiated, i.e., that

(5)   There is a possible world in which maximal greatness is instantiated. And the analogues of (3) and (4) spell out what is involved in maximal greatness:

(6)   Necessarily, a being is maximally great only if it has maximal excellence in every world

and

(7)   Necessarily, a being has maximal excellence in every world only if it has omniscience, omnipotence, and moral perfection in every world.

Notice that (6) and (7) do not imply that there are possible but nonexistent beings – any more than does, for example,

(8)   Necessarily, a thing is a unicorn only if it has one horn.

But if (5) is true, then there is a possible world W such that if it had been actual, then there would have existed a being that was omnipotent, omniscient, and morally perfect; this being, furthermore, would have had these qualities in every possible world. So it follows that if W had been actual, it would have been *impossible* that there be no such being. That is, if W had been actual,

(9)   There is no omnipotent, omniscient, and morally perfect being

would have been an impossible proposition. But if a proposition is impossible in at least one possible world, then it is impossible in every possible world; what is impossible does not vary from world to world. Accordingly (9) is impossible in the *actual* world, i.e., impossible *simpliciter*. But if it is impossible that there be no such being, then there actually exists a being that is omnipotent, omniscient, and morally perfect; this being, furthermore, has these qualities essentially and exists in every possible world.

What shall we say of this argument? It is certainly valid; given its premise, the conclusion follows. The only question of interest, it seems to me, is whether its main premise – that maximal greatness *is* possibly instantiated – is *true*. I think it *is* true; hence I think this version of the ontological argument is sound.

But here we must be careful, we must ask whether this argument is a successful piece of natural theology, whether it *proves* the existence of God. And the answer must be, I think, that it does not. An argument for God's existence may be *sound*, after all, without in any useful sense proving God's existence. Since I believe in God, I think the following argument is sound:

> **Either God exists or 7+5=14**
> **It is false that 7+5=14**
> **Therefore God exists.**

But obviously this isn't a *proof;* no one who didn't already accept the conclusion, would accept the first premise. The ontological argument we've been examining isn't just like this one, of course, but it must be conceded that not everyone who understands and reflects on its central premise – that the existence of a maximally great being is *possible* – will accept it. Still, it is evident, I think, that there is nothing *contrary to reason* or *irrational* in accepting this premise. What I claim for this argument, therefore, is that it establishes, not the *truth* of theism, but its rational acceptability. And hence it accomplishes at least one of the aims of the tradition of natural theology.

Perfection, All-Inclusive, Self-Caused*

BENEDICT SPINOZA

From *Short Treatise*

[T]here cannot be two infinites, but *only one;* [...] it cannot change into anything better, because it is perfect. [...]

God *is a cause of all things.* [...] [A]ll that he produces is within himself, and not outside him, because there is nothing outside him. [...] The *predisposing cause*

---

* From chapters 1, 3, and 6 of *Short Treatise*, Spinoza's *Short Treatise on God, Man, and his Well-Being*, trans. A. Wolf (New York: Russell & Russell, 1963), and from part 1 of *Ethics*, trans. James Gutmann (New York: Hafner, 1949).

[...] is his perfection itself; through it he is a cause of himself, and, consequently, of all other things. [...]

[I]t is just perfection in God, that he gives to all things, from the greatest to the least, their essence, or, to express it better, that he has all things perfectly in himself.

From *Ethics*

PROPOSITION XI. *God or substance consisting of infinite attributes, each one of which expresses eternal and infinite essence, necessarily exists.*

[...]

[T]he Being absolutely infinite, or God, has from Himself an absolutely infinite power of existence. [...] He therefore necessarily exists. [...] Perfection [...] does not prevent the existence of a thing but establishes it; imperfection, on the other hand, prevents existence, and so of no existence can we be more sure than of the existence of the Being absolutely infinite or perfect, that is to say, God. For since His essence shuts out all imperfection and involves absolute perfection, for this very reason all cause of doubt concerning His existence is taken away.

A Best Possible World*

GOTTFRIED WILHELM LEIBNIZ

Besides the world or the aggregate of finite things there is a certain unity which is dominant, not only as the soul is dominant in me or rather as the ego itself is dominant in my body, but also in a much higher sense. For the dominant unity of the universe not only rules the world but constructs or fashions it. It is higher than the world and, so to speak, extramundane, and is thus the ultimate reason of things. For the sufficient reason of existence cannot be found either in any particular thing or in the whole aggregate and series of things. Let us suppose that a book of the elements of geometry existed from all eternity and that in succession one copy of it was made from another, it is evident that although we can account for the present book by the book from which it was copied, nevertheless, going back through as many books as we like, we could never reach a complete reason for it, because we can always ask why such books have at all times existed, that is to say, why books at all, and why written in this way. What is true of books is also true of the different

---

* From *On the Ultimate Origination of Things*, in *Leibniz: The Monadology and Other Philosophical Writings*, trans. Robert Latta (London: Oxford University Press, 1898).

states of the world; for, in spite of certain laws of change, the succeeding state is, in some sort, a copy of that which precedes it. Therefore, to whatever earlier state you go back, you never find in it the complete reason of things, that is to say, the reason why there exists any world and why this world rather than some other.

You may indeed suppose the world eternal; but as you suppose only a succession of states, in none of which do you find the sufficient reason, and as even any number of worlds does not in the least help you to account for them, it is evident that the reason must be sought elsewhere. For in eternal things, even though there be no cause, there must be a reason which, for permanent things, is necessity itself or essence; but for the series of changing things, if it be supposed that they succeed one another from all eternity, this reason is, as we shall presently see, the prevailing of inclinations which consist not in necessitating reasons, that is to say, reasons of an absolute and metaphysical necessity, the opposite of which involves a contradiction, but in inclining reasons. From this it is manifest that even by supposing the eternity of the world, we cannot escape the ultimate extramundane reason of things, that is to say, God.

Accordingly the reasons of the world lie hid in something extramundane, different from the concatenation of states or the series of things, the aggregate of which constitutes the world. And thus we must go beyond the physical or hypothetical necessity, according to which the later things of the world are determined by the earlier, to something which is of absolute or metaphysical necessity, of which a reason cannot be given. For the present world is necessary physically or hypothetically, but not absolutely or metaphysically. That is to say, the nature of the world being such as it is, it follows that things must happen in it just as they do. Therefore, since the ultimate root of all must be in something which has metaphysical necessity, and since the reason of any existing thing is to be found only in an existing thing, it follows that there must exist one Being which has metaphysical necessity, one Being of whose essence it is to exist; and thus there must exist something different from that plurality of beings, the world, which as we admitted and showed, has no metaphysical necessity.

But to explain more distinctly how from eternal or essential or metaphysical truths there arise temporal, contingent or physical truths, we must first observe that, from the very fact that there exists something rather than nothing, it follows that in possible things, or in possibility or essence itself, there is a certain need of existence or, so to speak, a claim to exist, in a word, that essence of itself tends to existence. From this it further follows that all possible things, that is, things expressing essence or possible reality, with equal right tend to existence in proportion to the quantity of essence or reality, or in proportion to the degree of perfection which belongs to them. For perfection is nothing but quantity of essence.

Hence it is most evident that out of the infinite possible combinations and series of possible things there exists that one through which the greatest amount of essence or possibility is brought into existence. Indeed, there is always in things a principle of determination according to maximum and minimum, so that, for instance, the maximum effect is produced with the minimum outlay. And the time, the place, or, in a word, the receptivity or capacity of the world may here be considered as the outlay or ground on which the world is to be built as fittingly as possible, while the variety of forms corresponds to the fitness of the building and to the number and elegance of its rooms [...].

Thus it is wonderfully made known to us how in the very origination of things a certain Divine mathematics or metaphysical mechanics is employed and the greatest quantity is brought into existence [...].

[B]est of all is the illustration we get in ordinary mechanics, where, when several heavy bodies act against one another, the resultant motion is that which produces the greatest fall on the whole. For as possible things by an equal right tend to exist in proportion to their reality, so all weights by an equal right tend to fall in proportion to their gravity; and as in the case of the latter there is produced a motion which involves the greatest possible fall of the heavy bodies, so in the case of the former there is produced a world in which the greatest number of possible things comes into existence.

And thus we have physical necessity coming from metaphysical necessity; for although the world is not metaphysically necessary, so that its opposite involves a contradiction or logical absurdity, it is nevertheless physically necessary or so determined that its opposite involves imperfection or moral absurdity. And as possibility is the principle of essence, so perfection or degree of essence (through which more things are compossible the greater it is) is the principle of existence. Whence at the same time it is manifest how the Author of the world is free, although He does all things determinately, for He acts from a principle of wisdom or perfection. Indifference springs from ignorance, and the wiser a man is the more is he determined towards that which is most perfect.

But, you will say, however beautiful may seem this comparison of a certain metaphysical determining mechanism with the physical mechanism of heavy bodies, it nevertheless fails in this respect that heavy bodies really exist and act, but possibilities or essences anterior to existence or apart from it are imaginary or fictitious and therefore no reason of existence is to be sought in them. I reply that neither these essences nor what are called eternal truths regarding these essences are fictitious, but that they exist in a certain region (if I may so call it) of ideas, that is to say, in God Himself, the source of all essence and of the existence of other things [...].

And lest anyone should think that we are here confounding moral perfection or goodness with metaphysical perfection or greatness and, allowing the latter, should deny the former, it is to be observed that it follows from what has been said not only that the world is most perfect physically, or, if you prefer it, metaphysically, that is to say, that that series of things has come into existence in which the greatest amount of reality is actually manifested, but also that the world is most perfect morally because genuine moral perfection is physical perfection in minds themselves. Wherefore the world is not only the most admirable mechanism, but it is also, in so far as it is made up of minds, the best commonwealth, through which there is bestowed upon minds the greatest possible happiness or joy, in which their physical perfection consists.

But, you will say, we find that the opposite of this takes place in the world, for very often the best people suffer the worst things, and those who are innocent, both animals and men, are afflicted and put to death even with torture; and indeed the world, especially if we consider the government of the human race, seems rather a confused chaos than anything directed by a supreme wisdom. So, I confess, it seems at first glance, but when we look at it more closely the opposite conclusion manifestly follows *a priori* from those very considerations which have been adduced, the conclusion, namely, that the highest possible perfection of all things, and therefore of all minds, is brought about.

And indeed, as the lawyers say, it is not proper to judge unless we have examined the whole law. We know a very small part of eternity which is immeasurable in its extent; for what a little thing is the record of a few thousand years, which history transmits to us! Nevertheless, from so slight an experience we rashly judge regarding the immeasurable and eternal, like men who, having been born and brought up in prison or, perhaps, in the subterranean salt-mines of the Sarmatians, should think that there is no other light in the world than that of the feeble lamp which hardly suffices to direct their steps. If you look at a very beautiful picture, having covered up the whole of it except a very small part, what will it present to your sight, however thoroughly you examine it (nay, so much more, the more closely you inspect it), but a confused mass of colours laid on without selection and without art?

More Than Just a Right to Exist*

G.W.F. HEGEL

From *Section 6*

The object of philosophy is the Idea: and the Idea is not so impotent as merely to have a right or an obligation to exist without actually existing.

From *Section 59*

[T]he Idea, when all limitations were removed from it, would appear as follows. The universality moulded by Reason, and described as the absolute and final end or the Good, would be realised in the world [...]

---

* From *The Logic of Hegel*, trans. William Wallace, 2nd edn., revised (London: Oxford University Press, 1892). The work forms the first part of Hegel's *Encyclopaedia of the Philosophical Sciences*.

From *Section 235*

[T]he truth of the Good is laid down as the unity of the theoretical and practical idea in the doctrine that the Good is radically and really achieved, that the objective world is in itself and for itself the Idea, just as it at the same time eternally lays itself down as End, and by action brings about its actuality. [...]

From *Section 236*

The Idea, as unity of the Subjective and Objective Idea, is the notion of the Idea, – a notion whose object (*Gegenstand*) is the Idea as such, and for which the objective (*Objekt*) is Idea, – an Object which embraces all characteristics in its unity. This unity is consequently the absolute and all truth, the Idea which thinks itself [...]

God Exists by Ethical Necessity*

A.C. EWING

I do not think the existence of God can be proved in a strict sense, or even that the belief should be based mainly on argument, but I think that two at any rate of the three which have, since Kant at least, been classified as the traditional arguments for God have some force and are worthy of serious consideration. My view of the ontological argument is less favourable, and it surprises me very much that the argument has been revived not only by metaphysicians like Hartshorne but even by a philosopher who has been so much influenced by the linguistic school as Malcolm. As interpreted by them it is given at least a rather less implausible form by making the relevant property not existence but necessary existence. The objection that existence is not a predicate cannot, it is said, be applied to necessary existence, on the ground that the main reason for saying that existence is not a predicate is that a thing must exist before a predicate can be applied to it at all. The same obviously could not be said of necessary existence since many existent things do not exist necessarily. It also seemed obvious that a being whose existence was necessary would be more perfect than a being otherwise equally perfect whose existence depended on something else or who just "happened to be". [...] If the idea of a perfect being is not self-contradictory, Malcolm concludes, God must therefore exist, and while he does not see how the antecedent of this conditional can be proved, he makes rather light of that point, thinking that in view of its place in the

---

*   From chapter 7 of *Value and Reality* (London: George Allen & Unwin, 1973), pp. 146–147, 157, 161.

language, thought and lives of men there can be no more of a presumption that the idea of God is self-contradictory than there is with the concept of seeing a material thing. Hartshome's argument also skates too lightly over this.

I find more difficulty. Firstly, nothing has been done to overcome Kant's strongest objection to the proof of a necessary being, namely that there could not be any contradiction in something not existing, because you must ascribe conflicting attributes to something if you are to contradict yourself, but if you merely deny the existence of something you are not ascribing any attributes to anything, so there are no attributes to conflict. This seems to me a fatal objection to the view that the existence of God is logically necessary. [...]

I must admit that the concept of God for most philosophers who have reflected on it deeply does include necessity in some sense as an ingredient. The existence of God, it is felt, could not be merely a contingent fact; and, if it were, God could not be regarded as the completely supreme being but only as the being that *happened* to be strongest. But, I ask, need the necessity be logical necessity? Might not God be necessary in some sense other than that in which his necessity would mean that there was an internal contradiction in denying his existence? [...] If we are to meet the demand of the human intellect that there should be a reason, we seem to need a reason of such a kind as will give an explanation of existence without making the non-existence of anything logically self-contradictory. There remains only one alternative, as far as can be seen, which might do this, namely an explanation in terms of values. In that case God's existence will be necessary not because there would be any internal self-contradiction in denying it but because it was supremely good that God should exist. It is not indeed evident to us a priori that the best possible being must exist, but a universe determined by values would certainly be rational in a very important sense in which a universe not determined by values would quite fail to be so, and the hypothesis that complete perfection does constitute an adequate ground for existence does seem to be the only one which could make the universe intelligible and give an ultimate explanation of anything [...]

In traditional philosophical arguments about God too much stress, I think, has been laid on the metaphysical and too little on the ethical attributes of God. The thing that matters in religion and makes it worth having is that it tells us that the being on whom everything depends is absolutely and supremely good. The doctrine of the omnipotence of God is of great importance because it matters very much whether we can regard the supremely good being as in control of everything or as fighting a war in which he might well be defeated, but I do not see how any quality could give a title to worship except supreme goodness. The power and awesome mystery of God have often assumed the centre of the stage, but while a fully satisfying religious view does require the omnipotence of God, and a being so much above us as God is must be deeply mysterious to us, the worship of power as such is not good but evil and to worship mystery as such is to worship something simply because we do not know what it is like.

Goodness Could Be Self-Explanatory*

KEITH WARD

The biblical writers never raised the question of why God is as God is or why God does what God does. They encountered God in their history as a providential, glorious, loving, and holy being, who came to be seen as the creator of heaven and earth. The universe could be accounted for by tracing it to the will of God, though the prophets never claimed to understand that will in more than the tiny part of it which touched their own destiny. The question of what could account for God was never raised. It remained an ultimate mystery. It is clear, however, that nothing other than God can account for God. Either God cannot be accounted for – which makes the divine existence and nature something which just happens to be the case – or the divine nature accounts for its own existence. To "account for" is to give a reason; thus the reason for God's existence must lie in that existence itself. To that extent, a reflective theism does seem to point to an idea of a self-explanatory being, which is what Aristotle was seeking to articulate.

Aristotle sees that the best reason for the existence of anything is its goodness: "the real good is the primary object of rational wish." If I ask, "Why should X exist?", a good reason is that it is intrinsically valuable that it should exist. The good is that which can be reasonably desired; and it is good in itself that there should exist a state which consists in the contemplation of supreme beauty and goodness. This is the best of reasons for the existence of a being of supreme goodness, namely, that its existence is supremely desirable, not least to itself.

God's Creatively Effective Requiredness†

JOHN POLKINGHORNE

To say God is good cannot be just a tautology, making God a kind of celestial dictator whose will is "good" by mere definition, and woe betide those who question it. [...] God and his goodness are neither arbitrarily identical nor absolutely separable. I suspect this is what philosophical theologians are getting at in their celebrated equation of divine essence and divine existence – not just that the divine is Being with a capital B, but that God is self-subsistent perfection,

---

* From chapter 8 of *Religion and Creation* (Oxford: Clarendon Press, 1996), p. 195. Reprinted with permission of Oxford University Press.
† From chapter 3 of *The Faith of a Physicist: Reflections of a Bottom-Up Thinker*, Gifford Lectures 1993–4 (Princeton, N.J.: Princeton University Press, 1994).

identifying within himself not only cause and effect in the quality of aseity, but also supreme goodness and its instantiation in a divine bootstrap of virtue. Ward says of divine goodness that it is "a necessary part of the being of God and could not exist as necessary in isolation from the totality of Divine nature". If all that is right, John Leslie's extreme axiarchism (the creative effectiveness of supreme ethical requiredness) is not a Neoplatonic "Originating Principle" which might have as a consequence, in some emanating and descending chain of being, that there was "an all-powerful person, an omniscient Designer", but it is properly to be understood, purely and simply, as an insight into the divine nature itself.

Existing Because Ethically Required*

JOHN LESLIE

1. Three Very Basic Cosmological Questions

If eager to know the world's structure, ask the scientists. Science, however, seems unable to answer some key questions concerning the structure. For a start, why is the structure an orderly one? Why do events so often develop in fairly simple and familiar ways, leading us to talk of causal laws? Sure enough, we can often explain one causal regularity by pointing to another. We can say why gases regularly expand when heated. It is because faster-moving molecules regularly hit harder, as when colliding with pistons. Sooner or later, though, some regularities will presumably be fundamental, ultimate, rather than explicable by others that underlie them. Now, why do those regularities exist? Can events ever occur in orderly ways for absolutely no reason?

A next question is why the world's causal laws permit the existence of living organisms. It has long been a silly question in the eyes of many folk. Why, they have asked, should anyone think it strange, problematic, that the world's laws are life-permitting? But the question is typically viewed very differently today, thanks to what has come to be known as "cosmic fine tuning." Many cosmic parameters seem such that a lifeless universe would have resulted from even minimal changes to them. Minimal decreases, for instance, in the smoothness of our universe at early times (it was, it has been estimated, smooth to an accuracy of one part in one followed by a thousand trillion trillion trillion trillion trillion trillion trillion trillion trillion zeros, without which all would have remained tremendously hot); tiny alterations to the expansion speed early in the Big Bang; slight tinkering with

* From "A Cosmos Existing through Ethical Necessity," *Philo: A Journal of Philosophy*, 12(2), special issue: *Theism and Naturalism* (Fall/Winter, 2009), pp. 172–187. Reprinted by permission of *Philo* and of The Center for Inquiry.

the "weak" and "strong" interactions which control the atomic nucleus, or with Planck's constant which decides the size of the quantum packets in which energy is transferred, or with the relative masses of elementary particles such as the neutron and the proton, or with the relative strengths of forces such as electromagnetism and gravity – these and other minor modifications would have led to a universe in which life would almost certainly never have appeared. For there to be a scheme of things which avoids gravitational collapse for longer than a second, also failing to expand so fast as to become almost immediately composed only of near-vacuum, and for there to be atoms, steadily burning stars, chemistry, and so forth, the numbers featuring in the physical equations that describe our universe had seemingly to be brought inside narrow bounds. Now, how could such fine tuning have come about?

Admittedly there is much controversy over just what would have needed to be tuned. Some believe, for example, that the early cosmic expansion speed and degree of smoothness were made inevitable by a process called "inflation." Could inflation itself have occurred only thanks to very accurate tuning? Some say Yes, others No. Again, might it have been possible to get life without steadily burning stars? Could intelligent organisms exist on neutron star surfaces, maybe? Some think so, others think it ridiculous. It would seem, however, that accurate tuning was required even to get neutron stars instead of a universe composed almost entirely of light rays or of black holes. Well, why would ours be a universe characterized by such tuning?

A widely accepted answer is that there exist greatly many universes and that such factors as *scalar fields*, fields that could well vary from universe to universe, produce an immense variety of universe-types through influencing the force strengths and the particle masses of each particular universe. With any luck at least a few of the universes would then be tuned in life-permitting ways, and living beings could find themselves only among the universes that were. Problem solved? Unfortunately there is a conundrum here. In case after case, a force strength or a particle mass seems to require tuning to within the same tight limits for several different reasons at once. Look at electromagnetism. The strength of this force apparently needed to be tuned, often with great precision, *first* for matter to be significantly different from radiation (from which you presumably cannot construct living organisms); *second* for quarks to escape being converted into leptons, which would make atoms impossible; *third* for protons not to decay so swiftly that there would soon be no more atoms; *fourth* for there to be any such subject as chemistry; *fifth* for there to be sun-like stars, burning steadily for billions of years; *sixth* for stars to produce carbon in quantity, carbon being essential to all known organisms; *seventh* for there to be stellar explosions able to scatter carbon for making into living beings; *etcetera*. Now, how come that electromagnetism's actual strength can fulfil all these requirements simultaneously? Why did not this force need tuning in one way to fulfil a first requirement, in a different way to fulfil a second, in some still other way to fulfil a third, and so forth? Why was there any life-permitting strength to which electromagnetism could be tuned in some universe or other? The conundrum would seem only to get worse and worse, the further the picture was complicated by additional forces or elementary particles. How came there to be even just one potentially life-producing mixture of force strengths and particle masses? Why were not all possible mixture equally unsuitable?

Here we might try saying that not just force strengths and particle masses, but the basic laws of physics themselves, differed from universe to universe so that at least a few universes had laws that allowed for suitable mixtures. Yet wouldn't this risk being in severe conflict with trust in Induction, the scientific principle that local conditions are a guide to conditions elsewhere? It is easy enough to imagine factors such as scalar fields which might make things like the strength of electro-magnetism and the mass of the proton into matters that varied from universe to universe. But what factor could produce variation not just in (say) scalar fields and anything which those fields controlled, but in the basic laws of physics? And could we readily believe in any such factor, respectful of Induction as we very rightly are?

Then there is what can seem the biggest question of all. Science investigates the world's structure, but why is there anything at all to be structured? Why is there a cosmos, not a blank? Why is there something rather than nothing? Science cannot answer this. Imagine a universe obeying whatever physical laws you pleased; there would still be the problem of why there was any such universe. It has sometimes been suggested that our universe is a quantum fluctuation rather like the very short-lived particles that are for ever jumping into existence even in what we call "empty space" because of the Heisenberg uncertainty that connects energy and position in time. Since gravitational binding-energy is in some good enough sense "negative energy," a gravitationally bound universe that came into existence as a quantum fluctuation might have a total energy of zero or nearly zero, this permit-ting it to be very large and to survive for billions of years. Yet why would there be anything which the laws of quantum physics governed? It looks inadequate to pro-test that the laws *gave themselves* such and such a quantum-probability of actually having some universe to govern. Suppose I dream up a law that little red dragons will very probably exist. This surely does not mean there will in fact very likely be something (namely, little red dragons) for the law to describe. Now, why would the case of quantum laws be any different? Given various quantum-probabilistic equa-tions, what (in Stephen Hawking's words) breathes fire into those equations?

2.   Benevolent Omnipotence?

How could we possibly answer the questions I have raised? Could the world's explanation lie in God, understood as an omnipotent, world-creating person? Notoriously, this only generates the further question of why there is any such person. The idea that a deity must exist through logical necessity because *existence*, or perhaps *necessary existence*, is among the perfections he is defined as possessing, would appear not to work. Logical necessities look too *"IFfy-THENny."* If there are bachelors who are cannibals then there are wifeless non-vegetarians but this cannot itself explain why such individuals exist. The best line for a believer in God might therefore seem one taken by Richard Swinburne. Let us view God's existence as the ultimate brute fact; God is inexplicable not in the sense that we do not know his explanation, but in the sense that he just has no explanation. To make the brute fact more attractive let us call God supreme in his simplicity. Swinburne's idea is that God's ability to know, think and do everything that's logically possible *is simpler* – it is describable in fewer words, for a start – than knowing the rules of backgammon but not of baseball, being able to visualize a bar-room brawl but not a billion-man battle, and being able to create bears but not badgers and butterflies. Yet, I ask, would it not be simpler still, far simpler, if God did not exist?

God also presents the following difficulty. Supposedly, God's mental life is of the finest possible variety. God thinks about everything in the least worth thinking about. His thoughts include infinitely many worthwhile experiences because there is no difference between, for example, contemplating precisely how it would feel to experience beautiful music and actually experiencing beautiful music. Supposedly, too, God can create whatever he wills. Why then does he fail to create further beings like himself? Imagine there existed a mind infinite in negative value, perhaps because containing infinitely much suffering. Few would argue that the existence of further minds of the same terrible sort could be in no way unfortunate, bad, because it was already an infinite misfortune just by itself. But then, how odd it would be to fancy that the infinite *positive* value of a divine mind would mean there could be nothing *fortunate*, good, in the existence of further minds of *that* sort! So why ever would God create physical universes and their inhabitants? Would not each such inhabitant better be replaced by somebody else who thought about everything worth thinking about? Again, if God wanted to contemplate the beautiful structures of physical universes, why not contemplate them "just in his mind's eye"?

For anyone who accepts a deity both omnipotent and benevolent, this can look a very severe difficulty. Still, the more basic question is why there are any things at all, instead of a situation empty of all gods and other entities.

3.   Platonic Creation

Why, that is to say, is there more than just a Platonic realm of logical possibilities and facts concerning them? For please note: we must not fancy that any emptiness could be so very empty that even logical possibilities were banished from it. In order for our universe to exist, it had first to be logically possible. It must have been the case, unconditionally, that a universe of this sort, *if there were one*, would not be as self-contradictory as a round square. Likewise, in order for two sets of two roses to make four roses yesterday, it had first to be true that any two sets of two things, if they were ever to exist, necessarily would make four things. This was something unconditional, something eternal. Or consider afterimages produced by bright lights. Why are red ones more color-similar to purple ones than to blue ones? Answer: it is an unconditional, eternal reality that red, purple and blue afterimages, in the event of there ever being any, must have those degrees of greater and lesser similarity. There is a Platonic realm of necessary facts – logical facts, mathematical facts and countless other facts, for instance about possible afterimages – which depend not in the slightest on the actual existence of anything. If there is a creative factor explaining why there is "something rather than nothing," something (that is to say) in addition to the Platonic realm itself, then we must look for it in that realm. The factor in question must require the actual existence of this or that, without the sort of hypotheticality which infects the requirement that there must be fifteen lions *if* there are three sets of five such beasts.

Well, the Platonic realm might in fact supply what we are seeking. Necessarily, eternally, there can be ethical requirements for the existence of various things, needs for them to exist. You grasp the concept of goodness only when recognizing that the features which make a thing good provide a ground for it to exist and that this ground is not hypothetical through and through. It is not like the ground you would have for making poison gas if you happened to want to kill people. Ethical demands for the existence of this or that aren't to be understood just in terms of things happening to take our fancy. They are "out there in reality," unconditionally. That is to say, the only thing that could limit or set conditions to any such demand is that it might sometimes clash with other ethical demands, these then overruling it. [While *having people get what happens to take their fancy* could well be among the things which were ethically needful, things whose existence was called for, it presumably wouldn't be the only such thing; any need for it might therefore quite often conflict with further needs which outweighed it.] Ethical grounds for the existence of things, no matter how weighty, would of course still be "only ethical" in the sense that they weren't guaranteed by their very definition to give rise to any actual things or even to tend to give rise to them, for instance by giving people motives to produce them. But we must not say "only ethical" in the dismissive tones we could use for "just a matter of etiquette" or "just an affair weighty in the eyes of the fashion-conscious." Whenever not overruled by other ethical requirements, ethical requirements are absolutely firm calls for the existence of what they require. Might not Plato be right, therefore, when he suggests in Book Six of his *Republic* that The Good, something which is "itself beyond existence," is "what gives existence to things"?

Plato's suggestion, I take it, is that the actual world of existing things is a good one; that the existence of such a world is therefore required ethically, because calling a thing intrinsically good just is calling its existence required ethically; and that those seeking "what gives existence to things" need look no farther. The ethical requirement *that a good world exist* is "itself beyond existence" because even if nothing existed the presence of such a world would still be called for ethically. The requirement could therefore stand at least a chance of explaining the reality of any such world. An ethical requirement's ability to create something – to be directly responsible for the coming into existence or the eternal existence of, say, a good world, or maybe a divine being – is not immediately absurd, logically absurd, like a creative power attaching to *Three fives must make fifteen*. For acting creatively, an ethical requirement could be "in the right ballpark," something in the right category. And what other such something is there on the horizon? I have not managed to see one.

The Platonic suggestion would be nonsense were *a moral requirement* in question. Moral requirements, duties, exist just when there are gods, humans or other intelligent agents who ought to do things, yet when Plato searches for a creative factor what he seeks is a requirement such as could be present in a situation empty of absolutely all agents. It is a mistake, though, to make Ethics – the study of good and bad – into a field concerning only duties. For couldn't it have been fortunate, a good thing, that intelligent life evolved on Earth? Couldn't it have been unfortunate, bad, that animals burned in forest fires long before the evolution of humans with their duties? Yet who else was there to have duties here? Are we to say that such affairs could have been neither good nor bad unless some deity or some extraterrestrial had duties with respect to them? Surely not. The goodness of an actual or possible thing – of an entity, event or situation – is not something added to its other properties like sweetness to a cup of tea, but neither is it always a matter of how the thing stands to intelligent agents. It is an ethical status that the thing has, the status of *being marked out for existence*, while badness is the status of being marked out for *non-existence*. We can sometimes recognize this by acting morally, as when saving animals from forest fires. Even, however, when we cannot, good things satisfy ethical requirements by their presence, by being in existence, while bad ones violate them; though if by "ethical requirements" you prefer to mean duties only, then by all means say "axiological requirements" instead.

Even in an absence of all actually existing things, realities of some sort could be present in a way that really can seem fairly obvious. Suppose the entire cosmos suddenly vanished. Wouldn't it still be a reality that you personally had once been born? Whoever would want to deny this? Still, philosophers of today often assure us that ethical realities, at least, must always draw their being from the wants and needs of actually existing people. The idea that a situation empty of all things could be characterized as "the unfortunate absence of a good world," a case of an ethical requirement that had gone unsatisfied, must therefore be rejected, they insist. Yet why, when they would presumably agree that the emptiness *could be in a way fortunate* because no *bad* world was present in it? Imagine a world as horrible as you can, perhaps one whose infinitely many inhabitants have an existence inescapably filled with agony. In an emptiness of all things, couldn't it be fortunate that there existed no world where wants and needs were so thoroughly trampled upon? If a world crammed with torment were the sole thing in existence, couldn't it be right to press an annihilation button to get rid of it, for couldn't its subsequent absence be a fortunate affair? It surely makes sense to say that it could.

Can we move, though, from speaking of good or bad fortune, or even of ethical (or axiological) needs, to talk of "required existence" of a kind that might let The Good of Plato explain why there is a cosmos? Well, Plato's creation story would self-evidently be nonsense if it said that the concept of *being ethically required* was one and the same concept as that of *being required with creative success*. These are clearly two different concepts. So far as Logic is concerned, the cosmos could con- sist of infinitely many people all suffering frightful agonies. Compare the case of the intellectual requirement to respect Induction. Imagine a madman who kept touching red hot iron because doubting that the past was a guide to the future. While the madman would be reasoning in ways opposite to what was inductively required, he would be no logical impossibility. He would simply be mad. And evil people, folk who produce the opposite of what is ethically required, are simply evil instead of being comparable to spherical cubes or many-wived bachelors. Plato need not in the least deny such facts. His theory about why the world exists is not a grotesque mistake about the sheer meaning of the words "ethically required." It does not tell us that the absence of a good world would be logically impossible. Still, if the theory is right, why does the world contain such things as evil people? This is like the question, "In a world created by a benevolent deity, why is there anything bad?" A short answer could be that ethical requirements do often conflict with other ethical requirements and are then overruled by them. In due course we can look at how a longer answer might run.

For the moment please consider another two questions instead. First, if ethical requirements ever had creative power then this would surely be no mere matter of happenstance; yet how could it fail to be happenstance, were no logical necessity involved? Second, once the concepts of *ethically required existence* and of *creatively required existence* had been admitted to be two logically separate concepts, how could anyone imagine that some ethical requirement *as such* had acted creatively? For wouldn't it have been admitted that every ethical requirement could be exactly what it was – that it could carry exactly as much of the strictly ethical weight that makes a requirement merit the label "ethical" – even if it possessed no creative power whatever?

A reply to this second question is that words like "as such" can be very slippery. When a cow is brown, are we to say that "the cow as such" is brown, or shall we say only that cows as such, meaning cows each doing all that is strictly needed for meriting the label "cow," are female unlike bulls? Answer just as you please! There is a perfectly acceptable sense in which even a supremely weighty ethical require- ment would never "as such" act creatively: namely, that if it did act creatively then at least this wouldn't be *simply thanks to its very definition*. That, though, is no blunt denial that ethical requirements ever act creatively.

How about the first question, then? If The Good of Plato ever wielded creative power – if, in other words, a thing ever existed in direct response to its ethical requiredness – then how could this avoid the rocks both of happenstance and of logical necessity? An answer would be that the world is full of necessities that aren't logical necessities. "Synthetic necessities" is what philosophers call them. Take the fact that experienced red (the red of an afterimage, perhaps) is nearer to experienced purple than to experienced blue. Would that be logically necessary, assuming that by this you meant (as folk now typically would) that its ultimate ground was in definitions? Not at all. Our ability to define purple as "blue-red" is itself grounded on the fact, recognizable even by savages without languages, that experienced red really is nearer to experienced purple than to experienced blue. It is nearer not as a matter of logical, definitional necessity, but as a matter of necessity none the less. Look, too, at the truth that interestingly complex pleasures are intrinsically better than tediously simple miseries. That's a necessary truth, we could well claim, but not one provable by examining definitions. Definitions cannot establish that anything is ever any more good than anything else. Indeed, many clever philosophers think nothing ever is any more good than anything else, in the sense of the word "good" and equivalent words that Plato and his successors took seriously. J.L. Mackie, for example, acknowledged that this sense of the word "good" was standard in ordinary thought and in philosophical tradition yet he said it corresponded to a fiction.

In the course of two books of his, the first entitled *Ethics: Inventing Right and Wrong* and the second *The Miracle of Theism*, a book which spends a chapter discussing the Platonic theory about why the world exists, Mackie made the following points. (i) That, in the ordinary and traditional sense of the word "good," intrinsically good things were ones having a type of requiredness, *ethical requiredness*, otherwise called *ethically required existence*. Having the requiredness wasn't to be defined in terms of naturally detectable properties: for instance, that of being mental states of a pleasurable type. (ii) That such requiredness belonged necessarily to various things or else was (as he believed) fictitious, in which case it was absent necessarily from all things – for as pointed out in the first of the two books it would be absurd to see sheer happenstance in affairs of this sort so that the things of one world could be intrinsically good whereas the things of another world, like those of the first in all their qualities, were worthless or intrinsically bad. (iii) That neither the necessary presence of the requiredness, nor its necessary absence, could be a matter of mere logic. (iv) That the concept of *creative ethical requiredness* – of existing just because ethically required – was central to a tradition stretching back to Plato and that there was "no actual contradiction" in it. Either creative ethical requiredness was possessed somewhere, perhaps by a deity or by the cosmos, or else it failed to be possessed anywhere, but in neither case would any logical necessity be involved; and presumably, once again, sheer happenstance would not be involved either. (v) That while creative ethical requiredness was something *too queer to be real*, this wasn't because it would involve complex goings-on of one sort or another. The Platonic theory was that this or that existed simply through being ethically required rather than thanks to divine planning, acts of will, magical incantations, magnetic fields, rotating cogwheels or whatever.

I think Mackie correct in all this, with the exception of the charge of excessive queerness – a charge he brought not simply against *creative* ethical requiredness but also against the very idea of ethical requiredness in its ordinary and traditional form. Facing the alternatives that goodness of the good old sort, the sort ordinarily and traditionally believed in, either was necessarily possessed by various things or else was necessarily a fiction, he chose to think it a fiction despite accepting it as a logical possibility. Well, that's a position you and I might view as queer – and as arrived at, what's more, for rather a queer reason. For why does Mackie treat goodness of the good old sort as too bizarre to be taken seriously? What can seem crucial is that he pictures it as *supposedly knowable, but not by natural means*. Now, yes, folk believing in it have indeed often thought it detectable by some God-given ethical searchlight built into the human mind; yet why conclude that believing in it demands a belief in the searchlight? Treading in Mackie's footsteps, I look on my ethical views as mainly products of social pressures battering my brain. That brain's evolutionary history has disposed it to "internalize" the pressures by adopting the ordinary and traditional idea that various things are required not just by Society but in themselves. Yet cannot I join Mackie in thinking all this, and still have the idea in question? Just why should I reject my theory that, of the things I'd like to think required in themselves, quite a few truly are so? Just why must clinging to the theory be a claim to possess God-given knowledge or indeed anything much worth calling knowledge? While continuing to cling, why shouldn't I concede that my ethical hunches might conceivably one and all be wrong, the reality being that nothing was in itself better than anything else? True, it would be nice if we could *know* that various things were ethically needful in themselves – that intrinsic good and bad weren't the mere "inventions" that Mackie describes. Yet as Hume saw, we cannot even know that it is needful in itself (this time as a matter not of goodness but of right reasoning) to think that the future will resemble the past. Conceivably, then, Induction's requirements are merely invented; but are they too queer to be real, and would *you* touch red hot iron? And having just the brain you do have, thanks to evolutionary forces, social pressures and whatnot, mayn't you find it hard to accept the belief that saving happy children from drowning is only "by invention" better than drowning them for fun? Mayn't you view beliefs of that kind as peculiar, or worse? It could be how the social pressures etcetera almost force you to view them, but why should this make it a mistake to view them in that way?

Still, what if the cosmos does have goodness in the ordinary and traditional sense so that it can be said not only to exist, but to have an existence that is ethically required? Don't we nevertheless face a major problem in explaining what could make its existence required not just ethically, but creatively as well? Not in the least. The sole difficulty is in knowing whether the ethical requiredness of some-thing or other, maybe a deity or maybe the cosmos, is in fact creatively effective. Does the intrinsic worth of this or that provide a creatively adequate ground for it to exist, or is any such ground adequate only ethically, giving the thing *a right to exist* but that's all? Is "existing for no reason" a better label for a deity or for the cosmos than "existing for reasons of value"? This is an intriguing question, per-haps unlikely ever to be to answered by anything much better than guesswork, but there is absolutely no valid question of what could *make* the ethical requiredness creatively effective. You might equally well ask what magic wand "made" experi-enced red nearer to experienced purple than to experienced blue. Mackie under-stood the point. The Platonic theory, he emphasized, was that a thing's ethical requiredness could in some case or cases be creatively effective *by itself* instead of being important only thanks to something else such as a magic wand or complex clockwork or divinely injected nitroglycerine, something that "gave" creative weight to the fact of being ethically required.

Whether right or wrong, therefore, Plato's approach did at least have the charms of simplicity. Take any ethical requirement for a thing to exist which was not overruled by a requirement for something better to exist instead. Either that ethical requirement was creatively powerful or else it was creatively powerless, and it would be sheer confusion to think the one alternative simpler than the other.

We cannot argue that the second alternative would be simpler "through avoiding some strange necessity that was other-than-logical," because other-than-logical necessity simply cannot be avoided here. Both the being-powerful and the being-powerless would involve other-than-logical necessity. For remember, whether something's ethical requiredness itself sufficed to create it – to bring it into exist-ence or else bear responsibility for its having existed eternally – could hardly be sheer happenstance. It would have to be a matter of necessity; yet there is no logi-cal necessity in this area since (as Mackie noted) no conceptual maneuvers could show that all ethical requirements lacked creative power; hence to avoid viewing happenstance as settling the affair we must see ourselves as confronted with an other-than-logical necessity, a synthetic necessity, *one way or the other*. The ethical requiredness of some entity or entities – a divine person, or a universe or huge set of universes, or whatever – does as a matter of synthetic necessity have the power to create that entity or those entities, or else it does not, once again as a matter of synthetic necessity: necessity that isn't logical, yet is necessity none the less.

Now, why assume that the facts of synthetic necessity are such that even supremely weighty ethical requirements, ones not overruled by other ethical requirements, must never themselves be creatively sufficient? That they must always owe any influence they possess to, say, the goodwill of some reasonlessly existing benevolent deity? Why not instead speculate that they suffice whenever not opposed by malevolent demons?

4.   Pantheism

That the ethical requiredness of the cosmos *might itself* account for its existence has been a fairly widely accepted idea. It has been accepted not only by Neoplatonists of past ages but by various influential writers of recent times. By Paul Tillich and Hans Küng among the theologians, for instance, and by Derek Parfit and Nicholas Rescher among the philosophers – although Rescher much prefers to speak of "axiological" requiredness, thinking the word "ethical" too suggestive of the creative duty of some divine person, while for Parfit the world's evils could well be enough to show that the idea had theoretical interest only. Furthermore, other writers – they include Keith Ward, recently retired from Oxford's Regius Professorship of Divinity, and the idealist philosopher A.C. Ewing, and the physicist-turned-theologian John Polkinghorne – embrace an interesting variant of the idea. Believing in a divine mind, they think its existence quite probably due to its being ethically required. Anything else exists thanks to the divine mind's creative activity.

Is any of this plausible, though, in view of what we find actually existing? Here the crucial difficulty is one we came across earlier. Let us suppose for argument's sake that a divine person owed his existence to his ethical requiredness. And, although many a Platonist might well hesitate to join us, let us specify that any further entities could come to exist only through the divine person's creative prowess. If omnipotent and benevolent, why would he create a world like ours? Why wouldn't he produce other beings enjoying a mental life like his own, beings who each thought about everything in the least worth thinking about? Why would there ever exist anything apart from divine thinking, were Goodness in control?

The sole plausible answer is a Spinozistic one, I suggest. Why does there exist anything other than divine thinking? The answer is: *there doesn't*. Apart from divine thinking there exists nothing whatsoever. We live in the world of which physicists tell us, but they are concerned only with the world's structure. Physics avoids saying such scientifically useless things as that the structure is carried by "good, solid stuff, and not the stuff of divine thinking." The physicists of today seldom talk of "stuff." They describe Nature's patterns mathematically. As physicists doing physics they never so much as consider whether the patterns are, as Spinoza argues, carried by a mind that could be called divine, a mind infinite in its thinking. If, though, a mind of that type thought about everything in the least worth thinking about, then one of the things it might well think about would be the structure of a universe such as ours, causally organized and life-containing. This structure would be among countless logically possible matters that it could contemplate, and it might well be a structure fine enough to merit contemplation. However, the mind in question could not contemplate it without itself carrying a structure that was similar if not one and the same. The notion that

God is Pure Being, entirely unstructured, must be wrong if God's thoughts are immensely complex. A divine mind thinking of great structural complexities must itself be very complexly structured. And perhaps all the things of our universe are simply parts of such a mind's structure, as Spinoza believes.

Consider people blessed with eidetic imagery. They can recall passages in books so vividly that they seem to see them when they gaze at blank walls. Eidetic imagery has even been used for performing calculations with slide-rules "seen" on the walls. Now, what would you think of a philosopher who declared that minds could perform these feats without themselves carrying anything structurally comparable to book passages or slide-rules, because they were Pure Egos with no structures at all? What would you think of a theologian who held that the divine mind was one such Pure Ego? Spinoza at any rate is not of that ilk. In his *Ethics* Spinoza tells us that the order and connection of the divine ideas is the order and connection of the world's things – a point, he remarks, understood by those Jewish thinkers "who say that God, God's understanding and the things that God understands are all one and the same." Through thinking about the structure of our universe in full detail, God would ensure that the structure could not be termed "a merely possible structure," a structure not actually carried by anything. In thinking about it in full detail, God's mind would itself carry it, whether or not it were *carried also* by something that existed external to that mind. And Spinoza denies that it is carried also by any such external something. On his theory, the structure of our universe exists inside a divine mind and nowhere else.

It can still be a universe that includes the minds of you and me in all our ignorance. Our existing as patterns in the divine thoughts would by no means imply that we were omniscient or even that we knew a divine mind existed. People who lived, moved and had their being inside such a mind could easily be atheists. Spinoza's system is no denial of the world as we know it, atheists included.

A divine mind in which all the things of our universe exist as structures carried by its thinking – How can Spinoza find this plausible? The answer lies in his Platonic explanation of why there is a universe. Do not be misled by his *Ethics* which can seem to suggest that God exists purely through logical, definitional necessity. Look instead at his *Short Treatise of God, Man, and His Well-Being* in which the emphasis is always on Value rather than on Logic. Or at least concentrate on those passages in the *Ethics* where God's infinite power of existence is attributed to God's perfection, a term which, believe it or not, does have an ethical side to it in this book with *"Ethics"* as its title. Hegel, greatly influenced by Spinoza, speaks – in the *Logic* that forms the first part of his *Encyclopedia of the Philosophical Sciences* – of a cosmic "Idea that thinks itself," one "not so impotent as to have a mere right to exist, without actually existing." Spinoza believes in something on just those lines.

5.   Evils

Einstein admired Spinoza. Spinoza's divine mind is perfect and therefore (as the *Short Treatise* points out) it cannot change into anything better; hence it remains eternally the same. Spinoza believes that the mind in question is one and the same as the universe. It follows that the universe is *unchanging* in a sense. And Einstein, too, has a universe unchanging in a sense: a sense which is, however, compatible with recognizing that our surroundings alter from day to day and that sometimes one needs to run if wanting to catch a train. Our world, Einstein wrote, has "a four-dimensional structure," and "since there exist in this four-dimensional struc-ture no longer any sections which represent 'now' objectively, the concepts of hap-pening and becoming are indeed not completely suspended, but yet complicated," making it "natural to think of physical reality as a four-dimensional existence instead of, as hitherto, the evolution of a three-dimensional existence" (*Relativity: The Special and the General Theory*, Appendix Five to the Fifteenth Edition). This is a point he used when trying to comfort the relatives of his dead friend Michele Besso. Besso's life had not been rubbed out, Einstein considered, yet this was not to say that Besso was still alive. What can, however, be said is that the Problem of Evil may look rather less severe if Einstein is right. If Einstein is right, Besso's death did not mean that Besso's life had become annihilated in some absolute fash-ion: some way going beyond the mere fact of that life's being absent from various cross-sections of the world's four-dimensional reality.

Any Platonic theory of why the world exists will have to face up to the Problem of Evil, and that's a problem stretching far beyond the question of whether the lives of the dead are absent absolutely or (as Einstein thought) only relatively. Some might even argue that Einstein made the Problem of Evil *worse* because tell-ing us that terrible things which happened long ago still exist in all their awfulness "back there along the fourth dimension." If the cosmos is the product of an ethical requirement, how can anything be terrible? How can anything be the least bit unfortunate, in fact? Why is not everything so supremely good that efforts to improve it are pointless?

We can reply that theorizing that the cosmos is supremely good, maybe in part because so very much admiring the elegant physical laws which rule what we know of it, does not tell us we are powerless to improve things. Suppose that all the details of our thoughts and actions were governed by the physical laws in question. We could still have power over what we thought and did, plus a duty to use the power well and not badly. Calling us free – able to make up our minds, that's to say, in at least the sense in which a chess computer makes up its mind about whether to capture a pawn, and able to affect the world by our actions – need not be to adopt any opinion about whether the laws of physics are so all-governing that whether you will smoke tomorrow could in theory be foretold, calculated, by a demon who knew enough about today. Similarly, the world could have a four-dimensional existence without its following that you lack freedom with respect to stopping smoking "because whether you will smoke tomorrow is already a fact, farther along the fourth dimension." Neither could any supposed goodness of the world's plan mean that all efforts were pointless. If a Platonic ethical requirement is ultimately responsible for the existence of everything then it is ultimately responsible for the fact that humans are free in all the ways in which they are, instead of having their freedom destroyed by ethically guided thunderbolts that fry the wicked or by miracles that interfere with the workings of brains whenever they are tempted to be wicked, or as a consequence of the world's existing four-dimensionally. But this is not to say that wickedness is really just as good as moral decency – that its existence conflicts with no ethical requirement. Even in a supremely good scheme of things, one ethical requirement (perhaps the need for freedom) could often clash with another (such as the need not to drown children for fun), decent people being those who did their best to keep the clashes to a minimum. The Spinozistic theory that you and I are parts of an eternally unchanging divine mind, one that contemplates the pattern of our universe because it is a pattern worth contemplating, isn't something saying that trains are always motionless and humans lack all liberty, let alone something encouraging us to admire every avalanche, outbreak of plague or mass murderer.

6. Going beyond Spinoza

There are, though, various respects in which Spinoza's position could be judged unsatisfactory.

First, Spinoza's cosmic mind contemplates the structure of just one universe. What a preposterous restriction to place on the divine thoughts! As mentioned earlier, today's scientists often view the cosmos as divided into numerous universes, varying greatly in their characters. If a Platonic creation story leads us to believe in a cosmic mind inside which we humans exist because all the things of our universe are structures in its intricately structured thoughts, ones that extend to everything worth thinking about, then how unconvincing it must be to describe this mind as thinking about a single universe only! Very plausibly, there are infinitely many possible universes better than ours. Wouldn't it think about each of them, as well as about ours and countless others?

A second main difficulty is that Spinoza seems to view the divine thoughts as limited to ones about *universe-ingredients*. Why wouldn't divine thinking extend to infinitely many other things as well, things that failed to be collected into *universes*? For example, to countless board-games each hugely more complex than chess, or countless lives lived in what we could call "dream worlds rather than universes"? Why, indeed, is Spinoza so sure we are never immortal in the sense that our thoughts continue *outside our universe* after the deaths of our bodies? Imagine an extraterrestrial who creates a computer as powerful as a human brain, a fully conscious computer that takes joy in its existence. The fact of having created it doesn't bestow any right to smash it. Next, imagine that the extraterrestrial is clever enough to simulate such a computer's operations mentally, in all their details. The simulated computer's computations are merely ingredients of the extraterrestrial's own thinking. Does this bestow a right to put an end to the computations by ceasing to think about them? It is hard to see why. Even the simulated computer can compute, and why not with joy? Why not say that putting an end to its joy would be something ugly? And similarly, why not call it ugly if Spinoza's God failed to think about your thoughts and mine after our bodies had died? Why shouldn't a divine mind contemplate those thoughts continuing onwards outside the context of the universe in which we had been living? If personal identities are not firmly linked to brains, but instead concern thought-patterns such as happen to be carried by our brains yet which might perhaps be transferred to other substrates, then there is no clear need for a modern Spinozist to deny personal immortality. Even in a Spinozistic scheme of things our survival of bodily death would be a miracle in a sense, yet the miracle would not need to involve new and odd developments inside the universe we presently inhabit. The laws of that universe could continue to rule it at all times. It is just that those laws would be what governed the structure of the divine thoughts inside the tiny region of the divine thinking that was our universe. Now, patterns recognizable as those of your and my thinking, but which were no longer carried by brains, might well stretch onwards indefinitely beyond the boundaries of that tiny region, for wouldn't this be what was ethically required?

Third there is this. While I have been content to follow Spinoza in calling his cosmic mind "divine," I see no specially good reason for doing so. Many people consider Spinoza a philosophical trickster who writes "God otherwise known as Nature" when he really believes only in Nature, not in God. They may have understood him poorly, but nothing of importance hangs on whether "theist" or "atheist" is what we call him. Spinoza believes in a cosmic mind that is our universe. The mind in question exists, he thinks, simply because that's what's ethically required. Now, if you want to replace the term "divine mind" by the words "cosmic mind which exists because ethically required," then please yourself.

Fourth, Spinoza can look very badly mistaken when he suggests that a situation existing for ethical reasons would contain just a single infinite mind. Any modern defender of Plato's creation story ought to reject Spinoza's "proofs" that Reality is composed of one infinite mind only. What ought to be maintained instead is that there exist infinite minds in infinite number. You cannot have too many good things, and an infinite number of infinitely complex minds, each thinking about everything that's worth thinking about, is what is best. Or at any rate it is what is best so long as the Principle of Identity of Indiscernibles is mistaken. If it is not mistaken – if, that is to say, the Principle is right in insisting that no two existents can have exactly the same properties – then what is best is an infinite collection of infinitely complex minds, one of which thinks about *absolutely everything* worth thinking about whereas each of the others fails to think about some utterly trivial matter, a different matter in each individual case.

Either way, an infinite number of infinitely complex minds would seem to be what results when a Platonic creation story is developed with the help of modern philosophical techniques. It does not conflict with the findings of science. Instead it could get support from various of those findings, about cosmic fine tuning for example.

Here we could add that the universe described by today's scientists may well have *existential unity* such as Spinoza attributed to the divine thoughts, a unity where individual parts are abstractions only, no more capable of independent reality than are the length and the width of a table. Quantum physicists often say that such things as two electrons in a box, each in the same quantum state, and perhaps even all the particles visible to our telescopes, are not independently real. Naturally this isn't to suggest that the universe's parts are mashed together indistinguishably. Still, some of the parts may be so closely fused that their failure to exist independently can be detected by fairly simple experiments (as in the case of the electrons in the box) or even without any experiments. Just through acquaintance with our own mental states, such writers as David Bohm, Michael Lockwood, Roger Penrose and Abner Shimony have argued, we can know unity of the sort Descartes thought he had found in the human mind and which Spinoza then saw in the cosmos in its entirety.

Note

This has been a whirlwind tour of ideas that may look rather strange. For more about them, please consider consulting other writings of mine: in particular, *Value and Existence* (Oxford: Blackwell, 1979); *Universes* (London and New York: Routledge, 1989, paperback 1996); *Infinite Minds* (Oxford: Oxford University Press, 2001, paperback 2003); *Immortality Defended* (Blackwell, 2007); and "How many divine minds?," in *Consciousness, Reality and Value: Essays in Honour of Timothy Sprigge*, eds. P. Basile and L. McHenry (Heusenstamm: Ontos Verlag, 2007), pp. 123–134.

For further defenses of the notion that Value could perhaps be creatively active, see A.C. Ewing, *Value and Reality* (London: George Allen and Unwin, 1973) which uses this notion to explain the existence of a divine being; N. Rescher, *The Riddle of Existence* (Lanham and London: University Press of America, 1984) or *Nature and Understanding* (Oxford: Oxford University Press, 2000); D. Parfit, "The Puzzle of Reality," *The Times Literary Supplement* 3 July, 1992, pages 3–5; and H. Rice, *God and Goodness* (Oxford: Oxford University Press, 2000).

8

Fifth Solution
Mind/Consciousness as Ultimate

Editorial Introduction

Does an infinite mind supply the reason for all other existing things? Or are minds or conscious experiences in some way fundamental to all existence?

Richard SWINBURNE describes God as "a spirit," "a non-embodied person." God is omnipotent, able to do everything that is logically possible. God knows absolutely everything or (if this is different, perhaps because of future free choices) everything that can as yet be known. God is ultimately responsible for the existence of everything else at every moment. If God's power ceased to support a rock's existence, for instance, then the rock would disappear at once. And God's own existence, Swinburne tells us, is in no way "a matter of chance," something which could have been otherwise. Instead, he insists, God "could not not exist." *And yet* he writes that God's existence is just "a brute fact." You might think he is being flatly inconsistent, but his idea (many philosophers and quantum physicists would reject it) is that matters of chance, matters which could have been otherwise, *always depend on something else*. In contrast, God "depends on nothing." God's existence "is a brute fact that is inexplicable – not in the sense that we do not know its explanation, but in the sense that it does not have one." When Swinburne says God "could not not exist" he means that God has to exist eternally, *if* God exists at all. God could not suddenly vanish.

Can we reasonably believe in anything so wonderful? Yes, Swinburne replies, because God is the simplest conceivable being, far simpler than the God-created universe. God is a single substance, not a collection of separately existing things, and God's properties are all tied to one another in a simple fashion. God's omnipotence, for instance, requires God's omniscience. Lacking any complex

The Mystery of Existence: Why Is There Anything At All?, First Edition. Edited by John Leslie and Robert Lawrence Kuhn.
© 2013 John Wiley & Sons, Inc. Published 2013 by John Wiley & Sons, Inc.

internal mechanism, God's freedom is again something simple; God chooses good things because necessarily an agent who is perfectly free will do what he believes to be morally best. Above all, God's properties are simple through being infinite. Infinite power, for example, *power to do everything logically possible*, can be very simply described. Look at how few words (*six*) were just now used in describing it! Similarly with infinite knowledge, *knowing all that is now knowable*. Similarly with freedom that is infinite in the sense of being utterly unrestricted.

This package is undeniably elegant. Respect Simplicity is a principle that no scientist can afford to disregard. Swinburne's reasons for calling God simple are strong reasons. Still, simplicity can be defined in different ways, and a mind which knows all that is now knowable must *in some sense at least* be infinitely more complex than any human mind. It will be fully aware of infinitely many facts: of infinitely many mathematical facts, for example. Also of the difference in the number of hydrogen atoms, when you finished your breakfast yesterday, in your body and that of the world's fifth oldest rhinoceros, *plus* (since every relationship between facts is yet another fact, in an ever-exploding totality of ever-increasing messiness) the ratio between that number and the number of British Imperial ounces in the combined weights of Julius Caesar and of Brutus when they met for the last time. Also, God as pictured by Swinburne would – no matter how simplicity was defined – be less simple than a blank. Swinburne seems well along the road to admitting the importance of this when he writes, "Perhaps it seems *a priori* vastly improbable that there should exist anything at all logically contingent. But, given that there does exist something, the simple is more likely to exist." The simple, that is to say, in the sense of what is next simplest after the supreme simplicity of a blank. The point is that Swinburne's deity may not, after all, be all that very simple. Shouldn't we therefore keep searching for a factor that made God or the entire cosmos *inevitable*, absolutely necessary?

Timothy O'CONNOR defends the "absolutely necessary" existence of a divine mind or person, "a being which itself could not have failed to exist, since *that* it is is inseparable from *what* it is." Necessary existence "involves a superior mode of existing" and therefore is definitely a property, possessed by God alone. We have at least rudimentary understanding of it "as a property that directly grounds its possessor's own existence." Aquinas might well be wrong in his mysterious doctrine that all God's properties *are identical* – that God's necessary existence *just is* God's omnipotence which *just is* God's omniscience, and so forth. But we can at least see how apparently independent properties might have "an intimate internal connectedness short of identity." God's perfect power, perfect knowledge, perfect freedom, are all three of them understandably linked. So, too, with God's property of being the world's creator. God's perfect goodness may have made it inevitable that God would create a "super-universe" of infinitely many universes "disconnected save for their common origin within God's creative choice."

All the same, "our grasp on the property of necessary existence is tenuous," O'Connor says. And when his *Theism and Ultimate Explanation* makes God the ultimate explanation for everything, he risks rejecting the fairly obviously correct point that *not all truths* could be grounded in *existing things*. Even if – itself hard to swallow – God's eternal contemplation of mathematical truths were somehow essential to their being true, surely God himself couldn't exist unless it were *already a true possibility* for God to exist. To adopt the slogan "Truths Require Truthmakers Among Existing Things," then making that true possibility itself depend on God when God contemplated possibilities, simply wouldn't work. Might it not be better to see abstract factors, requirements needing nothing beyond themselves to "make" them real, as the ultimate explainers of why God truly is possible and of why God in fact exists?

The big question would then be whether O'Connor, writing of God's necessity, has recognized a requirement into which we could have some insight. Saying that necessary existence is "a property that directly grounds its possessor's own existence" can look better than nothing. It replaces a thing which just happens to exist by a thing which is somehow self-explaining. Yet what insight does it offer into the "somehow"? God's other properties may be understandably linked, but how about God's property of existing necessarily? To what is *that* understandably linked? Apart from indicating that there might be some truth in Aquinas's idea ("it is very hard," he comments, "to be sure just what it is supposed to come to") that all God's so-called *other properties* are ultimately one and the same as God's property of existing necessarily, O'Connor gives us no guidance here.

William Lane Craig views the physical universe as crying out to be explained. A translucent ball on a forest floor would require an explanation, and so would a universe-sized ball. Craig sees no need to join the followers of Aquinas in their belief that "being must be continually added" to the things of our world "lest they be spontaneously annihilated." Instead let us note that it is "easy to conceive of the non-existence of any and all of the objects we observe in the world," and that a world consisting of different fundamental particles "seems quite possible." However, even if no particular things that we observe were necessary, couldn't there still have to exist *at least one thing of some kind*? Not, Craig replies, unless there were some thing, somewhere, that existed necessarily. For, he asks, if all non-unicorns were absent, would a unicorn then have to exist, to stop there being *not even one thing of any kind*? He views that suggestion as ridiculous. Better, he thinks, to believe in God, "a transcendent, unembodied Mind which created the universe," a non-physical reality having its explanation "in the necessity of its own nature."

Craig considers that abstract objects – he gives The Number Seven as an example – can "transcend space and time." Like God, therefore, they "cannot be physical." Might such objects, instead of God, account for the physical universe? No, he answers, for "abstract objects don't stand in causal relations. This is part of what it means to be abstract." Yet when he says that God has an explanation in the necessity of God's own nature, isn't he himself introducing something markedly abstract? He seems to have in mind an absolute requirement, a requirement whose power was inevitable, that a being having God's characteristics *be more than a mere possibility*. Now, there might be nothing wrong in that idea, but the requirement in question would surely be "an abstract object" of a sort. And one would certainly like him to say something more about it.

In Islamic writings, Seyyed Hossein NASR tells us, "The Necessary Being" is a traditional term for God, and "one of the great masters of traditional Islamic philosophy" said he had found after a lifetime's study that Necessity "is none other than" Being. "That which exists is as it should be," and all existence is divine. Allah is "the only ultimate Reality," the source of everything that appears to possess reality. Wherever you turn, "there is the Face of God." All the things of our hugely complex world are only aspects of Allah's reality. Allah is "transcendent unity of Being."

Doesn't all this suggest a Mind underlying all things? Well, that Allah has been thought to be something as abstract as Necessity might count against any such suggestion. On the other hand, Allah has personhood, Allah is "He." Allah has our minds as constituents of Himself, and there is no claim that our minds are truly mental whereas Allah *isn't*. Furthermore, the *unity of being* that is traditionally ascribed to Allah – unity of elements which, like the size and the redness and the hardness of a ruby, are utterly incapable of existing each in isolation from the others – has been the sign of the mental in the eyes of countless philosophers. True, the theory that minds are nothing but brains has recently found numerous defenders who typically describe brains as collections of brain cells unified only in the way that the soldiers of a well disciplined army are unified, or the parts of a working steam engine, or the transistors of a digital computer. Yet there are many philosophers of today, even outside Islam, who continue to see *unity of being* as what characterizes minds or their experiences. They say that examining your own conscious life at any moment, but particularly when you experience something as complex as a countryside, a painting, a symphony, will show you such unity. Physicists such as David Bohm and Roger Penrose, together with philosophers of science such as Michael Lockwood and Abner Shimony, have linked this sort of unity ("globality," Penrose calls it) to the unity discovered in complex quantum realities. Others, however, say that talk of quantum realities is irrelevant. Instead they sometimes theorize that consciousness has the kind of "cosmic fundamentalness" which physicists ascribe to quantum theory or to General Relativity. This is a thesis defended particularly interestingly (on long roads running across philosophically complex landscapes) by Timothy Sprigge, writing in the tradition of Hegel and of F.H. Bradley, and by others such as Thomas Nagel.

Tenzin Gyatso, fourteenth DALAI LAMA, is among those advocating that thesis. Reality, he teaches, consists just of many separate centers of consciousness. They build up shared ideas about the world: about a particular glacier, for example. There is no single being "analogous to the non-Buddhist concept of Brahma as a substratum." "Inherent clear light, the essential nature of the mind," is merely "the ultimate clear light of each being" – each individually existing center of consciousness – so that we must not "deify" it. "Why is no creation possible in Buddhism?" It is because "causes have no beginning and stretch back to infinity." Similarly, consciousness has no beginning. It always has existed, but not joined always to the same bodies. [Remember, later Dalai Lamas are reincarnations of earlier ones.] It "penetrates the parental cells at the moment of conception."

Andrei LINDE, too, suspects that ours is a universe in which consciousness plays a crucial role. Physicists hope to describe the universe with the Wheeler–DeWitt equation, central to quantum mechanics. The equation seems, however, to state that the universe is "dead," "does not change" – not until you introduce observers and their clocks. John Wheeler found this kind of thing so important that he talked of a "self-observing universe." We have come to see space-time and matter as interdependent with "no longer any question which one of the two is more fundamental," Linde notes. He suggests that we should next stop treating consciousness as if it played "a secondary, subservient role, being just a function of matter and a tool for the description of the truly existing material world." Our perceptions, every bit as real as material objects, might actually in a sense be "even more real." After all, doesn't your knowledge of the world start with knowing your own pain, your own experience of green or of sweetness, and so forth, while "everything else is a theory"? Consciousness might even at times exist "in the absence of matter," just as gravitational waves may sometimes do.

Paul DAVIES is attracted by Wheeler's idea of a "self-observing" universe. Among the greatest oddities of the quantum world are the ones found by double-slit experiments. Fired towards a screen with two slits in it, streams of particles pass through it and then produce patterns like those of interacting waves. They do so even when the rate of fire is so slow that only a single particle is moving at any moment. Can each particle go through both slits, then interacting with itself? Strange indeed, but matters get stranger still. If the experimenter *looks* so as to try to discover which slit each particle went through, nothing like wave-interaction is detected. The particles instead behave like bullets. If the experimenter *doesn't look*, then we have apparent wave-interaction. And all of this remains true even when choosing whether to look is delayed until long after each particle has passed through the screen. Some say the particles are waves – they can do things like going through two slits at once – until they are observed, at which stage they appear to be bullets because of "wave collapse" at points that are decided by chance. Wheeler thinks instead that choices of what to observe *can cause past events*. When an experimenter chooses to investigate a particle's track, apparently discovering that it went through a left hand slit, then the particle did indeed traverse only that slit and not the right hand one; yet had there been no investigation, then the particle would have traversed both slits. Davies is among a small but growing number of physicists who accept such causation of the past by the present. He applies it to the question of why physical laws are what they are.

The question had long been "off-limits" for scientists: a question for theologians perhaps. Things are different today thanks to the discovery – Davies views it as well confirmed – that tiny changes to the actual laws of physics would have meant a lifeless universe. A currently popular theory is that there exist many universes *which vary in their laws*. Only a few have laws (they are really only "local by-laws") which are "just right" for permitting observers to evolve. It is then no surprise that we find ourselves in a universe among those few. But, Davies comments, this "merely shifts the mystery up a level." We now must ask why there are fundamental laws ("federal laws") that lead to such law-variation. Also, couldn't it be wrong to assume that the laws of a universe never depend on what goes on inside it, but are instead dictated from some "abstract other-worldly realm"? Davies is attracted by Seth Lloyd's idea that the laws are instead "software," so to speak, running on the "computer hardware" of the material world. Quantum theory tells us that such laws could never be infinitely precise. Indeed, at the universe's earliest moments the cosmic computer could process little information, making the laws markedly fuzzy. Which laws would emerge later, laws of far greater precision, could have been largely undetermined. This would be in line with Wheeler's longstanding conviction that the current laws of physics emerged over time, "congealing from the ferment of the big bang." Yet what if Wheeler were right, too, in his other conviction that present choices, present observations, cause events right back to the very early period when the laws were congealing? If so, then the sole laws that could have emerged would be laws permitting observers to evolve.

Very speculative, these ideas are still of great interest. Davies takes them further. Yes, there may be "a closed explanatory or causal loop" involving (with the help of causation of the past by the present) observers today and the earlier "congealing" of laws that permitted those observers to evolve. But, Davies asks, just why is there that loop? Do *all* self-consistent loops exist, whether or not they involve beings who can observe and understand them? Or can only universes involving Life and Mind breathe creative fire into themselves, taking themselves out of the realm of mere possibilities, because Mind is essential if a universe is to be "self-explaining"? He prefers that last suggestion. It is a fascinating instance of the idea that having a certain type of nature can turn possibilities into concretely existing things.

God's Maximal Simplicity★

RICHARD SWINBURNE

The Nature of God

[…] There exists now, and always has existed and will exist, God, a spirit, that is, a non-embodied person who is omnipresent. […] In essence, to say that God is not embodied is to deny that there is any volume of matter such that by his

★   From chapter 5 of *The Existence of God*, 2nd edn., revised (Oxford: Clarendon Press, 2004), pp. 93–101, 106, 108–109. Reprinted with permission of Oxford University Press.

basic actions he can control only it and such that he knows of goings-on elsewhere only by their effects on it. By contrast, to say that God is an omnipresent spirit is to say that he knows about goings-on everywhere without being dependent for that knowledge on anything, and can control by basic actions all states of affairs everywhere (in this or any other universe) without being dependent for that power on anything. God is creator of all things in that for all logically contingent things that exist (apart from himself) he himself brings about, or makes or permits other beings to bring about, their existence. He is, that is, the source of the being and power of all other substances. He is, for example, responsible for the past, present, and future existence of material objects and of the natural laws that they follow, of persons and their powers. And whatever else logically contingent there may be – devils and angels, and other universes – he makes them exist and behave as they do, or sustains in other beings the power so to do. Some thinkers have held that God created the world at a first moment of its history and imposed upon it then the laws of its future operation and thereafter left it to itself. This is the view of the deist. By contrast, in developing the theist's position, I postulate the more orthodox view that God is at each moment of the world's history responsible for its operation at that moment of its history. Of course the more orthodox theist does hold that, if the universe or anything else had a beginning of existence, God it was who brought that beginning about or permitted some other being so to do. God is perfectly free in the sense (which I introduce by definition) that nothing in any way causally influences his choices. Which choices he makes, that is, which intentions he adopts, depends on himself at the moment of choice alone (though he may form a particular intention – to cure your cancer, in order to fulfil another intention – to answer my prayers).

God is omnipotent in the sense (roughly) that he can do whatever it is logically possible that he do. The qualification in the last clause is important. There are some apparent states of affairs, the description of which involves a logical contradiction – for example, me existing and not existing at the same time. God cannot bring about such apparent states, not because he is weak, but because the description "me existing and not existing at the same time" does not really describe a state of affairs at all, in the sense of something that it is coherent to suppose could occur. [...] He is omniscient, at any rate in the sense that he knows at any time whatever it is logically possible that he know at that time. (It *may* be that there are true propositions that it is not logically possible that a person know at some time t – for example, propositions about some other person's future free actions. Then to claim that God is omniscient is not to claim that at t he knows these propositions.) He is perfectly good. I understand by this (roughly – in a way to be made precise shortly) that he is a being who always does a morally best action (where there is one) and does no morally bad action.

The theist holds that God possesses the properties described in some sense necessarily, and he is in some sense a necessary being. That is to say, God could not suddenly cease to be (for example) omnipotent. While God is God, he is omnipotent; nor could he cease to be God while remaining the same individual (as, for example, the Prime Minister can cease to be Prime Minister while remaining the same person). Further, while other things exist by chance or because of the action of yet other beings, God could not not exist. His existence is not dependent on any other being. Nor is it a matter of chance [...]

To say that "God exists" is necessary is, I believe, to say that the existence of God is a brute fact that is inexplicable – not in the sense that we do not know its explanation, but in the sense that it does not have one. [...] [T]here are two ways in which God's existence being an inexplicable brute fact can be spelt out. The first position is to say that God's essence is an eternal essence. God is a being of a kind such that if he exists at any time he exists at all times; his existence at all remains the one logically contingent fact. The alternative position is to say that the divine essence is a temporal essence; the ultimate brute fact is not God's existing as such, but his existing for a period of time without beginning. His subsequent existence would be due to his intentional choice at each moment of time to continue to exist subsequently. Theism has traditionally taken the former position, and I shall argue in favour of it shortly. In that case God will have the strongest kind of necessity compatible with his being a logically contingent being. Such necessary existence we may term factually necessary existence (in contrast to logically necessary existence) [...]

The Simplicity of Theism

Such is the hypothesis of theism, as I understand it. How simple a hypothesis is it? I propose to argue that it is a very simple hypothesis indeed. I shall begin to do this by showing how the divine properties that I have outlined fit together. A theistic explanation is a personal explanation. It explains phenomena in terms of the action of a person. Personal explanation explains phenomena as the results of the action of a person brought about in virtue of his basic powers, beliefs, and intentions. Theism postulates God as a person with intentions, beliefs, and basic powers, but ones of a very simple kind, so simple that it postulates the simplest kind of person that there could be.

To start with, theism postulates a God who is just one person,[1] not many. To postulate one substance is to make a very simple postulation. He is infinitely powerful, omnipotent. This is a simpler hypothesis than the hypothesis that there is a God who has such-and-such limited power (for example, the power to rearrange matter, but not the power to create it). It is simpler in just the same way that the hypothesis that some particle has zero mass, or infinite velocity is simpler than the hypothesis that it has a mass of 0.34127 of some unit, or a velocity of 301,000 km/sec. A finite limitation cries out for an explanation of why there is just that particular limit, in a way that limitlessness does not. [...] [S]cientists have always preferred hypotheses of infinite velocity to hypotheses of very large finite velocity, when both were equally compatible with the data. And they have always preferred hypotheses that some particle had zero mass to hypotheses that it had some very small mass, when both were equally compatible with the data. There is a neatness about zero and infinity that particular finite numbers lack. Yet a person with zero powers would not be a person at all. So in postulating a person with infinite power the theist is postulating a person with the simplest kind of power possible.

God's beliefs have a similar infinite quality. Human persons have some few finite beliefs, some true, some false, some justified, some not. In so far as they are true and justified (or at any rate justified in a certain way), beliefs amount to knowledge. It would seem most consonant with his omnipotence that an omnipotent being have beliefs that amount to knowledge. For, without true beliefs about the consequences of your actions, you may fail to realize your intentions. True beliefs fail to amount to knowledge only if they are true by accident. But, if the divine properties are possessed necessarily, God's beliefs could not be false, and so could not be true by accident. And, if an omnipotent being has knowledge, the simplest such supposition is to postulate that the omnipotent being is limited in his knowledge, as in his power, only by logic. In that case he would have all the knowledge that it is logically possible that a person have – that is, he would be omniscient.

For a person to act, he has to have intentions. A person could be omnipotent in the sense that whatever (logically possible) action he formed the intention to do, he would succeed in doing, and also omniscient so that he knew what were all the (logically possible) actions available to an omnipotent being in his situation, and yet be predetermined to form certain intentions. His intentions might be determined by causal factors outside his control, or at any rate, as are those of humans, greatly influenced by them. But, if a person is predetermined (or has an inbuilt probabilistic tendency) to act in certain specific ways, this means that a tendency to act in a particular way is built into him. But a person with an inbuilt detailed specification of how to act is a much more complex person than one whose actions are determined only by his uncaused choice at the moment of choice. Such a being I call a perfectly free being. Theism in postulating that God is perfectly free makes the simplest supposition about his choice of intentions.

A substance who is essentially omnipotent, omniscient, and perfectly free is necessarily a terminus of complete explanation [...]

I argue next that God's possession of the other properties ascribed to him – being an omnipresent spirit, being creator of all things, and (given a certain highly plausible assumption) being perfectly good all follow from his being omnipotent, omniscient, and perfectly free. His possession of the first two properties is easy enough to show. If God is omnipotent, then he must be able to control by basic actions all states of affairs everywhere. If God is omniscient, he must know what is going on everywhere. If he depended for this knowledge on the operation of nerves or eyes, then, if they were to behave in unusual ways, he would lack knowledge. But since, *ex hypothesi*, God's omniscience belongs to his essence, this could not happen. Hence God is an omnipresent spirit. Since God is omnipotent, then he could prevent anything from happening if he so chose. So whatever happens happens because he makes it or permits it to happen. Hence he is the creator of all things in the sense that I delineated.

Further, if one takes a certain view about the status of moral judgements, God's perfect goodness follows deductively from his omniscience and his perfect freedom. The view in question is the view that moral judgements to the effect that this action is morally good and that one is morally bad are propositions that are true or false. The truth of this view is, of course, a contentious philosophical issue, but it is highly plausible. Surely the person who says that there was nothing morally wrong in Hitler's exterminating the Jews is saying something false. For reasons of space I shall assume rather than argue for the view that moral judgements have truth values. But if they do not have truth values, it would be misleading to call perfect goodness a *property* of God, for it would be neither true nor false to say of him that (for example) he does no morally bad acts. If my view is correct, it follows that an omniscient being will know the truth value of all moral judgements – that is, will know of all moral judgements whether or not they are true or false. I now proceed to argue further that necessarily an agent who is perfectly free (that is free in the sense that nothing in any way causally influences which choices he makes) will do what he believes to be the morally best action or one of equal morally best actions, and will do no action that he believes to be morally bad. Thence it will follow that, if this agent is also omniscient, he will do the morally best action (if there is one) or one of the equal morally best actions (if there are such), and no morally bad action – for necessarily his beliefs about their status will be true ones.

To do an action an agent has to have a reason for acting. A movement brought about by an agent would not be an action unless the agent had some reason for bringing it about. The reason may be simply just to do that action, but normally an agent will have some further purpose in doing an action. Having a reason for an action consists in regarding some state of affairs as a good thing, and the doing of the action as a means to forwarding that state, and hence itself a good thing. If my reason for going to Oxford was to give a lecture, I must regard it as in some way a good thing that I give the lecture, and so a good thing that I go to Oxford. If I regarded it as in no way a good thing that I give the lecture, if I thought that giving the lecture was an event that would serve no useful function at all, giving the lecture could not have been my reason for going to Oxford. The point that to do an action I must (of logical necessity) see my performance of it as in some way a good thing is a very old one due to Aristotle, emphasized by Aquinas, and re-emphasized in our day by, among others, Stuart Hampshire. God, like man, cannot just act. He must act for a purpose and see his action as in some way a good thing. Hence he cannot do what he does not regard as in some way a good thing. This is not a physical constraint, but a logical limit. Nothing would count as an action of God unless God in some way saw the doing of it as a good thing [...]

The hypothesis of theism postulates not merely the simplest starting point of a personal explanation there could be (simpler than many gods or weak gods), but the simplest starting point of explanation for the existence of the universe [...] [T]he basic point is this. A scientific explanation will have to postulate as a starting point of explanation a substance or substances that caused or still cause the universe and its characteristics. To postulate many or extended such substances (an always existing universe; or an extended volume of matter-energy from which, uncaused by God, all began) is to postulate more entities than theism. The simplest scientific starting point would be an unextended point. This, however, would have to have some finite amount or other of power or liability to exercise it (since what it will create would not be constrained by rational considerations), and so it would not possess the simplicity of infinity.

Furthermore, if some actual or postulated entity other than God is to provide a complete (or ultimate) explanation of phenomena, it needs to have added to it (in the case of a person) specific powers, beliefs, and intentions, or (in the case of an inanimate substance) specific powers and liabilities to exercise them. We need both the "what" that causes, and the "why" it causes. The advantage of theism is that the mere existence of God provides most of that extra "why". The powers and beliefs of a God are part of his simple nature. And his perfect goodness constrains the intentions that he will form – he will, as we have seen, always do the best or equal best action or kind of action in so far as there are such, and no bad action. God chooses to bring about what he does in virtue of seeing the goodness of things; and, in so far as that still gives him an enormous choice of what to bring about, he chooses by a "mental toss up". Thus for the theist, explanation stops at what, intuitively, is the most natural kind of stopping place for explanation – the choice of an agent [...]

One final feature of great importance about the hypothesis of theism is this. What is at stake [...] is whether we ought to go beyond various phenomena to postulate a God who brings them about. This is a matter of whether the hypothesis of theism has sufficient prior probability and explanatory power. But, if it has, there is no similar issue of whether we ought to go beyond theism in order to provide a complete explanation. For, if theism is true, then, of logical necessity, God's action provides a complete and ultimate explanation of what it explains. For, as we saw earlier, it follows from God's omnipotence and perfect freedom that all things depend on him whereas he depends on nothing. If God features at all in explanation of the world, then explanation clearly ends with God.

[...] Perhaps it seems *a priori* vastly improbable, if one thinks about it, that there should exist anything at all logically contingent. But, given that there does exist something, the simple is more likely to exist than the complex.

Note

1   If the existence of that person entails the existence of other divine persons [...] the original hypothesis is no less simple for that. A simple hypothesis is none the less simple for entailing complicated consequences. But a hypothesis of three independent divine beings would be much more complicated than theism.

A Necessarily Existing Mind*

TIMOTHY O'CONNOR

Why is there anything (contingent) at all? Of course, this question admits distinct formulations of greater precision: What explains the fact that there are contingent things? What explains the fact that *these* contingent things exist? What explains the fact that *these* contingent things exist rather than *those* others that were possible? Why are there contingent things rather than there being nothing contingent at all? [...]

[T]here is undeniably a powerful impetus in human beings to ask the question (while waving one's hands all about) "Why is there *this* – why, indeed, is there anything at all?" [...] In its barest form, the traditional answer that I will defend is this: The reason that any contingent thing exists at all (and, in particular, the world of which we are part) is that it is a contingent causal consequence of an absolutely necessary being, a being which itself could not have failed to exist, since *that* it is is inseparable from *what* it is. [...] The claim that there is a necessary being is the claim that there is a being whose nature entails existence, so that *any* possible world would involve the existence of such an entity. Such a being, we might say, is absolutely invulnerable to nonexistence. By way of relevant contrast, were there a being which was causally immune from destruction (no existing thing or collection of things have the capacity indirectly or directly to destroy it), but whose existence was contingent, it would still, in the end, just *happen* to exist. Were such a being conscious, it could sensibly feel *fortunate* that it exists, even though it owes its existence to no existing thing. [...]

Having (wrongly) reduced the cosmological argument to the ontological argument, Kant famously responded to the latter with the objection that "existence is not a predicate." Since both arguments employ the concept of necessary being, it is worth responding to this complaint here. Kant's idea is that existence is not another quality or property on a par with extension, shape, or mass. If I contemplate two similar objects A and B in my mind, and add to the idea of A alone that it has existence, I am not thereby making it an idea of something different from, let alone greater than B. Whether Kant is right or not on the propertyhood of

*   From chapters 3, 4, and 5 of *Theism and Ultimate Explanation* (Malden, MA: Blackwell Publishing, 2009), pp. 65, 68–72, 88–89, 111–113, 116–117. Reprinted with permission of John Wiley & Sons, Ltd.

existence, however, is beside the point. For what is distinctive of necessary being is not the fact of its existing, but that it enjoys *necessary existence*. And this very much is a substantial, distinctive property, involving a superior mode of existing. […]

[I]t is overstating the shortcomings of the explanatory appeal to necessary being to say that we have no understanding at all what "necessary existence" is supposed to be. If that were the case, then appeal to it truly would be vacuous, as it would amount to no more than the claim that there is a being in whom the mystery of existence has its answer! We clearly do understand the rudimentary concept of necessary existence […] as a property that directly grounds its possessor's own existence and serves as a ground for the possibility of contingent things. […]

[M]ost medieval philosopher-theologians such as Aquinas went so far as to assert that […] [n]ecessary existence just *is* omnipotence, just is omniscience – and indeed, just is the necessary being Himself. […] [A]s intriguing as subsequent commentators have found this idea, it is very hard to be sure just what it is supposed to come to. In any case, prima facie it is possible to stop short of asserting the simplicity-identity thesis, and suppose instead only that there is an intimate internal connectedness short of identity. […] [O]ur grasp on the property of necessary existence is tenuous. But here is a quick example of how one might come to see subtle entailment relations between properties that at first seem mutually independent. In philosophical theology, God is often conceived as being perfectly powerful, perfectly free, and perfectly knowledgeable (where perfection entails maximality). One might think these are simply three impressive attributes that have no deep connection. After all, the corresponding attributes of more limited agents often fail to covary: powerful people are not always the most knowledgeable, nor the most free. We can plausibly argue, however, that perfect power entails perfect knowledge. […] Other things being equal, […] a causal agent endowed with free choice has greater power than one lacking it. So a perfectly powerful agent would also be free, indeed perfectly free. Further, freedom of choice requires knowledge of the possibilities and how they are to be achieved. Perfect power and freedom would require an essentially unlimited knowledge, corresponding to the unlimited range of possibilities. […]

In classical philosophical as well as religious theology, God is a personal being perfect in every way: absolutely independent of everything, such that nothing exists apart from God's willing it to be so; unlimited in power and knowledge; perfectly blissful, lacking in nothing needed or desired; morally perfect. If such a being were to create, on what basis would He choose?

Since there is a universe, we know that God did not in fact opt not to create anything at all. But was it really an open possibility that He might have done so? […] The most plausible understanding of God's being motivated to create at all (one which in places Aquinas himself comes very close to endorsing) is to see it as reflecting the fact that God's very being, which is goodness, necessarily diffuses itself. Perfect goodness will naturally communicate itself outwardly; God who is perfect goodness will naturally create, generating a dependent reality that imperfectly reflects that goodness. […] Perhaps it is inevitable, then, that a perfect God would create. But what? […]

Let a "single universe" be a concrete totality whose components are causally connected to each other but to nothing else save God. A universe is a relatively causally isolated part of the one actual world. Let us say that a "super-universe" is a collection of one or more totalities that are mutually disconnected save for their common origin within God's creative choice. Clearly, God's choice isn't between the single universes, but between the super-universes. […]

[A] perfect Creator would be disposed to create universes from among every significant type. So God has reason not to settle for creating a super-universe that has only one universe as member. Nor will it help for God to create a two- or three-membered super-universe, or, in fact, an n-membered super-universe, for any finite value n. But it would appear to help if God were to create an infinitely membered super-universe, provided there is no finite upper limit on the value of its members.

A World-Creating Mind*

WILLIAM LANE CRAIG

A simple statement of a Leibnizian cosmological argument might run as follows:

(1) Anything that exists has an explanation of its existence, either in the necessity of its own nature or in an external cause.
(2) If the universe has an explanation of its existence, that explanation is God.
(3) The universe exists.
(4) Therefore, the universe has an explanation of its existence. (from 1, 3)
(5) Therefore, the explanation of the existence of the universe is God. (from 2, 4)

Is this a good argument? The conclusion follows validly from the premises, so the only question is whether the three premises are more plausibly true than their denials.

The Principle of Sufficient Reason

Premise (1) is a modest version of the Principle of Sufficient Reason. It circumvents the typical objections to strong versions of that principle. For (1) merely requires any existing *thing* to have an explanation of its existence. This premise is compatible

* From chapter 3 of *Reasonable Faith*, 3rd edn. (Wheaton, IL: Crossway Publishing, 2006), pp. 106–111. Reprinted by permission of Crossway, a publishing ministry of Good News Publishers, Wheaton, IL 60187, www.crossway.org.

with there being brute *facts* about the world. What it precludes is that there could exist things which just exist inexplicably. According to (1) there are two kinds of being: necessary beings, which exist of their own nature and so have no external cause of their existence, and contingent beings, whose existence is accounted for by causal factors outside themselves. Numbers, sets, and other mathematical objects would be prime candidates for the first sort of thing, while familiar physical objects like people and planets and stars would be examples of the second kind of thing.

The principle enunciated in (1) seems quite plausible, at least more so than its denial. Richard Taylor gives the illustration of finding a translucent ball on the forest floor while walking in the woods. One would find the claim quite bizarre that the ball simply exists inexplicably; and just increasing the size of the ball, even until it becomes co-extensive with the cosmos, would do nothing to eliminate the need for an explanation of its existence.

Crispin Wright and Bob Hale agree that explicability is the default position and that exceptions to the principle therefore require justification. Nonetheless they maintain that an exception is justified in the case of the universe. Why? Because the explanation of any physical state of affairs *S* must be found in a causally prior state of affairs in which *S* does not exist. For example, the explanation why a certain horse exists is that two other horses were bred with the result that they caused the new horse to be conceived and come into existence. So any explanation of why the universe exists must be found in a causally prior state of affairs in which the universe does not exist. But, Wright and Hale object, since a physically empty world couldn't cause anything, the demand for an explanation of the universe becomes absurd. So the principle enunciated in (1) doesn't apply in the case of the universe.

This objection, however, plainly begs the question in favor of atheism. For unless one assumes in advance that the nuniverse is all there is, there's just no reason to think that the state of affairs causally prior to the existence of the universe which explains why the universe exists has to be a *physical* state of affairs. The explanation of why the physical universe exists could be some causally prior, non-physical state of affairs. If one assumes that that's impossible, then one is just begging the question in favor of atheism. The theist will regard Wright and Hale's maxim about the nature of explanation as not at all restrictive, since the explanation of why the physical universe exists can and should be provided in terms of a causally prior non-physical state of affairs involving God's existence and will.

The Explanation of the Universe

Premise (2) might seem at first blush to be a very bold assertion on the part of the theist. But, in fact, (2) is logically equivalent to the typical atheist response to Leibniz that on the atheistic worldview the universe simply exists as a brute contingent thing. Atheists typically assert that, since there is no God, it is false that everything has an explanation of its existence, for the universe, in this case, just exists inexplicably. So in affirming that

A. If atheism is true, then the universe has no explanation of its existence, atheists are also affirming the logically equivalent claim that

A'. If the universe has an explanation of its existence, then atheism is not true, that is to say, that God exists. Hence, most atheists are implicitly committed to (2).

Moreover, (2) seems quite plausible in its own right, for the universe, by definition, includes all of physical reality. So the cause of the universe must (at least causally prior to the universe's existence) transcend space and time and therefore cannot be physical or material. But there are only two kinds of things that could fall under such a description: either an abstract object (like a number) or else a mind (a soul, a self). But abstract objects don't stand in causal relations. This is part of what it means to be abstract. The number 7, for example, doesn't cause anything. So if the universe has an explanation of its existence, that explanation must be a transcendent, unembodied Mind which created the universe – which is what most people have traditionally meant by the word "God."

Finally, premise (3) states the obvious, that there is a universe. Since the universe exists, it follow that God exists.

The Contingency of the Universe

One way for the atheist or agnostic to try to escape the force of this argument is to say that while the universe has an explanation of its existence, as premise (1) requires, that explanation lies not in an external ground but in the necessity of its own nature. The universe exists necessarily. This is, however, an extremely bold suggestion which atheists have not been eager to embrace. We have, one can safely say, a strong sense of the universe's contingency. A possible world in which no concrete objects exist certainly seems conceivable. We generally trust our modal intuitions on other familiar matters (for example, our sense that the planet earth exists contingently, not necessarily, even though we have no experience of its non-existence). If we are to do otherwise with respect to the universe's contingency, then the non-theist needs to provide some reason for his skepticism other than his desire to avoid theism.

Still, it would be desirable to have some stronger argument for the universe's contingency than our modal intuitions alone. Could the Thomist cosmological argument help us here? The difficulty with appeal to the Thomist argument is that it is very difficult to show that things are, in fact, contingent in the special sense required by the argument. Certainly things are naturally contingent in that their continued existence is dependent upon a myriad of factors including particle masses and fundamental forces, temperature, pressure, entropy level, and so forth, but this natural contingency does not suffice to establish things' metaphysical contingency in the sense that being must be continually added to their essences lest they be spontaneously annihilated.

Nevertheless, I think we do have good grounds for thinking that the universe does not exist by a necessity of its own nature. It's easy to conceive of the non-existence of any and all of the objects we observe in the world; indeed, prior to a certain point in the past, when the universe was very dense and very hot, none of them did exist. What about the fundamental particles or the building blocks of matter, like quarks? Well, it's easy to conceive of a world in which all of the fundamental particles composing some macroscopic object were replaced by other quarks. A universe consisting of a totally different collection of quarks, say, seems quite possible. But if that's the case, then the universe does not exist by a necessity of its own nature. For a universe composed of a wholly different collection of quarks is not the same universe as ours. To illustrate, ask yourself whether the shoes you're wearing could have been made of steel? Certainly we can imagine that you could have had a pair of steel shoes in the same shape as the shoes you're wearing; but that's not the question. The question is whether the very shoes you're wearing could have been made of steel. I think the answer is obviously not. They would be a different pair of shoes, not the same pair of shoes you have on. The same is true of the universe. If it were composed of a different collection of quarks, then it would be a different universe, not the same universe. Since quarks are the fundamental building blocks of material objects, one cannot say, as we might say of macroscopic objects, that while they are contingent, the stuff of which they are made is necessary, for there is no further stuff beyond quarks. No atheist will, I think, dare to suggest that some quarks, though looking just like ordinary quarks, have the special occult property of being necessary, so that any universe that exists would have to include them. It's all or nothing here. But no one thinks that every quark exists by a necessity of its own nature. It follows that the universe does not exist by a necessity of its own nature either.

The Principle of Sufficient Reason Once More

There's one last way that the atheist might try to escape the argument. He might say that while there are no beings that exist necessarily, nevertheless it is necessary that something or other exist. Bede Rundle agrees with the theist that it is impossible that nothing exist. But he thinks that the proper conclusion to be drawn from this fact is not that a necessary being exists, but that, necessarily, some contingent being or other exists. (This is akin to saying that while, necessarily, every object has a shape, nonetheless there is no particular shape which everything necessarily has. In the same way, it's necessary that something or other exists but there isn't anything that exists necessarily.) In short, premise (1) is, on Rundle's view, false after all. The universe exists contingently and inexplicably. Some universe must exist, but there is no explanation why this universe exists.

Alexander Pruss has pointed out that Rundle's view has an extremely implausible consequence. It's plausible that no conjunction of claims about the non-existence of various things entails, say, that a unicorn exists. After all, how could the fact that certain things do *not* exists entail that some other contingent thing does exist? But on Rundle's view the conjunction "There are no mountains, there are no people, there are no planets, there are no rocks, ... [including everything that is not a unicorn]" entails that there is a unicorn! For if it is necessary that contingent being exist, and none of the other contingent beings listed exist, then the only thing left is a unicorn. Hence, a conjunction about the non-existence of certain things entails that a unicorn exists, which seems absurd.

Moreover, on Rundle's view there is nothing which would account for *why* there exist contingent beings in every possible world. Since there is no metaphysically necessary being, there is nothing that could cause contingent beings to exist in every possible world and no explanation why every world includes contingent beings. There is no strict logical inconsistency in the concept of a world devoid of contingent beings. What accounts for the fact that in every possible world contingent beings exist? Given the infinity of broadly logically possible worlds, the odds that in all of them contingent beings just happen inexplicably to exist in infinitesimal. Hence, the probability of Rundle's hypothesis is effectively zero.

Conclusion

Thus, the premises of this Leibnizian argument all seem to me to be more plausible than their negations. It therefore follows logically that the explanation for why the universe exists is to be found in God. It seems to me, therefore, that this is a good argument for God's existence.

A Necessary, All-Inclusive Unity*

SAYYED HOSSEIN NASR

There is no issue more central to Islamic philosophy and especially metaphysics than *wujūd* (at once Being and existence) in itself and in its relation to *māhiyyah* (quiddity or essence). [...] [T]he Necessary Being, which is a philosophical term for God, has been used throughout the centuries extensively by Islamic theologians,

* From chapter 4 of *Islamic Philosophy from its Origin to the Present: Philosophy in the Land of Prophecy* (Albany: State University of New York Press, 2006). Reprinted by permission. © 2006 State University of New York. All rights reserved.

Sufis, and even jurists and ordinary preachers. […] The quality of necessity in the ultimate sense belongs to God alone, as does that of freedom. One of the great masters of traditional Islamic philosophy of the beginning of the twentieth century, Mīrzā Mahdī Āshtiyānī who was devoted to the school of the "transcendent unity of being", in fact asserted that after a lifetime of study he had finally discovered that *wujūb* or necessity is none other than *wujūd* itself. […]

[A]ccording to most schools of Islamic philosophy what exists must exist and cannot not exist. Naṣīr al-Dīn al-Ṭūsī summarizes this doctrine in his famous poem:

> That which exists is as it should be,
> That which should not exist will not do so.

[…] [T]here is no divinity but Allah. This formula is the synthesis of all metaphysics and contains despite its brevity the whole doctrine of the Unity of the Divine Principle and the manifestation of multiplicity, which cannot but issue from that Unity before whose blinding Reality it is nothing. The Sufis and also Shi'ite esoterists and gnostics have asked, "What does divinity (*ilāh*) mean except reality or *wujūd?*" By purifying themselves through spiritual practice, they have come to realize the full import of the testimony and have realized that Reality or *wujūd* belongs ultimately to God alone, that not only is He One, but also that He is the only ultimate Reality and the source of everything that appears to possess *wujūd*. All *wujūd* belongs to God while He is transcendent vis-à-vis all existents. The Quran itself confirms this esotericdoctrine in many ways, such as when it asserts that God is "the First and the Last, the Outward and the Inward" or when it says, "Whithersoever ye turneth, there is the Face of God."

The experience of the "oneness of Being" or the "transcendent unity of Being" is not meant for everyone. Rather it is the crowning achievement of human existence […]

An Eternal Collection of Minds*

TENZIN GYATSO, DALAI LAMA XIV

I understand the Primordial Buddha, also known as Buddha Samantabhadra, to be the ultimate reality, the realm of Dharmakaya – the space of emptiness – where all phenomena, pure and impure, are dissolved. This is the explanation taught by the Sutras and Tantras. However, […] the tantric tradition is the only one which explains the Dharmakaya in terms of inherent clear light, the essential nature of the mind; this would seem to imply that all phenomena, samsara and nirvana, arise from this clear and luminous source. […] [T]his ultimate source, clear light, is close to the notion of

*   From parts 4 and 5 of *Beyond Dogma*, trans. A. Anderson, ed. Marianne Dresser (London: Souvenir Press, 1996), pp. 153–154, 191–192. Originally published as *Au-delà des dogmes* by Dalai Lama. © Éditions Albin Michel, Paris, 1994. Reprinted with permission of Souvenir Press and Éditions Albin Michel.

a Creator, since all phenomena, whether they belong to samsara or nirvana, originate therein. [...] I do not mean that there exists somewhere, there, a sort of collective clear light, analogous to the non-Buddhist concept of Brahma as substratum. We must not be inclined to deify this luminous space. We must understand that when we speak of ultimate or inherent clear light, we are speaking on an individual level.

Likewise, when we speak of karma as the cause of the universe we eliminate the notion of a unique entity called karma existing totally independently. Rather, collective karmic impressions, accumulated individually, are at the origin of the creation of a world. When, in the tantric context, we say that all worlds appear out of clear light, we do not visualize this source as a unique entity, but as the ultimate clear light of each being. [...]

Why is there no creation possible in Buddhism? [...] As causes have no beginning and stretch back to infinity, the same thing must apply for living beings. Creation is therefore not possible.

Let us now consider a particular phenomenon, a glacier for example: it does indeed have a beginning. How was it created? The outside world appears as a result of the acts of sentient beings who use this world. These acts, or karmas, in turn originate in the intentions and motivations of those beings who have not yet taken control of their minds.

The "creator of the world," basically, is the mind. In the Sutras, the mind is described as an agent. It is said that consciousness has no beginning, but we must distinguish here between gross consciousness and subtle consciousness. Many gross consciousnesses appear as dependents of the physical aggregates, of the body. This is evident when you consider the different neurons and the functioning of the brain, but just because physical conditions are met does not mean that this is enough to produce a perception. In order for a perception which will have the faculty to reflect and know an object to arise, it must have a consubstantial cause. The fundamental consubstantial cause, of the same substance as its result, will in this case be the subtle consciousness. It is this same consciousness or subtle mind which penetrates the parental cells at the moment of conception. The subtle mind can have no beginning. If it had one, the mind would have to be born of something that is not the mind.

Is Consciousness Basic to Reality?*

ANDREI LINDE

If quantum mechanics is universally correct, then one may try to apply it to the universe in order to find its wave function. This would allow us to find out which events are probable and which are not. However, it often leads to paradoxes. For

* From "Inflation, Quantum Cosmology, and the Anthropic Principle," in J.D. Barrow, P.C.W. Davies and C.L. Harper, eds., *Science and Ultimate Reality* (Cambridge: Cambridge University Press, 2004), pp. 449–451. © Cambridge University Press 2004. Reprinted with permission.

example, the essence of the Wheeler–DeWitt equation, which is the Schrödinger equation for the wave function of the universe, is that this wave function *does not depend on time* [...] Therefore if one would wish to describe the evolution of the universe with the help of its wave function, one would be in trouble: *The universe as a whole does not change in time.*

The resolution of this paradox suggested by Bryce DeWitt is rather instructive. The notion of evolution is not applicable to the universe as a whole since there is no external observer with respect to the universe, and there is no external clock that does not belong to the universe. However, we do not actually ask why the universe *as a whole* is evolving. We are just trying to understand our own experimental data. Thus, a more precisely formulated question is *why do we see* the universe evolving in time in a given way. In order to answer this question one should first divide the universe into two main pieces: (i) an observer with his clock and other measuring devices and (ii) the rest of the universe. Then it can be shown that the wave function of the rest of the universe does depend on the state of the clock of the observer, i.e., on his "time." [...] [W]ithout introducing an observer, we have a dead universe, which does not evolve in time. This example demonstrates an unusually important role played by the concept of an observer in quantum cosmology. John Wheeler underscored the complexity of the situation, replacing the word *observer* by the word *participant*, and introducing such terms as a "self-observing universe."

Most of the time, when discussing quantum cosmology, one can remain entirely within the bounds set by purely physical categories, regarding an observer simply as an automaton, and not dealing with questions of whether he/she/it has consciousness or feels anything during the process of observation. This limitation is harmless for many practical purposes. But we cannot rule out the possibility that carefully avoiding the concept of consciousness in quantum cosmology may lead to an artificial narrowing of our outlook.

Let us remember an example from the history of science that may be rather instructive in this respect. Prior to the invention of the general theory of relativity, space, time, and matter seemed to be three fundamentally different entities. Space was thought to be a kind of three-dimensional coordinate grid which, when supplemented by clocks, could be used to describe the motion of matter. [...] The general theory of relativity brought with it a decisive change in this point of view. Spacetime and matter were found to be interdependent, and there was no longer any question which one of the two is more fundamental. [...]

Now let us turn to consciousness. The standard assumption is that consciousness, just like spacetime before the invention of general relativity, plays a secondary, subservient role, being just a function of matter and a tool for the description of the truly existing material world. But let us remember that our knowledge of the world begins not with matter but with perceptions. I know for sure that my pain exists, my "green" exists, and my "sweet" exists. I do not need any proof of their existence, because these events are a part of me; everything else is a theory. Later we find out that our perceptions obey some laws, which can be most conveniently formulated if we assume that there is some underlying reality beyond our perceptions. This model of a material world obeying laws of physics is so successful that soon we forget about our starting point and say that matter is the only reality, and perceptions are nothing but a useful tool for the description of matter. This assumption is almost as natural (and maybe as false) as our previous assumption that space is only a mathematical tool for the description of matter. We are substituting *reality* of our feelings by the successfully working *theory* of an independently existing material world. And the theory is so successful that we almost never think about its possible limitations. [...]

Is it possible that consciousness, like spacetime, has its own intrinsic degrees of freedom, and that neglecting these will lead to a description of the universe that is fundamentally incomplete? What if our perceptions are as real as (or maybe, in a certain sense, are even more real than) material objects? What if my red, my blue, my pain, are really existing objects, not merely reflections of the really existing material world? Is it possible to introduce a "space of elements of consciousness," and investigate a possibility that consciousness may exist by itself, even in the absence of matter, just as gravitational waves, excitations of space, may exist in the absence of protons and electrons?

Note, that the gravitational waves usually are so small and interact with matter so weakly that we have not found any of them as yet. However, their existence is absolutely crucial for the consistency of our theory, as well as for our understanding of certain astronomical data. Could it be that consciousness is an equally important part of the consistent picture of our world, despite the fact that so far one could safely ignore it in the description of the well-studied physical processes?

Mind, Cosmos: A Self-Explaining Loop?*

PAUL DAVIES

From *"Laying Down the Laws"*

Science works because the universe is ordered in an intelligible way. The most refined manifestation of this order is found in the laws of physics, the fundamental mathematical rules that govern all natural phenomena. One of the biggest questions of existence is the origin of those laws: where do they come from, and why do they have the form that they do?

*   From "Laying Down the Laws," *New Scientist* (30 June 2007), pp. 301–303. © 2007 Reed Business Information UK. All rights reserved. Distributed by Tribune Media Services International; and from the Afterword to *The Goldilocks Enigma* (London: Allen Lane, 2006), pp. 301–303. Reprinted with permission of Penguin Books UK.

Until recently this problem was considered off-limits to scientists. Their job was to discover the laws and apply them, not inquire into their form or origin. Now the mood has changed. One reason for this stems from the growing realisation that the laws of physics possess a weird and surprising property: collectively they give the universe the ability to generate life and conscious beings, such as ourselves, who can ponder the big questions.

If the universe came with any old rag-bag of laws, life would almost certainly be ruled out. Indeed, changing the existing laws by even a scintilla could have lethal consequences. For example, if protons were 0.1 per cent heavier than neutrons, rather than the other way about, all the protons coughed out of the big bang would soon have decayed into neutrons. Without protons and their crucial electric charge, atoms could not exist and chemistry would be impossible.

Physicists and cosmologists know many such examples of uncanny bio-friendly "coincidences" and fortuitous fine-tuned properties in the laws of physics. Like Baby Bear's porridge in the story of Goldilocks, our universe seems "just right" for life. It looks, to use astronomer Fred Hoyle's dramatic description, as if "a super-intellect has been monkeying with physics". So what is going on?

A popular way to explain the Goldilocks factor is the multiverse theory. This says that a god's-eye-view of the cosmos would reveal a patchwork quilt of universes, of which ours is but an infinitesimal fragment. Crucially, each patch, or "universe", comes with its own distinctive set of local by-laws. Maybe the by-laws are assigned randomly, as in a vast cosmic lottery. It is then no surprise that we find ourselves living in a patch so well suited to life, for we could hardly inhabit a bio-hostile patch. Our universe has simply hit the cosmic jackpot. Those universes that can't support life – the vast majority in fact – go unobserved.

Goldilocks Enigma

The multiverse theory is a step forward, but it still leaves a lot unexplained. For a start, there has to be a universe-generating mechanism to make all those cosmic patches. There also has to be a process whereby each patch acquires a set of by-laws, perhaps at random, perhaps not. These requirements demand their own laws – which maybe we should refer to as federal laws or meta-laws – to govern the creation of law-driven universes.

In itself that is not an overriding objection. Cosmologists have concocted a way for an endless stream of big bangs to occur spontaneously throughout space and time, each triggering the birth of a "bubble" universe somewhere and somewhen in the boundless multiverse, with each bubble governed internally by its very own by-laws. However, their calculations appeal to quantum mechanics, relativity and a host of other conventional oddments from the standard tool kit of theoretical physics. Accepting such meta-laws as given – true without reason or explanation – merely shifts the mystery of the laws of physics in our universe up a level, to that of the meta-laws in the multiverse.

The basic difficulty can be traced back to the traditional concept of a physical law. Since at least the time of Isaac Newton, the laws of physics have been treated as immutable, universal, eternal relationships – infinitely precise mathematical rules that transcend the physical universe and inhabit an abstract other-worldly realm.

These perfect rules were supposedly imprinted on the universe – somehow – from outside, at the moment of cosmic creation, and haven't changed an iota since. In particular, the laws care nothing for what is actually happening in the universe, however violent the physical processes may be. So the universe depends on the laws, but the laws are strangely independent of the universe.

Four hundred years on, physicists still cling to this model of physical law, even though they have no idea what the external source of the laws might be. So long as science appeals to something outside the universe, we must abandon any hope of ultimately understanding why the universe is as it is. A large element of mystery will lie forever beyond our reach.

There is, however, another possibility: relinquish the notion of immutable, transcendent laws and try to explain the observed behaviour entirely in terms of processes occurring within the universe. As it happens, there is a growing minority of scientists whose concept of physical law departs radically from the orthodox view and whose ideas offer an ideal model for developing this picture. The burgeoning field of computer science has shifted our view of the physical world from that of a collection of interacting material particles to one of a seething network of information. In this way of looking at nature, the laws of physics are a form of software, or algorithm, while the material world – the hardware – plays the role of a gigantic computer.

Perfect Past

The mathematics of the laws may be the same, but the change in perspective leads to profoundly different conclusions, as we discover when we ask just how powerful the cosmic computer may be. Every computer's performance is limited by the finite speed of its processors and the finite storage capacity of its memory. The universe is no exception.

Bits of information, even in the subatomic domain, cannot be flipped faster than a maximum rate permitted by the Heisenberg uncertainty principle of quantum mechanics. Meanwhile the storage capacity depends on the physical size of the observable universe, which is limited to the maximum distance light can have travelled since the big bang 13.7 billion years ago. From this, Seth Lloyd of the

Massachusetts Institute of Technology in Cambridge has calculated that the observable universe can have processed no more than 10^{120} bits of information since its birth.

Does it matter that the universe commands only finite computational resources? Maybe not to the traditional view of the laws of physics, according to which Mother Nature computes the action of her laws in a transcendent heaven of infinitely precise mathematical relationships. But if we replace this highly idealised view with one in which nature computes in the real universe, then Lloyd's bound has serious implications. In effect, we have no reason to suppose any physical law can be more accurate than 1 part in 10^{120}. Beyond that we can expect the law to break down and become fuzzy.

For most practical purposes Lloyd's number is so big it might as well be infinite. For example, the law of conservation of electric charge has been tested to only about one part in a trillion, still 108 powers of 10 too crude to reveal any possible breakdown arising from the finite information bound.

However, Lloyd's bound isn't fixed: it grows with time, and at the instant of the big bang it was 0. At the time the large-scale structure of the universe was being laid down during the first split second, the bound was still only about 10^{20} – possibly small enough to have cosmological consequences. So we are led to a picture in which the laws of physics are inherent in the physical universe, and emerge with it. They start out unfocused, but rapidly sharpen and zero in on the form we observe today as the universe grows.

Flexi-laws of this sort are not a new idea. They were proposed 30 years ago by the physicist John Wheeler. The way he expressed it is that the laws of physics were not "cast in tablets of stone, from everlasting to everlasting". Rather, they emerged over time, congealing from the ferment of the big bang.

Can the flexibility in the laws explain the Goldilocks enigma? Is there enough wiggle room for the universe to somehow engineer its bio-friendliness? Freeman Dyson, one of the pioneers in the study of the biological fine-tuning mystery, wrote that the more he learned about the various accidents of physics and cosmology that permit life to arise, "the more it seems that in some sense the universe knew we were coming". Dyson's dramatic assertion raises the obvious question: how? In the first split second, when the laws were in the process of settling down, how could the universe "know about" life and consciousness coming along billions of years later? How can life today be relevant to the physics of the very early universe?

Surprisingly it can, thanks to the weirdness of quantum mechanics. Heisenberg's uncertainty principle says that even if you know the state of an atom at one moment, there is an irreducible uncertainty about what its properties will be when you observe them at a later moment. One way of expressing this is to say that the atom has many possible futures encompassed within the overall fuzziness of quantum uncertainty. What's more, the principle works just as well for the past as for the future, so an atom has many possible histories leading up to its present state. By the rules of quantum physics, all these parallel realities must meld together to yield the present state of the atom.

The same general conclusion holds if we apply quantum mechanics to the entire universe – a subject known as quantum cosmology, made famous by the work of Stephen Hawking. Since we cannot know the quantum state at the start of the universe, we must work backwards in time from our present observations and infer the past.

As Hawking has emphasised, it is a mistake to think there is a single, well-defined cosmic history connecting the big bang to the present state of the universe (*New Scientist*, 22 April 2006, p. 28). Rather, there will be a multiplicity of possible histories, and which histories are included in the amalgam will depend on what we choose to measure today. "The histories of the universe depend on the precise question asked," Hawking said in a paper last year with Thomas Hertog (www.arxiv.org/abs/hep-th/0602091). In other words, the existence of life and observers today has an effect on the past. "It leads to a profoundly different view of cosmology, and the relation between cause and effect," claims Hawking.

We can illustrate these abstract ideas from quantum physics with the help of a concrete demonstration suggested 25 years ago by Wheeler. His experiment is a variant of Thomas Young's famous 200-year-old double-slit experiment, designed to reveal the wave nature of light. A pinpoint source of light illuminates a screen punctured by a pair of parallel slits, projecting onto a second screen beyond. Light spreading out from each slit overlaps with that from the other. Where the light from both slits arrives at the image screen in phase, the waves reinforce to produce a bright band. Where they arrive out of phase, they interfere destructively, producing a dark band. The series of bright and dark bands are called interference fringes.

Mystery sets in when you turn the brightness right down. According to quantum theory, light may also be considered to consist of photons, which behave like a stream of particles. So what happens if you allow only one photon at a time to traverse the apparatus? Experiments show that although it takes a lot longer, an interference pattern does build up on the photographic screen, one photon at a time. Presumably each photon passes through only one slit, yet somehow it appears to "interfere with itself" and contribute to the pattern.

A wily experimenter might decide to place detectors at the slits to see which one each photon goes through. Nature, however, outmanoeuvres us. Whenever you determine the path of the photons, no interference pattern results. So you have a choice: look to see where the photon is heading and destroy its wavelike behaviour, or choose not to look, and allow the photon to manifest the wave aspect of its character. It essentially boils down to a choice of particle or wave. The photon can be both, but not at the same time. The experimenter gets to decide which.

So far so good. The novel twist that Wheeler added is that you can delay your decision to look at the wave or particle aspect until long after the light has passed through the slits. Using a pair of telescopes placed at the image screen, you can look back at the slits and infer which one any given photon emerged from. Do this and you destroy the interference pattern. In effect, the observation you make affects the nature of the past – specifically, whether the photon behaved as a wave or a particle. Physicists call this strange phenomenon "quantum post-selection".

There is a temptation to assume that the light "really was" either a wave or a particle in the past, but quantum physics denies this. It is simply not possible to ascribe a well-defined past to this system. Rather, your decision to make a particular observation – what Hawking meant by "the precise question asked" – determines the nature of the past. Crucially, however, the delayed-choice experiment cannot be used to change the past, or to send information back in time.

This aspect of quantum weirdness may appear startling, but it has been tested by experiments and found to be correct. In such experiments the quantum reach into the past is only a few nanoseconds, but in principle it could be extended to billions of years. And when it comes to quantum cosmology, it can penetrate right back to the big bang itself.

So how can this backward-in-time feature of quantum mechanics explain the bio-friendliness of the universe? Well, obviously we can rule out from the multiplicity of quantum histories any that don't lead to life, because that would conflict with the basic fact of our own existence. However, in the standard quantum cosmology advocated by Hawking, all of the alternative histories, without exception, conform to exactly the same laws of physics. So while a photon travelling from a source to a screen can take many different paths, the actual laws of motion that govern its path remain the same whichever route it takes.

Wheeler's idea was more radical. He claimed that the existence of life and observers in the universe today can help bring about the very circumstances needed for life to emerge by reaching back to the past through acts of quantum observation. It is an attempt to explain the Goldilocks factor by appealing to cosmic self-consistency: the bio-friendly universe explains life even as life explains the bio-friendly universe.

Flexi-Laws

As long as the laws of physics are fixed, as they are in Hawking's cosmology, their enigmatic bio-friendliness is left out of this explanatory loop. But with flexi-laws of the sort advocated by Wheeler, the way lies open for a self-consistent explanation. The fuzzy primordial laws focus in on precisely the form needed to give rise to the living organisms that eventually observe them. Cosmic bio-friendliness is therefore the result of a sort of quantum post-selection effect extended to the very laws of physics themselves.

Wheeler's ideas are far from properly worked out. They remain, as he quaintly referred to them, "an idea for an idea". However several theorists, including Yakir

Aharonov, Jeff Tollaksen and others at George Mason University in Fairfax, Virginia, and myself are attempting to place the concept of flexi-laws and quantum post-selection on a sound mathematical footing.

How can we test these outlandish ideas? If the fidelity of the laws of physics really is subject to a cosmological bound, then the structure of the universe might betray some remnant of the substantial primordial fuzziness. A more direct test could come from the phenomenon of quantum entanglement, in which the quantum states of a collection of particles are linked in such a manner that an observation performed on one affects all the others simultaneously.

The key point about an entangled state is that it requires many more parameters to define it. For example, 10 atoms may have their spins aligned with or against a magnetic field. In a non-entangled state, you only need 10 bits of information to define the state for each atom. But if the atoms are entangled, you must specify the values of 2^{10}, or 1024, parameters.

As the number of particles goes up, so the number of defining parameters escalates. A state with 400 entangled particles blows the Lloyd limit – it requires more bits of information to specify it than exist in the entire observable universe. If one takes seriously the inherent uncertainty in the laws implied by Lloyd's limit, then a noticeable breakdown in fidelity should manifest itself at the level of 400 entangled particles. Such a state is by no means far-fetched. Entangled states of about a dozen particles have already been created, and experimenters have set their sights on 10,000 as part of the effort to build a quantum computer.

In the orthodox view, the laws of physics are floating in an explanatory void. Ironically, the essence of the scientific method is rationality and logic: we suppose that things are the way they are for a reason. Yet when it comes to the laws of physics themselves, well, we are asked to accept that they exist "reasonlessly". If that were correct, then the entire edifice of science would ultimately be founded on absurdity. By bringing the laws of physics within the compass of science, and fusing nature and its laws into a mutually self-consistent explanation, we have some hope of understanding why the laws are what they are. In addition, we can begin to glimpse how we, the observers of this remarkable universe, fit into the great cosmic scheme.

From *The Goldilocks Enigma*

[...] Something unexplained has to be accepted as given and the rest of the explanatory scheme constructed on that ad hoc foundation. One way to avoid this trap is to appeal to a closed explanatory or causal loop. In effect, the universe (or multiverse – it can work at both levels) explains itself. There are even models involving causal loops or backwards-in-time causation, where the universe creates itself. The advantage of such a scheme is that it is self-contained [...] The disadvantage is that we are still left not knowing why this universe – *this* self-explaining, self-creating system – is the one that exists, as opposed to all other self-explanatory schemes. Perhaps *all* self-explanatory schemes exist and only ones like ours get observed because they are consistent with life – another variant on the multiverse. Or, better still, perhaps existence isn't something that gets bestowed from outside, by having "fire breathed" into a potentiality by some unexplained fire-breathing agency (i.e. a transcendent existence generator), but is also something self-activating. I have suggested that only self-consistent loops capable of understanding themselves can create themselves, so that only universes with (at least the potential for) life and mind really exist. [...]

I do take life, mind and purpose seriously, and I concede that the universe at least *appears* to be designed with a high level of ingenuity. I cannot accept these features as a package of marvels which just happen to be, which exist reasonlessly. It seems to me that there is a genuine scheme of things – the universe is "about" something. But I am equally uneasy about dumping the whole set of problems in the lap of an arbitrary god, or abandoning all further thought and declaring existence ultimately to be a mystery. [...] Many scientists will criticize my inclination as being crypto-religious. The fact that I take the human mind and our extraordinary ability to understand the world through science and mathematics as a fact of fundamental significance betrays, they will claim, a nostalgia for a theistic world view in which humankind occupies a special place. And this even though I do *not* believe *Homo sapiens* to be more than an accidental by-product of haphazard natural processes. Yet I do believe that life and mind are etched deeply into the fabric of the cosmos, perhaps through a shadowy, half-glimpsed life principle, and if I am to be honest I have to concede that this starting point is something I feel more in my heart than in my head. So maybe that is a religious conviction of sorts.

9

Fine-Tuning and Multiple Universes

Editorial Introduction

Our universe can look astonishingly well suited to the evolution of intelligent life. Tiny changes to numbers ("constants") occurring in the equations of physics and of cosmology would apparently have led to a lifeless universe. How might we explain what seems to be very precise "fine-tuning" of those numbers, without which the equations would fail to describe a universe in which life could appear? By a divine Fine-Tuner? By placing Mind at the world's foundations, but not a divine mind? By a Platonic creative principle which ensured that good things would come to exist? An alternative explanation now often accepted by physicists, and particularly by the ones who reject belief in God, runs as follows. There exist hugely many universes, varying greatly in their properties. Given sufficiently many universes and sufficiently much variation from universe to universe, tuning to absolutely any required degree of precision would be present in one or more universes. And observers of course couldn't find themselves in any universe *not* tuned with whatever accuracy was needed for intelligent life to exist in it.

John POLKINGHORNE, holder of a chair of mathematical physics before he became an Anglican priest, detects in the world "an astonishing drive towards fruitfulness." He suspects there could be "teleological laws of nature" directing events into fortunate channels. Even well-established science provides him with much that suggests a Creator's benevolence. For a start, our ability to understand physical reality "immensely exceeds" what could be expected of brains which evolved "to dodge sabre-toothed tigers."

The Mystery of Existence: Why Is There Anything At All?, First Edition. Edited by John Leslie and Robert Lawrence Kuhn.
© 2013 John Wiley & Sons, Inc. Published 2013 by John Wiley & Sons, Inc.

Critics could protest that dodging those tigers was no easy task. They might be more impressed by Polkinghorne's next point, that physical reality obeys beautiful equations. Yet might not a Creator have had more urgent priorities than producing beauty for physicists? Polkinghorne could be on firmer ground when he notes that the laws of quantum theory, laws almost incredible to many physicists, have the right properties for making the world neither too floppy nor too rigid for "the kind of flexible change that is the engine of evolution." And while that point might strike some folk as rather a loose one – its force would certainly be hard to quantify – actual *numbers* are provided by cosmic fine-tuning. For intelligent life to evolve, the strengths of physical forces "need to lie within very narrow limits," Polkinghorne reports. In particular the cosmological constant – it occurs in the equations of General Relativity – has to be *almost exactly* zero. For the universe to contain intelligent living beings, it must be zero to one part in ten followed by one hundred and nineteen zeros.

Other limits, "less exacting, but still tight," apply to the strength of electromagnetism (it controls chemical bonding, and it must be in the right balance to the strength of gravity for there to be long-lived, stable stars); to the strengths of the nuclear forces; to the masses of electrons, protons, and neutrons. Also to the early cosmic expansion speed. It had to be tuned to one part in ten followed by fifty-nine zeros – far less accurately, therefore, than the cosmological constant, but still with an accuracy equivalent to "hitting a target an inch wide on the other side of the observable universe." It is often theorized that at very early moments a process called Inflation led to the right expansion speed automatically. But, Polkinghorne argues, the process would itself have depended on whether the laws of nature took a particular form; one need for careful adjustment of Nature's properties "has been replaced by another." "There is, it seems to me, bound to be something specifically necessary to provide the basis of fertility." Quantum mechanics and gravity played "essential roles" in the processes governing the development of life, yet "the universe does not have *a priori* to be quantum mechanical, or gravitational." And "even if (as some speculate, but which does not seem all that likely to me) there is only one fundamental theory that could incorporate quantum gravity, it would still surely be remarkable that that unique possibility *also* provided all that was necessary for life's evolution."

Could the fine-tuning be explained by multiple universes which varied in their properties, combined with *observational selection* of a universe with observer-permitting properties? Although such selection has come to be called "anthropic" it need have little to do with *anthropos* – with humankind. What are important are the factors essential to the evolution *of observers*. The list of such factors is impressive enough to suggest that our life-permitting world was selected by God from a rich field of possibilities, yet it might be a sign of observational selection instead. Here it can help, Polkinghorne writes, if we think of "a single fly on a big blank wall." A bullet hits the fly. It could be a sign that a marksman had fired it. However, an alternative would be that many bullets were hitting the wall, which corresponds to the idea that there exist many universes or huge cosmic regions ("sub-universes") with different properties, most of them being places where observers could never be born. Polkinghorne sees a way in which physicists could develop that alternative. When the universe cooled after the Big Bang, "symmetries" described by a Grand Unified Theory may have broken in different ways in hugely many separate domains, each of vast size. We could exist deep inside one of the domains.

There could be another reason for leaving out God. Might not other possible universes have "their own forms of 'life', totally different from any that we can conceive"? Polkinghorne answers that this suggestion draws "intellectual blank cheques on totally unknown accounts." A stronger reply could be that the original fly-on-wall story, the one told in John Leslie's book *Universes*, did not involve a wall known to be blank except for the single unfortunate fly. Instead the wall was described as blank in *a largish but still fairly limited area surrounding the fly*, with the comment that *distant* areas of the wall could, for all one knew, be thick with flies. The point being that when we consider possible universes produced by *fairly limited changes* in the actual equations of physics, we can avoid the totally unknown. We can be fairly sure that such changes would be disastrous – so that we'd indeed want to understand "why the fly in this otherwise empty region was hit."

The possibility that there exist multiple universes does weaken our grounds for believing in a divine designer. The reason the fly was hit might be that many bullets were hitting the wall. But, Polkinghorne writes, the fine-tuning remains "a valuable hint" that there is "a divine meaning and purpose behind cosmic history."

Discussions of fine-tuning do quickly become very technical. Writers have argued that the amount of tuning required could be much less than is often thought, particularly if intelligent life could evolve in the absence of such things as carbon and maybe even in such places as the crusts of neutron stars. Matters become remarkably tricky when we imagine alterations to more than one of the figures embedded in some crucial equation. Might a potentially fatal change in one figure be fairly easily counterbalanced by a change in another? Perhaps not – for when (as seems probable) giving some new numerical value to an allegedly fine-tuned ingredient in the equation would dictate particular new values for various other ingredients, couldn't the continuance of life-permitting conditions be very hard to achieve, above all if those other ingredients had themselves seemed finely tuned? It might well take over a century for anything like full consensus to emerge in this field. Among those who have worked in it, however, it is now widely accepted that our universe would be lifeless had its physics been marginally different.

As Leonard SUSSKIND says, multiple universes came to be taken very seriously when Inflation – the theory that "the universe expanded spectacularly in the first fraction of a second" – was found to fit "a lot of data." Inflation would mean that the region we observe, "our universe," was probably a tiny patch in "a huge universe with patches that are very different from one another." The cosmological constant must be almost precisely zero for there to be anybody to observe anything. This, Susskind thought, could well indicate "anthropic" observational selection of a hospitable patch, large enough and different enough from other patches to be itself worth calling "a universe." Yet he was none too convinced until the constant was discovered to be *non-zero*, a fairly firm sign that no physically tidy principles had forced it to take its observed value. Even then it had seemed to him that String Theory – very popular nowadays, and suggesting the existence of universes that vary greatly in their properties – described not nearly enough universes for even a single universe to be "suitable for life." But Polchinski and Bousso found in the year 2000 that the figure string theorists had accepted until then, of roughly a million universes, was far too low. The actual figure could be 10^{500} – one followed by five hundred zeros. Numbers entering the basic equations of physics would differ from universe to universe instead of being dictated in the same way everywhere by "some deep mathematical principle." Fine-tuning that permitted observers to evolve could never be more than a local reality, yet the fact that it existed somewhere among those unimaginably many universes would not be astounding.

When Susskind wrote a paper saying all of this, the initial reaction was "very hostile," he tells us, yet he himself found it exciting that the cosmos could be much larger and more full of variety than physicists had ever expected. The dream of a Final Theory governing everything would not have to be abandoned. The theory would still be there, but it would dictate different things in different universes. We could never detect universes unlike ours – but this, Susskind points out, would be a poor reason for rejecting them, since if such universes *did not exist* then that fact, too, would be undetectable by us. And so far at least, "it looks bad" for those who hope that varied universes will not "make sense mathematically."

Susskind likes to reflect that Divine Design has become unnecessary. Still, he says, it might be difficult to avoid if the immensely rich String Theory "landscape" had to be abandoned. We could then be "in a very awkward position," hard pressed to answer the Intelligent Design community. [But note: "Intelligent Design" can mean many different things. Someone who thinks God chose Nature's laws is one sort of believer in Intelligent Design. Another may believe that God must constantly "conserve" the universe in its existence, almost as if creating it anew. When deciding at each new moment what the new, slightly changed situation would be, God would be faced with quantum indeterminism. Forced to choose from among the various alternatives allowed by the laws of quantum theory, God would presumably be inclined to conserve things in new quantum states that tended to lead to life and intelligence. Or again, it may be believed that God designed the eye and the eagle and the plague germ.]

Steven WEINBERG thinks it obvious that no mere need for mathematical consistency dictated what Nature's laws would be. The most we could ever hope to discover would be this: that only a single logically consistent theory was rich enough to allow for the existence of living beings such as humans. String Theory could have sufficient richness. It has dismayed many physicists by pointing to hugely many sub-universes that differ in their properties, asking us to accept "that much of what we had hoped to calculate are environmental parameters" of our own little sub-universe. Well, we may simply have to accept it. However – and this is quite an advantage – the richness of a String Theory cosmos would make it unsurprising that some places were "suitable for the appearance of life and its evolution into scientists." "Anthropic" reasoning, reasoning that links observed properties of our world to what was necessary for observers to evolve in it, is indeed, Weinberg writes, "a retreat from what we had hoped for: the calculation of all fundamental parameters from first principles." But we may have to live with it "just as Newton had to give up Kepler's hope of a calculation of the relative sizes of planetary orbits from first principles." Sure enough, "we will never be able to observe any subuni-verses except our own," yet "the test of a physical theory is not that everything in it should be observable and every prediction it makes should be testable."

Weinberg is puzzled when people view anthropic arguments as having "some of the flavor of religion," for isn't quite the opposite true? The gigantic String Theory landscape "may explain how the constants of nature that we observe can take values suitable for life without being fine-tuned by a benevolent creator."

The word "universe" once meant Absolutely Everything, with the possible excep-tion of God. It is now often used very differently. Everything inside our horizon, set by how far light could have traveled towards us since the Big Bang, counts as "inside our universe," yet most cosmologists of today feel sure that this is only a tiny frac-tion of the cosmos. How, then, are we to talk of regions beyond the horizon? They might be called "other large cosmic regions." However, straightforward cosmologi-cal models present them as being very similar to the region inside the horizon. They then probably contain observers like us. Max Tegmark calculates that if today's "simplest and most popular" model is right then you would probably even have a perfect twin, somebody exactly like you and surrounded by precise copies of every-thing inside your horizon, at a distance from you of "about 10 to the 10^{28} meters." [The figure is ten followed by a billion billion billion zeros, whereas a trillion is a mere 10^{12} – ten followed by only eleven zeros.] Why not say that the twin lived in "another universe"? Even when other large cosmic regions are pictured as having very different properties, why not call them "other universes" as well? And when cosmologists imagine groups of these large cosmic regions existing inside even larger cosmic regions, while those in turn exist inside regions larger still, why not do what most cosmologists do, calling *all* the regions "universes"? And why not then say that they are grouped into "multiverses" at many levels, with lower-level multi-verses nested inside higher-level ones? You can if you like name everything "the one and only universe," then saying it is divided into "sub-universes," "sub-sub-universes," and maybe even "sub-sub-sub-sub-sub-sub-universes." But forget about forcing every cosmologist to adopt your complicated terminology!

Tegmark has four levels in his cosmos – his sum total of all existing things. First come huge regions of a space that stretches far beyond our horizon. They are the universes of "the Level I multiverse." Next there is the Level II multiverse predicted by "the currently popular theory of chaotic eternal inflation." Inflation – expansion in which regions double in volume repeatedly and very quickly, each doubling occurring as rapidly as the one before – continues for ever in this scenario, but "some regions of space stop stretching and form distinct bubbles." The bubbles are universes varying in the qualities of their constituent particles and in the figures, "so-called physical constants," that appear in the equations governing them. The differences extend even to the number of large space-time dimensions each universe possesses. Several mechanisms, all of them connected with breaking of "symmetries" between physical properties, could have generated such variation among the universes. And a very varied multiverse accounts for the remarkable fact that "most, if not all" of the properties characterizing the universe that we observe "appear to be fine-tuned," meaning that it looks as if changing them slightly would have ruled out observers like ourselves. It would be no great surprise that such fine-tuning was present in one or more universes, and we couldn't observe ourselves to be anywhere else.

Tegmark's next level, Level III, is provided by Many-Worlds Quantum Theory. Here the various possible ways in which quantum events could occur are all of them ways in which they really do occur. The result is "superpositions of many such realities." With immense rapidity everything splits into more and more branches, these becoming more and more different from one another. The branches are the parallel universes of the Level III multiverse. We have no direct means of detecting its other universes but a powerful quantum computer, if we managed to develop it, would give us every excuse for believing in them, Tegmark argues. For, he tells us, the computer would operate through sharing its computational tasks between universes.

Up to Level III the fundamental laws of nature never vary from universe to universe. It is only the "derived" or "effective" laws that vary because of the variation in those "so-called constants." At Level IV the fundamental laws do vary, and to a very startling extent. Tegmark theorizes that his Level IV multiverse contains "all mathematical structures." Instead of being just abstract realities, "all mathematical structures exist physically as well." He notes the similarity between such a theory and the Modal Realism that David Lewis developed for philosophical reasons (see this volume's earlier pages). The Level IV multiverse might seem absurdly complex. Measured in a particular way, however, its simplicity would be delightful. Tegmark asks us to prefer "many worlds" to "many words." Just look at how simply the Level IV multiverse can be described! *Contains All Mathematical Structures* is four words only.

What is meant, though, by "all mathematical structures"? Leibniz wrote in his *Discourse on Metaphysics* that no matter how you scatter dots on paper there will be some mathematical formula, perhaps tremendously long and complicated, that generates a line passing through every one of them. As he saw, the point would apply also to events scattered through a huge universe. Inevitably, there would be a formula to fit them. Absolutely any universe, no matter how disorderly, might therefore count as having "a mathematical structure." If not, then very many words could be needed to explain why only orderly universes are "mathematically structured" and to specify all the forms that their mathematically structured orderliness could take.

It has seemed to many people – for example to the cosmologist Alex Vilenkin when he discusses Tegmark (see earlier pages) and to critics of David Lewis – that orderly universes *are untypical* among all conceivable universes rather as, among all whole numbers up to ninety-nine trillion (let's say), those that are multiples of forty-seven (for instance) are untypical. Here it might be useful to think of all the conceivable ways in which your future could be much less orderly than you would like. You might turn into a pile of dust, a goldfish, a cupcake, a miniature black hole. You might suddenly vanish or speed into outer space, and so on. Tegmark hopes that the structure of our world will be discovered to be not only typical but even "the most generic one" among whatever mathematical structures are "consistent with our observations." Yet if there is always some mathematical formula or other to fit *just any* dots scattered on a sheet of paper, no matter how large the sheet, then infinitely many different formulas can do the job, formulas some of which would fit not only the dots already scattered but also all the perhaps hundreds of trillions of dots that were going to be scattered later. Well, what if the dots already scattered looked "very orderly" through lying in a straight line so that a simple formula fitted them? Countless far more complicated formulas would fit those dots as well, mathematical equations predicting fantastically complex wriggling when the line was extended. So if he lived in a multiverse containing absolutely all mathematical structures, shouldn't Tegmark expect that the line of his future would wriggle wildly? That he would almost surely become a pile of dust or a goldfish or a cupcake or ... or ... or ... or ...?

Believers in God often dislike multiple universes, thinking they would remove all force from the new "fine-tuning" evidence for a Designer. (1) A first reason why any such thought could be wrong is that one and the same item of evidence can increase the probable correctness of *both* of two competing theories. Smith's pineapple goes missing on an island whose other inhabitants are Jones and Bloggs. It's new evidence for thinking Jones stole the coconuts that went missing yesterday. It increases, too, the suspicion that Bloggs stole them. (2) Another reason is that theories seeming to compete may in fact be fully compatible. Convinced that God designed our universe, Robin COLLINS judges that God could well want a multiverse, a far richer expression of divine creativity than a one and only universe. He finds the fine-tuning impressive, and a "multiverse-generator" might well have produced it. But the multiverse-generator, unless very carefully engineered, would nowhere, he thinks, have produced a life-permitting, fine-tuned situation. He describes this as "kicking the issue of design up one level" to the question of who designed the multiverse-generator. To illustrate the point, he examines a multiverse generated by Inflation. He argues that unless the inflationary process had properties that he lists, every universe in the multiverse would be lifeless. He points as well to how quantization and the Pauli exclusion principle help to make complex structures stable, and to how suited gravity is to building stars and planets. A lucky coming together of many brute facts? Divine Design strikes him as a far better explanation.

Collins could perhaps be correct. Yet wouldn't the mind of a divine designer itself need to be designed? And if not, why not? A reply might be that while such questions can be hard to answer, there is little need to answer them since there is so much "non-design" evidence of God's existence, in particular from religious experiences. Any indications of design merely add to our grounds for believing in God. Those grounds are forceful even without an answer to why God's mind is structured as it is. Yet many people, never themselves having had religious experiences, say that neurological disturbances sufficiently explain why others have them. And, their protest may be, God would be a Being *so atrociously complicated* that only extremely strong evidence could compensate for the "prior improbability" of God's existence. Now, these skeptics might be surprised to learn that numerous believers in God, including such major thinkers as Plotinus and Aquinas, doubt or deny that God has a mind of immense or infinite complexity. Yes, they say, God created just the sort of universe that a benevolent deity would design, but God could have created it without being *a designer*, or *a Being*, in any but an "analogical" sense – a sense very far from straightforward. Again, the skeptics might care to consider the argument that, while God really is a designer with a mind of vast intelligence that knows immensely much, and is therefore *immensely complicated* in an important sense, God's existence is nevertheless exceptionally likely because of being *extremely simple* in a more crucial sense. Richard Swinburne tells us that God has great simplicity through being very simply describable, for example with the words *Knows Everything Now Knowable*. And that, remember, is just the kind of simplicity Tegmark sees in his Level IV multiverse. When things have simplicity of this kind, it can strengthen our grounds for believing in them.

A Purpose behind Cosmic History?*

JOHN POLKINGHORNE

Cosmic Fruitfulness

There is an astonishing drive towards fruitfulness present in the unfolding process of the world, which has turned a newly formed Earth into the home of self-conscious beings in little more than three billion years. That may seem a long time, but astonishing things have to happen. The human brain (evolved in only a few hundred thousand years from a much more primitive hominid brain) is far and away the most complex physical system we have ever encountered in our exploration of the universe. It seems impossible in the state of current knowledge

* From chapter 6 of *Beyond Science* (Cambridge: Cambridge University Press, 1996), pp. 77–92. © Cambridge University Press 1996. Reprinted with permission.

to extract from evolutionary geneticists even the crudest estimates of the timescales over which such neural complexity might be expected to evolve. Nevertheless a number of physical scientists (and not just those who might be thought to have a covert religious agenda) believe it likely that neo-Darwinism is only *part* of the explanation. They suspect that other, hitherto undiscovered, organizing principles may be at work, driving the development of complexity [...]

I have considerable sympathy with the belief that the fruitfulness of cosmic and terrestrial history is such that it is reasonable to seek to supplement current received evolutionary ideas with the operation of possible teleological laws of nature (and, indeed, with the insights of a theology of nature seen as a creation). I have even speculated about how there might be room for the operation of such teleological influences without denying our current knowledge of natural process. Darwinian ideas provide partial insight into the developing history of a fruitful world but it is certainly not known that they tell the whole story. Rather than pursue these hypotheses once again, I prefer to turn to other, more clearly established, scientific insights which suggest that modern science is not in fact inhospitable to a metaphysical discernment of meaning and purpose lying behind cosmic history.

Beautiful Equations

The first consideration is that science is possible at all only because the physical world has proved to be remarkably rationally transparent to us. We are able to understand it to an astonishing degree. Most of the time we take this for granted. Of course, if we could not make sense of the *everyday* world, we would hardly have been able to survive in the struggle for existence. If we did not learn how to make generalizations such as "deadly nightshade is poisonous" or "jumping off a high cliff leads to disaster", we would not last long. Yet our ability to understand the physical world immensely exceeds anything that is required for the relatively banal purpose of survival. Think of the strange counter intuitive subatomic world of quantum theory. If you know where an electron is, you cannot know what it is doing; if you know what it is doing, you cannot know where it is. That is Heisenberg's uncertainty principle in a nutshell. The quantum world is totally unpicturable for us, but it is not totally unintelligible. I cannot believe that our ability to understand its strange character is a curious spin-off from our ancestors having had to dodge sabre-toothed tigers.

That seems even clearer when we recognize that it is *mathematics* which gives us the key to unlock the secrets of nature. Paul Dirac spent his life in the search for beautiful equations. That is a concept not all will find immediately accessible, but among those of us who speak the language of mathematics, mathematical beauty is a recognizable quality. It is hard to describe but easy to recognize – like most other kinds of beauty. Its essence lies in a certain economy and elegance that leads to the mathematical property of being "deep". Dirac once said that it is more important to have beauty in your equations than to have them fit experiment. Of course, he did not mean by that that empirical adequacy was unnecessary. No physicist could believe that. But if your equations did not appear to fit experiment, there were various possible ways out of the difficulty. Nearly always one has to solve the equations in some sort of approximation and maybe you had not hit on the right way to do that. Or maybe the experiments were wrong – we have known that to happen. At any rate, there was some sort of chance of snatching success from apparent failure. But if your equations are ugly, then there is really no hope for you. Time and again we have found that it is equations with that indispensable character of mathematical beauty which describe the nature of the physical world.

If you stop to think about it, that is a very significant thing to have discovered. After all, mathematics arises from the free rational exploration of the human mind. Yet it seems that our minds are so finely tuned to the structure of the universe that they are capable of penetrating its deepest secrets. Mathematicians have a very modest way of speaking, but even they are inclined to acknowledge this as a "non-trivial" fact about the world.

Einstein certainly saw it that way. He once said that the only incomprehensible thing about the universe is that it is comprehensible. In the rational beauty and rational transparency of the physical world we see the threads of a deep meaning woven into the empirical tapestry of science. Those physicists, like Stephen Hawking, who, in speaking of the mathematical order of the physical world like to refer to reading the Mind of God, are in my opinion speaking better than perhaps they know, though there remains much more to the divine mine than physics will ever disclose.

The Anthropic Principle

For a second consideration we should turn to the Anthropic Principle. In our scientific imaginations we can consider universes similar to ours but differing in some aspects of their physical fabric. One of the simplest variations to consider would be one in which the intrinsic strength of one of the forces of nature was different from the value it takes in our universe. For example, one could make the fine structure constant α (which measures the strength of electromagnetism) different from our value of about $1/137$. I would have guessed that this change would have no drastic effect on the history of that other world. If α were bigger, matter would be more dense (it is electromagnetism that holds bulk matter together), so the "people" of that world would be chunkier. But I would have expected that the evolutionary history of that universe would have produced its own kind of life – not *Homo sapiens*, of course, but maybe little green men. I would have been mistaken! A universe of that kind would have had a boring and sterile history. Evolution by itself is not enough. You cannot, if you want to fulfil the role of Creator, simply bring into being more or less any old world and just wait a few billion years for something interesting to happen. Only a very particular, a very "finely tuned", universe is capable of producing systems of the complexity and fruitfulness to make them comparable to *anthropoi*. The interplay of chance and necessity requires the necessity to have a very special form if anything worthy (by our standards) to be called "life" is to emerge. It is this surprising conclusion that has been called the Anthropic Principle.

It is worth looking in some detail at why a fruitful universe is thought to have to be so special in its physical constitution. Many reasons can be given and I shall only attempt to indicate something of the range of considerations involved.

In the first instance one needs to have the right kind of physical laws. Nature must not be too rigid, or else there will not be scope for the kind of flexible change that is the engine of evolution. Equally, nature must not be too floppy, or else there will be no persistence in the novel forms of organization that come into being. Quantum mechanical laws provide just that basic opportunity for the interplay of chance and necessity that seems essential for fertile development.

Fine-Tuning

Next, the intrinsic force strengths need to lie within very narrow limits. The most striking example of this is the cosmological constant. It corresponds to a term that logically can be present in the field equations of general relativity (the modern theory of gravity) but appears to be absent in our world to the extent that its value is zero to within one part in 10^{120}. Were the cosmological constant not virtually zero to this high degree of accuracy, that would make the evolution of life impossible, either by producing instantaneous cosmic collapse (if its sign were negative) or by inducing extremely rapid expansion and consequent dilution (if its sign were positive). This is the most stringent of all the anthropic requirements and it can result only from an exquisite degree of cancellation between two contributions that combine to produce the total effect.

Less exacting, but still tight, limits apply to the other forces of nature. Take electromagnetism. The nature of chemical bonding requires that it be not significantly weaker than it is, yet, if it were somewhat stronger, rates of chemical reactions would be appreciably slowed down and the evolution of life correspondingly retarded. There are many detailed properties of matter that depend on the electromagnetic force and have anthropic consequences. Crucial to the possibility of life in the waters of Earth is the remarkable property that ice is lighter than water, so that freezing takes place from the top downwards and not from the bottom upwards. In consequence, ice forms a skin on the surface, which easily melts at warmer temperatures and which protects the aquatic creatures living underneath while frost endures. A lake solidified from the bottom up would take a long time to melt and it could not be expected to sustain life.

Gravity must be strong enough to cause stars and galaxies to condense, but not so strong as to enforce a cosmic collapse. A particularly sensitive balance between gravity and electromagnetism controls the way in which stars burn (producing long-lived stable sources of energy, essential for the development of life). If electromagnetism were only slightly stronger than it is in relation to gravity, all stars would be red and probably too cold for supporting life; if electromagnetism were relatively slightly weaker, all stars would be blue, intensely hot, and they would live for only a few million years – far too short a time for an evolutionary history to develop on one of their planets.

There are two sorts of nuclear force at work in our universe: the strong nuclear force that holds nuclei together and the weak nuclear force that causes some of them to decay. The latter played an important role in early cosmic history. If it had been significantly stronger, hydrogen would have readily burnt to helium and only that element would have been left to constitute the galaxies and stars as they began to condense. There would then have been no water and no hydrogen-burning stars, which, we have noted, alone give the stable long-lived sources of energy needed for the development of life. If, on the contrary, the weak force had been a little weaker there would then have been no hydrogen left over after those hectic first three minutes in which the whole universe was hot enough to be the arena of nuclear reactions. The survival of some hydrogen requires an excess of protons over neutrons, which is derived from the decay of neutrons into protons, and a feebler weak nuclear force would have made that too slow a process to be effective. The strong nuclear force also has its anthropic bounds: a little stronger and protons would bind to form the diproton (again, no hydrogen); a little weaker and the deuteron becomes unbound, with disastrous consequences for the nuclear processes that make stars burn.

The nuclear processes in the stellar furnaces do not only provide energy. They also make the heavier elements, essential for the chemistry of life. We are made from the ashes of dead stars! Both of the nuclear forces play finely tuned roles in the delicate story of nucleosynthesis. The strong force is such that there is an enhancement (a resonance) in just the right place to enable three helium nuclei to stick together and make carbon. Fortunately, there is not another such enhancement present in the process whereby a further helium nucleus can stick to the carbon to make oxygen. This has the result that some oxygen is made but some carbon is also left behind. (It would be anthropically disastrous to turn all the carbon into oxygen.)

The weak nuclear force plays an essential role in the way some stars explode as supernovae (thus scattering their previous nuclear products out into the environment, where they can become part of the chemical composition of second-generation planets) and at the same time make essential heavier elements (such as zinc and iodine) that cannot be created in stellar interiors.

The sequence of reactions involved in synthesizing the range of nuclei needed for life is extremely complex and delicately balanced. Its unravelling has been a major achievement of twentieth century physics. One of the people who played a leading role in its discovery was the astronomer Fred Hoyle. In fact he *predicted* the existence of the carbon resonance that makes that link in the chain possible, before it was known experimentally, simply in order to make the process viable. Hoyle was very impressed with the "quirks" that occurred in just the right places to enable the sequence of element building to be completed. He wrote,

> I do not believe that any scientist who examined the evidence would fail to draw the conclusion that the laws of nuclear physics have been deliberately designed with regard to the consequences that they produce inside stars. If this is so, then my apparently random quirks have become part of a deep-laid scheme. If not, then we are back again at a monstrous sequence of accidents.

A Home for Life

We can also look to the circumstances of the universe in which we live, as well as to its physical laws, to see that it is not any old world that can be the home of life. One of the cosmos's most striking features is its size. We live on a planet circling an undistinguished star, lying among the hundred thousand million stars of the Milky Way galaxy, which is itself a pretty run-of-the-mill specimen among the hundred thousand million galaxies of the observable universe. Yet, we should resist the temptation to be daunted by the thought of such immensity. Those trillions of stars have to be around if we are to be around also to think about them. In modern cosmology there is a direct correlation between how big a universe is and how long it has lasted. Only a universe as large as ours could have been around for the fifteen billion years it takes to evolve life – ten billion years for the first generation of stars to generate the elements that are the raw materials of life, and about a further five billion years to reap the benefit of that chemical harvest.

One more example of fruitful circumstance must suffice. In our universe the neutron is about 0.1% more massive than the proton. Another way of saying it is that the neutron – proton mass difference is about twice the mass of an electron. If the difference were greater, neutrons would decay into protons inside nuclei, which would then be blown apart by electromagnetism, so that hydrogen would be the *only* possible element. If the difference were a little less, free neutrons would not decay into protons (an essential process in the early universe, as we have seen, for it yields the necessary cosmic presence of hydrogen). Incidentally, the fact that the electron mass is so much less than that of protons and neutrons implies that the nucleus of an atom is little affected by the motion of its orbiting electrons, permitting molecules to have a stable shape and position and so permitting solids to exist.

One could continue multiplying anthropic conditions of this kind but enough has been said to indicate the character of the scientific insights involved. We should now go on to ask what one makes of it all? Some reply that nothing can be learnt from one instance and we have only one universe accessible to our inquiry. Yet the whole nature of the argument has been that we can *imagine* universes that are similar to our own and that when we do so we find that only those extremely "nearby" in their physical characteristics would be capable of a fruitful history. In the space of ontologically conceivable universe, we are surrounded by a large sterile patch (so to speak). Adopting a philosophical parable told by the philosopher John Leslie, if there is a single fly on a big blank wall, its being hit by a bullet surely calls for some sort of explanation. Either a marksman has been at work or many shots were fired, one of which by chance hit this isolated target. I will return to the detail of this parable in due course.

Inflation

Another suggestion that has been made is that maybe the remarkable coincidences which the evolution of life seems to require are in fact entailments of a some deeper physical theory. It is possible to give an example of this happening. One anthropic necessity is that the very early universe should be characterized by a very precise balance between the explosive effect of the Big Bang, driving matter apart, and the attractive pull of gravity, drawing matter together. If these were out of kilter with each other, either the universe would rapidly become too dilute for anything interesting to happen (if expansion dominated) or it would recollapse before anything interesting had time to happen (if gravity predominated). If one makes the simplest extrapolation back to the Planck time when the universe was 10^{-43} second old (the earliest time at which one can even pretend to say anything sensible with current knowledge) the balance between the two seems to need to be better than one part in 10^{60}. Paul Davies neatly interprets this degree of accuracy as corresponding to hitting a target an inch wide on the other side of the observable universe! When this condition was first recognized, it was thought that this was a very delicate balance that had to be built into the initial conditions of the universe. Now, most physicists believe that it would be achieved, almost whatever the literally initial circumstances, by a process called inflation, which is thought to have intervened when the universe was about 10^{-35} seconds old. It is supposed that there was then a kind of boiling of space which would have had as its consequence that it subsequently left the universe in a perfect balance between expansion and gravitational attraction.

Yet not every conceivable universe could have had an inflationary scenario as part of its history. That possibility itself requires that the laws of nature (now referring to the Grand Unified Theory thought to lie behind presently observed forces) would have had to take a particular form. One anthropic condition has been replaced by another. There is, it seems to me, bound to be something specifically necessary to provide the basis of fertility. The universe does not have *a priori* to be quantum mechanical, or gravitational, though both of these aspects of its nature play essential roles in determining the character of its evolution of life. Even if (as some speculate, but which does not seem all that likely to me) there is only one fundamental theory incorporating quantum gravity, it would still surely be remarkable that that unique possibility *also* provided all that was necessary for life's evolution; that is to say that gravity and quantum theory were not only anthropically necessary but also anthropically sufficient.

The Carbon Principle

Much the most difficult to evaluate of the criticisms of anthropic arguments is that which points out that the principle should really be called the Carbon Principle, or at most the Nuclear Principle, since so many of its conditions relate to the generation of the chemical elements necessary for carbon-based life, together with the resulting properties of matter. Isn't this just a lack of imagination? Might not other universes have their own forms of "life", totally different from any that we can conceive but perfectly appropriate to their physical circumstances?

Something like consciousness seems to demand an immensely complicated physical carrier. There are as many neurons in our brains as there are stars in the Milky Way (10^{11}) and their interconnections are fantastically complex. It is impossible to say what radically different ways there might be for generating comparable complexity in totally different circumstances, but those who rely on this possibility to dismiss any significance in the fine-tuning of our own universe are drawing intellectual blank cheques on totally unknown accounts. I conclude that it is reasonable to continue to discuss the question of what significance attaches to these scientific insights.

A minimal response would be represented by what some call the Weak Anthropic Principle: the existence of human life imposes certain conditions on the universe and we observe that these must be consistent with our being here to do the observing. John Barrow and Frank Tipler give this formal expression:

> The observed values of all physical and cosmological quantities are not equally probable but they take on values restricted by the requirement that there exist sites where carbon-based life can evolve and by the requirement that the Universe be old enough for it to have already done so.

The Weak Anthropic Principle amounts to little more than tautology. "we're here and so things are the way that makes that possible." It fails adequately to encapsulate the remarkable degree of "fine-tuning" involved in spelling out the conditions that have permitted our evolution. Only a tiny fraction of conceivable universes could have been the homes of conscious beings.

Much too strong as a *scientific* principle is Barrow and Tipler's formulation of the Strong Anthropic Principle:

> The Universe must have those properties which allow life to develop within it at some stage of its history.

Where could such a necessity originate from within science alone, if that discipline has forsworn any consideration of purpose? The Strong Anthropic Principle is frankly teleological in its insistence that the world "must" have been that way.

A Philosophical Parable

In my restrained English way, I have suggested a Moderate Anthropic Principle:

> which notes the contingent fruitfulness of the universe as being a fact of interest calling for an explanation.

We are back with Leslie's fly on the blank wall. Why did the shot hit its apparent target so accurately? We should not merely shrug our shoulders and say it just happened that way. Actually we need to enhance the story somewhat. Let us replace the not intrinsically important fly with a tiny button, which on its being struck opens up the door of a secret treasure house. It is not long odds that make an event particularly notable, but only their combination with some other source of meaning that then makes that particular event the carrier of significance. Any specific layout of small white stones on green grass is hugely improbable, because there are so many possible configurations in which they might lie. It is only when there is something extra associated with such a pattern – such as its forming the letters SOS – that we think an explanation is called for. The evolution of conscious life seems the most significant thing that has happened in cosmic history and we are right to be intrigued by the fact that so special a universe is required for its possibility.

It is interesting how resistant some scientists are to seeking wider understanding. Heinz Pagels criticized the Anthropic Principle because it is not subject to experimental falsification, "a sure sign that it is not a scientific principle". One wonders if Pagels regarded the theory of evolution as as scientific principle and what was the experiment he thought would falsify it. When he goes on to say "I would opt for rejecting the anthropic principle as needless clutter in the conceptual repertoire of science", he displays a sad reluctance to lift his eyes beyond the horizon of the most narrow construal of scientific knowledge. We do not need to condemn ourselves to so impoverished a view. The question of the significance of the Anthropic Principle is a scientific *metaquestion*; that is to say it arises from the insights of scientific cosmology but it goes beyond what science alone is competent to discuss. We are concerned here, not with physics, but with metaphysics – and that is as true of those who deny a significance to the Principle as it is of those who wish to seek for a more profound understanding. In addressing questions of purpose or non-purpose, they are going beyond the self-limited domain of scientific discourse.

Leslie's philosophical story indicates the two possible lines along which a deeper intelligibility might be found. The fly was hit *either* because very many bullets were hitting the wall *or* because a marksman had taken careful aim.

The first explanation translates into a many-universes understanding of anthropic significance. If there are many, many different universes, each with its own physical laws and circumstances, then, somewhere in that vast portfolio of realized possibilities, there might well, "by chance", be a world with just the right conditions for the evolution of carbon-based life. That is the universe in which we live, of course, because we could not have appeared in any other. If you fire enough bullets, one of them may just happen to hit the fly.

Many Universes

The first thing to ask about this explanation is whether it is offered to us as physics or as metaphysics. One physical way of realizing a variety of different sets of effective laws of nature is provided by the concept of spontaneous symmetry breaking. When our universe was very hot and energetic, immediately after the Big Bang, it is supposed that the operative laws of nature were those of the (hypothesized) highly symmetrical Grand Unified Theory (GUT). As expansion cooled the universe, the symmetries present in the GUT were broken and the laws of nature as we now observe them crystallized out in the course of this process. Some of the details of the laws that we actually experience (including precise values of their force constants) depend upon the unpredictable way in which that symmetry breaking actually took place. It did not have to occur in a literally universal way. There could be different cosmic domains in which the details were different and, in consequence, the effective forces of nature would be different. It is supposed in this account that our experience of the universal character of natural law in that part of the universe where we are able to observe it is due to its domain wall (its interface with its differing neighbours) having been blown far away by the process of inflation.

If this speculative account is correct, it describes a universe that is a mosaic of (vast) sub-universes, in each of which a different set of force constants would be operating. These many sub-worlds would play the role of the bullets in the parable. We live in that domain where it has been possible for us to evolve. If true, this picture would go some way towards explaining anthropic coincidences. However, there would still be significant anthropic conditions to be satisfied by the universe as a whole. For example, its basic GUT would have to be such that under spontaneous symmetry breaking it could yield *appropriate* effective laws of nature. Not all GUTs would have this property. Thus, a total explanation of the Anthropic Principle would still call for an ensemble of different universes (in the large sense) and not just for an array of domains or sub-universes.

Other speculative attempts at a "physical" explanation clearly go beyond science itself. This is true of the proposal that the universe has been undergoing a sequence of expansions followed by collapses, a chain of Big Bangs followed by Big Crunches, and that from each crunch it bounces back with totally different physical laws. The singularity of Big Crunch/Big Bang is inaccessible to scientific thought and it is pure metaphysics to postulate that it wipes the physical slate clean and enables a quantitatively different universe to emerge.

Others have appealed to the highly contentious "many-worlds" interpretation of quantum theory. This supposes that the different outcomes of a quantum measurement all actually occur, but in disjoint worlds into which physical reality splits at each such act of measurement. Such speculative prodigality has appealed to comparatively few physicists, but even if it were true, the result would be the generation of worlds with different histories but not universes with different laws of nature. The many worlds differ only in the consequences of measurement, not in their physical fabric.

Thus, even after exploiting the ambiguities of spontaneous symmetry breaking, a full many-universes explanation of anthropic coincidences is metaphysical in character, depending upon an appeal to the existence of worlds of whose being we can have no direct, scientifically motivated, knowledge. It is a metaphysical guess that they might be there.

Creation

It is also a metaphysical guess that there might be a God whose will and purpose is expressed in a single universe, endowed by its Creator with just the physical fabric that will permit it to enjoy a fruitful history. This, of course, is the appropriate translation of the marksman solution to the problem of the shot that hit the fly on the wall. There was a purpose behind that careful aim. Notice that this theistic understanding of anthropic fruitfulness contains a complete answer to the anthropomorphic criticisms of David Hume, directed against less sophisticated accounts of creation. God's conferring on the natural world the power to make itself through an evolving history realizing that endowment of fertility is as far as could be from the image of human craft engaged in moulding pre-existing material. This new natural theology is not presented as a rival to science, as if it were an alternative explanation of the process of the world, but as a complement to science, making more deeply intelligible those fine-tuned natural laws that science must *assume* as the general basis of its explanations of particular occurrences. (We can note that the other main criticism made by Hume – that the existence of suffering in the world shows "creation" to be very imperfect – can at least be addressed by the insight that this is the necessary cost of a universe allowed to make itself, whose shuffling explorations of possibility will have to have ragged edges.) […] How are we to judge the matter? […] I believe that in the delicate fine-tuning of physical law, which has made the evolution of conscious beings possible, we receive a valuable, if indirect, hint from science that there is a divine meaning and purpose behind cosmic history.

Tuning in String Theory's Multiverse*

LEONARD SUSSKIND

Why are physicists taking the idea of multiple universes seriously now?

First, there was the discovery in the past few years that inflation seems right. This theory that the universe expanded spectacularly in the first fraction of a second fits a lot of data. Inflation tells us that the universe is probably extremely big and necessarily diverse. On sufficiently big scales, and if inflation lasts long enough, this diversity will produce every possible universe. The same process that forged our universe in a big bang will happen over and over. The mathematics are rickety, but that's what inflation implies: a huge universe with patches that are very different from one another. The bottom line is that we no longer have any good reason to believe that our tiny patch of universe is representative of the whole thing.

Second was the discovery that the value of the cosmological constant – the energy of empty space which contributes to the expansion rate of the universe – seems absurdly improbable, and nothing in fundamental physics is able to explain why. I remember when Steven Weinberg first suggested that the cosmological constant might be anthropically determined – that it has to be this way otherwise we would not be here to observe it. I was very impressed with the argument, but troubled by it. Like everybody else, I thought the cosmological constant was probably zero – meaning that all the quantum fluctuations that make up the vacuum energy cancel out, and gravity alone affects the expansion of the universe. It would be much easier to explain if they cancelled out to zero, rather than to nearly zero.

*   From Leonard Susskind, "Because We're Here." Interview in the *New Scientist*, vol. 188 no. 2530 (17 December 2005), pp. 48–50. © 2005 Reed Business Information UK. All rights reserved. Distributed by Tribune Media Services International.

The discovery that there is a non-zero cosmological constant changed everything. Still, those two things were not enough to tip the balance for me.

What finally convinced you?
The discovery in string theory of this large landscape of solutions, of different vacuums, which describe very different physical environments, tipped the scales for me. At first, string theorists thought there were about a million solutions. Thinking about Weinberg's argument and about the non-zero cosmological constant, I used to go around asking my mathematician friends: are you sure it's only a million? They all assured me it was the best bet.

But a million is not enough for anthropic explanations – the chances of one of the universes being suitable for life are still too small. When Joe Polchinski and Raphael Bousso wrote their paper in 2000 that revealed there are more like 10^{500} vacuums in string theory, that to me was the tipping point. The three things seemed to be coming together. I felt I couldn't ignore this possibility, so I wrote a paper saying so. The initial reaction was very hostile, but over the past couple of years people are taking it more seriously. They are worried that it might be true.

Steven Weinberg recently said that this is one of the great sea changes in fundamental science since Einstein, that it changes the nature of science itself. Is it such a radical change?
In a way it is very radical but in another way it isn't. The great ambition of physicists like myself was to explain why the laws of nature are just what they are. Why is the proton just about 1800 times heavier than the electron? Why do neutrinos exist? The great hope was that some deep mathematical principle would determine all the constants of nature, like Newton's constant. But it seems increasingly likely that the constants of nature are more like the temperature of the Earth – properties of our local environment that vary from place to place. Like the temperature, many of the constants have to be just so if intelligent life is to exist. So we live where life is possible.

For some physicists this idea is an incredible disappointment. Personally, I don't see it that way. I find it exciting to think that the universe may be much bigger, richer and full of variety than we ever expected. And it doesn't seem so incredibly philosophically radical to think that some things may be environmental.

In order to accept the idea that we live in a hospitable patch of a multiverse, must a physicist trade in that dream of a final theory?
Absolutely not. No more than when physicists discovered that the radii of planetary orbits were not determined by some elegant mathematical equation, or by Kepler's idea of nested Platonic solids. We simply have to reassess which things will be universal consequences of the theory and which will be consequences of cosmic history and local conditions.

**So even if you accept the multiverse and the idea that certain local
physical laws are anthropically determined, you still need a
unique mega-theory to describe the whole multiverse? Surely it
just pushes the question back?**

Yes, absolutely. The bottom line is that we need to describe the whole thing, the
whole universe or multiverse. It's a scientific question: is the universe on the
largest scales big and diverse or is it homogeneous? We can hope to get an
answer from string theory and we can hope to get some information from
cosmology.

There is a philosophical objection called Popperism that people raise against the
landscape idea. Popperism [after the philosopher Karl Popper] is the assertion that
a scientific hypothesis has to be falsifiable, otherwise it's just metaphysics. Other
worlds, alternative universes, things we can't see because they are beyond horizons,
are in principle unfalsifiable and therefore metaphysical – that's the objection. But
the belief that the universe beyond our causal horizon is homogeneous is just as
speculative and just as susceptible to the Popperazzi.

**Could there be some kind of selection principle that will emerge
and pick out one unique string theory and one unique universe?**

Anything is possible. My friend David Gross hopes that no selection principle
will be necessary because only one universe will prove to make sense mathematically, or something like that. But so far there is no evidence for this view.
Even most of the hard-core adherents to the uniqueness view admit that it
looks bad.

**Is it premature to invoke anthropic arguments – which assume that the
conditions for life are extremely improbable – when we don't know
how to define life?**

The logic of the anthropic principle required the strong assumption that our kind
of life is the only kind possible. Why should we presume that all life is like us –
carbon-based, needs water, and so forth? How do we know that life cannot exist
in radically different environments? If life could exist without galaxies, the argument that the cosmological constant seems improbably fine-tuned for life would
lose all of its force. And we don't know that life of all kinds can't exist in a wide
variety of circumstances, maybe in all circumstances. It is a valid objection. But
in my heart of hearts, I just don't believe that life could exist in the interior of a
star, for instance, or in a black hole.

Is it possible to test the landscape idea through observation?

One idea is to look for signs that space is negatively curved, meaning the geometry
of space-time is saddle-shaped as opposed to flat or like the surface of a sphere. It's
a long shot but not as unlikely as I previously thought. Inflation tells us that our
observable universe likely began in a different vacuum state, that decayed into our

current vacuum state. It's hard to believe that's the whole story. It seems more probable that our universe began in some other vacuum state with a much higher cosmological constant, and that the history of the multiverse is a series of quantum tunneling events from one vacuum to another. If our universe came out of another, it must be negatively curved, and we might see evidence of that today on the largest scales of the cosmic microwave background. So the landscape, at least in principle, is testable.

If we do not accept the landscape idea are we stuck with intelligent design?

I doubt that physicists will see it that way. If, for some unforeseen reason, the landscape turns out to be inconsistent – maybe for mathematical reasons, or because it disagrees with observation – I am pretty sure that physicists will go on searching for natural explanations of the world. But I have to say that if that happens, as things stand now we will be in a very awkward position. Without any explanation of nature's fine-tunings we will be hard pressed to answer the ID critics. One might argue that the hope that a mathematically unique solution will emerge is as faith-based as ID.

Tuning without God*

STEVEN WEINBERG

From *The New York Review of Books*

[I]t seems clear that we will never be able to explain our most fundamental scientific principles. (Maybe this is why some people say that science does not provide explanations, but by this reasoning nothing else does either.) I think that in the end we will come to a set of simple universal laws of nature, laws that we cannot explain. The only kind of explanation I can imagine (if we are not just going to find a deeper set of laws, which would then just push the question farther back) would be to show that mathematical consistency requires these laws. But this is clearly impossible, because we can already imagine sets of laws of nature that, as far as we can tell, are completely consistent mathematically but that do not describe nature as we observe it.

For example, if you take the Standard Model of elementary particles and just throw away everything except the strong nuclear forces and the particles on which they act, the quarks and the gluons, you are left with the theory known

*   "Can Science Explain Everything? Anything?", *New York Review of Books*, vol. 48 no. 9 (31 May 2011), pp. 47–50. © Steven Weinberg 2011, reprinted with kind permission of the author; and from "Living in the Multiverse," in B. Carr, ed., *Universe or Multiverse?* (Cambridge: Cambridge University Press, 2007), pp. 29–42. © Cambridge University Press 2007. Reprinted with permission.

as quantum chromodynamics. It seems that quantum chromodynamics is mathematically self-consistent, but it describes an impoverished universe in which there are only nuclear particles – there are no atoms, there are no people. If you give up quantum mechanics and relativity, then you can make up a huge variety of other logically consistent laws of nature, like Newton's laws describing a few particles endlessly orbiting each other in accordance with these laws, with nothing else in the universe, and nothing new ever happening. These are logically consistent theories, but they are all impoverished. Perhaps our best hope for a final explanation is to discover a set of final laws of nature and show that this is the only logically consistent rich theory, rich enough for example to allow for the existence of ourselves. This may happen in a century or two, and if it does then I think that physicists will be at the extreme limits of their power of explanation. [...]

From *Universe or Multiverse?*

Now we may be at a new turning point, a radical change in what we accept as a legitimate foundation for a physical theory. The current excitement is of course a consequence of the recent discovery of a vast number of solutions of string theory. The consistency conditions of string theory are most naturally satisfied in ten space-time dimensions. In order to account for the fact that we only perceive one time and three space dimensions, it is necessary to suppose that the extra six dimensions are tightly rolled up. The shape of this compact six-dimensional space is characterized by a large number of integers, which specify the way that various fields thread through holes and handles in the space, and each of these integers can take a large number of values. It has been estimated that the number of solutions for the way that the six extra dimensions are rolled up is of order 10^{100} to 10^{500} – that is, a one followed by one hundred to five hundred zeroes. String theorists have picked up the term "string landscape" for this multiplicity of solutions from biochemistry, where the possible choices of orientation of each chemical bond in large molecules leads to a vast number of possible configurations. Unless one can find a reason to reject all but a few of the string theory solutions, we may have to accept that much of what we had hoped to calculate are environmental parameters, characterizing the particular solution of the equations of string theory that describes our subuniverse. Then these constants would be like the distance of the Earth from the Sun, whose value we will never be able to deduce from first principles.

We lose some, and win some. The larger the number of possible values of physical parameters provided by the string landscape, the more string theory legitimates anthropic reasoning as a new basis for physical theories: Any scientists who study nature must live in a part of the landscape where physical parameters take values suitable for the appearance of life and its evolution into scientists, and it is likely that such parts of the landscape exist if physical parameters take sufficiently many different values in different parts of the string landscape. [...]

Some physicists have expressed a strong distaste for anthropic arguments. (I have heard David Gross say "I hate it.") This is understandable. Theories based on anthropic calculation certainly represent a retreat from what we had hoped for: the calculation of all fundamental parameters from first principles. It is too soon to give up on this hope, but without loving it we may just have to resign ourselves to a retreat, just as Newton had to give up Kepler's hope of a calculation of the relative sizes of planetary orbits from first principles.

There is also a less creditable reason for hostility to the idea of a multiverse, based on the fact that we will never be able to observe any subuniverses except our own. [...] There are various other ingredients of accepted theories that we will never be able to observe, without our being led to reject these theories. The test of a physical theory is not that everything in it should be observable and every prediction it makes should be testable, but rather that enough is observable and enough predictions are testable to give us confidence that the theory is right.

Finally, I have heard the objection that, in trying to explain why the laws of nature are so well suited for the appearance and evolution of life, anthropic arguments take on some of the flavor of religion. I think that just the opposite is the case. Just as Darwin and Wallace explained how the wonderful adaptations of living forms could arise without supernatural intervention, so the string landscape may explain how the constants of nature that we observe can take values suitable for life without being fine-tuned by a benevolent creator. [...]

I found a report of a discussion at a conference at Stanford, at which Martin Rees said that he was sufficiently confident about the multiverse to bet his dog's life on it, while Andrei Linde said he would bet his own life. As for me, I have just enough confidence about the multiverse to bet the lives of both Andrei Linde *and* Martin Rees's dog.

Varieties of Multiverse*

MAX TEGMARK

Is there a copy of you reading this article? A person who is not you but who lives on a planet called Earth, with misty mountains, fertile fields and sprawling cities, in a solar system with eight other planets? The life of this person has been identical

---

*   From "Parallel Universes," *Scientific American* (May 2003), pp. 3–13. Text only. © 2003 Scientific American, Inc. All rights reserved. Reprinted with permission of Scientific American.

to yours in every respect. But perhaps he or she now decides to put down this article without finishing it, while you read on.

The idea of such an alter ego seems strange and implausible, but it looks as if we will just have to live with it, because it is supported by astronomical observations. The simplest and most popular cosmological model today predicts that you have a twin in a galaxy about 10 to the 10^{28} meters from here. This distance is so large that it is beyond astronomical, but that does not make your droppelgänger any less real. The estimate is derived from elementary probability and does not even assume speculative modern physics, merely that space is infinite (or at least sufficiently large) in size and almost uniformly filled with matter, as observations indicate. In infinite space, even the most unlikely events must take place somewhere. There are infinitely many other inhabited planets, including not just one but infinitely many that have people with the same appearance, name and memories as you, who play out every possible permutation of your life choices.

You will probably never see your other selves. The farthest you can observe is the distance that light has been able to travel during the 14 billion years since the big bang expansion began. The most distant visible objects are now about 4×10^{26} meters away – a distance that defines our observable universe, also called our Hubble volume, our horizon volume or simply our universe. Likewise, the universes of your other selves are spheres of the same size centered on their planets. They are the most straightforward example of parallel universes. Each universe is merely a small part of a larger "multiverse."

By this very definition of "universe," one might expect the notion of a multiverse to be forever in the domain of metaphysics. Yet the borderline between physics and metaphysics is defined by whether a theory is experimentally testable, not by whether it is weird or involves unobservable entities. The frontiers of physics have gradually expanded to incorporate ever more abstract (and once metaphysical) concepts such as a round Earth, invisible electromagnetic fields, time slowdown at high speeds, quantum superpositions, curved space, and black holes. Over the past several years the concept of a multiverse has joined this list. It is grounded in well-tested theories such as relativity and quantum mechanics, and it fulfills both of the basic criteria of an empirical science: it makes predictions, and it can be falsified. Scientists have discussed as many as four distinct types of parallel universes. The key question is not whether the multiverse exists but rather how many levels it has.

Level I: Beyond Our Cosmic Horizon

The parallel universes of your alter egos constitute the Level I multiverse. It is the least controversial type. We all accept the existence of things that we cannot see but could see if we moved to a different vantage point or merely waited, like people watching for ships to come over the horizon. Objects beyond the cosmic horizon have a similar status. The observable universe grows by a light-year every year as light from farther away has time to reach us. An infinity lies out there, waiting to be seen. You will probably die long before your alter egos come into view, but in principle, and if cosmic expansion cooperated, your descendants could observe them through a sufficiently powerful telescope.

If anything, the Level I multiverse sounds trivially obvious. How could space *not* be infinite? Is there a sign somewhere saying "Space Ends Here – Mind the Gap"? If so, what lies beyond it? In fact, Einstein's theory of gravity calls this intuition into question. Space could be finite if it has a convex curvature or an unusual topology (that is, interconnectedness). A spherical, doughnut-shaped or pretzel-shaped universe would have a limited volume and no edges. The cosmic microwave background radiation allows sensitive tests of such scenarios [see "Is Space Finite?" by Jean-Pierre Luminet, Glenn D. Starkman and Jeffrey R. Weeks; *Scientific American*, April 1999]. So far, however, the evidence is against them. Infinite models fit the data, and strong limits have been placed on the alternatives.

Another possibility is that space is infinite but matter is confined to a finite region around us – the historically popular "island universe" model. In a variant on this model, matter thins out on large scales in a fractal pattern. In both cases, almost all universes in the Level I multiverse would be empty and dead. But recent observations of the three-dimensional galaxy distribution and the microwave background have shown that the arrangement of matter gives way to dull uniformity on large scales, with no coherent structures larger than about 10^{24} meters. Assuming that this pattern continues, space beyond our observable universe teems with galaxies, stars and planets.

Observers living in Level I parallel universes experience the same laws of physics as we do but with different initial conditions. According to current theories, processes early in the big bang spread matter around with a degree of randomness, generating all possible arrangements with nonzero probability. Cosmologists assume that our universe, with an almost uniform distribution of matter and initial density fluctuations of one part in 100,000, is a fairly typical one (at least among those that contain observers). That assumption underlies the estimate that your closest identical copy is 10 to the 10^{28} meters away. About 10 to the 10^{92} meters away, there should be a sphere of radius 100 light-years identical to the one centered here: all perceptions that we have during the next century will be identical to those of our counterparts over there. About 10 to the 10^{118} meters away should be an entire Hubble volume identical to ours.

These are extremely conservative estimates, derived simply by counting all possible quantum states that a Hubble volume can have if it is no hotter than 10^8 kelvins. One way to do the calculation is to ask how many protons could be packed into a Hubble volume at that temperature. The answer is 10^{118} protons. Each of those particles may or may not, in fact, be present, which makes for 2 to the 10^{118}

possible arrangements of the protons. A box containing that many Hubble volumes exhausts all the possibilities. If you round off the numbers, such a box is about 10 to the 10^{118} meters across. Beyond that box, universes – including ours – must repeat. Roughly the same number could be derived by using thermodynamic or quantum-gravitational estimates of the total information content of the universe.

Your nearest doppelgänger is most likely to be much closer than these numbers suggest, given the processes of planet formation and biological evolution that tip the odds in your favor. Astronomers suspect that our Hubble volume has at least 10^{20} habitable planets; some might well look like Earth.

The Level I multiverse framework is used routinely to evaluate theories in modern cosmology, although this procedure is rarely spelled out explicitly. For instance, consider how cosmologists used the microwave background to rule out a finite spherical geometry. Hot and cold spots in microwave background maps have a characteristic size that depends on the curvature of space, and the observed spots appear too small to be consistent with a spherical shape. But it is important to be statistically rigorous. The average spot size varies randomly from one Hubble volume to another, so it is possible that our universe is fooling us – it could be spherical but happen to have abnormally small spots. When cosmologists say they have ruled out the spherical model with 99.9 percent confidence, they really mean that if this model were true, fewer than one in 1,000 Hubble volumes would show spots as small as those we observe.

The lesson is that the multiverse theory can be tested and falsified even though we cannot see the other universes. The key is to predict what the ensemble of parallel universes is and to specify a probability distribution, or what mathematicians call a "measure," over that ensemble. Our universe should emerge as one of the most probable. If not – if, according to the multiverse theory, we live in an improbable universe – then the theory is in trouble. As I will discuss later, this measure problem can become quite challenging.

Level II: Other Postinflation Bubbles

If the Level I multiverse was hard to stomach, try imagining an infinite set of distinct Level I multiverses, some perhaps with different spacetime dimensionality and different physical constants. Those other multiverses – which constitute a Level II multiverse – are predicted by the currently popular theory of chaotic eternal inflation.

Inflation is an extension of the big bang theory and ties up many of the loose ends of that theory, such as why the universe is so big, so uniform and so flat. A rapid stretching of space long ago can explain all these and other attributes in one fell swoop [see "The Inflationary Universe," by Alan H. Guth and Paul J. Steinhardt;

Scientific American, May 1984; and "The Self-Reproducing Inflationary Universe," by Andrei Linde, November 1994]. Such stretching is predicted by a wide class of theories of elementary particles, and all available evidence bears it out. The phase "chaotic eternal" refers to what happens on the very largest scales. Space as a whole is stretching and will continue doing so forever, but some regions of space stop stretching and form distinct bubbles, like gas pockets in a loaf of rising bread. Infinitely many such bubbles emerge. Each is an embryonic Level I multiverse: infinite in size and filled with matter deposited by the energy field that drove inflation.

Those bubbles are more than infinitely far away from. Earth, in the sense that you would never get there even if you traveled at the speed of light forever. The reason is that the space between our bubble and its neighbors is expanding faster than you could travel through it. Your descendants will never see their doppelgängers elsewhere in Level II. For the same reason, if cosmic expansion is accelerating, as observations now suggest, they might not see their alter egos even in Level I.

The Level II multiverse is far more diverse than the Level I multiverse. The bubbles vary not only in their initial conditions but also in seemingly immutable aspects of nature. The prevailing view in physics today is that the dimensionality of spacetime, the qualities of elementary particles and many of the so-called physical constants are not built into physical laws but are the outcome of processes known as symmetry breaking. For instance, theorists think that the space in our universe once had nine dimensions, all on an equal footing. Early in cosmic history, three of them partook in the cosmic expansion and became the three dimensions we now observe. The other six are now unobservable, either because they have stayed microscopic with a doughnutlike topology or because all matter is confined to a three-dimensional surface (a membrane, or simply "brane") in the nine-dimensional space.

Thus, the original symmetry among the dimensions broke. The quantum fluctuations that drive chaotic inflation could cause different symmetry breaking in different bubbles. Some might become four-dimensional, others could contain only two rather than three generations of quarks, and still others might have a stronger cosmological constant than our universe does.

Another way to produce a Level II multiverse might be through a cycle of birth and destruction of universes. In a scientific context, this idea was introduced by physicist Richard C. Tolman in the 1930s and recently elaborated on by Paul J. Steinhardt of Princeton University and Neil Turok of the University of Cambridge. The Steinhardt and Turok proposal and related models involve a second three-dimensional brane that is quite literally parallel to ours, merely offset in a higher dimension [see "Been There, Done That," by George Musser; News Scan, *Scientific American*, March 2002]. This parallel universe is not really a separate universe, because it interacts with ours. But the ensemble of universes – past, present and future – that these branes create would form a multiverse, arguably with a diversity similar to that produced by chaotic inflation. An idea proposed by physicist Lee Smolin of the Perimeter Institute in Waterloo, Ontario, involves yet another multiverse comparable in diversity to that of Level II but mutating and sprouting new universes through black holes rather than through brane physics.

Although we cannot interact with other Level II parallel universes, cosmologists can infer their presence indirectly, because their existence can account for unexplained coincidences in our universe. To give an analogy, suppose you check into a hotel, are assigned room 1967 and note that this is the year you were born. What a coincidence, you say. After a moment of reflection, however, you conclude that this is not so surprising after all. The hotel has hundreds of rooms, and you would not have been having these thoughts in the first place if you had been assigned one with a number that meant nothing to you. The lesson is that even if you knew nothing about hotels, you could infer the existence of other hotel rooms to explain the coincidence.

As a more pertinent example, consider the mass of the sun. The mass of a star determines its luminosity, and using basic physics, one can compute that life as we know it on Earth is possible only if the sun's mass falls into the narrow range between 1.6×10^{30} and 2.4×10^{30} kilograms. Otherwise Earth's climate would be colder than that of present-day Mars or hotter than that of present-day Venus. The measured solar mass is 2.0×10^{30} kilograms. At first glance, this apparent coincidence of the habitable and observed mass values appears to be a wild stroke of luck. Stellar masses run from 10^{29} to 10^{32} kilograms, so if the sun acquired its mass at random, it had only a small chance of falling into the habitable range. But just as in the hotel example, one can explain this apparent coincidence by postulating an ensemble (in this case, a number of planetary systems) and a selection effect (the fact that we must find ourselves living on a habitable planet). Such observer-related selection effects are referred to as "anthropic," and although the "A-word" is notorious for triggering controversy, physicists broadly agree that these selection effects cannot be neglected when testing fundamental theories.

What applies to hotel rooms and planetary systems applies to parallel universes. Most, if not all, of the attributes set by symmetry breaking appear to be fine-tuned. Changing their values by modest amounts would have resulted in a qualitatively different universe – one in which we probably would not exist. If protons were 0.2 percent heavier, they could decay into neutrons, destabilizing atoms. If the electromagnetic force were 4 percent weaker, there would be no hydrogen and no normal stars. If the weak interaction were much weaker, hydrogen would not exist; if it were much stronger, supernovae would fail to seed interstellar space with heavy elements. If the cosmological constant were much larger, the universe would have blown itself apart before galaxies could form.

Although the degree of fine-tuning is still debated, these examples suggest the existence of parallel universes with other values of the physical constants [see "Exploring Our Universe and Others," by Martin Rees; *Scientific American*, December 1999]. The Level II multiverse theory predicts that physicists will never be able to determine the values of these constants from first principles. They will merely compute probability distributions for what they should expect to find, taking selection effects into account. The result should be as generic as is consistent with our existence.

Level III: Quantum Many Worlds

The Level I and Level II multiverses involve parallel worlds that are far away, beyond the domain even of astronomers. But the next level of multiverse is right around you. It arises from the famous, and famously controversial, many-worlds interpretation of quantum mechanics – the idea that random quantum processes cause the universe to branch into multiple copies, one for each possible outcome.

In the early 20th century the theory of quantum mechanics revolutionized physics by explaining the atomic realm, which does not abide by the classical rules of Newtonian mechanics. Despite the obvious successes of the theory, a heated debate rages about what it really means. The theory specifies the state of the universe not in classical terms, such as the positions and velocities of all particles, but in terms of a mathematical object called a wave function. According to the Schrödinger equation, this state evolves over time in a fashion that mathematicians term "unitary," meaning that the wave function rotates in an abstract infinite-dimensional space called Hilbert space. Although quantum mechanics is often described as inherently random and uncertain the wave function evolves in a deterministic way There is nothing random or uncertain about it.

The sticky part is how to connect this wave function with what we observe. Many legitimate wave functions correspond to counterintuitive situations, such as a cat being dead and alive at the same time in a so-called superposition. In the 1920s physicists explained away this weirdness by postulating that the wave function "collapsed" into some definite classical outcome whenever someone made an observation. This add-on had the virtue of explaining observations, but it turned an elegant, unitary theory into a kludgy, nonunitary one. The intrinsic randomness commonly ascribed to quantum mechanics is the result of this postulate.

Over the years many physicists have abandoned this view in favor of one developed in 1957 by Princeton graduate student Hugh Everett III. He showed that the collapse postulate is unnecessary. Unadulterated quantum theory does not, in fact, pose any contradictions. Although it predicts that one classical reality gradually splits into superpositions of many such realities, observers subjectively experience this splitting merely as a slight randomness, with probabilities in exact agreement with those from the old collapse postulate. This superposition of classical worlds is the Level III multiverse.

Everett's many-worlds interpretation has been boggling minds inside and outside physics for more than four decades. But the theory becomes easier to grasp when one distinguishes between two ways of viewing a physical theory: the outside view of a physicist studying its mathematical equations, like a bird surveying a landscape from high above it, and the inside view of an observer living in the world described by the equations, like a frog living in the landscape surveyed by the bird.

From the bird perspective, the Level III multiverse is simple. There is only one wave function. It evolves smoothly and deterministically over time without any kind of splitting or parallelism. The abstract quantum world described by this evolving wave function contains within it a vast number of parallel classical story lines, continuously splitting and merging, as well as a number of quantum phenomena that lack a classical description. From their frog perspective, observers perceive only a tiny fraction of this full reality. They can view their own Level I universe, but a process called decoherence – which mimics wave function collapse while preserving unitarity – prevents them from seeing Level III parallel copies of themselves.

Whenever observers are asked a question, make a snap decision and give an answer, quantum effects in their brains lead to a superposition of outcomes, such as "Continue reading the article" and "Put down the article." From the bird perspective, the act of making a decision causes a person to split into multiple copies: one who keeps on reading and one who doesn't. From their frog perspective, however, each of these alter egos is unaware of the others and notices the branching merely as a slight randomness: a certain probability of continuing to read or not.

As strange as this may sound, the exact same situation occurs even in the Level I multiverse. You have evidently decided to keep on reading the article, but one of your alter egos in a distant galaxy put down the magazine after the first paragraph. The only difference between Level I and Level III is where your doppelgängers reside. In Level I they live elsewhere in good old three-dimensional space. In Level III they live on another quantum branch in infinite-dimensional Hilbert space.

The existence of Level III depends on one crucial assumption: that the time evolution of the wave function is unitary. So far experimenters have encountered no departures from unitarity. In the past few decades they have confirmed unitarity for ever larger systems, including carbon 60 buckyball molecules and kilometer-long optical fibers. On the theoretical side, the case for unitarity has been bolstered by the discovery of decoherence [see "100 Years of Quantum Mysteries," by Max Tegmark and John Archibald Wheeler; *Scientific American*, February 2001]. Some theorists who work on quantum gravity have questioned unitarity; one concern is that evaporating black holes might destroy information, which would be a nonunitary process. But a recent breakthrough in string theory known as Ads/CFT correspondence suggests that even quantum gravity is unitary. If so, black holes do not destroy information but merely transmit it elsewhere.

If physics is unitary, then the standard picture of how quantum fluctuations operated early in the big bang must change. These fluctuations did not generate initial conditions at random. Rather they generated a quantum superposition of all possible initial conditions, which coexisted simultaneously. Decoherence then caused these initial conditions to behave classically in separate quantum branches. Here is the crucial point: the distribution of outcomes on different quantum branches in a given Hubble volume (Level III) is identical to the distribution of outcomes in different Hubble volumes within a single quantum branch (Level I). This property of the quantum fluctuations is known in statistical mechanics as ergodicity.

The same reasoning applies to Level II. The process of symmetry breaking did not produce a unique outcome but rather a superposition of all outcomes, which rapidly went their separate ways. So if physical constants, spacetime dimensionality and so on can vary among parallel quantum branches at Level III, then they will also vary among parallel universes at Level II.

In other words, the Level III multiverse adds nothing new beyond Level I and Level II, just more indistinguishable copies of the same universes – the same old story lines playing out again and again in other quantum branches. The passionate debate about Everett's theory therefore seems to be ending in a grand anticlimax, with the discovery of less controversial multiverses (Levels I and II) that are equally large.

Needless to say, the implications are profound, and physicists are only beginning to explore them. For instance, consider the ramifications of the answer to a long-standing question: Does the number of universes exponentially increase over time? The surprising answer is no. From the bird perspective, there is of course only one quantum universe. From the frog perspective, what matters is the number of universes that are distinguishable at a given instant – that is, the number of noticeably different Hubble volumes. Imagine moving planets to random new locations, imagine having married someone else, and so on. At the quantum level, there are 10 to the 10^{118} universes with temperatures below 10^8 kelvins. That is a vast number, but a finite one.

From the frog perspective, the evolution of the wave function corresponds to a never-ending sliding from one of these 10 to the 10^{118} states to another. Now you are in universe A, the one in which you are reading this sentence. Now you are in universe B, the one in which you are reading this other sentence. Put differently, universe B has an observer identical to one in universe A, except with an extra instant of memories. All possible states exist at every instant, so the passage of time may be in the eye of the beholder – an idea explored in Greg Egan's 1994 science-fiction novel *Permutation City* and developed by physicist David Deutsch of the University of Oxford, independent physicist Julian Barbour and others. The multiverse framework may thus prove essential to understanding the nature of time.

Level IV: Other Mathematical Structures

The initial conditions and physical constants in the Level I, Level II and Level III multiverses can vary, but the fundamental laws that govern nature remain the same. Why stop there? Why not allow the laws themselves to vary? How about a universe that obeys the laws of classical physics, with no quantum effects? How about time that comes in discrete steps, as for computers, instead of being continuous? How about a universe that is simply an empty dodecahedron? In the Level IV multiverse, all these alternative realities actually exist.

A hint that such a multiverse might not be just some beer-fueled speculation is the tight correspondence between the worlds of abstract reasoning and of observed reality. Equations and, more generally, mathematical structures such as numbers, vectors and geometric objects describe the world with remarkable verisimilitude. In a famous 1959 lecture, physicist Eugene P. Wigner argued that "the enormous usefulness of mathematics in the natural sciences is something bordering on the mysterious." Conversely, mathematical structures have an eerily real feel to them. They satisfy a central criterion of objective existence: they are the same no matter who studies them. A theorem is true regardless of whether it is proved by a human, a computer or an intelligent dolphin. Contemplative alien civilizations would find the same mathematical structures as we have. Accordingly, mathematicians commonly say that they discover mathematical structures rather than create them.

There are two tenable but diametrically opposed paradigms for understanding the correspondence between mathematics and physics, a dichotomy that arguably goes as far back as Plato and Aristotle. According to the Aristotelian paradigm, physical reality is fundamental and mathematical language is merely a useful approximation. According to the Platonic paradigm, the mathematical structure is the true reality and observers perceive it imperfectly. In other words, the two paradigms disagree on which is more basic, the frog perspective of the observer or the bird perspective of the physical laws. The Aristotelian paradigm prefers the frog perspective, whereas the Platonic paradigm prefers the bird perspective.

As children, long before we had even heard of mathematics, we were all indoctrinated with the Aristotelian paradigm. The Platonic view is an acquired taste. Modern theoretical physicists tend to be Platonists, suspecting that mathematics describes the universe so well because the universe is inherently mathematical. Then all of physics is ultimately a mathematics problem; a mathematician with unlimited intelligence and resources could in principle compute the frog perspective – that is, compute what self-aware observers the universe contains, what they perceive, and what languages they invent to describe their perceptions to one another.

A mathematical structure is an abstract, immutable entity existing outside of space and time. If history were a movie, the structure would correspond not to a single frame of it but to the entire videotape. Consider, for example, a world made up of pointlike particles moving around in three-dimensional space. In four-dimensional spacetime – the bird perspective – these particle trajectories resemble a tangle of spaghetti. If the frog sees a particle moving with constant velocity, the bird sees a straight strand of uncooked spaghetti. If the frog sees a pair of orbiting particles, the bird sees two spaghetti strands intertwined like a double helix. To the frog, the world is described by Newton's laws of motion and gravitation. To the bird, it is described by the geometry of the pasta – a mathematical structure. The frog itself is merely a thick bundle of pasta, whose highly complex intertwining corresponds to a cluster of particles that store and process information. Our universe is far more complicated than this example, and scientists do not yet know to what, if any, mathematical structure it corresponds.

The Platonic paradigm raises the question of why the universe is the way it is. To an Aristotelian, this is a meaningless question: the universe just is. But a Platonist cannot help but wonder why it could not have been different. If the universe is inherently mathematical, then why was only one of the many mathematical structures singled out to describe a universe? A fundamental asymmetry appears to be built into the very heart of reality.

As a way out of this conundrum, I have suggested that complete mathematical symmetry holds: that all mathematical structures exist physically as well. Every mathematical structure corresponds to a parallel universe. The elements of this multiverse do not reside in the same space but exist outside of space and time. Most of them are probably devoid of observers. This hypothesis can be viewed as a form of radical Platonism, asserting that the mathematical structures in Plato's realm of ideas or the "mindscape" of mathematician Rudy Rucker of San Jose State University exist in a physical sense. It is akin to what cosmologist John D. Barrow of the University of Cambridge refers to as "π in the sky," what the late Harvard University philosopher Robert Nozick called the principle of fecundity and what the late Princeton philosopher David K. Lewis called modal realism. Level IV brings closure to the hierarchy of multiverses, because any self-consistent fundamental physical theory can be phrased as some kind of mathematical structure.

The Level IV multiverse hypothesis makes testable predictions. As with Level II, it involves an ensemble (in this case, the full range of mathematical structures) and selection effects. As mathematicians continue to categorize mathematical structures, they should find that the structure describing our world is the most generic one consistent with our observations. Similarly, our future observations should be the most generic ones that are consistent with our past observations, and our past observations should be the most generic ones that are consistent with our existence.

Quantifying what "generic" means is a severe problem, and this investigation is only now beginning. But one striking and encouraging feature of mathematical structures is that the symmetry and invariance properties that are responsible for the simplicity and orderliness of our universe tend to be generic, more the rule than the exception. Mathematical structures tend to have them by default, and complicated additional axioms must be added to make them go away.

What Says Occam?

The scientific theories of parallel universes, therefore, form a four-level hierarchy, in which universes become progressively more different from ours. They might have different initial conditions (Level I); different physical constants and particles (Level II); or different physical laws (Level IV). It is ironic that Level III is the one that has drawn the most fire in the past decades, because it is the only one that adds no qualitatively new types of universes.

In the coming decade, dramatically improved cosmological measurements of the microwave background and the large-scale matter distribution will support or refute Level I by further pinning down the curvature and topology of space. These measurements will also probe Level II by testing the theory of chaotic eternal inflation. Progress in both astrophysics and high-energy physics should also clarify the extent to which physical constants are fine-tuned, thereby weakening or strengthening the case for Level II.

If current efforts to build quantum computers succeed, they will provide further evidence for Level III, as they would, in essence, be exploiting the parallelism of the Level III multiverse for parallel computation. Experimenters are also looking for evidence of unitarity violation, which would rule out Level III. Finally, success or failure in the grand challenge of modern physics – unifying general relativity and quantum field theory – will sway opinions on Level IV. Either we will find a mathematical structure that exactly matches our universe, or we will bump up against a limit to the unreasonable effectiveness of mathematics and have to abandon that level.

So should you believe in parallel universes? The principal arguments against them are that they are wasteful and that they are weird. The first argument is that multiverse theories are vulnerable to Occam's razor because they postulate the existence of other worlds that we can never observe. Why should nature be so wasteful and indulge in such opulence as an infinity of different worlds? Yet this argument can be turned around to argue *for* a multiverse. What precisely would nature be wasting? Certainly not space, mass or atoms – the uncontroversial Level I multiverse already contains an infinite amount of all three, so who cares if nature wastes some more? The real issue here is the apparent reduction in simplicity. A skeptic worries about all the information necessary to specify all those unseen worlds.

But an entire ensemble is often much simpler than one of its members. This principle can be stated more formally using the notion of algorithmic information content. The algorithmic information content in a number is, roughly speaking, the length of the shortest computer program that will produce that number as output. For example, consider the set of all integers. Which is simpler, the whole set or just one number? Naively, you might think that a single number is simpler, but the entire set can be generated by quite a trivial computer program, whereas a single number can be hugely long. Therefore, the whole set is actually simpler.

Similarly, the set of all solutions to Einstein's field equations is simpler than a specific solution. The former is described by a few equations, whereas the latter requires the specification of vast amounts of initial data on some hypersurface. The lesson is that complexity increases when we restrict our attention to one particular element in an ensemble, thereby losing the symmetry and simplicity that were inherent in the totality of all the elements taken together.

In this sense, the higher-level multiverses are simpler. Going from our universe to the Level I multiverse eliminates the need to specify initial conditions, upgrading to Level II eliminates the need to specify physical constants, and the Level IV multiverse eliminates the need to specify anything at all. The opulence of complexity is all in the subjective perceptions of observers – the frog perspective. From the bird perspective, the multiverse could hardly be any simpler.

The complaint about weirdness is aesthetic rather than scientific, and it really makes sense only in the Aristotelian worldview. Yet what did we expect? When we ask a profound question about the nature of reality, do we not expect an answer that sounds strange? Evolution provided us with intuition for the everyday physics that had survival value for our distant ancestors, so whenever we venture beyond the everyday world, we should expect it to seem bizarre.

A common feature of all four multiverse levels is that the simplest and arguably most elegant theory involves parallel universes by default. To deny the existence of those universes, one needs to complicate the theory by adding experimentally unsupported processes and ad hoc postulates: finite space, wave function collapse and ontological asymmetry. Our judgment therefore comes down to which we find more wasteful and inelegant: many worlds or many words. Perhaps we will gradually get used to the weird ways of our cosmos and find its strangeness to be part of its charm.

The Design of a Multiverse-Generator*

ROBIN A. COLLINS

From *Spiritual Information*

The fine-tuning of the cosmos for life refers to the fact that many of the fundamental parameters of physics and the initial conditions of the universe are balanced on a razor's edge for intelligent life to occur: If these parameters were slightly different, life of comparable intelligence to our own would not exist. The first major discovery along these lines was in 1956 – that the resonance states of carbon and oxygen had to fall within a narrow range for significant quantities of both carbon and oxygen to be produced in stars. Without enough carbon and oxygen, the existence of carbon-based life would be seriously inhibited. Many other instances of cosmic fine-tuning have been brought to light since then, and much work is continuing. One of the most impressive and discussed cases of fine-tuning is that of the cosmological constant, a term in Einstein's equation of general relativity that governs the rate at which space expands. For the universe to be hospitable to life, this constant must be fine-tuned to at least one part in 10^{53} – that is, one part in one hundred million billion billion billion billion – of what physicists consider its natural range of values. To get an idea of how precise this is, it would be like throwing a dart at the surface of the earth from the moon and hitting a bull's-eye one trillionth of a trillionth of an inch in diameter – less than the size of an atom!

Many physicists and others have taken the position that fine-tuning provides significant evidence that the cosmos is designed – and, furthermore, that one of the purposes of the designer was to create embodied, intelligent beings. Others have questioned this inference by saying that, as far as we know, the values of the fundamental parameters will eventually be explained by some grand unified theory. Hence, it is argued, we do not need to invoke a designer to explain why these parameters have life-permitting values. As astrophysicists Bernard Carr and Martin Rees note, however, "even if all apparently anthropic coincidences could be explained [in terms of such a unified theory], it would still be remarkable that the relationships dictated by physical theory happened also to be those propitious for life". For the theist, then, the development of a grand unified theory would not undercut the case for design, but would only serve to deepen our appreciation of the ingenuity of the creator: Instead of separately fine-tuning each individual parameter, in this view, the designer simply carefully chose those laws that would yield life-permitting values for each parameter.

---

* From C.L. Harper, ed., *Spiritual Information: 100 Perspectives on Science and Religion* (Philadelphia and London: Templeton Foundation Press, 2005), pp. 161–163. Reprinted with permission of Templeton Press; and from B. Carr, ed., *Universe or Multiverse?* (Cambridge: Cambridge University Press, 2007), pp. 464–466. © Cambridge University Press 2007. Reprinted with permission.

Another objection to considering fine-tuning as evidence for design is one that takes us almost into the realm of science fiction: the proposal that there are a very large number of universes, each with different values for the fundamental parameters of physics. If such multiple universes exist, it would be no surprise that the parameters in one of them would have just the right values for the existence of intelligent life – just as in the case where if enough lottery tickets were generated, it would be no surprise that one of them would turn out to be the winning number. [...]

I am not objecting to the notion of many universes itself. I actually believe that theists should be open to the idea that God created our universe by means of a universe generator. It makes sense that an infinitely creative deity would create other universes, not just our own. Further, the history of science is one in which our conception of nature keeps increasing in size in terms of both space and time – from believing that the universe consisted of the Earth and a few crystalline spheres created around six thousand years ago to positing a fifteen-billion-year-old universe with more than three hundred billion galaxies. For the theist, the existence of multiple universes would simply support the view that creation reflects the *infinite creativity* of the creator. This begins to bring us to an expanded notion of a designer, one far different and more interesting than the more anthropocentric and restrained God of much traditional and popular religious thought.

From *Universe or Multiverse?*

[...] [E]ven if a multiverse-generator exists, the argument for theism from the fine-tuning of the constants for intelligent life is not completely eliminated. The argument essentially goes as follows. The multiverse-generator itself, whether of the inflationary variety or some other type, seems to need to be "well designed" in order to produce life-sustaining universes. After all, even a mundane item like a bread machine, which only produces loaves of bread instead of universes, must be well designed as an appliance and must have the right ingredients (flour, water and yeast) to produce decent loaves of bread. If this is right, then invoking some sort of multiverse-generator as an explanation of the fine-tuning serves to kick the issue of design up one level, to the question of who designed the multiverse-generator.

The inflationary multiverse scenario, widely considered as the most physically viable, provides a good test case of this line of reasoning. The inflationary multiverse-generator can only produce life-sustaining universes (or regions of spacetime) because it has the following "components" or "mechanisms":

(1)   *A mechanism to supply the energy needed for the bubble universes.* This mechanism is the hypothesized inflaton field. By imparting a constant energy density to

empty space as space expands, the inflaton field can act "as a reservoir of unlimited energy" for the bubbles.

(2) *A mechanism to form the bubbles.* This mechanism relates to Einstein's equations of general relativity. Because of their peculiar form, Einstein's equations dictate that space expands at an enormous rate in the presence of a field – like the inflaton – which imparts a constant (and homogeneous) energy density to empty space. This causes both the formation of the bubble universes and the rapid expansion which keeps them from colliding.

(3) *A mechanism to convert the energy of the inflaton field to the normal mass/energy we find in our universe.* This mechanism is Einstein's equivalence of mass and energy, combined with an hypothesized coupling between the inflaton field and normal mass/energy fields we find in our universe.

(4) *A mechanism that allows enough variation in constants of physics among universes.* Currently, the most physically viable candidate for this mechanism is superstring or M-theory. Superstring theory might allow enough variation in the constants of physics among bubble universes to make it reasonably likely that a fine-tuned universe would be produced, but no one knows for sure.

Without all these "components", the multiverse-generator would almost certainly fail to produce a single life-sustaining universe. If, for example, the universe obeyed Newton's theory of gravity instead of Einstein's, the vacuum energy of the inflaton field would at best create a gravitational attraction causing space to contract rather than expand.

In addition to the four factors listed above, the inflationary multiverse generator can only produce life-sustaining universes because the right background laws are in place. Specifically, the background laws must be such as to allow the conversion of the mass/energy into the material forms required for the sort of stable complexity needed for life. For example, without the principle of quantization, all electrons would be sucked into the atomic nuclei and hence atoms would be impossible; without the Pauli exclusion principle, electrons would occupy the lowest atomic orbit and hence complex and varied atoms would be impossible; without a universally attractive force between all masses, such as gravity, matter would not be able to form sufficiently large material bodies (such as planets) for complex, intelligent life to develop or for long-lived stable energy sources like stars to exist.

In sum, even if an inflationary multiverse-generator exists, it must involve just the right combination of laws, principles and fields for the production of life-permitting universes; if one of the components were missing or different – such as Einstein's equation or Pauli's exclusion principle – it is unlikely that any life-permitting universes could be produced. In the absence of alternative explanations, it follows from the surprise principle that the existence of such a system could be considered to suggest design since it seems very surprising that such a system would have just the right components as a brute fact, but not surprising under the theistic design hypothesis. Thus, it does not seem that one can completely escape the suggestion of design merely by hypothesizing some sort of multiverse-generator.

It must be admitted, however, that if such a multiverse-generator could be verified, the sort of *quantitative* evidence for design based on the fine-tuning of the constants would be eliminated. Whereas the degree of fine-tuning of a particular constant of physics could arguably be assigned a number – such as that corresponding to the ratio of the length of its intelligent-life-permitting range to some non-arbitrarily specified "theoretically possible" range – we cannot provide a quantitative estimate for the degree of apparent design in the cases mentioned above. All we can say is that if certain seemingly highly specific sorts of laws were not in place, no life-sustaining universes could be generated. Thus, depending on the weight one attaches to such quantitative estimates, the evidence for design would be mitigated, although not completely eliminated.

10

The Problem Seems Genuine

Editorial Introduction

Now for five authors who survey possible reactions to why there exists anything at all. Does asking why even make sense? If it does, could it well have an answer beyond "that's just how matters are"?

To Derek PARFIT, "No question is more sublime than why there is a Universe: why there is something rather than nothing." "It can seem astonishing that anything exists," and what exists "might have been, in countless ways, different." A cosmos that had existed for ever, an infinite chain of events caused by earlier events, could still be in need of an explanation. The chain could not "explain itself." Physicists have suggested that everything started with "a random fluctuation in a vacuum," but "what physicists call a vacuum isn't really nothing"; "we can ask why it exists, and has the potentialities it does." There could never be "a causal explanation of why the Universe exists, why there are any laws of nature, or why these laws are as they are," or of why God was more than a fiction. Still, this need not mean that why there exists anything at all could never be explained.

Some claim that if nothing had existed, then there would have been nothing to explain. Strictly speaking that is wrong since there'd still have been "various truths, such as the truth that there were no stars or atoms." But of all possibilities, there existing nothing "would have needed the least explanation"; it would have been "much the simplest, and the least arbitrary" (there is only one way of being nothing). Nothingness would have raised "no problem" whereas the existence of anything worth calling God, or of the entire cosmos, "can seem mysterious."

The Mystery of Existence: Why Is There Anything At All?, First Edition. Edited by John Leslie and Robert Lawrence Kuhn.

Much excitement, Parfit notes, has greeted the apparent discovery that various features of our universe "must be almost precisely as they are" for living beings to exist in it. We mustn't just comment that any universe has to possess *some* features, so why not those? Reacting like that would disregard something impressive – the fact that the universe seemed of the sort that could have been aimed at by God or by some other factor specifically concerned with producing complex life-forms. If your jailer draws the only straw out of a thousand that would save you from being shot, suspect that "this lottery was rigged." Physicists have said there was less than a one in a billion billion chance that a universe obeying the laws which our universe obeys would have initial conditions permitting life to evolve. If that is right, then we ought to reflect that the probability of a divine Designer "cannot be as low as one in a billion billion." Such a Person might be replaced by "some impersonal force or fundamental law" which is "what some theists believe God to be," yet this would only broaden the argument. Our observation of a life-permitting universe might, however, be better explained by multiple universes, varying in their features, plus the fact that living beings would necessarily find themselves in a universe that was life-permitting. Universes additional to our own would be simply "more of the kind of reality that we can observe around us," which could make belief in them easier than believing in God. And while some have claimed that God would be a reality "simpler, and less arbitrary, than the uncaused existence of many highly complicated worlds," this possible reason for preferring belief in God would be outweighed by the Problem of Evil, the existence of what seems to be "much pointless suffering."

The theory that reality is *as full as possible* might explain any apparent evidence of divine design, for the existence of universes which looked as if designed would be part of what this theory proposed. The theory would also avoid the arbitrariness of there existing exactly fifty-eight universes, for instance, or exactly ninety-nine trillion universes. What the theory proposed could thus be "less puzzling" than other possibilities, Parfit comments. We'd still be left wondering why there hadn't instead been utter emptiness, but at least we could have made some progress.

Could any conceivable theory leave nothing to be explained? "It is sometimes claimed that God, or the Universe, make themselves exist," but that's impossible; "these entities cannot do anything unless they exist." And "for reasons that have been often given" we should reject the view that it is "logically necessary that God, or the Universe, exist." We should also dismiss the idea toyed with by Einstein when he said a Creator might have had no choice of what to create, there being only a single "coherent cosmic possibility."

How about the theory of "Plato, Plotinus and others" that the universe "exists because its existence is good"? This "Axiarchic" theory – that Value rules – can take the form of claiming "that God exists because his existence is good, and the rest of the Universe exists because God caused it to exist." In that case, however, God as a Creator "is redundant" since "if God can exist because his existence is good, so can the whole Universe." This threat to their beliefs "may be why some theists reject the Axiarchic View, and insist that God's existence is a brute fact, with no explanation." Axiarchists should admit that the *because* in "exists *because* its existence is good" is something which "cannot be easily explained," yet it is hardly an objection to their theory. Even ordinary causation "is mysterious"; "at the most fundamental level, we have no idea why some events cause others." And "if there is some explanation of the whole of reality, we should not expect this explanation to fit neatly into some familiar category. This extra-ordinary question may have an extra-ordinary answer." Axiarchism appeals "not to an existing entity, but to an explanatory law." We could still ask why the law applied to reality, but if finding that it applied "we would have made some progress."

Would we? Perhaps we would, but the position could look unsatisfactory even to axiarchists. Nicholas Rescher thinks he can do better. He has defended the variant of axiarchism that Parfit describes as follows: "Reality might be as good as it could be, and that might be true because its being true is best." In his recent *Axiogenesis: An Essay in Metaphysical Optimalism*, Rescher writes that what exists "is for the best" and that this principle "is self-sustaining": "the principle obtains because that is for the best." But in Parfit's eyes anything on those lines wrongly makes something "explain itself." The most, he writes, that we could reasonably think is instead this: that if reality possessed best-ness then so extreme a situation would be "no coincidence." Yet what, we could ask him, does he mean by *that*? Wouldn't there need to be some basis "out there in reality" for a best situation to exist not by coincidence, but instead because of its best-ness? Compare how there might have to be something "out there" that *made* events regularly conform to the fairly simple mathematical equations that physicists have discovered, for it to be more than a Cosmic Coincidence that events fitted those equations. So when saying "no coincidence" shouldn't Parfit be imagining *necessity* of some kind?

Well, he does accept that some necessities aren't *logical* necessities – they aren't set up by the mere need to avoid contradiction. An example he gives is "that undeserved suffering is bad." We could deny it without contradiction, yet it "could not have failed to be true." He notes that John Leslie is an axiarchist who "appeals to this kind of non-logical necessity," suggesting that Value "could not have failed to rule." But in Parfit's view the Problem of Evil tells us that in fact Value "does *not* rule." And certainly, the Problem of Evil is so large that it can be very hard to avoid that conclusion.

Apart from Value, Parfit sees various other possible "Selectors" of what is real. "Maximality," he writes, might be a Selector, as on the theory that all logically possible worlds exist. He recognizes, though, that a world need not be "wholly law-governed" for observers to exist in it. This would seem to show that Maximality could not rule supreme – that if it ruled, then only in company with one or more other Selectors which limited its power – because we observe far more orderliness than would be likely if all logically possible worlds existed. While of course a few of the worlds would be "wholly law-governed" we could hardly expect to find ourselves in one of those few.

Again, Parfit sees Simplicity as a possible Selector but it, too, could not rule supreme. For if it did, then there would exist nothing whatever.

Parfit gives Elegance in the world's fundamental laws as a further possible Selector. "Non-arbitrariness" could be another, he says. Also Selectors could exist at various levels, the higher-level ones selecting those lower down. But he thinks there are few plausible Selectors, so there would not be many levels of them. Could any highest-level Selector act by necessity? Certainly not by Logical Necessity, he answers. And after deciding that the world's evils apparently rule out Value as a Selector, he has not found another candidate for *non-logical* necessity.

After putting so much care into developing the idea of explanatory Selectors, Parfit can then cheerfully write that "the simplest explanatory possibility is that there is no Selector." As he points out, Reality would have to be of some sort, empty of things or otherwise, even if nobody and nothing had selected it. There just is "no conceivable alternative." Either Reality is thing-less, or else there exists at least one thing. One of those two possibilities must have won, whether or not any factor made it victorious. Reality couldn't be somehow uncertain about which of the two had triumphed.

"It is possible to think," writes Robert Nozick, "that one cannot answer any question if one cannot answer the question of why there is something rather than nothing. How can we know why something is (or should be) a certain way if we don't know why there is anything at all?"; "the answer to any other philosophical question is liable to be overturned or undermined or transformed by the answer to this one." Asking "Why is there something rather than nothing?" does in his view make a controversial assumption, namely, that "nothingness is a natural state requiring no explanation, while all deviations from nothingness are in need of explanation," yet he considers such an assumption far from foolish. Here he could have pointed to Hume, Kant, and the great philosopher-psychologist William James. As all three of them saw, we must start with various fundamental convictions if we are ever to make sense of the world instead of viewing it as what James called "blooming, buzzing confusion." Think once again of the philosophical baby described earlier in this volume. It keeps crawling into the fire. It lacks the fundamental conviction that the past will be a guide to the future. *In the past* such a conviction would have saved it from getting burned again and again. However, the baby tells itself, that's no logical guarantee that *in the future* the past will be a guide to the future. Now – and this was Hume's famous insight – the baby is correct in its Logic. It simply lacks the right fundamental conviction. And those who look on every pebble, every parrot, every galaxy, as needing an explanation, but who then state that the cosmos as a whole can do without one, may be similarly ill fitted for understanding reality. That every existing thing has an explanation is a Fundamental Conviction which has repeatedly served us well, and the cosmos as a whole is an existing thing.

Yet could "*Why Not Nothing?*" ever be answered? Nozick sees why some philosophers consider the question "ill formed or meaningless." "Any factor," they think, "introduced to explain why there is something will be part of the something to be explained," meaning that we could never explain "why there is *anything* at all." However they are assuming, for a start, that whatever did the explaining couldn't be a very special part of the cosmos, a part that existed *through necessity*. If it did exist in that fashion – though he finds it "difficult to see" how it could – then there would be no need for any further explanation of why there wasn't a blank. Again, he says, the philosophers might care to reflect that an explanatory principle could be "self-subsuming." Remember Nicholas Rescher's idea that a Principle of the Best rules because *that is itself best*? Nozick dreams up his own example of self-subsumption. Suppose that reality obeys a Fecundity Principle so that scattered across "parallel universes," "independent noninteracting realms," absolutely all possibilities are realized. Well, won't the Fecundity Principle itself then be something that is realized?

Might we instead treat nothingness as just one among countless possibilities, the others being the infinitely many conceivable forms that a cosmos might take? And if so, Nozick asks, could we conclude that nothingness had been *infinitely unlikely*? Here he has anticipated the argument which in due course occurred to Peter van Inwagen (consult earlier pages). As Nozick comments, it could need the Egalitarian assumption that the various possibilities all had equal chances of being realized. The assumption might conceivably be correct – but Nozick also thinks it might conceivably be true that in the beginning "a very powerful force towards nothingness" *nothinged itself*, thereby producing somethingness!

Looming larger, if only because so many have believed that Creation's secret can be found here, there is The Transcendent. If any factor explained the entire world of existing things, wouldn't it be beyond all of them? Nozick quotes the Hymn of Creation in Hinduism's *Vedas*. It begins, "Nonbeing then existed not, nor being." Or, in another translation, "There was then neither what is nor what is not." Well, he asks, why should *existent* and *nonexistent* be the sole available possibilities? After all, "the number 5, and Beethoven's Quartet Number 15, are neither colored nor uncolored." And while "the structure of all possibilities underlies existence and nonexistence," this structure itself "doesn't exist and it doesn't nonexist." In the West, "Plato says that God is 'beyond being'." And following in Plato's footsteps, Plotinus makes this same idea "central to his theory of the One."

Let us look at the point more closely. It can seem that Plato, trying to explain the cosmos, appeals to a realm filled with realities that are real not only eternally but also, in many instances, fairly uncontroversially – realities of what is logically possible, and of what's true about various logical possibilities. For instance it is true eternally, true unconditionally, that three sets of four unicorns could exist without contradiction, and that there would then be twelve unicorns. The eternal realm of possibilities and truths about possibilities fails to exist in the way that we ourselves do, yet we might hesitate to call it "nonexistent" since this could sound like saying "not real at all." We might prefer to imitate Nozick, saying that the Platonic realm "doesn't exist and also doesn't nonexist" since it is "beyond existence and nonexistence."

216 The Problem Seems Genuine

Plato searches the Platonic realm for possibilities whose reality *as more than mere possibilities* – as really existing things, in other words – could be "required" in some fashion which might account for the cosmos. His admirers can comment that unless things were already really possible, they would have no chance of existing. [Round squares and married bachelors wouldn't have one.] Hence Plato can appear fully justified when he assumes that the realm of possibilities "had to be there" completely independently of whether there existed anything. If it were wrong to assume it, then this would be enough to show that we faced an utterly unsolvable problem of why there is anything in existence, either a divine person or anything else, because not even deities could *first* exist and *then* cause it to be true that their existence really was possible.

Robert Lawrence Kuhn may have given himself just such a problem, at age twelve at any rate. He reports the frightening abyss that opened up when he first asked himself why there wasn't absolutely nothing, not even "abstract objects." There went, smashing through the window, all of Plato's eternal realities. Enough of the resultant "frigid blast" has remained for him to be very hesitant about tackling "*Why Not Nothing?*". He tries to limit himself to "*Why This Universe?*" which could seem "more accessible." It can be hard, though, to give answers to the second question which are not also answers to the first. Kuhn's survey of the area keeps wandering into "*Why Not Nothing?*" which even provides its title. The survey is an important companion to this volume's Suggestions for Further Reading. It mentions many writers listed in those suggestions, showing what you could expect to find in their writings. And it introduces themes which, even today, have been only obscurely developed although some of them feature prominently in the world's religions. These themes the volume could have discussed in detail only by becoming too heavy to lift.

Kuhn starts his survey by discussing the apparent cosmic fine-tuning. Even this first topic illustrates how difficult it is to separate "*Why This Universe?*" from "*Why Not Nothing?*". Our universe seems "fine-tuned for life" in the following technical sense: that slight changes to its basic features would have made it a lifeless universe. Suppose you bring in God as Creator of everything else, and Fine-Tuner of whatever needed fine-tuning. You may want to dodge the question of why there was God, creatively powerful, instead of a blank. An explanation can be a good first step, you announce, even when it raises new questions. Opponents, however, will say that advancing into a wasp nest isn't a good first step unless you can calm the wasps. They will want to hear your answer to why there exists so wondrous an individual as God. And many of them will take it for granted that everyone who talks of "fine-tuning" must believe in God as Fine-Tuner.

For a glorious illustration of this sort of thing, consider what has happened to the words "Strong Anthropic Principle." As originally defined by Brandon Carter, the Weak Anthropic Principle stated the fact, utterly obvious yet overlooked by many cosmologists, that our neck of the cosmic woods must (since we're in it) be capable of containing observers such as ourselves. Carter's Strong Anthropic Principle then made the equally obvious, equally often overlooked point that the cosmos must be capable of containing such observers somewhere, sometime. *Must*, that's to say, *since we're in it*, observing it. Just as a burglar *must* have paid a visit since your Picasso has disappeared. No suggestion that the burglar had been forced to visit you, or that God forced the universe to be life-permitting. As discussed earlier in this volume, the explanation of any fine-tuning could instead be that there exist multiple universes with varying properties. Our neck of those woods then *must be* a universe with life-permitting properties. Yet it is hard to say "evidence of fine-tuning," let alone "Strong Anthropic Principle," without being accused of claiming that God tuned the universe and that God's own existence presents no special problem. That fine-tuning is a reality – that our universe does balance on a razor edge between being life-permitting and being life-excluding – has been strongly resisted by physicists who viewed it as importing into physics an implausible divine magician. It gained wide acceptance only when people found what looked like suitably God-less physical mechanisms for creating multiple universes which differed in their properties. So, you see, "*Why is there Anything At All?*" interacts not only with "*Why is Our Universe Like This?*" but also with the question "*What is the This that Our Universe is Like?*." The question, in other words, of what we can reasonably think our universe's properties really are. Asking whether it balances on a razor edge gets us into such theoretical difficulties that we cannot settle the affair by collecting more and more evidence about the universe's nature. Questions about how it could have got its nature – through the choice of a Creator? through a mechanism creating a trillion trillion universes, tuned in different ways? – simply cannot be dismissed as irrelevant.

Not just there but in many other cases as well, collecting more and more evidence might never protect even the best brains against reaching mistaken conclusions. Kuhn's survey contains intriguing illustrations of this. Might our universe be, for example, simply a pattern inside a gigantic computer? It could certainly seem that it isn't – but if it were, would it definitely look any different? John Barrow has suggested that his fellow physicists should look hard for irregularities of kinds very difficult to avoid in computer-simulations. Yet if they found none, the matter still wouldn't have been settled firmly.

Kuhn's survey article is very wide-ranging. Some of the themes he lists are such gems that some later edition of this volume perhaps ought to be too heavy to lift.

Michael HELLER notes that Kuhn's real interest is often more in "*Why Is There Something?*" than in "*Why a Universe Like This?*". "Why is there something rather than nothing?" is what Leibniz so famously asked. Heller mentions three ways in which people have protested against asking it. A first protest has been that any answer would involve deducing something "from non-existent premises." A second, that the word "nothingness" does not refer to anything, so we can't sensibly ask why nothingness is absent. A third, that there is "a syntax error" in the apparent assumption that something other than Something could explain Something. Heller counters the objections by saying we must not expect to answer great philosophical problems "solely by means of linguistic resources."

Heller next examines what he calls Peter van Inwagen's "rather peculiar answer" to why there exists anything at all. Remember, van Inwagen suggests that since An Absence of All Existing Things had been just one possibility, in contrast to infinitely many possible versions of There Existing Something, it follows that an empty cosmos had been ruled out by its *infinite improbability*. Heller comments that "we should not treat probability theory as an absolute and turn it into an ontology which governs everything." He considers the case of throwing a true die. We typically assume that there are just six possible results, all equiprobable, yet this would be wrong in the case of dice which behaved in ways we'd find odd: sometimes coming to rest on their beveled corners, for instance.

Suppose we thought there was no reason why the world exists. In Heller's eyes this would be a case of accepting not just "a brute fact," but "a brutal fact," a fact brutal because violating "the principle that we should go on asking questions for as long as there is still something left to explain."

Nicholas RESCHER sees that questions like *"Why is there anything at all?"* and *"Why does the world obey these laws instead of others?"* are unanswerable inside "the standard causal framework." "Rejectionists" conclude that such questions are illegitimate; the so-called explanatory problem "vanishes as meaningless." Carl Hempel writes that "what seems to be wanted is an explanatory account which does not assume the existence of something or other," yet that such an account seems to him "a logical impossibility." And Rescher grants that if *"Why Anything?"* goes as far as to ask why there are *any facts at all*, then of course it cannot possibly be answered. But he thinks we could make progress if we distinguished between the existence of things, on the one hand, and the reality of facts on the other – facts including ones about "states of affairs that are not dependent on the operation of preexisting things." Sure enough, "we cannot explain one *fact* without involving other *facts* to do the explaining," but it is sheer prejudice to assume that "the reason for anything must always inhere in the operation of things" so that "no *thing* can emerge from a thingless condition." He points to how "in Plato and the Presocratics, the causal efficacy of *principles* is recognized." Principles and not things, when *things* could never explain why there are any things at all.

Rescher adds that other routes to Rejectionism include Kant's view that "it is illegitimate to try to account for the phenomenal universe as a whole" – the entire universe as it appears to our senses. Yet such a view strikes him as "deeply problematic." For do we not try to explain the age, the structure, the volume, the laws, and the composition of the universe in its entirety? "Why not then its *existence* as well?" The decree that explanations can throw light only on parts of the universe, not the whole, "seems a mere device for sidestepping embarrassingly difficult questions." Rejectionism "is not a particularly appealing course," for there is "nothing patently meaningless about this 'riddle of existence'." While it may be optimistic to think "that there are always reasons why things are as they are," it is too early to classify *"Why Existence?"* as an improper question. Try as we may to get rid of it, the question "comes back to haunt us."

Here is a final editorial comment. People sometimes argue that human brains evolved only for such things as escaping predators, and that therefore *"Why Existence?"* will long remain unanswerable. But surely, we can protest, avoiding being killed by a leopard wasn't just a matter of having enough sense to jump sideways when the beast sprang. Interpreting almost invisible tracks, tiny changes in the behavior of birds, faint noises in the forest, was vitally important. Cavemen could not afford to be stupid. Moreover there were very few humans in those distant times. Today there are over seven billion. They can tackle hard questions as large teams and as heirs to many centuries of hard thinking by writers whose ideas can be found not just in libraries but also on the Internet where search engines can find them. Have you hit on an answer to *"Why Existence?"* that strikes you as rather good? Search engines may soon be able to advise you – they can perhaps do so already if you help them by repeatedly refining the words you put into their search slots – that your idea in fact dates from the early Middle Ages or has been around for over two thousand years. But you may also discover that the idea has been developed only in rough ways that you think you could improve on, or you may find that nothing like it appears to have occurred to anybody. Describe it on the Internet, and you may soon get messages from many potential allies. The human race can now rapidly enlist thousands of its members for reacting to interesting suggestions.

While, however, cavemen could have found it helped to be terribly smart, might it not be that intelligence such as theirs, intelligence of the kind that has become *ours*, intelligence adequate for getting humans to the moon, probing the interior of the atom, constructing very long mathematical proofs, was not *the kind of intelligence* that could give us the solution to why the world exists? Well, there could be grounds for suspecting that our intelligence was indeed "of the wrong kind," yet how could we ever know whether it was? Only by proposing some answer to why the world exists and then demonstrating firmly that this answer *was correct*. In other words, we could settle whether we had the wrong kind of intelligence only by discovering that our intelligence *clearly wasn't* of the wrong kind, because we knew it had enabled us to find the solution. Simply getting into a time machine, getting out at a point ten thousand years in the future, and observing that no particular answer to *"Why Existence?"* had become generally accepted, wouldn't settle anything. Long before the twenty-first century the correct answer might have been found, then failing to gain general acceptance. The possibility, for instance, that the cosmos *just happens to be non-empty* is an idea that has been around for centuries; since the cosmos had to be *somehow*, empty or otherwise, whether or not there was a reason for its being like that, this idea isn't obviously mistaken; and our intelligence is plainly of the right kind for understanding it since any bright seven-year-old could understand it. It has never gained general acceptance but perhaps it is right – yet any one of many further ideas, all easy enough to understand and some of them appearing in this edited volume, might be right instead. So, provably unable to know that we have "the wrong kind of intelligence," we may as well keep trying to solve the mystery of existence, the riddle of why there's anything at all.

Making Existence Less Puzzling*

DEREK PARFIT

Why does the Universe exist? There are two questions here. First, why is there a Universe at all? It might have been true that nothing ever existed: no living beings, no stars, no atoms, not even space or time. When we think about this possibility, it can seem astonishing that anything exists. Second, why does this Universe exist? Things might have been, in countless ways, different. So why is the Universe as it is?

These questions, some believe, may have causal answers. Suppose first that the Universe has always existed. Some believe that, if all events were caused by earlier events, everything would be explained. That, however, is not so. Even an infinite series of events cannot explain itself. We could ask why this series occurred, rather than some other series, or no series. Of the supporters of the Steady State Theory, some welcomed what they took to be this theory's atheistic implications. They assumed that, if the Universe had no beginning, there would be nothing for a Creator to explain. But there would still be an eternal Universe to explain.

Suppose next that the Universe is not eternal, since nothing preceded the Big Bang. That first event, some physicists suggest, may have obeyed the laws of quantum mechanics, by being a random fluctuation in a vacuum. This would causally explain, they say, how the Universe came into existence out of nothing. But what physicists call a vacuum isn't really nothing. We can ask why it exists, and has the potentialities it does. In Hawking's phrase, "What breathes fire into the equations?"

Similar remarks apply to all suggestions of these kinds. There could not be a causal explanation of why the Universe exists, why there are any laws of nature, or why these laws are as they are. Nor would it make a difference if there is a God, who caused the rest of the Universe to exist. There could not be a causal explanation of why God exists.

Many people have assumed that, since these questions cannot have causal answers, they cannot have any answers. Some therefore dismiss these questions, thinking them not worth considering. Others conclude that they do not make sense. They assume that, as Wittgenstein wrote, "doubt can exist only where there is a question; and a question only where there is an answer."

These assumptions are all, I believe, mistaken. Even if these questions could not have answers, they would still make sense, and they would still be worth considering. I am reminded here of the aesthetic category of the sublime, as applied to the highest mountains, raging oceans, the night sky, the interiors of some cathedrals, and other things that are superhuman, awesome, limitless. No question is more sublime than why there is a Universe: why there is anything rather than nothing.

---

*   "Why Anything? Why This?", a two-part essay in *The London Review of Books* (22 January and 5 February 1998). Reprinted with kind permission of the author.

Nor should we assume that answers to this question must be causal. And, even if reality cannot be fully explained, we may still make progress, since what is inexplicable may become less baffling than it now seems.

One apparent fact about reality has recently been much discussed. Many physicists believe that, for life to be possible, various features of the Universe must be almost precisely as they are. As one example, we can take the initial conditions in the Big Bang. If these conditions had been more than very slightly different, these physicists claim, the Universe would not have had the complexity that allows living beings to exist. Why were these conditions so precisely right?

Some say: "If they had not been right, we couldn't even ask this question." But that is no answer. It could be baffling how we survived some crash even though, if we hadn't, we could not be baffled.

Others say: "There had to be some initial conditions, and the conditions that make life possible were as likely as any others. So there is nothing to be explained." To see what is wrong with this reply, we must distinguish two kinds of case. Suppose first that, when some radio telescope is aimed at most points in space, it records a random sequence of incoming waves. There might be nothing here that needed to be explained. Suppose next that, when the telescope is aimed in one direction, it records a sequence of waves whose pulses match the number π, in binary notation, to the first ten thousand digits. That particular number is, in one sense, just as likely as any other. But there *would* be something here that needed to be explained. Though each long number is unique, only a very few are, like π, mathematically special. What would need to be explained is why this sequence of waves exactly matched such a special number. Though this matching might be a coincidence, which had been randomly produced, that would be most unlikely. We could be almost certain that these waves had been produced by some kind of intelligence.

On the view that we are now considering, since any sequence of waves is as likely as any other, there would be nothing to be explained. If we accepted this view, intelligent beings elsewhere in space would not be able to communicate with us, since we would ignore their messages. Nor could God reveal himself. Suppose that, with an optical telescope, we saw a distant pattern of stars which spelled out in Hebrew script the first chapter of Genesis. According to this view, this pattern of stars would not need to be explained. That is clearly false.

Here is another analogy. Suppose first that, of a thousand people facing death, only one can be rescued. If there is a lottery to pick this one survivor, and I win, I would be very lucky. But there might be nothing here that needed to be explained. Someone had to win, and why not me? Consider next another lottery. Unless my gaoler picks the longest of a thousand straws, I shall be shot. If my gaoler picks that straw, there would be something to be explained. It would not be enough to say, "This result was as likely as any other." In the first lottery, nothing special happened: whatever the result, someone's life would be saved. In this second lottery, the result *was* special, since, of the thousand possible results, only one would save a life. Why was this special result also what happened? Though this might be a coincidence, the chance of that is only one in a thousand. I could be almost certain that, like Dostoevsky's mock execution, this lottery was rigged.

The Big Bang, it seems, was like this second lottery. For life to be possible, the initial conditions had to be selected with great accuracy. This *appearance of fine-tuning*, as some call it, also needs to be explained.

It may be objected that, in regarding conditions as special if they allow for life, we unjustifiably assume our own importance. But life is special, if only because of its complexity. An earthworm's brain is more complicated than a lifeless galaxy. Nor is it only life that requires this fine-tuning. If the Big Bang's initial conditions had not been almost precisely as they were, the Universe would have either almost instantly recollapsed, or expanded so fast, and with particles so thinly spread, that not even stars or heavy elements could have formed. That is enough to make these conditions very special.

It may next be objected that these conditions cannot be claimed to be improbable, since such a claim requires a statistical basis, and there is only one Universe. If we were considering all conceivable Universes, it would indeed be implausible to make judgments of statistical probability. But our question is much narrower. We are asking what would have happened if, with the same laws of nature, the initial conditions had been different. That provides the basis for a statistical judgment. There is a range of values that these conditions might have had, and physicists can work out in what proportion of this range the resulting Universe could have contained stars, heavy elements and life.

This proportion, it is claimed, is extremely small. Of the range of possible initial conditions, fewer than one in a billion billion would have produced a Universe with the complexity that allows for life. If this claim is true, as I shall here assume, there is something that cries out to be explained. Why was one of this tiny set also the one that actually obtained?

On one view, this was a mere coincidence. That is conceivable, since coincidences happen. But this view is hard to believe, since, if it were true, the chance of this coincidence occurring would be below one in a billion billion.

Others say: "The Big Bang *was* fine-tuned. In creating the Universe, God chose to make life possible." Atheists may reject this answer, thinking it improbable that God exists. But this probability cannot be as low as one in a billion billion. So even atheists should admit that, of these two answers to our question, the one that invokes God is more likely to be true.

This reasoning revives one of the traditional arguments for belief in God. In its strongest form, this argument appealed to the many features of animals, such as eyes or wings, that look as if they have been designed. Paley's appeal to such features much impressed Darwin when he was young. Darwin later undermined this form of the argument, since evolution can explain this appearance of design. But evolution cannot explain the appearance of fine-tuning in the Big Bang.

This argument's appeal to probabilities can be challenged in a different way. In claiming it to be most improbable that this fine-tuning was a coincidence, the argument assumes that, of the possible initial conditions in the Big Bang, each was equally likely to obtain. That assumption may be mistaken. The conditions that allow for complexity and life may have been, compared with all the others, much more likely to obtain. Perhaps they were even certain to obtain.

To answer this objection, we must broaden this argument's conclusion. If these life-allowing conditions were either very likely or certain to obtain, then – as the argument claims – it would be no coincidence that the Universe allows for complexity and life. But this fine-tuning might have been the work, not of some existing being, but of some impersonal force, or fundamental law. That is what some theists believe God to be.

A stronger challenge to this argument comes from a different way of explaining the appearance of fine-tuning. Consider first a similar question. For life to be possible on Earth, many of Earth's features have to be close to being as they are. The Earth's having such features, it might be claimed, is unlikely to be a coincidence, and should therefore be regarded as God's work. But such an argument would be weak. The Universe, we can reasonably believe, contains many planets, with varying conditions. We should expect that, on a few of these planets, conditions would be just right for life. Nor is it surprising that we live on one of these few.

Things are different, we may assume, with the appearance of fine-tuning in the Big Bang. While there are likely to be many other planets, there is only one Universe. But this difference may be less than it seems. Some physicists suggest that the observable Universe is only one out of many different worlds, which are all equally parts of reality. According to one such view, the other worlds are related to ours in a way that solves some of the mysteries of quantum physics. On the different and simpler view that is relevant here, the other worlds have the same fundamental laws of nature as our world, and they are produced by Big Bangs that are broadly similar, except in having different initial conditions.

On this *Many Worlds Hypothesis*, there is no need for fine-tuning. If there were enough Big Bangs, we should expect that, in a few of them, conditions would be just right to allow for complexity and life; and it would be no surprise that our Big Bang was one of these few. To illustrate this point, we can revise my second lottery. Suppose my gaoler picks a straw, not once but many times. That would explain his managing, once, to pick the longest straw, without that's being an extreme coincidence, or this lottery's being rigged.

On most versions of the Many Worlds Hypothesis, these many worlds are not, except through their origins, causally related. Some object that, since our world could not be causally affected by such other worlds, we can have no evidence for their existence, and can therefore have no reason to believe in them. But we do have such a reason, since their existence would explain an otherwise puzzling feature of our world: the appearance of fine-tuning.

Of these two ways to explain this appearance, which is better? Compared with belief in God, the Many Worlds Hypothesis is more cautious, since its claim is merely that there is more of the kind of reality that we can observe around us. But God's existence has been claimed to be intrinsically more probable. According to most theists, God is a being who is omnipotent, omniscient and wholly good. The uncaused existence of such a being has been claimed to be simpler, and less arbitrary, than the uncaused existence of many highly complicated worlds. And simpler hypotheses, many scientists assume, are more likely to be true.

If such a God exists, however, other features of our world become hard to explain. It may not be surprising that God chose to make life possible. But the laws of nature could have been different, so there are many possible worlds that would have contained life. It is hard to understand why, out of all these possibilities, God chose to create our world. What is most baffling is the problem of evil. There appears to be suffering which any good person, knowing the truth, would have prevented if he could. If there is such suffering, there cannot be a God who is omnipotent, omniscient and wholly good.

To this problem, theists have proposed several solutions. Some suggest that God is not omnipotent, or not wholly good. Others suggest that undeserved suffering is not, as it seems, bad, or that God could not prevent such suffering without making the Universe, as a whole, less good.

We must ignore these suggestions here, since we have larger questions to consider. I began by asking why things are as they are. Before returning to that question, we should ask how things are. There is much about our world that we have not discovered. And, just as there may be other worlds that are like ours, there may be worlds that are very different.

It will help to distinguish two kinds of possibility. Cosmic possibilities cover everything that ever exists, and are the different ways that the whole of reality might be. Only one such possibility can be actual, or the one that obtains. Local possibilities are the different ways that some part of reality, or local world, might be. If some local world exists, that leaves it open whether other worlds exist.

One cosmic possibility is, roughly, that every possible local world exists. This we can call the *All Worlds Hypothesis*. Another possibility, which might have obtained, is that nothing ever exists. This we can call the *Null Possibility*. In each of the remaining possibilities, the number of worlds that exist is between none and all. There are countless of these possibilities, since there are countless combinations of particular possible local worlds.

Of these different cosmic possibilities, one must obtain, and only one can obtain. So we have two questions: which obtains, and why? These questions are connected. If some possibility would be easier to explain, we have more reason to believe that this possibility obtains. This is how, rather than believing in only one Big Bang, we have more reason to believe in many. Whether we believe in one or many, we have the question why any Big Bang has occurred. Though this question is hard, the occurrence of many Big Bangs is not more puzzling than the occurrence of only one. Most kinds of thing, or event, have many instances. We also have the question why, in the Big Bang that produced our world, the initial conditions allowed for complexity and life. If there has been only one Big Bang, this fact is also hard to explain, since it is most unlikely that these conditions merely happened to be right. If, instead, there have been many Big Bangs, this fact is easy to explain, since it is like the fact that, among countless planets, there are some whose conditions allow for life. Since belief in many Big Bangs leaves less that is unexplained, it is the better view.

If some cosmic possibilities would be less puzzling than others, because their obtaining would leave less to be explained, is there some possibility whose obtaining would be in no way puzzling?

Consider first the Null Possibility, in which nothing ever exists. To imagine this possibility, it may help to suppose first, that all that ever existed was a single atom. We then imagine that even this atom never existed.

Some have claimed that, if there had never been anything, there wouldn't have been anything to be explained. But that is not so. When we imagine how things would have been if nothing had ever existed, what we should imagine away are such things as living beings, stars and atoms. There would still have been various truths, such as the truth that there were no stars or atoms, or that 9 is divisible by 3. We can ask why these things would have been true. And such questions may have answers. Thus we can explain why, even if nothing had ever existed, 9 would still have been divisible by 3. There is no conceivable alternative. And we can explain why there would have been no such things as immaterial matter, or spherical cubes. Such things are logically impossible. But why would *nothing* have existed? Why would there have been no stars or atoms, no philosophers or bluebell woods?

We should not claim that, if nothing had ever existed, there would have been nothing to be explained. But we can claim something less. Of all the global possibilities, the Null Possibility would have needed the least explanation. As Leibniz pointed out, it is much the simplest, and the least arbitrary. And it is the easiest to understand. It can seem mysterious, for example, how things could exist without their existence having some cause, but there cannot be a causal explanation of why the whole Universe, or God, exists. The Null Possibility raises no such problem. If nothing had ever existed, that state of affairs would not have needed to be caused.

Reality, however, does not take its least puzzling form. In some way or other, a Universe has managed to exist. That is what can take one's breath away. As Wittgenstein wrote, "not how the world is, is the mystical, but *that* it is." Or, in the words of a thinker as unmystical as Jack Smart: "That anything should exist at all does seem to me a matter for the deepest awe."

Consider next the All Worlds Hypothesis, in which every possible local world exists. Unlike the Null Possibility, this may be how things are. And it may be the next least puzzling possibility. This hypothesis is not the same as – though it includes – the Many Worlds Hypothesis. On that more cautious view, many other worlds have the same elements as our world, and the same fundamental laws, and differ only in such features as their constants and initial conditions. The All Worlds Hypothesis covers every conceivable kind of world, and most of these other worlds would have very different elements and laws.

If all these worlds exist, we can ask why they do. But, compared with most other cosmic possibilities, the All Worlds Hypothesis may leave less that is unexplained. For example, whatever the number of possible worlds that exist, we have the question, "Why that number?" This question would have been least puzzling if the number that existed were none, and the next least arbitrary possibility seems to be that *all* these worlds exist. With every other cosmic possibility, we have a further question. If ours is the only world, we can ask: "Out of all the possible worlds, why is this the one that exists?" On any version of the Many Worlds Hypothesis, we have a similar question: "Why do just these worlds exist, with these elements and laws?" But, if *all* these worlds exist, there is no such further question.

It may be objected that, even if all possible local worlds exist, that does not explain why our world is as it is. But that is a mistake. If all these worlds exist, each world is as it is in the way in which each number is as it is. We cannot sensibly ask why 9 is 9. Nor should we ask why our world is the one it is: why it is *this* world. That would be like asking, "Why are we who we are?", or "Why is it now the time that it is?" Those are not good questions.

Though the All Worlds Hypothesis avoids certain questions, it is not as simple, or unarbitrary, as the Null Possibility. There may be no sharp distinction between worlds that are and are not possible. It is unclear what counts as a kind of world. And, if there are infinitely many kinds, there is a choice between different kinds of infinity.

Whichever cosmic possibility obtains, we can ask why it obtains. All that I have claimed so far is that, with some possibilities, this question would be less puzzling. Let us now ask: could this question have an answer? Might there be a theory that leaves nothing unexplained?

It is sometimes claimed that God, or the Universe, make themselves exist. But this cannot be true, since these entities cannot do anything unless they exist.

On a more intelligible view, it is logically necessary that God, or the Universe, exist, since the claim that they might not have existed leads to a contradiction. On such a view, though it may seem conceivable that there might never have been anything, that is not really logically possible. Some people even claim that there may be only one coherent cosmic possibility. Thus Einstein suggested that, if God created our world, he might have had no choice about which world to create. If such a view were true, everything might be explained. Reality might be the way it is because there was no conceivable alternative. But, for reasons that have been often given, we can reject such views.

Consider next a quite different view. According to Plato, Plotinus and others, the Universe exists because its existence is good. Even if we are confident that we should reject this view, it is worth asking whether it makes sense. If it does, that may suggest other possibilities.

This *Axiarchic View* can take a theistic form. It can claim that God exists because his existence is good, and that the rest of the Universe exists because God caused it to exist. But in that explanation God, qua Creator, is redundant. If God can exist because his existence is good, so can the whole Universe. This may be why some theists reject the Axiarchic View, and insist that God's existence is a brute fact, with no explanation.

In its simplest form, this view makes three claims: "(1) It would be best if reality were a certain way. (2) Reality is that way. (3) (1) explains (2)." (1) is an ordinary evaluative claim, like the claim that it would be better if there was less suffering. The Axiarchic View assumes, I believe rightly, that such claims can be in a strong sense true. (2) is an ordinary empirical or scientific claim, though of a sweeping kind. What is distinctive in this view is claim (3), according to which (1) explains (2).

Can we understand this third claim? To focus on this question, we should briefly ignore the world's evils, and suspend our other doubts about claims (1) and (2). We should suppose that, as Leibniz claimed, the best possible Universe exists. Would it then make sense to claim that this Universe exists because it is the best?

That use of "because", Axiarchists should admit, cannot be easily explained. But even ordinary causation is mysterious. At the most fundamental level, we have no idea why some events cause others; and it is hard to explain what causation is. There are, moreover, non-causal senses of "because" and "why", as in the claim that God exists because his existence is logically necessary. We can understand that claim, even if we think it false. The Axiarchic View is harder to understand. But that is not surprising. If there is some explanation of the whole of reality, we should not expect this explanation to fit neatly into some familiar category. This extra-ordinary question may have an extraordinary answer. We should reject suggested answers which make no sense; but we should also try to see what might make sense.

Axiarchy might be expressed as follows. We are now supposing that, of all the countless ways that the whole of reality might be, one is both the very best, and is the way that reality is. On the Axiarchic View, *that is no coincidence*. This claim, I believe, makes sense. And, if it were no coincidence that the best way for reality to be is also the way that reality is, that might support the further claim that this was why reality was this way.

This view has one advantage over the more familiar theistic view. An appeal to God cannot explain why the Universe exists, since God would himself be part of the Universe, or one of the things that exist. Some theists argue that, since nothing can exist without a cause, God, who is the First Cause, must exist. As Schopenhauer objected, this argument's premise is not like some cabdriver whom theists are free to dismiss once they have reached their destination. The Axiarchic View appeals, not to an existing entity, but to an explanatory law. Since such a law would not itself be part of the Universe, it might explain why the Universe exists, and is as good as it could be. If such a law governed reality, we could still ask why it did, or why the Axiarchic View was true. But, in discovering this law, we would have made some progress.

It is hard, however, to believe the Axiarchic View. If, as it seems, there is much pointless suffering, our world cannot be part of the best possible Universe.

Some Axiarchists claim that, if we reject their view, we must regard our world's existence as a brute fact, since no other explanation could make sense. But that, I believe, is not so. If we abstract from the optimism of the Axiarchic View, its claims are these: "Of the countless cosmic possibilities, one both has a very special feature, and is the possibility that obtains. That is no coincidence. This possibility obtains because it has this feature." Other views can make such claims. This special feature need not be that of being best. Thus, on the All Worlds Hypothesis, reality is maximal, or as full as it could be. Similarly, if nothing had ever existed, reality would have been minimal, or as empty as it could be. If the possibility that obtained were either maximal or minimal, that fact, we might claim, would be most unlikely to be a coincidence. And that might support the further claim that this possibility's having this feature would be why it obtained.

Let us now look more closely at that last step. When it is no coincidence that two things are both true, there is something that explains why, given the truth of one, the other is also true. The truth of either might make the other true. Or both might be explained by some third truth, as when two facts are the joint effects of a common cause.

Suppose next that, of the cosmic possibilities, one is both very special and is the one that obtains. If that is no coincidence, what might explain why these things are both true? On the reasoning that we are now considering, the first truth explains the second, since this possibility obtains because it has this special feature. Given the kind of truths these are, such an explanation could not go the other way. This possibility could not have this feature because it obtains. If some possibility has some feature, it could not fail to have this feature, so it would have this feature whether or not it obtains. The All Worlds Hypothesis, for example, could not fail to describe the fullest way for reality to be.

While it is necessary that our imagined possibility has its special feature, it is not necessary that this possibility obtains. This difference, I believe, justifies the reasoning that we are now considering. Since this possibility must have this feature, but might not have obtained, it cannot have this feature because it obtains, nor could some third truth explain why it both has this feature and obtains. So, if these facts are no coincidence, this possibility must obtain *because* it has this feature.

When some possibility obtains because it has some feature, its having this feature may be why some agent, or process of natural selection, made it obtain. These we can call the *intentional* and *evolutionary* ways in which some feature of some possibility may explain why it obtains.

Our world, theists claim, can be explained in the first of these ways. If reality were as good as it could be, it would indeed make sense to claim that this was partly God's work. But, since God's own existence could not be God's work, there could be no intentional explanation of why the whole of reality was as good as it could be.

So we could reasonably conclude that this way's being the best explained directly why reality was this way. Even if God exists, the intentional explanation could not compete with the different and bolder explanation offered by the Axiarchic View.

Return now to other explanations of this kind. Consider first the Null Possibility. This, we know, does not obtain; but, since we are asking what makes sense, that does not matter. If there had never been anything, would that have had to be a brute fact, which had no explanation? The answer, I suggest, is No. It might have been no coincidence that, of all the countless cosmic possibilities, what obtained was the simplest, and least arbitrary, and the only possibility in which nothing ever exists. And, if these facts had been no coincidence, this possibility would have obtained because – or partly because – it had one or more of these special features. This explanation, moreover, could not have taken an intentional or evolutionary form. If nothing had ever existed, there could not have been some agent, or process of selection, who or which made this possibility obtain. Its being the simplest or least arbitrary possibility would have been, directly, why it obtained.

Consider next the All Worlds Hypothesis, which may obtain. If reality is as full as it could be, is that a coincidence? Does it merely happen to be true that, of all the cosmic possibilities, the one that obtains is at this extreme? As before, that is conceivable, but this coincidence would be too great to be credible. We can reasonably assume that, if this possibility obtains, that is because it is maximal, or at this extreme. On this *Maximalist View*, it is a fundamental truth that being possible, and part of the fullest way that reality could be, is sufficient for being actual. That is the highest law governing reality. As before, if such a law governed reality, we could still ask why it did. But, in discovering this law, we would have made some progress.

Here is another special feature. Perhaps reality is the way it is because its fundamental laws are, on some criterion, as mathematically beautiful as they could be. That is what some physicists are inclined to believe.

As these remarks suggest, there is no clear boundary here between philosophy and science. If there is such a highest law governing reality, this law is of the same kind as those that physicists are trying to discover. When we appeal to natural laws to explain some features of reality, such as the relations between light, gravity, space and time, we are not giving causal explanations, since we are not claiming that one part of reality caused another part to be some way. What such laws explain, or partly explain, are the deeper facts about reality that causal explanations take for granted. In the second half of this essay, I shall ask how deep such explanations could go.

***

In the first half of this essay, I suggested how reality's deepest features might be partly explained. Of the countless cosmic possibilities, or ways that reality might be, a few have very special features. If such a possibility obtained, that might be no coincidence. Reality might be this way because this way had this feature. Thus, if nothing had ever existed, that might have been true because it was the simplest way for reality to be. And if reality is maximal, because all possible local worlds exist, this may be true because it is the fullest way for reality to be. The highest law may be that being possible, and part of the fullest way reality might be, is sufficient for being actual.

If some cosmic possibility obtains because it has some special feature, we can call this feature the *Selector*. If there is more than one such feature, they are all partial Selectors. Just as there are various cosmic possibilities, there are various explanatory possibilities. For each of these special features, there is the explanatory possibility that this feature is the Selector, or is one of the Selectors. Reality would then be the way it is because, or partly because, this way had this feature.

There is one other explanatory possibility: that there is no Selector. If that is true, it is random that reality is as it is. Events may be in one sense random, even though they are causally inevitable. That is how it is random whether a meteorite strikes the land or the sea. Events are random in a stronger sense if they have no cause. That is what most physicists believe about some features of events involving subatomic particles. If it is random what reality is like, the Universe not only has no cause. It has no explanation of any kind. This claim we can call the *Brute Fact View*.

Few features can be plausibly regarded as possible Selectors. Though plausibility is a matter of degree, there is a natural threshold to which we can appeal. If we suppose that reality has some special feature, we can ask which of two beliefs would be more credible: that reality merely happens to have this feature, or that reality is the way it is because this way has this feature. If the second would be more credible, this feature can be called a *credible Selector*. Return, for example, to the question of how many possible local worlds exist. Of the different answers to this question, *all* and *none* give us, I have claimed, credible Selectors. If either all or no worlds existed, that would be unlikely to be a coincidence. But suppose that 58 worlds existed. This number has some special features, such as being the smallest number that is the sum of seven different primes. It may be just conceivable that this would be why 58 worlds existed; but it would be more reasonable to believe that the number that existed merely happened to be 58.

There are, I have claimed, some credible Selectors. Reality might be some way because that way is the best, or the simplest, or the least arbitrary, or because its obtaining makes reality as full and varied as it could be, or because its fundamental laws are, in some way, as elegant as they could be. Presumably there are other such features, which I have overlooked.

In claiming that there are credible Selectors, I am assuming that some cosmic and explanatory possibilities are more probable than others. That assumption may be questioned. Judgments of probability, it may again be claimed, must be grounded on facts about our world, so such judgments cannot be applied either to how the whole of reality might be, or to how reality might be explained.

This objection is, I believe, unsound. When we choose between scientific theories, our judgments of their probability cannot rest only on predictions based on established facts and laws. We need such judgments in trying to decide what these facts and laws are. And we can justifiably make such judgments when considering different ways in which the whole of reality may be, or might have been. Compare two such cosmic possibilities. In the first, there is a lifeless Universe consisting only of some spherical iron stars, whose relative motion is as it would be in our world. In the second, things are the same, except that the stars move together in the patterns of a minuet, and they are shaped like either Queen Victoria or Cary Grant. We would be right to claim that, of these two possibilities, the first is more likely to obtain.

In making that claim, we would not mean that it is more likely that the first possibility obtains. Since this possibility is the existence of a lifeless Universe, we know that it does not obtain. We would be claiming that this possibility is intrinsically more likely, or that, to put it roughly, it had a greater chance of being how reality is. If some possibility is more likely to obtain, that will often make it more likely that it obtains; but though one kind of likelihood supports the other, they are quite different.

Another objection may again seem relevant here. Of the countless cosmic possibilities, a few have special features, which I have called credible Selectors. If such a possibility obtains, we have a choice of two conclusions. Either reality, by an extreme coincidence, merely happens to have this feature, or – more plausibly – this feature is one of the Selectors. It may be objected that, when I talk of an extreme coincidence, I must be assuming that these cosmic possibilities are all equally likely to obtain. But I have now rejected that assumption. And, if these possibilities are not equally likely, my reasoning may seem to be undermined.

As before, that is not so. Suppose that, of the cosmic possibilities, those that have these special features are much more likely to obtain. As this objection rightly claims, it would not then be amazing if such a possibility merely happened to obtain. But that does not undermine my reasoning, since it is another way of stating my conclusion. It is another way of saying that these features are Selectors.

These remarks do show, however, that we should distinguish two ways in which some feature may be a Selector. *Probabilistic Selectors* make some cosmic possibility more likely to obtain, but leave it open whether it does obtain. On any plausible view, there are some Selectors of this kind, since some ways for reality to be are intrinsically more likely than others. Thus, of our two imagined Universes, the one consisting of spherical stars is intrinsically more likely than the one with stars that are shaped like Queen Victoria or Cary Grant. Besides Probabilistic Selectors, there may also be one or more *Effective Selectors*. If some possibility has a certain feature, this fact may make this possibility, not merely intrinsically more likely, but the one that obtains. Thus, if simplicity had been the Effective Selector, that would have made it true that nothing ever existed. And, if maximality is the Effective Selector, as it may be, that is what makes reality as full as it could be. When I talk of Selectors, these are the kind I mean.

There are, then, various cosmic and explanatory possibilities. In trying to decide which of these obtain, we can in part appeal to facts about our world. Thus, from the mere fact that our world exists, we can deduce that the Null Possibility does not obtain. And, since our world seems to contain pointless evils, we have reason to reject the Axiarchic View.

Consider next the Brute Fact View, on which reality merely happens to be as it is. No facts about our world could refute this view. But some facts would make it less likely that this view is true. If reality is randomly selected, what we should expect to exist are many varied worlds, none of which had features that, in the range of possibilities, were at one extreme. That is what we should expect because, in much the largest set of cosmic possibilities, that would be what exists. If our world has very special features, that would count against the Brute Fact View.

Return now to the question whether God exists. Compared with the uncaused existence of one or many complicated worlds, the hypothesis that God exists has been claimed to be simpler, and less arbitrary, and thus more likely to be true. But this hypothesis is not simpler than the Brute Fact View. And, if it is random which cosmic possibility obtains, we should not expect the one that obtains to be as simple, and unarbitrary, as God's existence is claimed to be. Rather, as I have just said, we should expect there to be many worlds, none with very special features. Ours may be the kind of world that, on the Brute Fact View, we should expect to observe.

Similar remarks apply to the All Worlds Hypothesis. Few facts about our world could refute this view; but, if all possible local worlds exist, the likely character of our world is much the same as on the Brute Fact View. That claim may seem surprising, given the difference between these two views. One view is about *which* cosmic possibility obtains, the other is about *why* the one that obtains obtains. And these views conflict, since, if we knew either to be true, we would have strong reason not to believe the other. If all possible worlds exist, that is most unlikely to be a brute fact. But, in their different ways, these views are both *non-selective*. On neither view do certain worlds exist because they have certain special features. So, if either view is true, we should not expect our world to have such features.

To that last claim, there is one exception. This is the feature with which we began: that our world allows for life. Though this feature is, in some ways, special, it is one that we cannot help observing. That restricts what we can infer from the fact that our world has this feature. Rather than claiming that being life-allowing is one of the Selectors, we can appeal to some version of the Many Worlds Hypothesis. If there are many worlds, we would expect a few worlds to be life-allowing, and our world is bound to be one of these few.

Consider next other kinds of special feature, ones that we are not bound to observe. Suppose we discover that our world has such a feature, and we ask whether that is no coincidence. It may again be said that, if there are many worlds, we would expect a few worlds to have this special feature. But that would not explain why that is true of our world. We could not claim – as with the feature of being life-allowing – that our world is bound to have this feature. So the appeal to many worlds could not explain away the coincidence. Suppose, for example, that our world were very good, or were wholly law-governed, or had very simple natural laws. Those facts would count against both of the unselective views: both the All Worlds Hypothesis and the Brute Fact View. It is true that, if all worlds exist, or there are very many randomly selected worlds, we should expect a few worlds to be very good, or wholly law-governed, or to have very simple laws. But that would not explain why our world had those features. So we would have some reason to believe that our world is the way it is because this way has those features.

Does our world have such features, ones that count against the unselective views? Our world's moral character seems not to count against these views, since it seems the mixture of good and bad that, on the unselective views, we should expect. But our world may have the other two features: being wholly law-governed, and having very simple laws. Neither feature seems to be required in order for life to be possible. And, among possible life-containing worlds, a far greater range would not have these features. Thus, for each law-governed world, there are countless variants that would fail in different ways to be wholly law-governed. And, compared with simple laws, there is a far greater range of complicated laws. So, on both the unselective views, we should not expect our world to have these features. If it has them, as physicists might discover, that would give us reasons to reject both the All Worlds Hypothesis and the Brute Fact View. We would have some reason to believe that there are at least two partial Selectors: being law-governed and having simple laws.

There may be other features of our world from which we can try to infer what reality is like, and why. But observation can take us only part of the way. If we can get further, that will have to be by pure reasoning.

Of those who accept the Brute Fact View, many assume that it must be true. According to these people, though reality merely happens to be some way, that it merely happens to be some way does not merely happen to be true. There could not be an explanation of why reality is the way it is, since there could not be a causal explanation, and no other explanation would make sense.

This assumption, I have argued, is mistaken. Reality might be the way it is because this way is the fullest, or the most varied, or obeys the simplest or most elegant laws, or has some other special feature. Since the Brute Fact View is not the only explanatory possibility, we should not assume that it must be true.

When supporters of this view recognise these other possibilities, they may switch to the other extreme, claiming that their view's truth is another brute fact. If that were so, not only would there be no explanation of reality's being as it is, there would also be no explanation of there being no such explanation. As before, though this might be true, we should not assume that it must be true. If some explanatory possibility merely happens to obtain, the one that obtains may not be the Brute Fact View. If it is randomly selected *whether* reality is randomly selected, and there are other possibilities, random selection may not be selected.

There is, moreover, another way in which some explanatory possibility may obtain. Rather than merely happening to obtain, this possibility may have some feature, or set of features, which explains why it obtains. Such a feature would be a Selector at a higher level, since it would apply not to factual but to explanatory possibilities. It would determine, not that reality be a certain way, but that it be determined in a certain way how reality is to be.

If the Brute Fact View is true, it may have been selected in this way. Of the explanatory possibilities, this view seems to describe the simplest, since its claim is only that reality has no explanation. This possibility's being the simplest might make it the one that obtains. Simplicity may be the higher Selector, determining that there is no Selector between the ways that reality might be.

Once again, however, though this may be true, we cannot assume its truth. There may be some other higher Selector. Some explanatory possibility may obtain, for example, because it is the least arbitrary, or is the one that explains most. The Brute Fact View has neither of those features. Or there may be no higher Selector, since some explanatory possibility may merely happen to obtain.

These alternatives are the different possibilities at yet another, higher explanatory level. So we have the same two questions: which obtains, and why?

We may now become discouraged. Every answer, it may seem, raises a further question. But that may not be so. There may be some answer that is a necessary truth. With that necessity, our search would end.

Some truth is logically necessary when its denial leads to a contradiction. It cannot be in this sense necessary either that reality is a brute fact, or that there is some Selector. Both these claims can be denied without contradiction.

There are also non-logical necessities. The most familiar, causal necessity, cannot give us the truth we need. It could not be causally necessary that reality is, or isn't, a brute fact. Causal necessities come lower down. Similar remarks apply to the necessities involved in the essential properties of particular things, or natural kinds. Consider next the metaphysical necessity that some writers claim for God's existence. That claim means, they say, that God's existence does not depend on anything else, and that nothing else could cause God to cease to exist. But these claims do not imply that God must exist, and that makes such necessity too weak to end our questions.

There are, however, some kinds of necessity that would be strong enough. Consider the truths that undeserved suffering is bad, and that, if we believe the premises of a sound argument, we ought rationally to believe this argument's conclusion. These truths are not logically necessary, since their denials would not lead to contradictions. But they could not have failed to be true. Undeserved suffering does not merely happen to be bad.

When John Leslie defends the Axiarchic View, he appeals to this kind of non-logical necessity. Not only does value rule reality, Leslie suggests, it could not have failed to rule. But this suggestion is hard to believe. While it is inconceivable that undeserved suffering might have failed to be in itself bad, it seems clearly conceivable that value might have failed to rule, if only because it seems so clear that value does not rule.

Return now to the Brute Fact View, which is more likely to be true. If this view is true, could its truth be non-logically necessary? Is it inconceivable that there might be some Selector, or highest law, making reality be some way? The answer, I have claimed, is No. Even if reality is a brute fact, it might not have been. Thus, if nothing had ever existed, that might have been no coincidence. Reality might have been that way because, of the cosmic possibilities, it is the simplest and least arbitrary. And, as I have also claimed, just as it is not necessary that the Brute Fact View is true, it is not necessary that this view's truth be another brute fact. This view might be true because it is the simplest of the explanatory possibilities.

We have not yet found the necessity we need. Reality may happen to be as it is, or there may be some Selector. Whichever of these is true, it may happen to be true, or there may be some higher Selector. These are the different possibilities at the next explanatory level, so we are back with our two questions: which obtains, and why?

Could these questions continue for ever? Might there be, at every level, another higher Selector? Consider another version of the Axiarchic View. Reality might be as good as it could be, and that might be true because its being true is best, and that in turn might be true because its being true is best, and so on for ever. In this way, it may seem, everything might be explained. But that is not so. Like an infinite series of events, such a series of explanatory truths could not explain itself. Even if each truth were made true by the next, we could still ask why the whole series was true, rather than some other series, or no series.

The point can be made more simply. Though there might be some highest Selector, this might not be goodness but some other feature, such as non-arbitrariness. What could select between these possibilities? Might goodness be the highest Selector because that is best, or non-arbitrariness be this Selector because that is the least arbitrary possibility? Neither suggestion, I believe, makes sense. Just as God could not make himself exist, no Selector could make itself the one that, at the highest level, rules. No Selector could settle whether it rules, since it cannot settle anything unless it does rule.

If there is some highest Selector, this cannot, I have claimed, be a necessary truth. Nor could this Selector make itself the highest. And, since this Selector would be the highest, nothing else could make that true. So we may have found the necessity we need. If there is some highest Selector, that, I suggest, must merely happen to be true.

Supporters of the Brute Fact View may now feel vindicated. Have we not, in the end, accepted their view?

We have not. According to the Brute Fact View, reality merely happens to be as it is. That, I have argued, may not be true, since there may be some Selector which explains, or partly explains, reality's being as it is. There may also be some higher Selector which explains there being this Selector. My suggestion is only that, at the end of any such explanatory chain, some highest Selector must merely happen to be the one that rules. That is a different view.

This difference may seem small. No Selector could explain reality, we may believe, if it merely happened to rule. But this thought, though natural, is a mistake. If some explanation appeals to a brute fact, it does not explain that fact; but it may explain others.

Suppose, for example, that reality is as full as it could be. On the Brute Fact View, this fact would have no explanation. On the Maximalist View, reality would be this way because the highest law is that what is possible is actual. If reality were as full as it could be, this Maximalist View would be better than the Brute Fact View, since it would explain reality's being this way. And this view would provide that explanation even if it merely happened to be true. It makes a difference where the brute fact comes.

Part of the difference here is that, while there are countless cosmic possibilities, there are few plausible explanatory possibilities. If reality is as full as it could be, that's being a brute fact would be very puzzling. Since there are countless cosmic possibilities, it would be amazing if the one that obtained merely happened to be at the maximal extreme. On the Maximalist View, this fact would be no coincidence. And, since there are few explanatory possibilities, it would not be amazing if the Maximalist highest law merely happened to be the one that rules.

We should not claim that, if some explanation rests on a brute fact, it is not an explanation. Most scientific explanations take this form. The most that might be true is that such an explanation is, in a way, merely a better description.

If that were true, there would be a different defence of the kind of reasoning that we have been considering. Even to discover *how* things are, we need explanations. And we may need explanations on the grandest scale. Our world may seem to have some feature that would be unlikely to be a coincidence. We may reasonably suspect that this feature is the Selector, or one of the Selectors. That hypothesis might lead us to confirm that, as it seemed, our world does have this feature. And that might give us reason to conclude either that ours is the only world, or that there are other worlds, with the same or related features. We might thus reach truths about the whole Universe.

Even if all explanations must end with a brute fact, we should go on trying to explain why the Universe exists, and is as it is. The brute fact may not enter at the lowest level. If reality is the way it is because this way has some feature, to know *what* reality is like we must ask *why*.

We may never be able to answer these questions, either because our world is only a small part of reality, or because, though our world is the whole of reality, we could never know that to be true, or because of our own limitations. But, as I have tried to show, we may come to see more clearly what the possible answers are. Some of the fog that shrouds these questions may then disappear.

It can seem astonishing, for example, how reality could be made to be as it is. If God made the rest of reality be as it is, what could have made God exist? And, if God does not exist, what else could have made reality be as it is? When we think about these questions, even the Brute Fact View may seem unintelligible. It may seem baffling how reality could be even randomly selected. What kind of process could select whether, for example, time had no beginning, or whether anything ever exists? When, and how, could any selection be made?

This is not a real problem. Of all the possible ways that reality might be, there must be one that is the way reality actually is. Since it is logically necessary that reality be some way or other, it is necessary that one way be picked to be the way reality is. Logic ensures that, without any kind of process, a selection is made. There is no need for hidden machinery.

Suppose next that, as many people assume, the Brute Fact View must be true. If our world has no very special features, there would then be nothing that was deeply puzzling. If it were necessary that some global possibility be randomly selected, while there would be no explanation of why the selection went as it did, there would be no mystery in reality's being as it is. Reality's features would be inexplicable, but only in the way in which it is inexplicable how some particle randomly moves. If a particle can merely happen to move as it does, reality could merely happen to be as it is. Randomness may even be less puzzling at the level of the whole Universe, since we know that facts at this level could not have been caused.

The Brute Fact View, I have argued, is not necessary, and may not be true. There may be one or more Selectors between the ways that reality might be, and one or more Selectors between such Selectors. But, as I have also claimed, it may be a necessary truth that it be a brute fact whether there are such Selectors, and, if so, which the highest Selector is.

If that is a necessary truth, similar remarks apply. On these assumptions, there would again be nothing that was deeply puzzling. If it is necessary that, of these explanatory possibilities, one merely happens to obtain, there would be no explanation of why the one that obtains obtains. But, as before, that would be no more mysterious than the random movement of some particle.

The existence of the Universe can seem, in another way, astonishing. Even if it is not baffling that reality was made to be some way, since there is no conceivable alternative, it can seem baffling that the selection went as it did. Why is there a Universe at all? Why doesn't reality take its simplest and least arbitrary form: that in which nothing ever exists?

If we find this astonishing, we are assuming that these features should be the Selectors: that reality should be as simple and unarbitrary as it could be. That assumption has, I believe, great plausibility. But, just as the simplest cosmic possibility is that nothing ever exists, the simplest explanatory possibility is that there is no Selector. So we should not expect simplicity at both the factual and explanatory levels. If there is no Selector, we should not expect that there would also be no Universe. That would be an extreme coincidence.

Of several discussions of these questions, I owe most to John Leslie's *Value and Existence* (1979), and to Robert Nozick's *Philosophical Explanations* (1981); then to Richard Swinburne's *The Existence of God* (1979), John Mackie's *The Miracle of Theism* (1982), Peter Unger's article in *Mid-West Studies in Philosophy*, Volume 9 (1989), and some unpublished work by Stephen Grover.

Ways of Explaining Existence*

ROBERT NOZICK

Why is there something rather than nothing? The question appears impossible to answer. Any factor introduced to explain why there is something will itself be part of the something to be explained, so it (or anything utilizing it) could not explain all of the something – it could not explain why there is *anything* at all. Explanation proceeds by explaining some things in terms of others, but this question seems to preclude introducing anything else, any explanatory factors. Some writers conclude from this that the question is ill-formed and meaningless. But why do they cheerfully reject the question rather than despairingly observe that it demarcates a limit of what we can hope to understand? So daunting is the question that even a recent urger of it, Heidegger, who terms it "the fundamental question of metaphysics", proposes no answer and does nothing toward showing how it might be answered.

This chapter considers several possible answers to the question. My aim is not to assert one of these answers as correct (if I had great confidence in any one, I wouldn't feel the special need to devise and present several); the aim, rather, is to loosen our feeling of being trapped by a question with no possible answer – one impossible to answer yet inescapable. (So that one feels the only thing to do is gesture at a Mark Rothko painting.) The question cuts so deep, however, that any approach that stands a chance of yielding an answer will look extremely weird. Someone who proposes a non-strange answer shows he didn't understand this question. Since the question is not to be rejected, though, we must be prepared to accept strangeness or apparent craziness in a theory that answers it.

Still, I do not endorse here any one of the discussed possible answers as correct. It is too early for that. Yet it is late enough in the question's history to stop merely asking it insistently, and to begin proposing possible answers. Thereby, we at least show how it is possible to explain why there is something rather than nothing, how it is possible for the question to have an answer.

Explaining Everything

The question "why is there something rather than nothing?" quickly raises issues about the limits of our understanding. Is it possible for everything to be explained? It often is said that at any given time the most general laws and theories we know (or believe) are unexplained, but nothing is unexplainable in principle. At a later

* From chapter 2 of *Philosophical Explanations* (Cambridge, MA: The Belknap Press of Harvard University Press, 1981), pp. 115–129, 131, 150, 152–153, 156–157. Reprinted by permission of the Publisher. Copyright © 1981 by Robert Nozick.

time we can formulate a deeper theory to explain the previous deepest one. This previous theory wasn't unexplainable, and though the new deepest theory is unexplained, at least for the time being, it too is not unexplainable.

The question about whether everything is explainable is a different one. Let the relation E be the relation *correctly explains*, or *is the (or a) correct explanation of*. [...] How is the set of truths structured by the explanatory relation E? There appear to be only two possibilities. Either (1) there is some truth that no further truth stands in E to, or (2) there are infinite explanatory chains, and each truth has something else that stands in E to it. Either there are no foundations to science, no most fundamental or deep explanatory principles (the second possibility) or there are some truths without any explanation (the first possibility); these actually will be unexplainable in that *no* truths (known or not) explain them. About such truths *p* lacking further explanation, there also appear to be two possibilities. First, that such truths are necessarily true, and could not have been otherwise. (Aristotle, as standardly interpreted, maintained this.) But it is difficult to see how this would be true. It is not enough merely for it to be of the essence of the things which exist (and so necessarily true of them) that *p*. There would remain the question of why those and only those sorts of things (subject to *p*) exist; only if *p* must be true of everything possible would this question be avoided.

The second possibility is that *p* is a brute fact. It just happens that things are that way. There is no explanation (or reason) why they are that way rather than another way, no (hint of) necessity to remove this arbitrariness.

One way to remove some arbitrariness from the end of the explanatory chain is illustrated by the program of deriving moral content from the form of morality, a persistent attempt since Kant. [...] Within the factual realm, the parallel endeavor would derive particular empirical content from the form of facts, or more narrowly from the form of scientific laws or theories. This would show that if there are ultimate scientific laws, so nothing else does or can stand in the explanatory relation E to them, then these must have particular content. Such a project might formulate various symmetry and invariance conditions as holding of fundamental scientific laws, showing that only particular content satisfied all these conditions about form. This would render the particular content less arbitrary, but the question would remain of why there were any ultimate scientific laws, any truths of that specified form. In any case, there will be the question of why there are any laws at all. This question is narrower than our title question but raises similar problems. If all explanation utilizes laws, then in the explanation of why there are any laws, some law will appear. Will not the question of why it holds, and hence of why any law holds, thereby go unanswered?

Is there any way at all to remove these last unexplained bits? Since a fact that nothing explains is left dangling, while a fact explained by something else leaves the problem of explaining that something else, only one thing could leave nothing at all unexplained: a fact that explains itself. [...]

Suppose a principle P presented sufficient conditions for a fundamental law's holding true; any lawlike statement that satisfies these conditions, such as invariance and symmetry, will hold true. P says: any lawlike statement having characteristics C is true. Let us imagine this is our deepest law; we explain why other fundamental laws hold true in accordance with the deep principle P, by their having the characteristic C. Those laws are true because they have C.

Next we face the question of why P holds true, and we notice that P itself also has characteristics C. This yields the following deduction.

P: any lawlike statement having characteristic C is true.
P is a lawlike statement with characteristic C.
Therefore P is true.

This is not presented to justify P or as a reason for believing P. Rather, granting that P *is* true, the question is whether what explains its being true, is its having characteristics C (since everything with C is true). [...] Our question is not whether such self-subsumption as an instance of itself can constitute a proof, but whether it can constitute an explanation; *if* the statement is true, can the reason why be the very content it itself states?

Explanatory self-subsumption, I admit, appears quite weird – a feat of legerdemain. When we reach the ultimate and most fundamental explanatory laws, however, there are few possibilities. Either there is an infinite chain of different laws and theories, each explaining the next, or there is a finite chain. If a finite chain, either the endmost laws are unexplainable facts or necessary truths or the only laws there can be if there are laws of a certain sort at all (the fact that there are laws of that sort is classified under one of the other possibilities) – or the endmost laws are self-subsuming.

We face two questions about such self-subsumption: does it reduce the arbitrariness and brute-fact quality of the endpoint at all? If so, does it remove that quality completely? It does reduce that quality, I believe, though I cannot quite say it removes it altogether. If a brute fact is something that cannot be explained by anything, then a self-subsumable principle isn't a brute fact; but if a brute fact is something that cannot be explained by anything *else*, such a principle counts as a brute fact [...]

Inegalitarian Theories

There is one common form many theories share: they hold that one situation or a small number of states N are natural or privileged and in need of no explanation, while all other states are to be explained as deviations from N, resulting from the action of forces F that cause movement away from the natural state. For Newton, rest or uniform rectilinear motion is the natural state requiring no explanation, while all other motions are to be explained by unbalanced forces acting upon bodies. For Aristotle, rest was the natural state, deviations from which were produced by the continual action of impressed forces. This pattern is not, however, restricted to theories of motion.

Let us call a theory of this sort an inegalitarian theory. An inegalitarian theory partitions states into two classes: those requiring explanation, and those neither needing nor admitting of explanation. Inegalitarian theories are especially well geared to answer questions of the form "why is there X rather than Y?" There is a non-N state rather than an N state because of the forces F that acted to bring the system away from N. When there is an N state, this is because there were no unbalanced forces acting to bring the system away from N.

Inegalitarian theories unavoidably leave two questions unanswered. First, why is it N that is the natural state which occurs in the absence of unbalanced external forces, rather than some other (type of) state N'? Second, given that N is a natural or privileged state, why is it forces of type F, not of some other type F', that produce deviations from N? If our fundamental theory has an inegalitarian structure, it will leave as brute and unexplained the fact that N rather than something else is a natural state, and that F rather than something else is the deviation force.

However special a state appears, to assume it is a natural state within an inegalitarian theory has significant content. We should be very suspicious of a priori arguments purporting to demonstrate that a state is a natural one, and we should search such arguments carefully for the covert assumption that the state is natural or that only certain types of forces can produce deviations from whatever the natural state happens to be. We cannot assume any particular inegalitarian theory as our fundamental theory.

The question "why is there something rather than nothing?" is posed against the background of an assumed inegalitarian theory. If there were nothing, then about this situation would there also be the question (though without anyone to ask it) of why there is nothing rather than something? To ask "why is there something rather than nothing?" assumes that nothing(ness) is the natural state that does not need to be explained, while deviations or divergences from nothingness have to be explained by the introduction of special causal factors. There is, so to speak, a presumption in favor of nothingness. The problem is so intractable because any special causal factor that could explain a deviation from nothingness is itself a divergence from nothingness, and so the question seeks its explanation also.

Is it possible to imagine nothingness being a natural state which itself contains the force whereby something is produced? One might hold that nothingness as a natural state is derivative from a very powerful force toward nothingness, one any other forces have to overcome. Imagine this force as a vacuum force, sucking things into non-existence or keeping them there. If this force acts upon itself, it sucks nothingness into nothingness, producing something or, perhaps, everything, every possibility. If we introduced the verb "to nothing" to denote what this nothingness force does to things as it makes or keeps them nonexistent, then (we would say) the nothingness nothings itself. (See how Heideggerian the seas of language run here!) Nothingness, hoisted by its own powerful petard, produces something. In the Beatles' cartoon *The Yellow Submarine*, a being like a vacuum cleaner goes around sucking up first other objects, next the surrounding background; finally, turning upon itself, it sucks itself into nothingness, thereby producing with a pop a brightly colored variegated scene.

On this view, there is something rather than nothing because the nothingness there once was nothinged itself, thereby producing something. Perhaps it nothinged itself just a bit, though, producing something but leaving some remaining force for nothingness. [...]

Thus far I have been considering the inegalitarian theory that assumes nothingness is the natural state. It is time to undermine the picture of nothingness as natural, first by imagining inegalitarian theories where it is not. We might imagine that some fullness of existence is the natural state, and that the actual situation deviates from this fullness because of special forces acting. Whether this theory allows nothingness to result eventually will depend upon whether the force producing deviations from fullness, once it has performed the rest of its task, can act upon itself thereby annihilating itself, the very last vestige of any fullness. (Or perhaps several forces operate to diverge from fullness that, after the rest of their job is done, can simultaneously annihilate each other.) The western philosophical tradition tends to hold that existence is better or more perfect than nonexistence, so it tends to view forces that cause divergence from fullness as malignant. But one can imagine another view, wherein the movement from thick and dense matter to more ethereal and spiritual modes of energy and existence is a movement of increasing perfection. The limit of such movement toward more and more insubstantial existence will be the most perfect: nothingness itself. Since reaching such perfection might take hard work and spiritual development, the answer to the question "why is there something rather than nothing?" might be that the universe is not yet spiritually developed enough for there to be nothing. The something is not enlightened yet. Perfection is not the natural state, and there is something rather than nothing because this is not the best of all possible worlds. Against the background of some such theory, the opposite question "why is there nothing rather than something?" (as applied to the appropriate situation) would make sense, and the correct answer would specify the forces that produced the deviation from somethingness, bringing about nothingness.

Apart from any such specific background theory, we should note a general reason or argument for *something's* being the natural state. (This argument was pointed out to me by Emily Nozick, then age twelve.) If something cannot be created out of nothing, then, since there is something, it didn't come from nothing. And there never was a time when there was only nothing. If ever nothing was the natural state, which obtained, then something could never have arisen. But there is something. So nothingness is not the natural state; if there is a natural state, it is somethingness. (If nothingness were the natural state, we never could have gotten to something – we couldn't have gotten here from there.)

It is possible to think that one cannot answer any question if one cannot answer the question of why there is something rather than nothing. How can we know why something is (or should be) a certain way if we don't know why there is anything at all? Surely this is the first philosophical question that has to be answered. It doesn't seem to assume anything (other than that there is something), while the answer to any other philosophical question is liable to be overturned or undermined or transformed by the answer to this one. However, to ask this question is to presume a great deal, namely, that nothingness is a natural state requiring no explanation, while all deviations from nothingness are in need of explanation. This is a very strong assumption, so strong that we cannot merely extrapolate from more limited contexts (such as argument, where the burden of proof is on the person who makes an existence claim) and build the assumption into our fundamental theory, one not restricted within an understood wider context [...]

Egalitarianism

One way to dissolve the inegalitarian class distinction between nothing and something, treating them on a par, is to apply a version of the principle of indifference from probability theory. There are many ways w_1, w_2, ... for there to be something, but there is only one way w_0 for there to be nothing. Assign equal probability to each alternative possibility w_i, assuming it is a completely random matter which one obtains. The chances, then, are very great that there will be something, for "there is something" holds of every possibility except w_0. On some views of statistical explanation, by (correctly) specifying a random mechanism that yields a very high probability of there being something, we thereby would have explained why there is. ("Why is there something? It is just what you would expect that random mechanism to produce.")

In regard to the use of principles of indifference within probability theory, it often has been pointed out that much rests upon the initial partitioning into (what will be treated as equiprobable) states. A state that is single in one partition can encompass many states in another partition. Even the many ways of there being something might be viewed as just one state in the two-membered partition: there is nothing, there is something. Yet while we can shrink there being something down to only one alternative, we cannot, even artificially, expand there being nothing up to more than one alternative. If there is nothing(ness), there just are no aspects of it to use to divide it into two alternatives.

So on the worst assumptions about how the partitioning goes, yielding the two-membered partition, there initially is a one-half chance that something exists. Since all other partitions are at least three-membered, on these other partitionings the initial chance of something's existing is at least two-thirds. Can we go up one level and assign probabilities to the different partitionings themselves? If we go up levels, assigning equal probabilities to the worst case partitioning and to all others (equally), then the probability of something existing increases, and tends toward the probability in the previous equal-chance large partitioning under the principle of indifference. The larger the number of alternatives partitioned, the closer the probability that something exists approaches to one.

This model of a random process with one alternative being that nothing exists (N), is illuminating. However, it does not sufficiently shake off inegalitarian assumptions. Though the model treats its possibilities on a par, it assumes a possibility will not be realized unless at random. It assumes that the natural state for a possibility is nonrealization, and that a possibility's being realized has to be explained by special factors (including, at the limit, random ones). At this deep level the presented model remains inegalitarian. What would a thoroughgoing egalitarian theory be like?

Fecundity

A thoroughgoing egalitarian theory will not treat nonexisting or non-obtaining as more natural or privileged, even for a possibility – it will treat all possibilities on a par. One way to do this is to say that all possibilities are realized.

For the most fundamental laws and initial conditions C of the universe, the answer to the question "why C rather than D?" is that *both* independently exist. We happen to find ourselves in a C universe rather than a D universe; perhaps this is no accident for a D universe might not produce or support life such as ours. There is no explanation of why C rather than D, for there is no fact of C rather than D. All the possibilities exist in independent noninteracting realms, in "parallel universes". We might call this the fecundity assumption. It appears that only such an egalitarian view does not leave any question "why X rather than Y?" unanswered. No brute fact of X rather than Y is left unexplained for no such fact holds [...]

Fecundity and Self-Subsumption

As an ultimate and very deep principle, the principle of fecundity can subsume itself within a deductive explanation. It states that all possibilities are realized, while it itself is one of those possibilities [...]

Beyond

The important hymn from the Vedas, the Hymn of Creation, begins "Nonbeing then existed not nor being". This is the translation by Radhakrishnan and Moore.

In the Griffith translation, we find this as "Then was not nonexistent nor existent"; in the Max Müller translation, "There was then neither what is nor what is not."

How can what there was "then", that is, in the beginning or before everything else, be neither nonbeing nor being, neither nonexistent nor existent, neither is nor is not? For being and nonbeing, existent and nonexistent, is and is not, seem exhaustive. There does not seem to be any other possibility. In accordance with the law of the excluded middle, everything is either one or the other.

However, sometimes things that seem to exhaust the possibilities do not, rather they do so only within a certain realm. Consider color. Everything is either colored (singly colored or multicolored) or uncolored, that is, transparent. Either a thing is colored or it is uncolored, what other possibility is there? Yet the number 5, and Beethoven's Quartet Number 15, are neither colored nor uncolored. These are not the sort of things that can have or fail to have colors – they are not physical or spatial objects or events. (Do not confuse them with numerals or written musical scores, which can be colored.) [...]

I suggest we understand the beginning of the Hymn of Creation, "nonbeing then existed not nor being", as saying that the pairs being and nonbeing, existent and nonexistent, and is and isn't have presuppositions, that the terms within these pairs apply and exhaust the possibilities only within a certain domain, while outside this domain a thing may be neither. Such theories are not unknown in the West: Plato says God is "beyond being" (*Republic* VI, 509b), and Plotinus makes this central to his theory of the One [...]

It is plausible that whatever every existent thing comes from, their source, falls outside the categories of existence and nonexistence. Moreover, we then avoid the question: why does *that* exist? It doesn't *exist*. Strictly, that which is beyond those categories neither exists nor doesn't exist. But if you had to say one, you would mention whichever of existence and nonexistence was closer to its status. If both were equally close or distant, if it was equidistant from both, you might say: it exists *and* it doesn't exist. [...]

Consider, as an analogy, the structure of all possibilities. A particular possibility is realized or is actual or exists, and another is not realized and so nonexists. What exists and nonexists are particular possibilities. The structure of all possibilities underlies existence and nonexistence. That structure itself doesn't exist and it doesn't nonexist. [...]

Mystical Experience

Assertions of something beyond existence and nonexistence, infinite and unbounded, appear in the writings of (some) mystics, not as hypotheses to answer questions of cosmogony but to describe what they have experienced and encountered.

How much credence should we give to these experiences? Undoubtedly such experiences are had and are sincerely reported, and they strike the mystic as revelatory of reality, of a deeper reality. Why deeper? What is experienced is different, but this does not show that it is deeper, rather than more superficial even than the reality we normally know. The experiences come as revelatory of something deeper. Should we believe the report of mystics that there is this reality? Should the mystics themselves believe it?

There are two major approaches to these experiences: first, to explain them away, to offer an explanation of why they occur that doesn't introduce (as an explanatory factor) anything like what the mystics claim to experience; and second, to see them as revelatory of a reality that is as it is encountered. To notice that there are special conditions under which such experiences occur, for example, after yogic practice or ingestion of certain drugs, does not settle which approach should be taken. What the first approach treats as a cause of the experience, the second will see as removing the veil from reality so that it can be perceived as it really is. Does the unusual physio-chemical state of the brain produce an illusion, or does it enable us to experience reality?

Why Not Nothing?*

ROBERT LAWRENCE KUHN

When I was 12, in the summer between seventh and eighth grades, a sudden realization struck such fright that I strove desperately to blot it out, to eradicate the disruptive idea as if it were a lethal mind virus. My body shuddered with dread; an abyss had yawned open. Five decades on I feel its frigid blast still.

Why not Nothing?[1] What if everything had always been Nothing? Not just emptiness, not just blankness, and not just emptiness and blankness forever, but not even the existence of emptiness, not even the meaning of blankness, and no forever. Wouldn't it have been easier, simpler, more logical, to have Nothing rather than something?[2]

Lump together everything that exists and might exist – physical, mental, platonic, spiritual, God. As for the physical, include all matter, energy, space and time, and all the laws and principles that govern them (known and unknown); as for the mental, imagine all kinds of consciousness and awareness (known and unknown); as for the platonic, gather all forms of abstract objects (numbers, logic, forms, propositions – known and unknown); and as for the spiritual and God, embrace anything that could possibly fit these nonphysical categories (if anything

* Derived and developed further from "How Ultimate Reality Works for Us: A Taxonomy of Possible Explanations," in R.L. Kuhn, *Closer to Truth: Science, Meaning and the Future* (Westport, CT: Praeger, 2007), and "Why This Universe: Toward a Taxonomy of Possible Explanations," *Skeptic* vol. 13 no. 2 (2007). With kind permission of ABC-CLIO LLC and Skeptic Magazine.

does). Lump together literally everything contained in ultimate reality. Now call it all by the simple name "Something." Why is there "Something" rather than "Nothing?"

The question would become my life partner, and even as I learned the rich philosophical legacy of Nothing,[3] I do not pass a day without its disquieting presence. I am haunted. Here we are, human beings, conscious and abruptly self-aware, with lives fleetingly short, engulfed by a vast, seemingly oblivious cosmos of unimaginable enormousness.[4]

While "Why Not Nothing?" may seem impenetrable, "Why This Universe?", revivified by remarkable advances in precision cosmology, may be accessible. Even though they are not at all the same question, perhaps if we can begin to decipher the latter, we can begin to decrypt the former. Why This Universe? assumes there is Something and seeks the root reason of why this universe exists and works for us.

I am the creator and host of the public television/PBS series *Closer To Truth*, which brings together scientists and philosophers to examine the meaning and implications of state-of-the-art science and diverse forms of new knowledge. The current production – *Closer To Truth: Cosmos, Consciousness, God*[5] – focuses on cosmology, fundamental physics, philosophy of cosmology/physics, nature of consciousness, mind/body problem, philosophy of religion, and philosophical theology, and thus I have been meeting cosmologists, physicists, neuroscientists, philosophers and theologians, and asking them ultimate questions. From their multifarious and insightful answers, and from my own night musings, I have constructed a taxonomy that I present here as a heuristic to help get our minds around this perennial and terminal question.[6]

The Problem to be Solved

In recent years, the search for scientific explanations of reality has been energized by increasing recognition that the laws of physics and the constants that are embedded in these laws all seem exquisitely "fine tuned" to allow, or to enable, the existence of stars and planets and the emergence of life and mind. If the laws of physics had much differed, if the values of their constants had much changed, or if the initial conditions of the universe had much varied, what we know to exist would not exist since all things of size and substance would not have formed. Stephen Hawking presented the problem this way:

> Why is the universe so close to the dividing line between collapsing again and expanding indefinitely? In order to be as close as we are now, the rate of expansion early on had to be chosen fantastically accurately. If the rate of expansion one second after the Big Bang had been less by one part in 10^{10}, the universe would have

collapsed after a few million years. If it had been greater by one part in 10^{10}, the universe would have been essentially empty after a few million years. In neither case would it have lasted long enough for life to develop. Thus one either has to appeal to the anthropic principle or find some physical explanation of why the universe is the way it is.[7]

To Roger Penrose, the "extraordinary degree of precision (or 'fine tuning') that seems to be required for the Big Bang of the nature that we appear to observe [....] in phase-space-volume terms, is one part in $\mathbf{10^{10^{123}}}$ at least." Penrose sees "two possible routes to addressing this question [...] We might take the position that the initial condition was an 'act of God'. [...] or we might seek some scientific/ mathematical theory." His strong inclination, he says, "is certainly to try to see how far we can get with the second possibility."[8]

To Steven Weinberg, it is "peculiar" that the calculated value of the vacuum energy of empty space (due to quantum fluctuations in known fields at well-understood energies) is "larger than observationally allowed by 10^{56}," and if this were to be cancelled "by simply including a suitable cosmological constant in the Einstein field equations [General Relativity], the cancellation would have to be exact to 56 decimal places." Weinberg states that "No symmetry argument or adjustment mechanism could be found that would explain such a cancellation."[9]

To Leonard Susskind, "the best efforts of the best physicists, using our best theories, predict Einstein's cosmological constant incorrectly by 120 orders of magnitude!" "That's so bad, "he says, "it's funny." He adds that "for a bunch of numbers, none of them particularly small, to cancel one another to such precision would be a numerical coincidence so incredibly absurd that there must be some other answer."[10]

The problem to be solved is even broader. Sir Martin Rees, Britain's Astronomer Royal, presents "just six numbers" that he argues are necessary for our emergence from the Big Bang. A minuscule change in any one of these numbers would have made the universe and life, as we know them, impossible.[11] Deeper still, what requires explanation is not only this apparent fine-tuning but also the more fundamental fact that there are laws of physics at all, that we find regularity in nature.

What to make of our astonishingly good fortune? In 1938 Paul Dirac saw coincidences in cosmic and atomic physics;[12] in 1961 Robert Dicke noted that the age of the universe "now" is conditioned by biological factors;[13] and in 1973 Brandon Carter used the phrase "Anthropic Principle," which in his original formulation simply draws attention to such uncontroversial truths as that the universe must be such as to admit, at some stage, the appearance of observers within it.[14] Others then took up this oddly evocative idea, calling what seems to be a tautological statement the "Weak Anthropic Principle," as distinguished from what they defined as the "Strong Anthropic Principle," which makes the teleological claim that the universe *must* have those properties that allow or require intelligent life to develop.[15] Steven Weinberg used anthropic reasoning more rigorously to provide an upper limit on the vacuum energy (cosmological constant) and to give some idea of its expected value. He argued that "it is natural for scientists to find themselves in a subuniverse in which the vacuum energy takes a value suitable for the appearance of scientists."[16]

Although the (Weak) Anthropic Principle appears perfectly obvious – some say that a logical tautology cannot be an informative statement about the universe – inverting its orientation may elicit an explanatory surprise: What we can expect to observe must be restricted by the conditions necessary for our presence as observers. Such expectations then suggest, perhaps inevitably, the startling insight that there could be infinite numbers of separate regions or domains or "universes," each immense in its own right, each with different laws and values – and because the overwhelming majority of these regions, domains or universes would be non-life-permitting, it would be hardly remarkable that we do not find ourselves in them nor do we observe them. One could conclude, therefore, that while our universe seems to be so incredibly fine-tuned for the purpose of producing human beings, and therefore so specially designed for us, it is in fact neither.

Since the 1970s, theists have invoked this fine-tuning argument as empirical evidence for a creator by asserting that there are only two explanations: God or chance. However to pose such a stark and simplistic choice is to construct a false and misleading dichotomy. Since the Anthropic Principle leads to multiple universes, a "multiverse," other possible explanations are made manifest. I have documented 27 such explanations, a constellation of what I'll call "ultimate reality generators," in a kind of typology of cosmological conjecture. I'm sure there are more, or some could be subdivided, but generally the taxonomy can be structured with four overarching categories: One Universe Models, Multiple Universe Models, Nonphysical Causes, and Illusions.[17]

My claim is that the set of these four categories is universally exhaustive, meaning that whatever the true explanation of Why This Universe?, it would have to be classified into one (or more) of these categories (irrespective of whether we ever discover or discern that true explanation).[18]

Yet the set of the 27 possible explanations which compose the categories is not universally exhaustive nor is there practical hope of making it so. Therefore unless we can ever answer the Why-This-Universe question with certainty and finality (a dubious prospect), there will be other explanations out there that cannot be logically excluded. Further, while it might seem tidy for these explanations to be mutually exclusive – meaning that no two can both be right – such simplicity cannot be achieved. The explanations, and their categories, can be combined in any number of ways – in series, in parallel, and/or nested.

The 27 possible explanations, or ultimate reality generators, that follow are based on criteria that are logically permissible, criteria that for some may seem too lenient. I do not, however, confuse speculation with science. Logical possibilities should not be mistaken for scientific theories or even scientific possibilities.[19] A physicist's musings do not morph, as if by cosmological alchemy or professional courtesy, from speculative metaphysics into established physics. That said, some of the more intriguing metaphysical possibilities are being proffered by physicists.[20]

Some claim that while there may be ultimate answers, human beings will never be able to discern them because human brains are limited in capacity.[21] This conjecture is less relevant here because I only lay out the landscape of possible explanations, not select among them. I do try, however, to capture *all* possible explanations, and so it may be that due to my neural limitations, whether personally or species specific, I am incapable of discerning a category or two (or three).

I provide scant analysis of the explanations; all are subject to withering attack from experts, as well they should be. And to the critique that the lines of the taxonomy are drawn too sharply, or that my explanations overlap, I can only empathize and encourage my critic to offer a more refined version.

1. One Universe Models

We begin with traditional nontheistic explanations (traditionally, one recalls, there was only one universe), which also include a radically nontraditional explanation and the philosophical positions that the question makes no sense and that even if it did make sense it would still be unanswerable.

1.1 Meaningless Question.   Big "Why" questions such as Why Ultimate Reality? or Why This Universe? are words without meaning and sounds without sense; this emptiness of content is epitomized by the supreme Why question, Why Not Nothing?[22] As a matter of language, to ask for the ultimate explanation of existence is to ask a question that has no meaning. Human semantics and syntax, and perhaps the human mind itself, are utterly incapable of attaching intelligibility to this concept. Words transcend boundaries of ordinary usage so as to lose their grounding.[23] The deep incoherence here is confirmed by the fact that only two kinds of possible answers are permissible – an infinite regress of causation or something that is inherently self-existing – neither of which can be confirmable or even cogent. (Logical positivism, which holds this position but is internally inconsistent, verifies propositions as cognitively meaningful only by sensory facts or logical grammar.) Any apparent answers, when unpacked properly, are but tautological restatements of the original question.

1.2 Brute Fact.   The big Why questions make sense but answering them is not possible, not even in principle. There has been and is only one universe and its laws seem fine-tuned to human existence simply because this is the way it is; the universe and all its workings stand as a "brute fact"[24] of existence, a terminus of a series of explanations that can brook no further explanation.[25] All things just happen to be and "there is no hint of necessity to reduce this arbitrariness" (Robert Nozick's description of this view).[26] My favorite is Bertrand Russell's stark "[...] the universe is just there, and that's all."[27]

1.3 Necessary/Only One Way. There has been and is only one universe and its laws seem fine-tuned to human existence because, due to the deep essence of these laws, they must take the form that they do and the values of their constants must be the only quantities they could have. It could never be the case that these laws or values could have any other form or quantity. Finding this "deep essence" is the hope of Grand Unification Theory (GUT) or Theory of Everything (TOE); in technical terms, there would be no free parameters in the mathematical equations; all would be determined, derived or deduced from fundamental principles.[28] As for the existence of life and mind in this only-one-way explanation, the laws of biology must be embedded within the laws of physics either inextricably or by happenstance. (And in either case we would be fortunate, wildly fortunate, I would guess).

1.4 Almost Necessary/Limited Ways. Physical laws have only a small range in which they can vary, such that the number of possible universes is highly constrained. This means that what would appear on the surface to be most improbable, i.e., a universe that just happens to be hospitable for life and mind, is in its deep structure most probable. (As with 1.3, of which this is a variant, the presence of life and mind cries out for explanation.)

1.5 Temporal Selection. Even though physical laws or the values of their constants may change, regularly or arbitrarily, we have been living during (or at the end of) an extended period of time during which these laws and values happen to have been, for some reason or for no reason, within a range consistent with the existence of stars and planets and the emergence of life and mind. This temporal selection can operate during periods of time following one Big Bang in a single universe or during vastly greater periods of time following sequential Big Bangs in an oscillating single universe of endless expansions and contractions.

1.6 Self Explaining. The universe is self-creating and self-directing, and therefore self-explaining. In Paul Davies' formulation, the emergence of consciousness (human and perhaps other forms) somehow animates a kind of backward causation (e.g., via post or delayed selection of quantum "histories" of the universe) to select from among the untold laws and countless values that seem possible at the beginning of the universe to actualize those that would prove consistent with the later evolution of life and mind. In this teleological schema the universe and mind would eventually meld and become one, so that it could be the case that the purpose of the universe is to allow or enable it, in some retroactive sense, to engineer its own self-awareness.[29]

Note: Quentin Smith theorizes that the "universe caused itself to begin to exist." By this he means that the universe is a succession of states, each state is caused by earlier states, and, as he tells it, the Big Bang singularity prevents there from being a first instant. Thus in the earliest hour, there are infinitely many zero-duration instantaneous states of the universe, each caused by earlier states, but with no earliest state.[30] This model, like other atheistic mechanisms that claim to obviate the need for a First Cause or preclude the possibility that God exists, could empower any of these One Universe Models. Similarly, if information is somehow fundamental to reality (as opposed to it being constructed by the human mind to allow us to represent reality), an idea proposed by John Wheeler ("It from Bit"),[31] Seth Lloyd[32] and others, information *per se* would undergird or endow these One Universe models (and, for that matter, Multiverse Models as well). Independently, should limitless spaces of our possibly infinite universe exist beyond our visible horizon,[33] which cosmologists acknowledge to be a virtual certainty, these continuing and contiguous spaces would still be included in One Universe Models.[34] We would have an inestimably larger universe to be sure but we would still have only one universe to explain.

2.   Multiple Universe (Multiverse) Models

There are innumerable universes (and/or, depending on one's definition of "universe," causally disconnected domains within one spatiotemporal setting), each bringing forth new universes ceaselessly, boundlessly, in an immense multiverse.[35] What's more, there are perhaps immeasurable extra dimensions, with all universes and dimensions possessing different sets of laws and values in capricious combinations and yet all somehow coexisting in the never-ending, unfurling fabric of the totality of reality. Our reality is the only reality, but there is a whole lot more of it than ever imagined. This means that in the context of this multi-universe, multi-dimensional amalgam, the *meaningful* fine-tuning of our universe is a mirage. The fine-tuning itself is real, but it is not the product of purpose. Rather it is instead a statistical surety that is predicted by force, since only in a universe in which observers exist could observers observe (the Weak Anthropic Principle).[36] Thus, the laws and values engendering sentient life in our universe are not a "fortuitous coincidence" but rather a guaranteed certainty, entirely explained by natural principles and physical processes.

2.1   Multiverse by Disconnected Regions (Spatial).   Generated by fundamental properties of spacetime that induce mechanisms to spawn multiple universes – for example, eternal chaotic inflation (i.e., unceasing phase transitions and bubble nucleations of spacetime) which causes spatial domains to erupt, squeeze off in some way, expand (perhaps), and separate themselves forever without possibility of causal contact (Alan Guth,[37] Andre Linde,[38] Alex Vilenkin[39]).

2.2   Multiverse by Cycles (Temporal).   Generated by an endless sequence of cosmic epochs, each of which begins with a "bang" and ends with a "crunch."

In the Steinhardt-Turok model, it involves cycles of slow accelerated expansions followed by contractions that produce the homogeneity, flatness, and energy needed to begin the next cycle (with each cycle lasting perhaps a trillion years).[40] Roger Penrose postulates a "conformal cyclic cosmology," where an initial space-time singularity can be represented as a smooth past boundary to the conformal geometry of space-time. With conformal invariance both in the remote future and at the Big-Bang origin, he argues, the two situations are physically identical, so that the remote future of one phase of the universe becomes the Big Bang of the next. Though the suggestion is his own, he calls it "outrageous."[41]

2.3 Multiverse by Sequential Selection (Temporal). Generated by fertile black holes out of which new universes are created continuously by "bouncing" into new Big Bangs (instead of collapsing into stagnant singularities). Applying principles of biological evolution to universal development, and assuming that the constants of physics could change in each new universe, Lee Smolin hypothesizes a cosmic natural selection that would favor black holes in sequential ("offspring") universes, thus increasing over time the number of black holes in sequential universes, because the more black holes there are, the more universes they generate.[42] A multiverse generating system that favors black holes might also favor galaxies and stars (rather than amorphous hydrogen gas), but jumping all the way to favor life and mind, however, is a leap of larger magnitude.

2.4 Multiverse by String Theory (with Minuscule Extra Dimensions). String theory postulates a vast "landscape" of different "false vacua," with each such "ground state" harboring different values of the constants of physics (such that on occasion some are consistent with the emergence of life). Structured with six, seven or more extra dimensions of subatomic size, string theory thus generates its own kind of multiple universes (Leonard Susskind).[43]

2.5 Multiverse by Large Extra Dimensions. Generated by large, macroscopic extra dimensions which exist in reality (not just in mathematics), perhaps in infinite numbers, forms and structures, yet which cannot be seen or apprehended (except perhaps by the "leakage" of gravity).[44] Multiple universes generated by extra dimensions may also be cyclical.[45]

2.6 Multiverse by Quantum Branching or Selection. Generated by the many-worlds interpretation of quantum theory as formulated by Hugh Everett and John Wheeler, in which the world forks at every instant (perhaps every Planck time instant) so that different and parallel "histories" are forming continuously and exponentially, with all of them existing in some meta-reality.[46] This means that whenever any quantum object is in any quantum state a new universe will form so that in this perpetual process an unimaginably vast number of parallel universes come into existence, with each universe representing each unique possible state of every possible object. Stephen Hawking has conceptualized this staggering cascade of "branching universes" as a kind of retro-selection, in which current decisions or observations in some sense select from among immense numbers of possible universal histories that exist simultaneously and represent every state of every object and through which the universe has somehow already lived.[47]

2.7   Multiverse by Mathematics.   Generated by Max Tegmark's hypothesis that every conceivable consistent mathematical form or structure corresponds to a physical parallel universe which actually exists.[48]

2.8   Multiverse by All Possibilities.   Generated by the hypothesis that each and every logically possible mode of existence is a real thing and really exists, that possible worlds are as real as the world we inhabit, since the things that we call merely possible (from our perspective) are all of them things truly existing somewhere else (David Lewis's "modal realism";[49] Robert Nozick's "principle of fecundity"[50]).

Note: For Paul Davies, "The multiverse does not provide a complete account of existence, because it still requires a lot of unexplained and very 'convenient' physics to make it work." There has to be, he says, a "universe-generating mechanism" and "some sort of ingenious selection still has to be made," and unless all possible worlds really exist (2.7 and 2.8), "a multiverse which contains less than everything implies a rule that separates what exists from what is possible but does not exist," a rule that "remains unexplained." And regarding all possible worlds really existing, Davies states, "A theory which can explain anything at all really explains nothing."[51] According to Richard Swinburne, arguing for theism, the problem is not solved by invoking multiple universes: the issue that would remain, he says, is why our multiple universe would have the particular characteristic it does, that is, of producing at least one universe fine-tuned for life. And to postulate a mechanism that produces every kind of universe, he adds, would be to postulate a mechanism of enormous complexity in order to explain the existence of our universe, which would go far beyond the simplest explanation of the data of our universe as well as raise the question of why things are like that.[52] According to Quentin Smith, arguing for atheism, it cannot yet be determined if a multiverse, which he calls speculation not science, is even logically possible.[53]

3.   Nonphysical Causes

This universe, however unfathomable, is fine-tuned to human existence because a nonphysical Cause made it this way. The nonphysical Cause may be a Person, Being, Mind, Force, Power, Value, Entity, Unity, Presence, Principle, Law, Proto-Law, Stuff or Feature. It is likely transcendent and surely irreducible; it exists beyond the boundaries and constraints of physical law, matter, energy, space and time; and while it is the Cause it does not itself have or need a cause. The Cause is the absolute bedrock of ultimate reality beyond which, by logic or fact, there can be nothing further. There is blur and overlap among these nonphysical Cause explanations, yet each is sufficiently different in how it claims to generate ultimate reality, and sufficiently opposed to the claims of its competitors, to warrant distinction.

3.1   Theistic Person.   A Supreme Being who in Christian philosophy is portrayed as incorporeal, omnipotent, omniscient, perfectly free, perfectly good, necessarily existent and the creator of all things, and who is also a "person" with person-like characteristics such as beliefs, intents and purposes; a "divine being" (as defined by Richard Swinburne[54]), a theistic God (as defended by Alvin Plantinga[55]) with a "nature."[56] In Judaic-Christian tradition, the existence-as-essence Name offered to Moses – "I am that I am."[57] In Islamic philosophy, the concepts of Unity, the Absolute, Beyond-Being.[58] In modern thought, God as underlying fundamental reality, entailing the meaning of universe and life (George Ellis);[59] God as working through special divine action, interventionist (creationism) or noninterventionist (Robert John Russell).[60] The affirmative creative act of this theistic God may bring the universe into being by a creation from nothing (*creatio ex nihilo*),[61] or may be a continuing creative sustenance of the universe (*creatio continua*), or both.[62] A theistic explanation of ultimate reality is logically compatible with both One Universe and Multiverse Models.[63]

3.2   Ultimate Mind.   A Supreme Consciousness that hovers between a personal theistic God and an impersonal deistic first cause; a nonpareil artist who contemplates limitless possibilities; a quasi Being with real thoughts who determines to actualize certain worlds (Keith Ward).[64] Understanding this kind of God does not begin with an all-powerful "person" but rather with an unfathomable reservoir of potentialities as expressed in all possible universes, for which Ultimate Mind is the only and necessary basis.

3.3   Deistic First Cause.   An impersonal Primal Force, Power or Law that set the universe in motion but is neither aware of its existence nor involved with its constituents. The idea requires initializing powers but rejects beliefs, intents and purposes, active consciousness, self-awareness or even passive awareness. There is no interaction with creatures (humans) or activities (universe).[65]

3.4   Pantheistic Substance.   Pantheism equates God with nature in that God is all and all is God.[66] The universe (all matter, energy, forces and laws) is identical with a ubiquitous metaphysical entity or stuff, which to Baruch Spinoza possessed unlimited attributes and was the uncaused "substance" of all that exists. The pantheistic "God," nontheistic and impersonal, is the paragon of immanence in that it is neither external to the world nor transcendent of it. In diverse forms, pantheism appears in Western philosophy (Plotinus's "One," Hegel's "Absolute"), process theology, and some Eastern religions (Taoism; later Buddhism; Hinduism where Brahman is all of existence).[67] Pantheism finds a unity in everything that exists and in this unity a sense of the divine.[68]

3.5   Spirit Realms.   Planes, orbs, levels, domains and dimensions of spirit existence as the true, most basic form of reality. Described by mystics, mediums, and occult practitioners, and exemplified by mystic, polytheistic and animistic religions, these spirit realms are populated by the presence of sundry spirit beings and laced with complex spiritual rituals and schemas (some good, some evil).[69]

3.6   Consciousness as Cause.   Pure Consciousness as the fundamental stuff of reality out of which the physical world is generated or expressed.[70] It is the explanation claimed or typified by certain philosophical and quasi-theological systems, Eastern religions, mystic religions, and cosmic consciousness devotees, and by some who accept the actuality of paranormal phenomena.[71] For example, Buddhism and Rigpa in Tibetan Buddhism[72] (omniscience or enlightenment without limit).[73] Even some physicists ponder the pre-existence of mind.[74]

3.7   Principle or Feature of Sufficient Power.   An all-embracing cosmic principle beyond being and existence, such as Plato's "the Good" or John Leslie's "ethical requiredness"[75] or Nicholas Rescher's "cosmic values,"[76] or some defining characteristic so central to ultimate reality and so supremely profound that it has both creative imperative and causative potency to bring about being and existence. Derek Parfit says it might be no coincidence if, of the countless cosmic possibilities, or ways that reality might be, one has a very special feature and is the possibility that obtains (actually exists). "Reality might be this way," he says, "because this way had this feature." He calls this special feature the "Selector," and two candidates he considers are "being law-governed and having simple laws."[77] Schellenberg's non-theistic "Ultimism" might be housed here.[78]

3.8   Abstract Objects/Platonic Forms as Cause.   Although philosophers deny that abstract objects can have causal effects on concrete objects (abstract objects are often defined as causally inert), their potential, say as a collective, to be an explanatory source of ultimate reality cannot be logically excluded. (This assumes that abstract objects – such as numbers, logic, universals, propositions – manifest real existence on some plane of existence not in spacetime.) Platonic Forms, abstract entities that are perfect and immutable and exist independently of the world of perceptions, are occasionally suspected of possessing some kind of causal or quasi-causal powers.[79]

3.9   Being and Non-Being as Cause.   Being and Non-Being as ineffable dyadic states that have such maximal inherent potency that they (either one) can somehow bring all things into existence. In Taoism, the invisible Tao (Way) gives rise to the universe; all is the product of Being, and Being is the product of Not-being.[80] In Hinduism, it is the Brahman (unchanging, infinite, immanent, transcendent).[81] The Ground of All Being; Great Chain of Being; Great Nest of Spirit (Ken Wilbur).[82]

3.10   Beyond Concepts and Categories.   Approaching ultimate reality is impossible for human thought, even "more impossible" for human language, because whatever fundamental existence may be, it must escape all our concepts and categories. This is not a matter of limited knowledge, but rather of absolute unknowability, a boundary that is in principle impenetrable. Included would be John Hick's "The Real," which is his transcendant, "transcategorical" common denominator of all religions.[83] Related are ineffable realms of Eastern religions and negative (apophatic) theology in Western religions (where it is only possible to state what God is not).

Note: Cyclical universes of Eastern religious traditions can be consistent with all of these nonphysical ultimate reality generators,[84] although the Western Theistic Person (3.1) would normally be excluded. To Derek Parfit, if we take the apparent fine-turning of the universe to support, not some multiverse or many-worlds hypothesis, but the traditional theistic hypothesis, this should invoke a creator who may be omnipotent and omniscient, but who isn't wholly good or even significantly good. What we can see of reality (with its enormity of evil), he says, counts very strongly against this hypothesis of the fine-tuner being an all-good God.[85]

4. Illusions

This universe, everything we think we know, is not real. Facts are fiction; nothing is fundamental; all is veneer, through and through.

4.1   Idealism.   As argued by generations of idealistic philosophers, all material things are manifestations of consciousness or assemblies of mind, so that while the physical world appears to be composed of non-mental stuff, it is not.[86]

4.2   Simulation in Actual Reality.   We exist merely or marginally in someone's or something's simulation, in an artificial world that actually exists in terms of having physical particles and forces and galaxies and stars, but that entirety is not what it seems because that entirety is derivative not original. Andre Linde analyzes "baby universe formation" and then asks, "Does this mean that our universe was created not by a divine design but by a physicist hacker?"[87] Paul Davies speaks of "fake universes," and of those beings who created them as "false gods;" and he ponders that if multiple universes really exist, the great majority of them may be fakes because some of them (there are so many) would have spawned, at some time or another, unthinkably superior beings who would have had the capacity to create these fake universes – and once they could have done so they would have done so, creating innumerably many fake universes and thereby swamping the real ones.[88]

4.3   Simulation in Virtual Reality.   We exist merely or marginally in someone's or something's simulation, in an artificial sensory construction that is an imitation of what reality might be but is not; for example, a Matrix-like world in which all perceptions are fed directly into the human nervous system ("brains in vats") or into our disembodied consciousness. Alternatively, we exist as processes generated by pure software running inside cosmic quantum supercomputers.[89]

4.4   Solipsism.   The universe is wholly the creation of one's own mind and thereby exists entirely in and for that mind.[90]

Note: Even if every thing in *this* universe were illusion (4.1 to 4.4), there would still have to be something outside of this universe that generates the illusion, which would bring us back to something fundamental in One Universe Models, Multiple Universe Models or Nonphysical Causes.

What is it About Nothing?

If it seems improbable that human thought can make distinguishing progress among these categories and explanations, consider the formulating progress already made. Two centuries years ago the available options were largely Nonphysical Causes (Category 3) structured simplistically. A century ago scientists assumed that our own galaxy, the Milky Way, was the entire universe. Today we grasp the monumental immensity of the cosmos.

I now return to Nothing, asking yet again, Why Not Nothing? A taxonomy of possible explanations for Why This Universe? may suggest new seas to sail, if only by loosening our mental moorings from the one or two cultural conditioned explanations that are generally and uncritically accepted.[91] Nonetheless there remains a great gulf between the two questions: even if we eventually obtain the actual explanation of this universe we may still have made no progress at all on why there is Something rather than Nothing.[92]

What guides me here is gut feeling, not complex reasoning, which is why no argument has ever dissuaded me from continuing to think, following Leibniz,[93] that Nothing, no world, is simpler and easier than any world, that Nothing would have been the least arbitrary and "most natural" state of affairs.

As I have continued to think about Nothing, I have continued to think that Nothing "should," in some sense, have obtained, and the only reason I accept the fact that Nothing does not obtain is not because of any of the arguments against Nothing,[94] but because of the raw existence of Something – because in my private consciousness I am forced to recognize that real existents compose Something. In other words, an a priori weighing of Nothing vs. Something (from a timeless, explanatorily earlier perspective) would, for me, tip the balance heavily to Nothing, but for the fact of the matter.

Thus, since I have no choice but to recognize that there is Something, I have no choice but to conclude that there is some deep reason, force, productive principle or type of necessity that brings about the absence of Nothing. I cannot rid myself of the conviction that Nothing would have obtained had not something special somehow superseded or counteracted it. Yes, many well-regarded philosophers say, "So there's a world not a blank; what's in any way surprising about that?"[95] But I just can't help feeling that they are passing right over the problem most probative of ultimate reality.[96]

Levels of Nothing

Defining "Nothing" may seem simple – no thing, not a thing. But what's a "thing?" I invoke the term "thing" in the most general possible way, and therefore, given some possible notions of Nothing, it is no contradiction to find "things" of which these different Nothings are comprised. Teasing apart these constituent things, as if scaffolds or sinews of Nothings, may help deepen understanding of the nature of Nothing, yielding a taxonomy that arrays opposing kinds of Nothing that could be conceived and might have existed.

This taxonomy is structured as a deconstruction, or as a dissection, as it were, a reverse layering, a peeling, a progressive reduction of the content of each Nothing in a hierarchy of Nothings. As such, this taxonomy takes its heritage from the so-called Subtraction Argument, which seeks to show that the absence of all concrete objects would be metaphysically possible. (Stated simply, the Subtraction Arguments works by imagining a sequence of possible worlds each containing one less concrete object than the world before, so that in the very last world even the very last object has vanished. It is no surprise that complexities emerge.[97])

Developing this way of thinking, there might be nine levels of Nothing, with a general progression from Nothing most simplistic (Nothing One) to Nothing most absolute (Nothing Nine).

There are criticisms of each of these Nothings. My point here is not so much to argue the legitimacy of any one kind of Nothing but rather to construct an exhaustive taxonomy of all potential or competing Nothings, and perhaps a taxonomy in which those Nothings are mutually exclusive.

Following are nine levels of Nothings.

(1)   Nothing as existing space and time that just happens to be totally empty of all visible objects (particles and energy are permitted – an utterly simplistic view).

(2)   Nothing as existing space and time that just happens to be totally empty of all matter (no particles, but energy is permitted – flouting the law of mass-energy equivalence).

(3)   Nothing as existing space and time that just happens to be totally empty of all matter and energy.[98]

(4)   Nothing as existing space and time that is by necessity – irremediably and permanently in all directions, temporal as well as spatial – totally empty of all matter and energy.

(5)   Nothing of the kind found in some theoretical formulations by physicists, where, although space-time (unified) as well as mass-energy (unified) do not exist, pre-existing laws, particularly laws of quantum mechanics, do exist. And it is these laws that somehow make it the case that universes can and do, from time to time, pop into existence from "Nothing," creating space-time as well as mass-energy. (It is standard physics to assume that empty space must seethe with virtual particles, a consequence of the uncertainty principle of quantum physics, where particle-antiparticle pairs come into being and then, in a fleetingly brief moment, annihilate each other.)

(6)   Nothing where not only there are no space-time and no mass-energy, but also there are no pre-existing laws of physics that could generate space-time or mass-energy (universes).

(7)   Nothing where not only there are no space-time, no mass-energy, and no pre-existing laws of physics, but also there are no non-physical things or kinds that are concrete (rather than abstract) – no God, no gods, and no consciousness (cosmic or otherwise). This means that there are no physical or non-physical beings or existents of any kind – nothing, whether natural or supernatural, that is concrete (rather than abstract).

(8)   Nothing where not only there are none of the above (so that, as in Nothing 7, there are no concrete existing things, physical or non-physical), but also there are no *abstract objects* of any kind – no numbers, no sets, no logic, no general propositions, no universals, no Platonic forms (perhaps no value[99]).

(9)   Nothing where not only there are none of the above (so that, as in Nothing 8, there are no abstract objects), but also there are no *possibilities* of any kind (recognizing that possibilities and abstract objects overlap, though allowing that they can be distinguished).

Nothings One through Seven progressively remove or eliminate existing things, so that a reasonable stopping point – a point at which we might well be thought to have reached (what I hesitate to call) "Real Nothing", the metaphysical limit – would be Nothing Seven, which features no concrete existing things (no physical or non-physical concrete existents) of any kind.

Nothings Eight and Nine go further, eliminating *non-concrete* objects, things, existents and realities. Do they go too far? Many philosophers assert that neither Nothing Eight nor Nothing Nine are metaphysically possible, arguing that the claimed absence of abstract objects and/or possibilities would constitute a logical contradiction and hence abstract objects and/or possibilities exist necessarily.[100] This could be important because, as John Leslie points out, among the realities which aren't concrete things, or which do not depend on the existence of concrete things, and thus cannot be eliminated, there may be some realities that are plausible candidates for explaining the world of concrete things. (See sections 3.7, 3.8 and 3.9 in the Why This Universe? taxonomy.) In this way of thinking, the crucial distinction is between realities that seemingly can be eliminated and realities that seemingly cannot be eliminated, rather than any particular way of distinguishing between levels of nothingness or particular ways of defining nothingness.

Note that of all these levels of Nothing, one of the "lesser Nothings" – that is, a kind of Nothing with more "things" in it – is the Nothing of physicists. What physicists contemplate – the sudden emergence or "tunneling" of universes from "Nothing" – is fascinating and indeed may be cosmogenic, but the tunneling process or capacity is not Nothing.[101] The Nothing of physicists is thick with the complete set of the laws of physics, and so between physicists' Nothing and Real Nothing lies a vast, unbridgeable gulf. Physicists' Nothing is Nothing Five on this taxonomic scale, barely half way to utterly Nothing. If physicists' Nothing were in reality Real Nothing (i.e., ultimate reality), the laws of quantum physics (or whatever might turn out to be the most fundamental laws underlying quantum physics) would have to be either impossible to remove (meaning that eliminating them would involve logical contradiction) or a brute fact about existence beyond which explanation would be meaningless. I doubt I could ever get over the odd idea that something so intricate, so involved, so organized and so accessible as the laws of physics would be the ultimate brute fact.

As a separate consideration, some philosophers of religion argue that God is a "necessity" – meaning that it would be impossible for God not to exist – thus precluding Nothing Seven (which has no non-physical concrete things such as God but still has abstract objects) and crowning Nothing Six (which has no space-time, no mass-energy, no laws of physics but still has God and other nonphysical things) as the metaphysical limit of what is to be explained.[102] I find the move challenging. Moreover, based on the levels of Nothing in this taxonomy, it would seem less of a leap to imagine a world without God (Nothing Seven) than to imagine a world without abstract objects (Nothing Eight). For the traditional God, that won't do.[103]

Why Not Nothing?

Cosmic visions are overwhelming, but I am oddly preoccupied with another conundrum. How is it that we humans have such farsighted understanding after only a few thousand years of historical consciousness, only a few hundred years of effective science, and only a few decades of cosmological observations? Maybe it's still too early in the game. Maybe answers have been with us all along. This is a work in process and diverse contributions are needed.

Now for my secret. No matter how sensible and controlled I may seem to be, Why Not Nothing still drives me nuts. Every time I revisit the stupefying question, I want to scream. Why this Universe? Does God Exist? In comparison, both questions are small beer. Why is there anything at all? That's the magisterial Question.

Setting aside my taxonomy and consulting my gut, I come to only two kinds of answers. The first is that there can be no answer: Existence is a brute fact without explanation. The second is that at the primordial beginning, explanatorily and timelessly prior to time, something was *self*-existing. The essence of this something was its existence such that non-existence to it would be as inherently impossible as physical immortality to us is factually impossible. (Various things or substances could conceivably harbor this deeply centered self-existing essence, from the most fundamental meta-laws of physics to diverse kinds of consciousness, one of which could be God or a kind of god.)

Why is there Something rather than Nothing? Why Not Nothing? If you don't get dizzy, you really don't get it.

Endnotes and References

The author thanks John Leslie, Paul Davies, Derek Parfit, Robert John Russell, Michael Shermer, Quentin Smith, Richard Swinburne, and Keith Ward for their comments and suggestions.

1   Quentin Smith would reformulate my awestruck "Why not Nothing? [....]" so as to satisfy an analytical philosopher. He points out (in a personal communication) that it is a logical fallacy to talk about "nothing," to treat "nothing" as if it were "something" (with properties). To say "there might have been nothing" implies "it is possible that there is nothing". "There is" means "something is." So "there is nothing" means "something is nothing," which is a logical contradiction. His suggestion is to remove "nothing" and replace it by "not something" or "not anything", since one can talk about what we mean by "nothing" by referring to *something* or *anything* of which there are no instances (i.e., the concept of "something" has the property of not being instantiated). The common sense way to talk about Nothing is to talk about something and negate it, to deny that there is something. Smith would rewrite my lines about like this: "*There is something. But why? There might not ever have been anything at all. Why are there existents rather than no existents?*" As for Nothing being "easier," Smith says that the word connotes that it would have been easier for "God," and God he does not like at all. So my passage would become, "*Wouldn't it have been easier if there were not even one thing, in the sense that there is no causal activity, whereas things require causes to bring them into existence? Wouldn't it have been simpler in the sense that there are zero things if there are no things, and that as a number zero is simpler than one, two, three or any other number? Wouldn't it have been more logical in the sense that the laws of logic do not imply there are things and if there are things, that fact is inexplicable in terms of the laws of logic?*" (For euphony, as well as simplicity, I will continue to use "Nothing" – Quentin, my appreciation and apology.)

2   Leibniz, Gottfried. 1714. *The Principles of Nature and Grace.*

3   Martin Heidegger famously called "Why is there something rather than nothing?" the fundamental question of metaphysics. Heidegger, Martin, 1959. *Introduction to Metaphysics.* New Haven: Yale University Press. Leibniz. 1714. Parfit, Derek. 1998. "Why Anything? Why This?" *London Review of Books.* January 22, pp. 24–27 and February 5, pp. 22–25. Van Inwagen. 1996. (van Inwagen says "we can make some

progress […] if we do not panic.") Leslie, John. 1998. *Modern Cosmology and Philosophy*. Amherst, N.Y: Prometheus Books. Rundle, Bede. 2004. *Why there is Something rather than Nothing*. Oxford: Clarendon Press. (Rundle seeks "what might be possible in areas where it is so easy to think that we have come to a dead end." He concludes that there must be "something or other"; there cannot be Nothing; Nothing is an impossible state of affairs.) Leslie, John. 2005. Review of *Why there is Something rather than Nothing* by Bede Rundle. *MIND*. January 2005. Nagel, Thomas. 2004. Review of *Why there is Something rather than Nothing* by Bede Rundle. *Times Literary Supplement*. May 7. "*Nothing.*" Stanford Encyclopedia of Philosophy. http://plato.stanford.edu/entries/nothingness/. Carlson, Erik and Erik J. Olsson. 1998. "The Presumption of Nothingness." *Ratio, XIV,* 2001: 203–221. Nozick, Robert. 1981. "Why is there Something Rather than Nothing?" *Philosophical Explanations*. Cambridge, MA: Harvard University Press, Ch. 2. Nozick's aim is "to loosen our feeling of being trapped by a question with no possible answer." He says, "the question cuts so deep, however, that any approach that stands a chance of yielding an answer will look extremely weird. Someone who proposes a non-strange answer shows he didn't understand the question." "Only one thing," he says, "could leave nothing at all unexplained: a fact that explains itself"; he calls this "explanatory self-subsumption."

4   To Quentin Smith, grasping the universe as a world-whole and asking Why? engenders global awe, feeling-sensations that tower and swell over us in response to the stunning immensity of it all. The more we consider this ultimate question of existence, he believes, the more our socio-culture would improve. (Personal communication and Smith, Quentin. 1986. *The Felt Meanings of the World: A Metaphysics of Feeling*. West Lafayette, Indiana: Purdue University Press.) Arthur Witherall argues "that a feeling of awe [wonder, astonishment, and various other affective states] at the existence of something rather than nothing is appropriate and desirable," perhaps because "there is a fact-transcendent meaning to the existence of the world." (Witherall, Arthur. *Journal of Philosophical Research* – http://www.hedweb.com/witherall/existence.htm, *2006*). Santayana describes existence as "logically inane and morally comic" and "a truly monstrous excrescence and superfluity." (Santayana, George. 1955. Scepticism and Animal Faith. New York: Dover Publications, p. 48). Paul Tillich talks about the "ontological shock of confronting nonbeing" (Tillich, Paul. 1973. *Systematic Theology, Volume One*, Chicago: University of Chicago Press.), which, according to Robert John Russell, is more the realization that we needn't exist than just the fact that one day we will die.

5   *Closer To Truth: Cosmos, Consciousness, God* presents over 200 television episodes which have been broadcast on PBS and other noncommercial stations (since the year 2000), and offers over 2500 videos of scientists and philosophers addressing the big questions of existence. See www.closertotruth.com. For videos on "Why is there Something Rather than Nothing?" see www.closertotruth.com/topic/Why-is-There-Something-Rather-than-Nothing-/45.

6   This is new territory and the first step in methodical exploration is often to construct a taxonomy. Here is the challenge: How can we (i) discern and describe all possible explanations of ultimate reality (devised by human intelligence or imagined by human speculation), and then (ii) classify and array these possible explanations into categories so that we might assess and compare their essence, efficacy, explanatory potency and interrelationships?

7   Hawking, Stephen. 1996. "Quantum Cosmology." In Hawking, Stephen and Roger Penrose. *The Nature of Space and Time*. Princeton, NJ: Princeton University Press, pp. 89–90.

8   Penrose, Roger. 2005. *The Road to Reality: A Complete Guide to the Laws of the Universe*. New York: Knopf, p. 726–732, 762–765. Penrose's analysis of the "extraordinary 'specialness' of the Big Bang" is based on the Second Law of Thermodynamics and the "absurdly low entropy" [i.e. highly organized] state of the very early universe.

9   Weinberg, Steven. 2007. "Living in the Multiverse." In Carr, Bernard, ed. *Universe or Multiverse*. Cambridge, UK: Cambridge University Press.

10 Susskind, Leonard. 2005. *The Cosmic Landscape: String Theory and the Illusion of Intelligent Design*. Boston MA: Little, Brown, p. 66, 78–82.

11 Rees, Martin. 2000. *Just Six Numbers: The Deep Forces That Shape the Universe*. New York: Basic Books. Following are Rees' six numbers.

$N = 10^{36}$, the ratio of the strength of electric forces that hold atoms together to the force of gravity between them such that if N had just a few less zeros, only a short-lived and miniature universe could exist, which would have been too young and too small for life to evolve.

E (epsilon) $= .007$, a definition of how firmly atomic nuclei bind together such that if E were .006 or .008 matter could not exist as it does.

Ω (omega) $= \sim 1$, the amount of matter in the universe, such that if Ω were too high the universe would have collapsed long ago and if Ω were too low no galaxies would have formed.

Λ (lambda) $= \sim 0.7$, the cosmological constant, the positive energy of empty space, an "antigravity" force that is causing the universe to expand at an accelerating rate, such that if Λ were much larger the universe would have expanded too rapidly for stars and galaxies to have formed.

$Q, = 1/100,000$, a description of how the fabric of the universe depends on the ratio of two fundamental energies, such that if Q were smaller the universe would be inert and featureless and if Q were much larger the universe would be violent and dominated by giant black holes.

$D = 3$, the number of dimensions in which we live such that if D were 2 or 4 life could not exist.

12 Dirac, P.A.M. 1938. *Proceedings of the Royal Society* A165, 199–208. Dirac noted that for some unexplained reason the ratio of the electrostatic force to the gravitational force between an electron and a proton is roughly equal to the age of the universe divided by an elementary time constant, which suggested to him that the expansion rate of the macroscopic universe was somehow linked to the microscopic subatomic world (and that gravity varied with time). Although his inference was in error, Dirac's observation enabled a novel way of grand thinking about the universe.

13 Dicke, Robert H. 1961. "Dirac's cosmology and Mach's principle." *Nature* 192: 440. In order for the universe to host biological observers, it has to be sufficiently old so that carbon would already have been synthesized in stars and sufficiently young so that main sequence stars and stable planetary systems would still continue to exist ("golden age"). Dicke, Robert H. 1970. *Gravitation and the Universe*. Philadelphia: American Philosophical Society.

14 Carter, Brandon. 1973. "Large Number Coincidences and the Anthropic Principle in Cosmology," reprinted in Leslie, John. 1998. *Modern Philosophy and Cosmology*. Amherst, NY: Prometheus Books.

15 Barrow, John D. and Frank Tipler. 1986. *The Anthropic Cosmological Principle*. New York: Oxford University Press.

16 Weinberg, 2007, op cit. Weinberg, Steven. 1987, "Anthropic Bound on the Cosmological Constant." *Physical Review Letters* 59, 22 2607–2610.

17 The reason I distinguish One Universe Models from Multiple Universe Models by classifying them in separate categories is because of the implicative and potentially disruptive power of fine-tuning. Irrespective of whether multiple universes really exist, multiple universes are the most "natural" explanation for the fine-tuning of our universe. Moreover, theoretical evidence (and some observational data) has been accumulating in their support.

18 Methodologically, I first try to expand the possible explanations and their categories, striving to be universally exhaustive – which is my objective here – and then only later try, in some way, to cull them by data, analysis or reasoning. (To set the scientific standard of falsification for most of these "ultimate reality generators" is to be unrealistically reliant on a single way of thinking.) After Paul Davies presents the pros and cons of the various main positions he proffers to answer the ultimate questions of existence, he asks a droll but deeply profound question, "Did I leave any out?" Davies, Paul. 2006. *The Goldilocks Enigma: Why is the Universe Just Right for Life*. London: Allen Lane / Penguin Books, p. 302.

19 "Modal logic" allows an infinite number of logical possibilities that are (or seem) scientifically impossible. Smith, Quentin. Personal communication.

20 That the explanation for the universe may be hard to understand is no surprise to Derek Parfit. "If there is some explanation of the whole of reality, we should not expect this explanation to fit neatly into some familiar category. This extra-ordinary question may have an extra-ordinary answer." Parfit. January 22, 1998.

21 The argument goes like this: Why should we expect that brains, which evolved for very different purposes (for hunting and surviving), would be capable of penetrating all the unfathomable layers of reality to reach the ultimate? Perhaps, the argument continues, if our brains evolve much further, in a million years or in a billion years, or with unimaginablly more powerful non-biological intelligences, whatever species may then exist may stand a better chance. Martin Rees has speculated about human brain limitations (on *Closer To Truth*) and for similar (and other) reasons Colin McGinn is a "mysterian" about consciousness (McGinn, Colin. 1989. "Can We Solve the Mind-Body Problem," *Mind*, New Series, Volume 98, Issue 391, pp. 349–366. McGinn, Colin. 2000. *The Mysterious Flame: Conscious Minds in a Material World*. New York: Basic Books.) I think I do not agree. I contend that the human brain, having come so far so fast in comprehending fundamental physics and cosmology, *can* approach ultimate reality, whatever "it" may be as long as it is purely physical or natural. However, if ultimate reality were to be found among Nonphysical Causes, then all bets would be off.

22 Those who contend that "Why Not Nothing?" is a Meaningless Question (1.1) often rely on what they believe to be logical contradictions in the concepts "Nothing" and "Something." For example, they argue that the statement "There is Nothing" has no

referent and makes no legitimate claim; something more, such as a location of the Nothing, must be specified to complete it and make it meaningful, but any such addition contradicts itself in that by specifying Something it destroys Nothing (as it were). Rundle. 2004. Olsson, Erik, J. 2005. *Notre Dame Philosophical Reviews*. March 3. http://ndpr.nd.edu/review.cfm?id=2081. See Endnote 1. In like manner, the question "Why is there Something?" makes a simple logical mistake in that it presupposes an antecedent condition that can explain that Something, but there can be no such antecedent condition because it too must be subsumed in the Something which must be explained, thus embedding circular reasoning. Edwards, Paul. 1967. "Why" in Edwards, Paul, ed. *The Encyclopedia of Philosophy*. New York: Macmillan, vol. 8, pp. 300–301. Witherall, 2006.

23   Nagel, 1981. As John Leslie puts this view, "Metaphysical efforts to explain the cosmos offend against *grammar* in Wittgenstein's sense." Leslie. 2005.

24   To be a brute fact, a universe does not depend on any particular universe-generating mechanism – Big Bang, steady state, complex cyclicals can all fit the brute fact framework. A multiverse or surely a God can be a brute fact. The point is that there must be a terminal explanation: a brute fact is as far as you can get, even in principle, ever.

25   Parfit states, "If it is random what reality is like, the Universe not only has no cause, it has no explanation of any kind." Of the explanatory possibilities, he later notes that brute fact "seems to describe the simplest, since its claim is only that reality has no explanation." Parfit. February 5, 1998. Smith, Quentin. 1997. "Simplicity and Why the Universe Exists." *Philosophy* 71: 125–32.

26   Nozick, 1981.

27   "I should say that the universe is just there, and that's all," Bertrand Russell, in the classic 1948 BBC Radio debate on the existence of God between Father Frederick Copleston, a Jesuit priest and historian of philosophy, and Bertrand Russell, the agnostic philosopher and logician. The entire debate is my all-time favorite on God. Many sources. Russell, Bertrand and F.C. Copleston. 1964. "The Existence of God." In Hick, John, ed., *Problems of Philosophy Series*. New York: Macmillan & Co., p. 175.

28   Weinberg, Steven. 1983. *Dreams of a Final Theory: The Scientist's Search for the Ultimate Laws of Nature*. New York: Vintage Books. Witten, Edward. 2002. "Universe on a String." *Astronomy* magazine (June 2002). Gell-Mann, Murray. 1994. *The Quark and the Jaguar*. New York: W.H. Freeman. Greene, Brian. 2003. *The Elegant Universe: Superstrings, Hidden Dimensions, and the Quest for the Ultimate Theory*. Reissue edition. New York: W.W. Norton. String theory is modern physics' best bet to find the Grand Unification Theory or Theory of Everything, but the desire to find a "Necessary / Only One Way" mathematical mechanism for string theory seems shattered by $\sim 10^{500}$ different string theories (which correspond to a vast array of different geometries of the compact manifolds that describe string theory's compactified extra six or seven dimensions beyond the common four).

29   Davies, 2006. Davies. Paul. 1993. *The Mind of God*. London: Penguin. Davies, Paul. 2005. In Harper, Charles L., Jr., ed. *Spiritual Information: 100 Perspectives on Science and Religion*. West Conshohocken, PA: Templeton Foundation Press. On *Closer To Truth*.

30 Smith, Quentin. 2007. "Kalam Cosmological Arguments for Atheism." In Martin, Michael, ed., *The Cambridge Companion for Atheism*. Smith, Quentin. 1999. "The Reason the Universe Exists is that it Caused Itself to Exist", *Philosophy*, Vol. 74, pp. 136–146. Personal communication. To Quentin, whereas "no thing existing" might have been the case, "some things existing" is the case. The reason is trivial, he says: each and every thing was caused by a prior thing. The theistic counterargument, which goes back to at least Aquinas, is that even if the universe is infinitely old – even if a real infinity of prior events really obtains – existence itself would still require God because contingent being always requires necessary being. Atheists hit right back: some reject the contingent-necessary dichotomy; others claim that the problems of a self-existing universe are no more troubling than those of a self-existing god, and at least we know the universe exists, they continue, which is more than we can say about God.

31 Wheeler, John Archibald, 1990. "Information, physics, quantum: The search for links" in W. Zurek (ed.) *Complexity, Entropy, and the Physics of Information*. Boston: Addison-Wesley.

32 Lloyd, Seth. 2006. *Programming the Universe: A Quantum Computer Scientist Takes On the Cosmos*. New York: Knopf.

33 To observers at any given time, the distance to the visible horizon, meaning the farthest they can in principle see at that time, is set by the speed of light and the age of the universe, since light could have traveled towards them only so far in so long. (In special relativity, a "light cone" is the geometric pattern describing the temporal evolution of a flash of light in Minkowski spacetime. Wikipedia, http://en.wikipedia.org/wiki/Light_cone.)

34 These continuing and contiguous spaces included in the One Universe would be causally connected, though communication between any given coordinates would always be limited by the speed of light and the expansion of the universe.

35 Rees, Martin J. 1998. *Before the Beginning: Our Universe and Others*. New York: Perseus Books. Rees, Martin J. 2004. *Our Cosmic Habitat*. Princeton, NJ: Princeton University Press. Rees, Martin J. 1999. "Exploring Our Universe and Others," *Scientific American*, December. Leslie, John. 1989. *Universes*. London: Routledge. Davies, 2006, p. 299. On *Closer To Truth*.

36 Weinberg, 1987. Weinberg, 2007. On *Closer To Truth*. There is hardly unanimity about the Anthropic Principle among physicists, some of whom characterize it as betraying the quest to find fundamental first principles that can explain the universe and predict its constituents. David Gross "hates" it, comparing it to a virus – "Once you get the bug, you can't get rid of it." Overbye, Dennis. 2003. "Zillions of Universes? Or Did Ours Get Lucky?" *New York Times*. October 28. On *Closer To Truth*.

37 Guth, Alan. 1981. "The Inflationary Universe: A Possible Solution to the Horizon and Flatness Problems." *Phys. Rev. D* 23, 347. Guth, Alan. 1997. *The Inflationary Universe: The Quest for a New Theory of Cosmic Origins*. Boston: Addison-Wesley. On *Closer To Truth*.

38 Linde, Andrei. 1982. "A New Inflationary Universe Scenario: A Possible Solution of the Horizon, Flatness, Homogeneity, Isotropy and Primordial Monopole Problems." *Phys. Lett.* B 108, 389. Linde, Andrei. 1990. *Particle Physics and Inflationary Cosmology*. Chur, Switzerland: Harwood. Linde, Andrei. 2005. "Inflation and String Cosmology."

J. Phys. Conf. Ser. 24 151–60. Linde, Andrei. 1991. "The Self-Reproducing Inflationary Universe." *Scientific American*, November 1991, 48–55. Linde, Andrei. 2005. "Current understanding of inflation." *New Astron. Rev.* 49:35–41. Linde, Andrei. 2005. "Choose Your Own Universe," in Harper, 2005. On *Closer To Truth*.

39   Vilenkin, Alex. 2006. *Many Worlds in One: The Search for Other Universes*. New York: Hill and Wang. On *Closer To Truth*.

40   Steinhardt, Paul J. and Neil Turok. 2002. "A Cyclic Model of the Universe." *Science*, May 2002: Vol. 296. no. 5572, pp. 1436–1439. The authors claim that a cyclical model may solve the cosmological constant problem – why it is so vanishingly small and yet not zero – by "relaxing" it naturally over vast numbers of cycles and periods of time exponentially older than the Big Bang estimate. Steinhardt, Paul J. and Neil Turok. 2006. "Why the Cosmological Constant is Small and Positive." *Science* 26 May 2006: Vol. 312. no. 5777, pp. 1180–1183. On *Closer To Truth*. The oscillating universe hypothesis was earlier suggested by John Wheeler, who in the 1960s posited this scenario in connection with standard recontracting Friedman cosmological models (I thank Paul Davies for the reference).

41   Penrose, Roger. "Before the Big Bang: An Outrageous New Perspective and Its Implications for Particle Physics." Proceedings of the EPAC 2006, Edinburgh, Scotland. On *Closer To Truth*.

42   Smolin, Lee. 1992. "Did the universe evolve?" *Classical and Quantum Gravity* 9, 173–191. Smolin, Lee. 1997. The Life of the Cosmos. New York: Oxford University Press. Since a black hole is said to have at its center a "singularity," a point at which infinitely strong gravity causes matter to have infinite density and zero volume and the curvature of spacetime is infinite and ceases to exist as we know it, and since the Big Bang is said to begin under similar conditions, the idea that the latter is engendered by the former seems less far-fetched. In 1990 Quentin Smith proposed that our Big Bang is a black hole in another universe, but said that it could not be a genuine scientific theory unless a new solution to Einstein's ten field equations of general relativity could be developed, Smith, Quentin. 1990. "A Natural Explanation of the Existence and Laws of Our Universe," *Australasian Journal of Philosophy* 68, pp. 22–43. It is a theory that Smith has since given up. Smolin called his own theory a "fantasy." On *Closer To Truth*.

43   Susskind, Leonard, "The anthropic landscape of string theory." arXiv:hep-th/0302219. Susskind, 2005. The string theory landscape is said to have ~10^{500} expressions. On *Closer To Truth*.

44   Randall, Lisa. 2006. *Warped Passage: Unraveling the Mysteries of the Universe's Hidden Dimensions*. New York: Harper Perennial. Krauss, Lawrence. 2005. *Hidden in the Mirror: The Mysterious Allure of Extra Dimensions, from Plato to String Theory and Beyond*. New York: Viking.

45   An "ekpyrotic" mechanism for generating universes postulates immeasurable three-dimensional "branes" (within one of which our universe exists) moving through higher-dimensional space such that when one brane in some way collides with another, a contracting, empty universe is energized to expand and form matter in a hot Big Bang. Khoury, Justin, Burt A. Ovrut, Paul J. Steinhardt and Neil Turok. 2002. "Density Perturbations in the Ekpyrotic Scenario." *Phys. Rev.* D66 046005. Ostriker, Jeremiah P. and Paul Steinhardt, "The Quintessential Universe." *Scientific American*, January 2001, pp. 46–53.

46 Everett, Hugh. 1957. "Relative State' Formulation of Quantum Mechanics." *Reviews of Modern Physics* 29, No.3, 1957, pp. 454–462. Reprinted in DeWitt. B.S. and N. Graham, eds. 1973. *The Many-Worlds Interpretation of Quantum Mechanics*. Princeton NJ: Princeton University Press, pp. 141–149. Wheeler, John Archibald. 1998. *Geons, Black Holes & Quantum Foam*. New York: W.W. Norton, pp. 268–270. Deustch, David. 1997. *The Fabric of Reality*. London: Penguin Books.

47 Getler, Amanda. 2006. "Exploring Stephen Hawking's Flexiverse." *New Scientist*, April 2006.

48 Tegmark, Max. 2003. "Parallel Universes." *Scientific American*, May 2003, pp. 41–51.

49 Lewis, David. 1986. *On the Plurality of Worlds*. Oxford, UK: Blackwell Publishing, p.2. Lewis writes, "I advocate a thesis of plurality of worlds, or *modal realism*, which holds that our world is but one world among many. There are countless other worlds [...] so many other worlds, in fact, that absolutely *every* way that a world could possibly be is a way that some world *is*."

50 Nozick. 1981. Nozick seeks to "dissolve the inegalitarian class distinction between nothing and something, treating them on a par [....], not treating nonexisting or nonobtaining as more natural or privileged [...]" One way to do this, he proposes, "is to say that all possibilities are realized." He thus defines the "principle of fecundity" as "All possible worlds obtain." Nozick, 1981, p. 127–128, 131.

51 Davies, 2006, pp. 298–299.

52 On *Closer To Truth*. Personal communication

53 On *Closer To Truth*. Personal communication.

54 Swinburne, Richard. 2004. *The Existence of God* (second edition). Oxford: Clarendon / Oxford University Press. Swinburne, Richard. 1993. *The Coherence of Theism* (revised edition). Oxford: Clarendon / Oxford University Press. Swinburne, Richard. 1994. *The Christian God*. Oxford: Clarendon / Oxford University Press. Swinburne, Richard. 1996. *Is There a God?* Oxford: Clarendon / Oxford University Press. On *Closer To Truth*. In his influential book, *The Existence of God*, Swinburne builds a "cumulative case" of inductive arguments to assert (not prove) the claim that the proposition "God exists" is more probable than not. He begins with a description of what he means by God. ("In understanding God as a person, while being fair to the Judaic and Islamic view of God, I am oversimplifying the Christian view.") Swinburne states: "I take the proposition 'God exists' (and the equivalent proposition 'There is a God') to be logically equivalent to 'there exists necessarily a person without a body (i.e. a spirit) who necessarily is eternal, perfectly free, omnipotent, omniscient, perfectly good, and the creator of all things'. I use 'God' as the name of the person picked out by this description." Swinburne then defines each of his terms. By God being a person, Swinburne means "an individual with basic powers (to act intentionally), purposes, and beliefs." By God's being eternal, that "he always has existed and always will exist." By God's being perfectly free, that "no object or event or state (including past states of Himself) in any way causally influences him to do the action that he does – his own choice at the moment of action alone determines what he does." By God's being omnipotent, that "he is able to do whatever it is logically possible (i.e., coherent to suppose) that he can do." By God's being omniscient, that "he knows whatever it is logically possible that he know." By God's being perfectly good, that "he always does a morally best action (when there is one), and does no morally bad action." By his being the creator of all things, that "everything that

exists at each moment of time (apart from himself) exists because, at that moment of time, he makes it exist, or permits it to exist." The claim that there is a God, Swinburne states, is called theism.

55   Plantinga, Alvin. 1983. "Reason and Belief in God," in Plantinga, Alvin and Nicholas Wolterstorff, eds. *Faith and Rationality: Reason and Belief in God*. Notre Dame, IN: University of Notre Dame Press. Plantinga argues famously that theistic belief does not, in general, need argument or evidence to be rational and justified; belief in God, in Plantinga's well-known terminology, is "properly basic." This means that belief in God is such that one may properly accept it without evidence, that is, without the evidential support of other beliefs. "Perhaps the theist," Plantinga asserts, "is entirely within his epistemic rights in *starting from* belief in God [even if he has no argument or evidence at all]; perhaps that proposition is one of the ones with respect to whose probability he determines the rational propriety of *other* beliefs he holds." (Tomberlin, James E. and Peter van Inwagen, eds. 1985. Alvin Plantinga. Holland: D. Reidel Publishing Company.) Notwithstanding this position, Plantinga presents his own arguments for God's existence: Plantinga, Alvin. "Two Dozen (or so) Theistic Arguments." Lecture notes. http://www.calvin.edu/academic/philosophy/virtual_library/articles/plantinga_alvin/two_dozen_or_so_theistic_arguments.pdf.

56   Philosophical discussions of God's Nature, which much occupied medieval theologians (Scholastics), seem arcane and irrelevant today but may probe the structure and meaning of a theistic God, and as such may help advise whether such a Being really exists. Take the traditional doctrine of "Divine Simplicity" (which is anything but simple): God is utterly devoid of complexity; no distinctions can be made in God; God has no "parts." Plantinga describes the doctrine: "We cannot distinguish him from his nature, or his nature from his existence, or his existence from his other properties; he is the very same thing as his nature, existence, goodness, wisdom, power, and the like. And this is a dark saying indeed." Plantinga, Alvin. 1980. *Does God Have a Nature?* Milwaukee: Marquette University Press. On *Closer To Truth*.

57   In the Bible, names are often declarations of the essence of things. "Adam" means earth, soil, reddish-brownish stuff, from which, as the story goes, God made Adam – "Adam" the stuff was what Adam the man literally *was*. The Hebrew words often translated "I am that I am" could perhaps be more intensely (but less euphonically) rendered "I-am-continuing to-be that which I-am-continuing to-be." Hence, since name is essence, and here the Name means existence, God's existence is his essence. A God of this Name can claim to be without need of further explanation, not in the sense that a further explanation cannot be known but in the sense that a further explanation cannot exist.

58   Nasr, Seyyed Hossein. 2006. *Islamic Philosophy from Its Origin to the Present: Philosophy in the Land of Prophecy*. SUNY Series in Islam. Albany, NY: State University of New York Press. Nasr, Seyyed Hossein, Randall E. Auxier and Luican W. Stone, eds. 2000. *The Philosophy of Seyyed Hossein Nasr*. Library of Living Philosophers Series. Chicago and La Salle, IL: Open Court Publishing Company. On *Closer To Truth*.

59   Ellis, George F. R. 2002. "Natures of Existence (Temporal and Eternal)." In Ellis, George F. R., ed., *The Far-Future Universe: Eschatology from a Cosmic Perspective*. Philadelphia, PA: Templeton Foundation Press. On *Closer To Truth*.

60 Russell, Robert John. 2002. "Eschatology and Physical Cosmology – A Preliminary Reflection." In Ellis. 2002. Russell, Robert John, Nancey Murphy and Arthur Peacocke, eds. 1997. *Chaos and Complexity: Scientific Perspectives on Divine Action.* Vatican City State: Vatican Observatory Publications. On *Closer To Truth.*

61 Craig, William Lane. 1991. "The Existence of God and the Beginning of the Universe." *Truth: A Journal of Modern Thought* 3: 85–96. Copan, Paul and William Lane Craig. 2004. Creation out of Nothing: *A Biblical, Philosophical and Scientific Exploration.* Grand Rapids, MI: Baker Academic. Craig, William Lane and Quentin Smith. 1993. *Theism, Atheism, and Big Bang Cosmology.* Oxford: Clarendon Press. On *Closer To Truth.*

62 To John Polkinghorne, a mathematical physicist turned Anglican priest, the Big Bang is "scientifically very interesting but theologically neutral." He asserts that Christian doctrine, which he says never had a stake in the Big Bang vs. Steady State debate, has often erroneously been supposed to be "principally concerned with initiation, with the primary instant." Rather, he says, its concern is "not just with what God did, but with what God is doing; its subject is ontological origin, not temporal beginning." Polkinghorne, John. 1995. *Serious Talk: Science and Religion in Dialogue.* Valley Forge, PA: Trinity Press International, p. 64. On *Closer To Truth.*

63 Theists debate among themselves whether the Judeo-Christian God is theologically compatible with a multiverse. While many theists denounce multiple universes as a naturalistic substitute for God – they argue that accepting a God is far simpler than postulating a multiverse – some theists now break tradition by claiming that a multiverse reveals an even grander grandeur of the Creator. Collins, Robin. 2007. "A Theistic Perspective on the Multiverse Hypothesis." In Carr, 2007. Collins, Robin. 2005. "Design and the Designer: New Concepts, New Challenges." In Harper, 2005. On *Closer To Truth.*

64 Ward, Keith. 2006. *Pascal's Fire: Scientific Faith and Religious Understanding.* Oxford: Oneworld Publications. On *Closer To Truth.* Ward's blurring of personal / impersonal models of God, he says, is influenced by the Brahman / Isvara distinction in Indian philosophy, with resonances in Eastern Orthodox theology (the distinction between *ousia* and *economia*). On *Closer To Truth.*

65 "Deism," *Dictionary of the History of Ideas*, http://etext.lib.virginia.edu/cgi-local/DHI/dhi.cgi?id=dv1-77. Deist website: http://www.deism.com/.

66 Levine, Michael, "Pantheism", *The Stanford Encyclopedia of Philosophy (Spring 2006 Edition)*, Edward N. Zalta (ed.), http://plato.stanford.edu/archives/spr2006/entries/pantheism/. H. P. Owen proposes a more formal definition: "'Pantheism' [...] signifies the belief that every existing entity is only one Being; and that all other forms of reality are either modes (or appearances) of it or identical with it." Owen, H. P. 1971. *Concepts of Deity.* London: Macmillan. Pantheism is distinguished from Deism in that, while both sport nontheistic, impersonal Gods, the former allows no separation between God and the world while the latter revels in it. Pantheism's many variations take contrasting positions on metaphysical issues: its fundamental substance can be real or unreal, changing or changeless, etc.

67 *Panentheism*, a word that is a manufactured cognate of pantheism, is the doctrine that the universe is in God but God is more than the universe – i.e., it combines the robust immanence of pantheism (God is truly "in" the world) with the ultimate transcendence

of theism (God exceeds the world in His ontological "otherness"). More formally, panentheism is "The belief that the Being of God includes and penetrates the whole universe, so that every part of it exists in Him, but (against pantheism) that His Being is more than, and is not exhausted by, the universe." Cross, F. L. and E. A. Livingstone, eds. 1985. *Oxford Dictionary of the Christian Church*. 2nd ed. Oxford: Oxford University Press, p. 1027. Panentheism, a recent formulation, is the guiding philosophy of Charles Hartshorne, process theologians, and some who seek harmony between science and religion. Clayton, Philip and Arthur Peacocke, eds. 2004. *In Whom We Live and Move and Have Our Being: Panentheistic Reflections on God's Presence in a Scientific World*, Grand Rapids, MI: Eerdmans. *Acosmic pantheism* considers the world merely an appearance and fundamentally unreal (it is more characteristic of some Hindu and Buddhist traditions). *Panpsychism*, the belief that every entity in the universe is to some extent sentient, amalgamates Pantheism (3.4) with Consciousness as Cause (3.6).

68   MacIntyre, Alasdair. 1967. "Pantheism." In *Encyclopedia of Philosophy*. Edwards, Paul, ed. New York: Macmillan and Free Press. John Leslie derives pantheism from his thesis that "ethical requiredness" (see Endnote 75) is the ultimate reality generator. Leslie, John. 2001, *Infinite Minds: A Philosophical Cosmology*. Oxford: Oxford University Press, pp. 39–41, 126–130, 215–216. On *Closer To Truth*.

69   A wide range of conflating examples include Spiritualism, Spiritism, Animism, Occultism, New Age religions of all kinds, Edgar Cayce and those like him, Theosophy and its sort, forms of Gnosticism – the list is as tedious as it is endless.

70   According to Amit Goswami, a quantum physicist inspired by Hindu philosophy, "everything starts with consciousness. That is, consciousness is the ground of all being" which imposes "downward causation" on everything else. Goswami, Amit. 1995. *The Self-Aware Universe: How Consciousness Creates the Material World*. New York: Tarcher.

71   There are copious, fanciful schemes that attempt to make consciousness fundamental; many disparate philosophies and world systems take "cosmic mind" as the source of all reality (e.g., http://primordality.com/).

72   Rigpa is considered to be a truth so universal, so primordial, that it goes beyond all limits, and beyond even religion itself (http://www.rigpa.org/).

73   To the Dalai Lama, consciousness (in its subtle form), which has no beginning, explains the world. Although he rejects any commencement of creation ("Creation is therefore not possible"), he asserts that the "creator of the world" in Buddhism is "the mind" and "collective karmic impressions, accumulated individually, are at the origin of the creation of a world." Dalai Lama XIV, Marianne Dresser and Alison Anderson. 1996. *Beyond Dogma: Dialogues & Discourses*. Berkeley, CA: North Atlantic Books.

74   Linde, Andrei, "Inflation, Quantum Cosmology and the Anthropic Principle," p. 25–27, arXiv:hep-th/0211048v2; Vilenkin, 2006, p. 205. On *Closer To Truth*.

75   Leslie, John. 2001. Leslie, John. 1979. *Value and Existence*. Oxford: Blackwell. On *Closer To Truth*. Leslie states, "A force of *creative ethical requirement* or [...] a principle that consistent groups of ethical requirements, ethical demands for the actual presence of this or that situation, can sometimes bring about their own fulfillment. The cosmos might exist because its existence was ethically necessary, without the aid of an omnipotent being who chose to do something about this." Although Leslie surmises,

"a divine person might well head the list of the things that the creative force would have created," his preferred position is "a cosmos of infinitely many unified realms of consciousness, each of them infinitely rich [...] a picture of *infinitely many minds each one worth calling 'divine'* and each one "expected to include knowledge of absolutely everything worth knowing." Leslie, 2002, p. v-vi. On *Closer To Truth*.

76   Rescher, Nicholas. 1984. *The Riddle of Existence: An Essay in Idealistic Metaphysics*. Lanham, MD: University Press of America. Rescher's "cosmic values" are simplicity, economy, elegance, harmony, and the like, which are maximized by what he calls "protolaws" as they bring about the existence of the spatiotemporal laws and concrete objects of the actual universe. Witherall. 2006.

77   Parfit. January 22, 1998 and February 5, 1998. Parfit suggests that if reality were as full as it could be ("All Worlds Hypothesis"), that would not be a coincidence. "We can reasonably assume that, if this possibility obtains, that is because it is maximal, or at this extreme. On this Maximalist View, it is a fundamental truth that being possible, and part of the fullest way that reality could be, is sufficient for being actual. That is the highest law governing reality." It does not stop there. Parfit conceptualizes the "Selector" as some special feature that actualizes a real world from among countless cosmic possibilities. "It would determine, not that reality be a certain way, but that it be determined in a certain way how reality is to be." Then, to the extent that there are competing credible Selectors, rules would be needed to select among them, which may be followed by higher level Selectors and rules. Can it ever stop? Parfit concludes by stating "just as the simplest cosmic possibility is that nothing ever exists, the simplest explanatory possibility is that there is no Selector. So we should not expect simplicity at both the factual and explanatory levels. If there is no Selector, we should not expect that there would also be no Universe." It seems that we arrive back at Brute Fact, which radiates a bit more color now, and we are enlightened by the journey.

78   Schellenberg defines ultimism as "the claim that there is a metaphysically and axiologically ultimate reality (one representing both the deepest fact about the nature of things and the greatest possible value), in relation to which an ultimate good can be attained." ' Schellenberg, J. L. 2009. *The Will to Imagine: A Justification of Skeptical Religion*. Ithaca: Cornell University Press.) On *Closer To Truth*.

79   Penrose, Roger. 2006. "The Big Questions: What is Reality?" *New Scientist*, November 18.

80   Taoism, an indigenous religion of China, is centered on "The Way," the path to understanding of the foundations and true nature of heaven and earth. Its scriptures are the relatively short (81 chapters, 5000 Chinese characters) *Dao De Jing* (*Tao Te Ching*), its essence signaled by its famous first verse: "The Tao that can be told is not the eternal Tao" (chapter 1; translation, Gia-Fu Feng & Jane English, 1972). "For though all creatures under heaven are the products of Being, Being itself is the product of Not-being" (chapter 40; translation, Arthur Waley).

81   Wikipedia, http://en.wikipedia.org/wiki/Brahman. Robert Nozick, in his exploration of "Why is there Something Rather Than Nothing," quotes the beginning of the Hindu Vedas' Hymn of Creation, "Nonbeing then existed not nor being," and then shows how Being and Nonbeing do not exhaust all possibilities – outside a certain domain, he says, a thing may be neither. Nozick thus suggests that "It is

plausible that whatever every existent thing comes from, their source, falls outside the categories of existence and nonexistence." Nozick. 1981, p. 150, 152.

82   Wilber, Ken. 1995. *Sex, Ecology, Spirituality: The Spirit of Evolution*. Boston: Shambhala Publications. Thompson, William Irwin. 1996. *Coming into Being: Artifacts and Texts in the Evolution of Consciousness*. New York: St. Martin's Press.

83   Hick, John, "The Real and Its Personae and Impersonae," *John Hick: The Official Website*, http://www.johnhick.org.uk/article10.html. On *Closer To Truth*.

84   In Tao, the only motion is returning. *Dao De Jing*, chapter 6; translation, Arthur Waley.

85   Personal communication. To give the other side equal time, theists have a plethora of explanations or justifications of evil – some of them innovative and sophisticated, the "Free-Will Defense" being only the most common among a legion of others (a summary of which would exhaust an article about like this one).

86   "Idealism" *Wikipedia*, http://en.wikipedia.org/wiki/Idealism. Goswami, 1995.

87   Linde, Andrei. 1992. "Hard Art of the Universe Creation." *Nucl. Phys.* B372 421–442. Using a stochastic approach to quantum tunneling, Linde develops a method to create "the universe in a laboratory." He concludes by observing that this would be "a very difficult job," but if it is true, "Hopefully, he [the other-worldly physicist hacker] did not make too many mistakes […]" On *Closer To Truth*.

88   Davies, 2006.

89   Bostrom, Nick. 2003. "Are You Living in a Computer Simulation?" *Philosophical Quarterly*, Vol. 53, No. 211, pp. 243–255. Bostrom, Nick. 2005. "Why Make a Matrix? And Why You Might Be In One." In Irwin, William, ed. *More Matrix and Philosophy: Revolutions and Reloaded Decoded*. Chicago: IL: Open Court Publishing Company. "Life's a Sim and Then You're Deleted" *New Scientist*, 27 July 2002. On *Closer To Truth*. Another kind of Simulation in Virtual Reality (4.3) is Frank Tipler's notion of a general resurrection just before a Big Crunch at what he calls the "Omega Point," which would be brought about by an almost infinite amount of computational power generated by a universe whose inward gravitational rush is accelerating exponentially. Tipler, Frank. 1997. *The Physics of Immortality: Modern Cosmology, God and the Resurrection of the Dead*. New York: Anchor Books. On *Closer To Truth*.

90   "Solipsism" *Wikipedia*, http://en.wikipedia.org/wiki/Solipsism.

91   If the problem is turned from explaining the fundamental essence or existence of this universe, including its apparent fine-tuning, to the exquisitely more profound problem of explaining why there is anything at all – Why Not Nothing? – the categories and explanations, and their organization, shift. To try to get at Why Not Nothing, the new taxonomy would ask, in a first cut, two overarching questions: (i) "Of What Things does Ultimate Reality Consist?" and (ii) "By What (If Anything) is Ultimate Reality Caused?" or "For What Reason (If Any) Does Ultimate Reality Exist?" Under the "Consist" question, I include all four of the categories – One Universe Models, Multiple Universe Models, Nonphysical Causes, and Illusions – in that prior to trying to fill the set of all possible explanations of the most fundamental or primitive cause of (or reason for) why anything at all exists in ultimate reality, we should try to fill the set of all possible constituents of ultimate reality (i.e., all the things that collectively compose the Something-rather-than-Nothing that does in fact really exist). (I include Illusion under the Consist question even though by definition

it is not "ultimate" because, if any of the Illusions obtains, it might reveal deeper layers of reality.) Under the "Cause" or "Reason" question, I have two categories: "Natural Explanations" (which subsumes One Universe Models and Multiple Universe Models) and "Nonphysical Causes." The subcategory possible explanations under each category remain largely the same. (I do not include Illusions under the Cause or Reason question for obvious reasons.)

92 van Inwagen, Peter. 2002. *Metaphysics* (Second Edition). Boulder, CO: Westview Press, p. 132. See also Endnotes 3 and 77. Derek Parfit states: "Reality might be some way because that way is the best, or the simplest, or the least arbitrary, or because its obtaining makes reality as full and varied as it could be, or because its fundamental laws are, in some way, as elegant as they could be." Parfit, February 5, 1998.

93 Leibniz, Gottfried. 1714. *The Principles of Nature and Grace*.

94 Arguments against Nothing include saying that Nothing is unimaginable, nonsense, meaningless or absurd, or as soon as something is possible it must exist somewhere. Some would have God's necessary existence as proscribing Nothing.

95 Peter van Inwagen argues that since there can be infinitely many non-empty worlds (populated by things, any things at all), but only one empty world ("Nothing"), the probability that any given world is non-empty (not Nothing) is infinite and the probability of Nothing is zero. In other words, because there are infinitely many potential worlds, each specific world would have a zero probability of actually existing – and because Nothing is only one of these potential worlds – there is only one kind of Nothing – therefore the probability of Nothing is zero. van Inwagen, Peter. 1996. "Why Is There Anything at All?" *Proceedings of the Aristotelian Society*, pp. 95–110. The argument is intriguing and hinges on two assumptions: (i) all possible populated worlds have the same probability and (ii) the probability of the empty world (Nothing) is no different than that of any of the infinite number of possible populated worlds. While recognizing that the empty world is vastly, even infinitely, easier to *describe*, van Inwagen reasons that this should not increase its relative probability unless "one is covertly thinking that there is something that is outside the 'Reality' […] [like] a 'pre-cosmic selection machine', not a part of Reality" (for Leibniz this was God) [….] or "something that determines that *there being nothing* is the 'default setting' on the control-board of Reality." "But there could be no such thing," van Inwagen argues, "for nothing is outside Reality," and he concludes, tentatively, that "the simplicity of the empty world provides us with no reason to regard it as more probable than any other possible world." Yet I find it hard to get out of my head the sense that the a priori probability of an empty world (Nothing) is greater than that of any possible populated world (Something) in that to have Something seems to require a second step (and likely many more steps), a process or rule or capricious happening that generates whatever is populating whatever world. If so, any given possible world (Something) would be less simple than the empty world (Nothing), which would mean that the probability of the empty world (Nothing) would be greater than zero. According to John Leslie, worlds of Somethings call for explanation because they consist of things that are actually there, whereas Nothing would be the absence of all such things; it would be a case of there not being anything there, and therefore of there being, prima facie, nothing to explain, and equally, of there being, prima facie, no situation whose production would be hard.

96   An empty world, Nothing, would then be followed by, in order of increasing complexity (or oddity) and explanatory difficulty, the following categories: infinitely many universes (for simplicity, "all" is second only to "none"); one universe (it's all we know but its life-friendly nature would be challenging to explain [other than by theism, which has its own challenges]); few-but-not-many universes (maybe there's some simple generating principle at work); an unimaginably large number of universes (but still a finite number); and universes in some number that, though very great, could still be called "a normal number". When one ponders the alternatives, all are baffling.

97   For the Subtraction Argument, see the following. Baldwin, T. 1996. "There might be nothing", *Analysis* 56, pp. 231–8. Rodriguez-Pereyra, G. 1997. "There might be nothing: the subtraction argument improved", *Analysis* 57, pp. 159–66. Rodriguez-Pereyra, G. 2002. "Metaphysical nihilism defended: reply to Lowe and Paseau," *Analysis* 62, pp. 172–80. Paseau, Alexander. 2006. "The Subtraction Argument(s)," *Dialectica* 60(2), 2006, pp. 145–156. For the opposing view, that it is metaphysically not possible that there would be no concrete objects, see the following. Armstrong, D.M. 1989. A Combinatorial Theory of Possibility. Cambridge: Cambridge University Press. Lewis, D. 1986. *On the Plurality of Worlds*. Oxford: Blackwell. Lowe, E. J. 1996. "Why is there anything at all?" *Aristotelian Society Supplementary Volume* 70: 111–20. See also, Sorensen, Roy. 2009. "Nothingness," *Stanford Encyclopedia of Philosophy*.

98   As an example of an objection to a kind of Nothing, some would resist the idea that there could be space and time that had been emptied of existing things. The "relational" theories of space and of time assume that emptying space and time of existing things is impossible, because space is the system of spatial relations between things, and time is the system of temporal relations between things.

99   I struggle with the place of value in this taxonomy. It would always seem to be the case, as John Leslie stresses, that a world composed entirely and continuously of suffering sentient beings would be an existence worse than nothing. But I am not convinced that this true human sensibility ipso facto elevates value to being an abstract object; I cannot rid myself of the opposing notion that our reading into reality an absolute value imposes a human or sentient sense on an otherwise oblivious, value-free existence. However, Leslie makes the point that if the cosmos as a whole has a value, whether positive or negative, that is not simply relative to the individual tastes of sentient beings, then even in the absence of all existing things it would presumably have been a fact that a *possible* cosmos like this would possess that same value, were it to come into existence, so that its not having come into existence would be really fortunate (if its net existence would be bad) or really unfortunate (if its net existence would be good). Of course, this would not lead straight to the more speculative notion that the reason why the cosmos exists is that its existence was "required" in an ethical sense (i.e., that value was explanatorily prior to the cosmos and somehow brought about all things). However, it would support the idea that value is something ineradicable and fundamental (primitive) and would thus give me pause. Furthermore, it could help show that the absence of all existing things need not be a Nothing in which all realities were absent.

100 Distinguishing Nothings Eight and Nine may be artificial in that abstract objects and possibilities are both non-existent things, but I make the distinction for clarity and

explanatory depth, not for fundamental essence. I also do so because of a naïve sense, which I take the liberty of having, that I can imagine (just barely) a possible world where there were no abstract objects but where there were still possibilities (though what those possibilities would be without abstract objects I've no idea). I cannot, however, imagine the reverse: a world where there were abstract objects but no possibilities. In fact, I cannot conceive of a possible world in which there were no possibilities.

101 That the universe may have popped into existence via some sort of cosmic spontaneous combustion, emerging from the "nothing" of empty space (i.e., vacuum energy generated by quantum fluctuations, unstable high energy "false vacua") or from "quantum tunneling" (Vilenkin, 2006), may be the proximal cause of why we have a universe in the first place, but of itself it cannot be the reason why the universe we have works so well for us. Universe-generating mechanisms of themselves, such as unprompted eternal chaotic inflation or uncaused nucleations in spacetime, do not address, much less solve, the fine-tuning problem. Nor can vacuum energy or quantum tunneling or anything of the like be the ultimate cause of the universe, because, however hackneyed, the still-standing, still-unanswered question remains "from where did those laws come?"

102 The question of whether God, assuming God exists, would be "necessary" – which means that God would exist in all possible worlds – has beset philosophers and theologians for centuries. The much-debated Ontological Argument for the existence of God, which defines God as "a being than which no greater can be conceived," leads to the claim that God is necessary because necessity is a higher perfection than contingency. Richard Swinburne asserts that God is a "factual necessity" but not a "logical necessity" in that the non-existence of God would introduce no logical contradiction. On *Closer To Truth*. Timothy O'Connor defends God's necessity in his monograph on the topic. O'Connor, Timothy. 2008. *Theism and Ultimate Explanation: The Necessary Shape of Contingency*. Oxford: Blackwell.

103 The relationship between God and abstract objects is particularly troublesome for those who believe that God created and sustains *all* things and who privilege above all else God's absolute sovereignty (aseity). The reason is that abstract objects, many philosophers believe, exist necessarily, which means that it is impossible for abstract objects not to exist, which further means that it makes no sense for even God to have created them. What would it take to create the idea of the number 3 or the truth that $1 + 2 = 3$ or the reality that squares are not round? How could such ideas, truths, realities even conceivably be created? Peter van Inwagen calls abstract objects "putative counterexamples" to the thesis that God has created everything. But if abstract objects do exist necessarily, then wouldn't God's mental life be encompassed by infinities of infinities of abstract objects, not only which God would not have created but also over which God would exercise no control? The problem posed by abstract objects for a God whose sovereignty must be absolute is complex and requires metaphysical analysis. Consider two of the more general ways to defend God's sovereignty (aseity): 1) Deny that abstract objects are real, in that numbers, universals, propositions and the like are mere human-invented names with no correspondence in reality (nominalism); and/or 2) claim that abstract objects are thoughts in the mind of God. Van Inwagen rejects both ways; he must therefore

defend the position that there are besides God other uncreated beings and thus prefers to restrict God's creation of "all things visible and invisible" to "objects that can enter into causal relations" (which excludes abstract objects). Van Inwagen, Peter. 2009. "God and Other Uncreated Things," in *Metaphysics and God*, ed. Kevin Timpe. London: Routledge. On the other hand, William Lane Craig rejects the view that "there might be things, such as properties and numbers, which are causally unrelated to God as their Creator." Craig says that "Abstract objects have at most an insubstantial existence in the mind of the Logos," adding, "If a Christian theist is to be a platonist, then, he must, it seems, embrace absolute creationism, the view that God has created all the abstract objects there are." However, Craig himself resolves the conundrum by espousing nominalism, by judging platonism to be false – so that those pesky abstract objects no longer exist and thus no longer undermine God's sovereignty. Craig, William Lane. 2011. "Van Inwagen On Uncreated Beings (http://www.reasonablefaith.org/van-inwagen-on-uncreated-beings). Craig, William Lane. 2011. "Nominalism and Divine Aseity," *Oxford Studies in Philosophy of Religion* 4: 44–65. Craig, William Lane. 2004. "*Creatio ex Nihilo* and Abstract Objects" in Copan, Paul and William Lane Craig (eds). *Creation out of Nothing* (Baker). Craig, William Lane. 2011. "Why are (some) Platonists so insouciant?" *Philosophy* 86:2 (2011): 213–229. Cambridge University Press. See also Davidson, Matthew. 2009. "God and Other Necessary Beings," *Stanford Encyclopedia of Philosophy*.

Leibniz's Question*

MICHAEL HELLER

1.   R.L. Kuhn's Catalogue of Explanations

In No. 2 of Volume 13 of the well-known journal *Skeptic* there is an article by Robert Lawrence Kuhn entitled "Why This Universe? Toward a Taxonomy of Possible Explanations." Kuhn is patently excited by the prospects opened up by contemporary theoretical physics and cosmology. These prospects transcend the method employed in the empirical sciences in the narrow sense, well-nigh compelling the more inquisitive mind at least to ask questions. The anthropic principles have drawn attention to the exceptionality of our universe within the space of all the possibilities, and the idea of a multiverse has thrown the gate open to speculation. Kuhn decided to compile a "taxonomy" of all the explanations various authors have put forward for the amazing fact that the universe we live in is what it is and no other. As one reads Kuhn's "catalogue of explanations" [...] one develops the impression that for Kuhn the question why the universe is what

* From chapter 21 of *Ultimate Explanations of the Universe*, translated from the Polish by T. Bałuk-Ulewiczowa (Heidelberg: Springer, 2009), pp. 177–184. Reprinted with permission of Springer (www.springer.com) and TAIWPN UNIVERSITAS.

it is was a surrogate question. His real question comes at the beginning and end of his article. In his introduction Kuhn admits that already when he was twelve he was suddenly struck by the question *why there was something in existence rather than nothing* [...]

This question haunted Kuhn. In his catalogue of explanations it is implied rather than expressly formulated. "Why is the universe what it is?" is only the inevitable sequel of "Why is it at all?" [...]

[C]osmology, the contemporary science of the universe, cannot break free from asking ultimate questions. Admittedly, more insistent versions of such questions transcend the borders of the mathematical and experimental method employed in cosmology, but the representatives of this science often cross these boundaries themselves and indulge in speculation that is not so constrained by methodology. Nonetheless in all of these speculations there has to be a point of departure; you have to make some initial assumptions: maybe mathematics, the rules of deduction, the laws of nature, an infinite number of universes. If your initial assumption is NOTHING, then you stay with NOTHING forever [...]

2.   Leibniz's Question

[T]he question of why something rather than nothing has been present in Christian thought from the very beginning, but this form of the question and its dramatisation comes from Leibniz. A word of explanation is needed for the expression "dramatisation." Leibniz formulated his question in a fairly short treatise entitled "Principles of Nature and Grace, Based on Reason," and he did so dryly and with no drama whatsoever. But apparently the contrast between the brevity of the question itself and the intensity of the sense – dramatic in itself – that this question carries itself so firmly in the memories of the following generations of thinkers that afterwards they were never able to ask for the reason of the existence of anything at all other than in the way Leibniz had done. So let's consult the original text. After rather briefly introducing the reader to the main ideas in his monadology, Leibniz states:

> So far I have spoken only of what goes on in the natural world: now I must move up to the metaphysical level, by making use of a great though not very widely used principle, which says that *nothing* comes about without a sufficient reason [...]

[...][T]he principle of sufficient reason (along with the principle of contradiction) is what determines the whole of Leibniz's thought. And it makes him ask the following question:

> Why is there something rather than nothing? *After all, nothing is simpler and easier than something.*

Leibniz's answer to this question is perhaps rather hasty (at least so it seems if read without the context of his other works), and may seem to us too flimsily grounded. According to Leibniz the universe is made up of a "series of contingent things," hence

> *a sufficient reason that has no need of any further reason – a "Because" that doesn't throw up a further "Why?" – and this must lie outside the series of contingent things, and must be found in a substance which is the cause of the entire series. It must be something that exists necessarily, carrying the reason for its existence within itself.*

Perhaps that is precisely the fate of that question: every unsatisfactory answer makes the question become more and more vexing.

3.   The Domino Effect

There have been several attempts to "neutralise" Leibniz's question. I shall present a few of them. Here is the first, frequently invoked in discussions:

> *We shall simply have to reconcile ourselves not so much to there being no answer to this question, as to there being no possibility of obtaining an answer to it. Expecting an answer to Leibniz's question would mean calling for the deducing of something from non-existent premises. You can hardly hold it against the logician if he is incapable of doing that.*

[...] The author of the entry in the *Stanford Encyclopedia of Philosophy* I have just quoted writes with what looks like a touch of irony that there is not much consolation in Hume's observation that although we can't explain the existence of all things, we can explain the existence of every thing separately. Imagine an infinite row of dominoes standing upright and then tumbling in an avalanche-like manner, each pushing down the domino behind it. We know what caused the fall of each domino, even though we don't know what made the whole row start to tumble. Hume was being optimistic in trusting that we are able to explain the existence of each thing on its own. Science tries to explain "the existence of every thing," certainly not "on its own" or "separately," but in far-reaching association with other things. And alas [...] it is still a long way off from the final success. But it has scored some remarkable successes "on the way." Which makes Leibniz's question even more dramatic: not only should we be asking why something exists, but also why that something is open to rational methods of examination. This is the source of Leibniz's principle of sufficient reason – only in a rational world can we ask for reasons, also for the reasons why anything at all exists.

4. The Existence of the Universe and the Rules of Language

One of the variations of the above objection invokes the "philosophical syntax of language." Leibniz's question is a combination of words which are meaningless. The syntactic error consists in the fact that the word "nothingness" does not refer to anything and we can neither ask a sensible question about "nothing," nor can we say anything at all about nothingness. Also the question "Why does something exist?" carries a syntax error, since it assumes that there exists a "something else," apart from "something," which could explain that "something."

The dispute over the philosophical (or logical) syntax of language separates off analytical philosophers from practically all other trends in philosophy, and even within the analytical fold there is no unanimity on this issue. Hence resorting to the rules of logical syntax in order to neutralise Leibniz's question has the character of an "intra-systemic" criterion; outside the system it is not regarded as legitimate. I am far from querying the achievements of analytical philosophy, in the field of the philosophy of language as well. But it is one thing to determine the principles of "philosophical grammar," and quite another to apply them to specific cases.

Philosophical issues certainly have a "linguistic component," and ignoring it is a serious fault on the part of many philosophers. Every philosopher should be analytical as regards this component. But then resolving philosophical problems, including the Great Philosophical Problems (and Leibniz's question is one of them) solely by means of linguistic resources is a serious fault on the part of many (not all) analytical philosophers. Often such solutions consist in getting rid of the problem as meaningless. One may not assume a priori that everything that cannot be formulated in ordinary language, even as rigorously defined as the language of philosophy, is not a genuine problem. Try formulating an advanced mathematical structure, e.g. describe the structure of spinor space, in ordinary though rigorously defined language. It is self-evient that mathematics is the language that has been created specifically for the description of structures like spinor structure, though this in no way alters the fact that spinor structure is a good example to show the limitations of ordinary language.

It is good to bear in mind Quine's warning. After a rather arduous analysis of certain ontological problems he wrote: "But we must not jump to the conclusion that what there is depends on words."

5. The Probability of Nothing

Peter van Inwagen proposed a rather peculiar answer to the question why there exists anything at all. His reasoning is as follows. There may exist an infinite number of worlds full of diverse beings, but only one empty world. Therefore the probability of the empty world is zero, while the probability of a (non-empty) world full of beings is one.

This apparently simple reasoning is based on very strong and essentially arbitrary assumptions. First of all, that there may exist an infinite number of worlds (that they have at least a potential existence); secondly, that probability theory as we know it may be applied to them (in other words that probability theory is in a sense aprioristic with respect to these worlds); and thirdly, that they come into being on the principle of "greater probability." The following question may be put with respect to this mental construct: "why does it exist, rather than nothing?"

[...] [W]e should not treat probability theory as an absolute and turn it into an ontology which governs everything, even the decisions made by God. Probability theory is simply a very good mathematical theory and the fact that it may be successfully applied to the world is truly astonishing. [...] Let's consider the example of throwing a true die. In connection with van Inwagen's argument, let's ask what is the probability of throwing none of the numbers. The answer is self-evident: there is no such possibility at all. But why? Because we ourselves have defined the distribution function for the probabilities, on the grounds of many experiments, for the set of all possible outcomes of throwing the die. That function assigns the same probability, $1/6$, to each of the possible outcomes, that is 1, 2, 3, 4, 5, and 6. On the grounds of the definition of the distribution function we have ruled out the occurrence of any other outcomes except for the above-mentioned ones. Of course we could have given a different definition of the probability function, but it would not be applicable to the throwing of a true die. For instance, it might apply to the throwing of a die with bevelled corners, in which case we would have the grounds for a definition of a probability function with a value assigned for the probability of not throwing any of the numbers.

Rather that treat probability theory as an absolute, it might be worthwhile to stop and think for a moment how it actually works.

6.   A Brute Fact

There is one further way out of the situation. To present it, I shall refer to Helena Eilstein, who in her recent book *Biblia w ręku ateisty* (The Bible in the Hands of an Atheist) made her position plain. In her introduction she writes that she considers herself an atheist, not an agnostic, and gives an extensive explanation that there are many ways in which a given attitude may be rejected. She also explains in what sense she rejects the belief in the existence of God. It's an interesting question, but not so relevant to our reflections right now. What is of interest to us is the manner in which someone who denies the existence of God tackles Leibniz's question.

Helena Eilstein starts her "approach" to the question with a remark that every scientific hypothesis which is to explain something is based on "certain assumptions" which are treated as "given" and in themselves not subject to explanation. Sometimes an explanation may be obtained for them thanks to subsequent theories, but it may happen that "their explanation is beyond the cognitive powers of the human intellect." There follows a cogent observation:

> *In fact, one of the characteristic features of contemporary science is that the limitation of the human cognitive powers is becoming more and more comprehensively apparent. Our observations cannot encompass the universe, irrespectively of whether it is constrained in terms of space-time or not. Our experiments cannot "directly" reach all the layers of physical existence, because, for instance, it is impossible for us physically to achieve the energy necessary for this. Moreover, sometimes it happens in science that asking for an explanation becomes warranted cognitively only once we have achieved the capacity to obtain an explanation.*

Eilstein "extrapolates" these undeniably true observations back to a more extreme case:

> *We cannot rule out that some of the givens relied on by science are unexplainable for ontological reasons; they are "ontologically primary" and therefore do not call for an explanation, but merely for confirmation.*

Note that the supposition that there are certain problems which science will never solve (and certain facts it will never explain) is quite natural, and many scientists and philosophers concur; but the claim that some of these problems relate to "ontologically primary givens" is a very strong ontological assertion.

Eilstein gradually approaches the central issue:

> *In the scientific presentation of reality we should take into consideration the inevitability of having to acknowledge the conjecture that in certain of its most essential aspects the universe simply is what it is, and that we shall have to base our scientific explanations on this.*

She calls answers to questions why this or that thing exists "existential explanations." An existential explanation may refer to the laws of science or the initial conditions for the given issue. The property that all explanations, including existential explanations, have in common

> *is that they take for granted that something exists and is what it is, and that this acknowledgement needs no further explanation, at least within the bounds of the given explanatory procedure.*

Again a relevant observation, but it should be supplemented with the remark that science never withdraws from the possibility of explaining what has been accepted as "initially given" in the explanations obtained hitherto. In the opinion of many, even "the ultimate theory" will not bring an end to questions.

And for this reason what Helena Eilstein goes on to write may not be inferred from these remarks. She continues in this way:

> From the above it may be inferred that the question why something exists rather than nothing is illegitimate. The question is illegitimate since by the very nature of things there can be no answer to it. The fact that it exists is the ultimate, brute fact.

In the original Polish text Eilstein adds a footnote to explain that she had the English expression "brute fact" in mind, but could find no good Polish equivalent (she uses the phrase "naked fact"). Sympathising with her translation problems, I would recommend following the phonetics and writing *brutalny fakt* ("brutal fact"). Indeed, for anyone concurring with Helena Eilstein's opinion, the existence of anything whatsoever is a brutal fact – brutal because it violates the principle which for me is the expression of rationality: that we should go on asking questions for as long as there is still something left to explain. And in philosophy it often happens that even if there is no answer to some questions, their examination may lead to progress.

The Rejectionist Approach*

NICHOLAS RESCHER

Questions like "Why is there anything at all?" "Why are things-in-general as they actually are?", and "Why is the law structure of the world as it is?" cannot be answered within the standard causal framework. For causal explanations need inputs: they are essentially *transformational* (rather than *formational* pure and simple). They can address themselves to specific issues distributively and seriatim, but not collectively and holistically. If we persist in posing the sorts of global questions at issue, we cannot hope to resolve them in orthodox causal terms. Does this mean that such questions are improper?

On the rejectionist approach, the entire question of obtaining the (or *a*) reason for the existence of things is simply dismissed as illegitimate. Even to inquire into the existence of the entire universe is held to be somehow illegitimate. It is just a mistake to ask for a causal explanation of existence *per se*; the question should be abandoned as improper – as not representing a legitimate issue. We are assured that in the light of closer scrutiny the explanatory "problem" vanishes as meaningless.

---

*   From *The Riddle of Existence* (Lanham, MD, and London: University Press of America, 1984). Reprinted with permission of University Press of America, a member of the Rowman & Littlefield Publishing Group.

Dismissal of the problem as illegitimate is generally based on the idea that the question at issue involves an illicit presupposition. It looks to answers of the form "Z is the (or *an*) explanation for the existence of things." Committed to this response-schema, the question has the thesis "There is a ground for the existence of things – existence-in-general is the sort of thing that has an explanation." And this presumption – we are told – might well be false. In principle its falsity could emerge in two ways:

(1)   on grounds of deep general principle inherent in the conceptual "logic" of the situation; or
(2)   on grounds of a concrete doctrine of substantive metaphysics or science that precludes the prospect of an answer – even as quantum theory precludes the prospect of an answer to "Why did that atom of Californium decay at that particular time?"

Let us begin by considering if the question of existence might be invalidated by considerations of the first sort and root in circumstances that lie deep in the conceptual nature of things. Consider the following discussion by C. G. Hempel:

> Why is there anything at all, rather than nothing? ... But what kind of an answer could be appropriate? What seems to be wanted is an explanatory account which does not assume the existence of something or other. But such an account, I would submit, is a logical impossibility. For generally, the question "Why is it the case that *A*? is answered by "Because *B* is the case" [...] [*A*]*n answer to our riddle which made no assumptions about the existence of anything cannot possibly provide adequate grounds.* [...] The riddle has been constructed in a manner that makes an answer logically impossible [...][1]

But this plausible line of argumentation has shortcomings. The most serious of these is that it fails to distinguish appropriately between the *existence of things* on the one hand and the *obtaining of facts* on the other,[2] and supplementarily also between specifically substantival facts regarding existing *things*, and nonsubstantival facts regarding *states of affairs* that are not dependent on the operation of preexisting things.

We are confronted here with a principle of hypostatization to the effect that the reason for anything must ultimately always inhere in the operations of things. And at this point we come to a prejudice as deep-rooted as any in Western philosophy: the idea that things can only originate from things, that nothing can come from nothing (*ex nihilo nihil fit*) in the sense that no *thing* can emerge from a thingless condition.[3] Now, this somewhat ambiguous principle is perfectly unproblematic when construed as saying that if the existence of something real has a correct explanation at all, then this explanation must pivot on something that is really and truly so. Clearly, we cannot explain one *fact* without involving other *facts to* do the explaining. But the principle becomes highly problematic when construed in the manner of the precept that *"things* must come from *things,"* that *substances* must inevitably be invoked to explain the existence of *substances.* For we then become committed to the thesis that everything in nature has an efficient cause in some other natural thing that is its causal source, its reason for being.

This stance is implicit in Hempel's argument. And it is explicit in much of the philosophical tradition. Hume, for one, insists that there is no feasible way in which an existential conclusion can be obtained from nonexistential premisses.[4] And the principle is also supported by philosophers of a very different ilk on the other side of the channel – including Leibniz himself, who writes:

> [T]he sufficient reason [of contingent existence] [...] must be outside this series of contingent things, and *must reside in a substance which is the cause of this series* [...][5]

Such a view amounts to a thesis of genetic homogeneity which says (on analogy with the old but now rather obsolete principle that "life must come from life") that "things must come from things," or "stuff must come from stuff," or "substance must come from substance." What, after all, could be more plausible than the precept that only real (*existing*) causes can have real (*existing*) effects?

But despite its appeal, this principle has its problems. It presupposes that there must be a type-homogeneity between cause and effect on the lines of the ancient Greek principle that "like must come from like." This highly dubious principle of genetic homogeneity has taken hard knocks in the course of modern science. Matter can come from energy, and living organisms from complexes of inorganic molecules. If the principle fails with matter and life, need it hold for substance as such? The claim that it does so would need a very cogent defense. None has been forthcoming to date.

Is it indeed true that only *things* can engender things? Why need a ground of change always inhere in a *thing* rather than in a nonsubstantival "condition of things-in-general"? Must substance inevitably arise from *substance*? Even to state such a principle is in effect to challenge its credentials. For why must the explanation of facts rest in the operation of *things*? To be sure, fact-explanations must have inputs (*all* explanations must). Facts must root in facts. But why thing-existential ones? A highly problematic bit of metaphysics is involved here. Dogmas about explanatory homogeneity aside, there is no discernible reason why an existential fact cannot be grounded in nonexistential ones, and why the existence of substantial *things* cannot be explained on the basis of some nonsubstantival circumstance or principle whose operations can constrain existence in something of the way in which equations can constrain nonzero solutions. Once we give up the principle of genetic homogeneity and abandon the idea that existing things must originate in existing things, we remove the key prop of the idea that asking for an explanation of things in general is a logically inappropriate demand. The footing of the rejectionist approach is gravely undermined.

There are, of course, other routes to rejectionism. One of them turns on the doctrine of Kant's *Antinomy* that it is illegitimate to try to account for the phenomenal universe as a whole (the entire *Erscheinungswelt*). Explanation on this view is inherently partitive: phenomena can only be accounted for in terms of other phenomena, so that it is in principle improper to ask for an account of phenomena-as-a-whole. The very idea of an explanatory science of nature-as-a-whole is illegitimate. Yet this view is deeply problematic. To all intents and purposes, science strives to explain the age of the universe-as-a-whole, its structure, its volume, its laws, its composition, etc. Why not then its *existence* as well? The decree that explanatory discussion is by nature necessarily partial and incapable of dealing with the whole lacks plausibility. It seems a mere device for sidestepping embarrassingly difficult questions.

Rejectionism is not a particularly appealing course. Any alternative to rejectionism has the significant merit of retaining for rational inquiry and investigation a question that would otherwise be abandoned. The question of "the reason why" behind existence is surely important. If there is any possibility of getting an adequate answer – by hook or by crook – it seems reasonable that we would very much like to have it. There is nothing patently meaningless about this "riddle of existence." And it does not seem to rest in any obvious way on any particularly problematic presupposition – apart from the epistemically optimistic yet methodologically inevitable idea that there are always reasons why things are as they are (the "principle of sufficient reason"). To dismiss the question as improper or illegitimate is fruitless. Try as we will to put the question away, it comes back to haunt us.[6]

Notes

1   Carl G. Hempel, "Science Unlimited," *The Annals of the Japan Association for Philosophy of Science*, vol. 14(1973), pp. 187–202. (See p. 200). Our italics.

2   Note too that the question of the existence of facts is a horse of a very different color from that of the existence of things. There being no *things* is undoubtedly a possible situation, there being no *facts* is not (since if the situation were realized, this would itself constitute a fact).

3   Aristotle taught that every change must emanate from a "mover," i.e., a substance whose machinations provide the cause of change. This commitment to causal reification is at work in much of the history of Western thought. That its pervasiveness is manifest at virtually every juncture is clear from William Lane Craig's interesting study of *The Cosmological Argument from Plato to Leibniz* (London, 1980).

4   David Hume, Dialogues Concerning Natural Religion (ed. N. K. Smith; London, 1922), p. 189.

288 The Problem Seems Genuine

5   G. W. Leibniz, "Principles of Nature and of Grace," sect. 8, italics supplied. Compare
St. Thomas:

> Of necessity, herefore, anything in process of change is being changed by something
> else. (S.T., IA 2,3)

The idea that only substances can produce changes goes back to Thomas' master,
Aristotle. In Plato and the Presocratics, the causal efficacy of *principles* is recognized
(e.g., the love and strife of Empedocles).

6   For criticisms of ways of avoiding the question "Why is there something rather than
nothing?" see Chap. III of William Rowe, *The Cosmological Argument* (Princeton, 1975).
Cf. also Donald R. Burrill (ed.), *The Cosmological Argument* (Garden City, 1967), esp.
"The Cosmological Argument" by Paul Edwards.

Bibliography and Further Reading

Adams, R.M. (1971) "Has It Been Proved that All Real Existence is Contingent?" *American Philosophical Quarterly*, July: 284–291.

Adams, R.M. (1972) "Must God Create the Best?" *Philosophical Review*, July: 317–332.

Adler, R. (2011) "The Many Faces of the Multiverse." *New Scientist*, 26 November, 43–47.

Almeida, M.J. (2008) *The Metaphysics of Perfect Beings*. New York: Routledge.

Alston, W.P. (1960) "The Ontological Argument Revisited." *Philosophical Review*, October: 452–474.

Anselm (1903) *Proslogium and Monologium: in Saint Anselm: Basic Writings*, trans. S.N. Deane. La Salle: Open Court.

Anthony, L.M., ed. (2007) *Philosophers without Gods*. Oxford: Oxford University Press.

Aquinas (1945) *Summa Theologica*. In A.C. Pegis, ed., *Basic Writings of Saint Thomas Aquinas*. New York: Random House.

Aquinas (1955) *On the Truth of the Catholic Faith: Summa contra Gentiles* (book 1, trans. A.C. Pegis; book 2, trans. J.F. Anderson). New York: Image Books.

Aquinas (1962) *On Interpretation: Commentary by St. Thomas and Cajetan* [the Commentary is on Aristotle's *Peri Hermeneias*], trans. J.T. Oesterle. Milwaukee: Marquette University Press.

Aquinas (1964) *On the Eternity of the World*. Selections from Aquinas (trans. C. Vollert), Siger of Brabant (trans. L.H. Kendzierski) and Bonaventure (trans. P.M. Byrne), Milwaukee: Marquette University Press.

Aristotle (1928) *Metaphysica*, in vol. 8 of *The Works of Aristotle*, 2nd edn., ed. W.D. Ross. Oxford: Clarendon Press.

Armour, L. (1987) "Values, God, and the Problem About Why There is Anything at All." *Journal of Speculative Philosophy*, vol. 1 no. 2: 147–162.

Armstrong, D.M. (1989) *A Combinatorial Theory of Possibility*. Cambridge: Cambridge University Press.

Atkatz, D., and H. Pagels (1982) "Origin of the Universe as Quantum Tunneling Event." *Physical Review D*, 15 April: 2065–2073.

The Mystery of Existence: Why Is There Anything At All?, First Edition. Edited by John Leslie and Robert Lawrence Kuhn.
© 2013 John Wiley & Sons, Inc. Published 2013 by John Wiley & Sons, Inc.

Atkins, P.W. (1981) *The Creation*. Oxford: W.H. Freeman.

Atkins, P.W. (1992) *Creation Revisited*. Oxford: W.H. Freeman.

Atkins, P.W. (2011) *On Being*. Oxford: Oxford University Press.

Augustine (1967) *Confessions*, trans. J.K. Ryan. New York: Image Books. See esp. book 11.

Baggini, J. (2003) *Atheism: A Very Short Introduction*. Oxford: Oxford University Press.

Balashov, Y.V. (1991) "Resource Letter AP–1: The Anthropic Principle." *American Journal of Physics* vol. 59 no. 12: 1069–1076.

Baldwin, T. (1996) "There Might Be Nothing." *Analysis*, October: 231–238.

Balslev, A.N. (1990) "Cosmology and Hindu Thought." *Zygon*, March: 47–58.

Barrow, J.D. (1988) *The World within the World*. Oxford: Oxford University Press.

Barrow, J.D. (1994) *The Origin of the Universe*. New York: HarperCollins.

Barrow, J.D. (2001) "Cosmology, Life and the Anthropic Principle," pp. 139–153 of J.B. Miller, ed., *Cosmic Questions*, New York: New York Academy of Sciences.

Barrow, J.D. (2007a) *New Theories of Everything*. Oxford: Oxford University Press.

Barrow, J.D. (2007b) "Living in a Simulated Universe," pp. 481–486 of B. Carr, ed., *Universe or Multiverse?*, Cambridge: Cambridge University Press.

Barrow, J.D. (2011) *The Book of Universes*. New York: W.W. Norton.

Barrow, J.D., P.C.W. Davies, and C.L. Harper, eds. (2004) *Science and Ultimate Reality*. Cambridge: Cambridge University Press.

Barrow, J. D., and F.J. Tipler (1986) *The Anthropic Cosmological Principle*. Oxford: Oxford University Press.

Basile, P., and L.B. McHenry, eds. (2007) *Consciousness, Reality and Value: Essays in Honour of T.L.S. Sprigge*. Frankfurt: Ontos Verlag. See esp. the articles by Mander, Leslie, Forrest, and Sprigge.

Bergson, H. (1935) *The Two Sources of Morality and Religion*, trans. R.A. Audra and C. Brereton. New York: Henry Holt.

Bergson, H. (2007) *Creative Evolution*, trans. A. Michell. New York: Palgrave Macmillan. See esp. ch. 4.

Bertola, F., and U. Curi, eds. (1993) *The Anthropic Principle*. Cambridge: Cambridge University Press.

Blackburn, S. (2009) *The Big Questions*. London: Quercus Publishing. See section "Why Is There Something and Not Nothing?"

Blackford, R., and U. Schüklenk, eds. (2009) *50 Voices of Disbelief: Why We Are Atheists*. Malden MA: Wiley-Blackwell.

Boethius (1969) *The Consolation of Philosophy*, trans. V.E. Watts. Harmondsworth: Penguin Books. See esp. book 3.

Bohm, D., and B.J. Hiley. (1993) *The Undivided Universe*. London and New York: Routledge.

Bojowald, M. (2010) *Once Before Time: A Whole Story of the Universe*. New York: Alfred A. Knopf.

Bondi, H., W.B. Bonnor, R.A. Lyttleton, and G.J. Whitrow (1960) *Rival Theories of Cosmology*. London: Oxford University Press.

Bonnor, W.B. (1960) "The Problem of Evolution in General Relativity." *Journal of Mathematics and Mechanics*, vol. 9: 439–445.

Borchert, D.M., ed. (2006) *The Encyclopedia of Philosophy*, 2nd edn. (expanded). Detroit: Thomson Gale/Macmillan Reference USA. See "Anthropic Principle," "Atheism," "Augustine," "Averroes," "Bonaventure," "Brahman," "Conway, Anne," "Cosmological Argument for the Existence of God," "Cosmology," "Creation and Conservation,"

"Duns Scotus, John," "Edwards, Jonathan," "Erigena, John Scotus," "Epistemology, Religious," "Eternity," "Existence," "Eckhart, Meister," "Geulincx, Arnold," "God/ Isvara in Indian Philosophy," "Grosseteste, Robert," "Islamic Philosophy," "Jewish Philosophy," "Maimonides," "Malebranche, Nicolas," "Nature, Philosophical Ideas of," "Nicholas of Cusa," "Pantheism," "Parmenides of Elea," "Peter Lombard," "Philosophy of Religion," "Philosophy of Religion, History of," "Physicotheology," "Thomas Aquinas," "Tillich," "Time," "Voltaire," "Why," and "William of Auvergne."

Bostrom, N. (2002a) *Anthropic Bias: Observation Selection Effects in Science and Philosophy.* London and New York: Routledge.

Bostrom, N. (2002b) "Self-Locating Belief in Big Worlds: Cosmology's Missing Link to Observation." *Journal of Philosophy*, December: 607–623.

Bostrom, N. (2003) "Are You Living in a Computer Simulation?" *Philosophical Quarterly*, vol. 53 no. 211: 243–255.

Bradley, F.H. (1897) *Appearance and Reality*, 2nd edn. Oxford: Clarendon Press.

Bradley, F.H. (1922) *Principles of Logic*, 2nd edn., revised. London: Oxford University Press.

Brooks, D. (1992) "Why This World?" *Philosophical Papers*, November: 259–273.

Brout, R., F. Englert, and E. Gunzig (1978) "The Origin of the Universe as a Quantum Phenomenon." *Annals of Physics, vol.* 115: 78–106.

Brown, P. (1966) "Infinite Causal Regression." *Philosophical Review*, October: 510–525.

Bunge, M. (1962) "Cosmology and Magic." *The Monist*, Fall: 116–141.

Burke, M.B. (1984) "Hume and Edwards on 'Why Is There Something Rather Than Nothing?'" *Australasian Journal of Philosophy*, December: 355–362.

Burrell, D.B. (1993) *Freedom and Creation in Three Traditions.* Notre Dame: University of Notre Dame Press.

Burrell, D.B, C. Cogliati, J.M. Soskice, and W.R. Stoeger, eds. (2010) *Creation and the God of Abraham.* Cambridge: Cambridge University Press.

Burrill, D.R., ed. (1967) *The Cosmological Arguments.* New York: Doubleday.

Cameron, R.P. (2000) "Much Ado About Nothing: A Study of Metaphysical Nihilism." *Erkenntnis*, vol. 64 no. 2: 99–113.

Cameron, R.P. (2007) "Subtractability and Concreteness," *Philosophical Quarterly*, April: 273–279.

Campbell, C.A. (1957) *On Selfhood and Godhood.* London: George Allen & Unwin. See esp. Lectures 18 and 19.

Carlson, E., and E.J. Olsson (2001) "The Presumption of Nothingness." *Ratio*, September: 203–221.

Carr, B., ed. (2007) *Universe or Multiverse?* Cambridge: Cambridge University Press. Includes B. Carr, "The Anthropic Principle Revisited," pp. 77–89.

Carr, B.J., and M.J. Rees (1979) "The Anthropic Principle and the Structure of the Physical World." *Nature*, 12 April: 605–612.

Carter, B. (1974) "Large Number Coincidences and the Anthropic Principle in Cosmology," pp. 291–298 of M.S. Longair, ed., *Confrontation of Cosmological Theories with Observational Data*, Dordrecht: Reidel.

Carter, B. (1989) "Self-selection as an Adjunct to Natural Selection," pp. 185–206 of S.K. Biswas, D.C.V. Mallik and C.V. Vishveshwara, eds., *Cosmic Perspectives*. Cambridge: Cambridge University Press.

Carter, B. (2007) "Micro-anthropic Principle for Quantum Theory," pp. 285–319 of B. Carr, ed., *Universe or Multiverse?* Cambridge: Cambridge University Press.

Carroll, S.M. (2005) "Why (Almost) All Cosmologists Are Atheists." *Faith and Philosophy,* vol. 22 no. 5: 622–635.

Chalmers, D., D. Manley, and R. Wasserman, eds. (2009) *Metametaphysics: New Essays on the Foundations of Ontology.* Oxford: Clarendon Press.

Chen, E.M. (1969) "Nothingness and the Mother Principle in Early Chinese Taoism." *International Philosophical Quarterly,* September: 391–405.

Chiao, R.Y., M.L. Cohen, A.J. Leggett, W.D. Phillips, and C.L. Harper, eds. (2011) *Visions of Discovery: New Light on Physics, Cosmology and Consciousness.* Cambridge: Cambridge University Press.

Chisholm, R.M. (1964) "The Ethics of Requirement." *American Philosophical Quarterly,* April: 147–153.

Clark, S.R.L. (1990) "Limited Explanations," pp. 195–200 of D. Knowles, ed., *Explanation and its Limits,* Cambridge: Cambridge University Press.

Clark, S.R.L. (1998a) "The Cosmic Priority of Value" (Aquinas Lecture, Leuven). *Tijdschrift voor Filosofie,* 62: 681–700.

Clark, S.R.L. (1998b) *God, Religion and Reality.* London: SPCK.

Clarke, S. (1998) *A Demonstration of the Being and Attributes of God, and Other Writings,* ed. E. Vailati. Cambridge: Cambridge University Press.

Clayton, P., and A. Peacocke, eds. (2004) *In Whom We Live and Move and Have Our Being: Panentheistic Reflections on God's Presence in a Scientific World.* Grand Rapids: Eerdmans.

Closer to Truth: Cosmos, Consciousness, God. (2009 and later) Public television series created and hosted by Robert Lawrence Kuhn (www.closertotruth.com). See television shows "Why is there Something Rather than Nothing?"; "Why Is There Anything At All?"; "Why the Cosmos?"; "Asking Ultimate Questions"; "What Would Multiple Universes Mean?"; "Does the Cosmos Provide Meaning?"; "Why Not Nothing?"; "Explaining Existence"; and other shows. See also uncut video discussions on these and further topics by, among others, Peter Atkins, Philip Clayton, Robin Collins, William Lane Craig, Paul Davies, Hubert Dreyfus, Owen Gingerich, Alan Guth, Michio Kaku, Lawrence Krauss, John Leslie, Andrei Linde, Seth Lloyd, Colin McGinn, Ernan McMullin, John Polkinghorne, Bede Rundle, Robert John Russell, Quentin Smith, Lee Smolin, Russell Stannard, Victor Stenger, Leonard Susskind, Richard Swinburne, Max Tegmark, Peter van Inwagen, Alexander Vilenkin, Keith Ward, Steven Weinberg, and Frank Wilczek.

Coggins, G. (2010) *Could There Have Been Nothing?* New York: Palgrave Macmillan.

Collins, R. (2005) "Design and the Designer: New Concepts, New Challenges," in C.L. Harper, ed., *The Spiritual Information Project: 100 Perspectives.* Radnor: Templeton Foundation Press.

Collins, R. (2007) "The Multiverse Hypothesis: A Theistic Perspective," pp. 459–480 of B. Carr, ed., *Universe or Multiverse?* Cambridge: Cambridge University Press.

Collins, R. (2008) "The Teleological Argument," pp. 98–111 of P. Copan and C. Meister, eds., *Philosophy of Religion,* Malden, MA: Wiley-Blackwell.

Conee, E., and T. Sider (2005) *Riddles of Existence.* Oxford: Oxford University Press. See esp. ch. 5, "Why Not Nothing?"

Craig, E., ed. (1998) *Routledge Encyclopedia of Philosophy.* See "Contingency," "Cosmology," "Creation and Conservation," "Religion and Science," "Religion, History of."

Craig, W.L. (1979) *The Kalam Cosmological Argument*. London: Macmillan.

Craig, W.L. (1980) *The Cosmological Argument from Plato to Leibniz*. London: Macmillan.

Craig, W.L. (1993) "What Place, then, for a Creator? Hawking on God and Creation," pp. 279–300 of W.L. Craig and Q. Smith, *Theism, Atheism and Big Bang Cosmology*, Oxford: Oxford University Press..

Craig, W.L. (1999) " Timelessness, Creation, and God's Real Relation to the World." *Laval Théologique et Philosophique*, February: 93–112.

Craig, W.L. (2001) "Professor Grünbaum on the 'Normalcy of Nothingness' in the Leibnizian and Kalam Cosmological Arguments." *British Journal for the Philosophy of Science*, June: 371–386.

Craig, W.L. (2004) *Creation Out of Nothing*. Grand Rapids: Baker Academic.

Craig, W.L. (2008) *Reasonable Faith*, 3rd edn., revised. Wheaton: Crossway Books

Craig, W.L., and J.P. Moreland, eds. (2009) *The Blackwell Companion to Natural Theology*. Oxford and Malden, MA: Wiley-Blackwell.

Crosby, J.F. (1983) "Are Being and Good Really Convertible?" *The New Scholasticism*, Autumn: 465–500.

Cudworth, R. (1978) *The True Intellectual System of the Universe*. New York: Garland Publishing.

Dalai Lama XIV. (1996) *Beyond Dogma*, trans. A. Anderson. Berkeley: North Atlantic Books.

Dalai Lama XIV. (2005) *The Universe in a Single Atom*. New York: Morgan Road Books. See ch. 4, "The Big Bang and the Buddhist Beginningless Universe."

Davidson, H.A. (1987) *Proofs for Eternity, Creation, and the Existence of God in Medieval Islamic and Jewish Philosophy*. New York: Oxford University Press.

Davies, B. (1982) *An Introduction to Philosophy of Religion*. Oxford: Oxford University Press. See ch. 5, "The Cosmological Argument."

Davies, B. (1997) "Aquinas, God and Being." *The Monist*, October: 500–517.

Davies, P.C.W. (1972) "Closed Time as an Explanation of the Black Body Background Radiation." *Nature Physical Science*, vol. 240, p. 3.

Davies, P.C.W. (1982) *The Accidental Universe*. Cambridge: Cambridge University Press.

Davies, P.C.W. (1984) *Superforce*. London: William Heinemann. See esp. ch. 12, "What Caused the Big Bang?"

Davies, P.C.W. (1992) *The Mind of God*. New York: Simon & Schuster. See esp. ch. 2, "Can the Universe Create Itself?"

Davies, P.C.W. (2006) *The Goldilocks Enigma: Why is the Universe Just Right for Life?* London: Allen Lane.

Davies, P.C.W. (2007) "Laying Down the Laws." *New Scientist*, 30 June: 30–34.

Davies, P.C.W. (2007) "Universes Galore: Where will it All End?," pp. 487–505 of B. Carr, ed., *Universe or Multiverse?*, Cambridge: Cambridge University Press.

Dawkins, R. (2007) *The God Delusion*. New York: Houghton Mifflin.

Deltete, R.J. (1993) "Hawking on God and Creation." *Zygon*, December: 485–506.

Deltete, R.J. (2000) "Is the Universe Self-Caused?" *Philosophy*, December: 599–603.

Deltete, R.J., and R.A. Guy (1997) "Hartle-Hawking Cosmology and Unconditioned Probabilities." *Analysis*, October: 304–315.

Demaret, J., ed. (1987) *Origin and Early History of the Universe*. Liège: Presses of the University of Liège.

Demaret, J. (1991) *Univers*. Aix-en-Provence: Éditions Le Mail.

Demaret, J., and D. Lambert. (1994) *Le Principe Anthropique*. Paris: Armand Colin.

Descartes, R. (1984) *Meditations, and Replies to Objections*. In vol. 2 of *The Philosophical Writings of Descartes*, trans. J. Cottingham, R. Stoothoff, and D. Murdoch. Cambridge: Cambridge University Press.

Deutsch, D. (1997) *The Fabric of Reality*. London: Penguin Books.

Deutsch, D. (2004) "It from Qubit," pp. 90–102 of J.D. Barrow, P.C.W. Davies, and C.L. Harper, eds., *Science and Ultimate Reality*, Cambridge: Cambridge University Press.

Deutsch, D. (2009) *The Beginning of Infinity*. London: Penguin Books. See esp. chs. 4 and 11.

DeWitt, B.S. (2004) "The Everett Interpretation of Quantum Mechanics," pp. 167–197 of J.D. Barrow, P.C.W. Davies, and C.L. Harper, eds., *Science and Ultimate Reality*, Cambridge: Cambridge University Press.

Dick, S., ed. (2000) *Many Worlds*. Philadelphia: Templeton Foundation Press.

Dionysius (1940) *Dionysius the Areopagite on the Divine Names*, trans. C.E. Rolt. London: SPCK.

Drees, W. (2010) *Religion and Science in Context*. Abingdon: Routledge.

Dunham, J., Grant, I.H., and S. Watson (2011) *Idealism*. Montreal: McGill-Queen's University Press.

Duns Scotus, John (1966) *Treatise on God as First Principle*, trans. A. Wolter, 2nd edn. Chicago: Franciscan Herald Press.

Eddington, A.S. (1928) *The Nature of the Physical World*. Cambridge: Cambridge University Press.

Eddington, A.S. (1929) *Science and the Unseen World*. New York: Macmillan.

Edwards, D.L., ed. (1963) *The Honest to God Debate*. London: SCM Press.

Edwards, P. (1987) "A Critique of the Cosmological Argument," pp. 12–20 of L.P. Pojman, ed., *Philosophy of Religion: An Anthology*. Belmont: Wadsworth.

Edwards, P. (1967) "Why," vol. 8: 296–302 of P. Edwards, ed., *The Encyclopedia of Philosophy*, New York: Macmillan.

Efird, D., and T. Stoneham (2005) "The Subtraction Argument for Metaphysical Nihilism." *Journal of Philosophy*, vol. 102 no. 6: 303–325.

Efird, D., and T. Stoneham (2006) "Combinatorialism and the Possibility of Nothing." *Australasian Journal of Philosophy*, vol. 84 no. 2: 269–280.

Einstein, A. (1962) *Relativity: The Special and the General Theory*, 15th edn., enlarged. London: Methuen. See appendix 5 for the world as having "a four-dimensional existence."

Ellis, G.F.R. (1993) *Before the Beginning*. London: Bowerdean Press / Marion Boyers.

Ellis, G.F.R. (2000) "Before the Beginning: Emerging Questions and Uncertainties," in D. Block et al., eds., *Toward a New Millennium in Galactic Morphology*. Dordrecht: Kluwer.

Ellis, G.F.R., ed. (2002) *The Far-Future Universe*. Philadelphia: Templeton Foundation Press. Contributions by Barrow, Davies, Ellis, Heller, Morris, and Rees discuss cosmic beginnings as well as endings.

Ellis, G.F.R. (2007) "Multiverses: Description, Uniqueness and Testing," pp. 387–409 of B. Carr, ed., *Universe or Multiverse?* Cambridge: Cambridge University Press.

Epicurus (1964) Letter to Herodotus. In *Epicurus: Letters, Principal Doctrines and Vatican Sayings*, trans. R.M. Geer, Indianapolis: Bobbs-Merrill.

Erhardt, A. (1968) *The Beginning: A Study in the Greek Philosophical Approach to the Concept of Creation from Anaximander to St. John*. New York: Barnes & Noble.

d'Espagnat, B. (2006) *On Physics and Philosophy*. Princeton: Princeton University Press.

Everitt, N. (2004) *The Non-Existence of God*. London: Routledge.

Ewing, A.C. (1966) "Two 'Proofs' of God's Existence." *Religious Studies, no.* 1: 29–46.

Ewing, A.C. (1973) *Value and Reality*. London: George Allen & Unwin. See esp. ch. 7.

Farrer, A. (1943) *Finite and Infinite*. London: Dacre Press.

Ferguson, K. (1995) *The Fire in the Equations: Science, Religion and the Search for God*. Grand Rapids: Eerdmans.

Findlay, J.N. (1958) *Hegel: A Re-examination*. London: Allen & Unwin.

Findlay, J.N. (1970) *Ascent to the Absolute*. London: Allen & Unwin.

Fleming, N. (1988) "Why Is There Something Rather than Nothing?" *Analysis*, January: 32–35.

Flew, A. (1966) *God and Philosophy*. London: Hutchinson. See esp. ch. 4.

Flew, A. (1976) *The Presumption of Atheism*. London: Pemberton.

Forrest, P. (1996) *God without the Supernatural*. Ithaca: Cornell University Press.

Forrest, P. (2007) *Developmental Theism*. Oxford: Oxford University Press.

Forrest, P. (2012) "Replying to the Anti-God Challenge." *Religious Studies*, March: 36–43.

Foster, J. (1982) *The Case for Idealism*. London: Routledge & Kegan Paul.

Foster, J. (2004) *The Divine Lawmaker*. Oxford: Oxford University Press.

Franklin, R.L. (1957) "Necessary Being." *Australasian Journal of Philosophy*, August: 97–110.

Gale, R.M. (1974) "Bergson's Analysis of the Concept of Nothing." *The Modern Schoolman*, May: 269–300.

Gale, R.M. (1991) *On the Nature and Existence of God*. Cambridge: Cambridge University Press.

Gale, R.M., and A.R. Pruss, eds. (2003) *The Existence of God*. Aldershot: Ashgate.

Gamow, G. (1954) "Modern Cosmology." *Scientific American*, March: 55–63.

Gardner, M. (1975) "How the Absence of Anything Leads to Thoughts of Nothing." *Scientific American*, February: 98–101.

Gardner, M. (1983) *The Whys of a Philosophical Scrivener*. New York: Quill.

Gardner, M. (2003) *Are Universes Thicker Than Blackberries?* New York: Norton.

Gaskin, J.C.A. (1988) "Philosophy and the Existence of God," pp. 327–335 of G.H.R. Parkinson, ed., *An Encyclopaedia of Philosophy*, London: Hutchinson.

Gaskin, J.C.A., ed. (1989) *Varieties of Unbelief*. New York: Macmillan. See esp. selections from Epicurus, Lucretius, d'Holbach, Russell, Ayer.

Gasperini, M. (2008) *The Universe before the Big Bang: Cosmology and String Theory*. New York: Springer.

Geach, P. (1962) "Causality and Creation." *Sophia*, April: 1–8.

Genz, H. (2006) *War es ein Gott? Zufall, Notwendigkeit und Kreativität in der Entwicklung des Universums*. Munich: Carl Hanser.

Gilson, E. (1952) *Being and Some Philosophers*, 2nd edn., enlarged. Toronto: Pontifical Institute of Medieval Studies.

Gingerich, O. (2006) *God's Universe*. Cambridge, MA: Harvard University Press.

Goldschmidt, T. (2011) "The New Cosmological Argument: O'Connor on Ultimate Explanation." *Philosophia*, June: 267–288.

Goldschmidt, T., ed. (2013) *The Puzzle of Existence*. London and New York: Routledge.

Goldstick, D. (1979) "Why is there Something Rather than Nothing?" *Philosophy and Phenomenological Research*, vol. 40: 265–271.

Goldstick, D. (1981) "Realism about Possible Worlds." *Pacific Philosophical Quarterly*, July: 272–273.

Gott, J.R., and L.-X. Li. (1998) "Can the Universe Create Itself?" *Physical Review D*, 29 May: 23501–23543.

Greene, B. (2011) *The Hidden Reality: Parallel Universes and the Deep Laws of the Cosmos*. New York: Alfred A. Knopf.

Grover, S. (1998) "Cosmological Fecundity." *Inquiry*, September: 277–299.

Grünbaum, A. (1990) "Pseudo-creation of the Big Bang." *Nature, vol.* 344: 821–822.

Grünbaum, A. (1993) "Creation in Cosmology," pp. 126–136 of N.S. Hetherington, ed., *Encyclopedia of Cosmology*, New York: Garland.

Grünbaum, A. (2004) "The Poverty of Theistic Cosmology." *British Journal for the Philosophy of Science*, October: 561–614.

Grünbaum, A. (2009) "Why is there a Universe AT ALL, Rather than Just Nothing?", pp. 5–17 of C. Glymour et al., eds., *Logic, Methodology, and Philosophy of Science: Proceedings of the XIIIth International Congress*. London: King's College Publications.

Guerry, H. (1997) "Sommers' Ontological Proof ." *Analysis*, December: 60–61.

Guth, A. (1997) *The Inflationary Universe: The Quest for a New Theory of Cosmic Origins*. Boston: Addison-Wesley.

Guth, A. (2001) "Eternal Inflation," pp. 66–82 of J.B. Miller, ed., *Cosmic Questions*, New York: New York Academy of Sciences.

Guth, A. (2002) "Inflation and the New Era of High-Precision Cosmology," pp. 28–39 of *MIT Physics Annual 2002*.

Haack, S. (1977) "Lewis' Ontological Slum." *Review of Metaphysics*, March: 415–429.

Halliwell, J.J. (1992) *Quantum Cosmology*. Cambridge: Cambridge University Press.

Halliwell, J.J. (1993) "Quantum Cosmology and the Creation of the Universe," pp. 547–558 of N.S. Hetherington, ed., *Encyclopedia of Cosmology*, New York: Garland.

Hartle, J.B., and S.W. Hawking (1983) "Wave Function of the Universe." *Physical Review D* 28, 15 December: 2960–2975.

Hartshorne, C. (1976) *Aquinas to Whitehead: Seven Centuries of Metaphysics of Religion*. Milwaukee: Marquette University Press.

Hartshorne, C. (1984) *Omnipotence and Other Theological Mistakes*. Albany: SUNY Press.

Hassing, R., ed. (1997) *Final Causality in Nature*. Washington: Catholic University of America Press.

Hawking, S.W. (1987) "Quantum Cosmology," pp. 631–651 of S.W. Hawking and W. Israel, eds., *Three Hundred Years of Gravitation*, Cambridge: Cambridge University Press.

Hawking, S.W. (1988) *A Brief History of Time*. New York: Bantam.

Hawking, S.W. (1993) *Black Holes and Baby Universes*. New York: Bantam. See esp. ch. 9, "The Origin of the Universe."

Hawking, S.W. (1996) "Quantum Cosmology," ch. 3 of S. Hawking and R. Penrose, *The Nature of Space and Time*, Princeton: Princeton University Press.

Hawking, S.W. (2001) *The Universe in a Nutshell*. New York: Bantam.

Hawking, S., and L. Mlodinow (2005) *A Briefer History of Time*. New York: Bantam.

Hawking, S., and L. Mlodinow (2010) *The Grand Design*. New York: Bantam.

Hawthorne, J. (2006) *Metaphysical Essays*. Oxford: Oxford University Press. See pp. 265–283, "What Would Teleological Causation Be?".

Hegel, G.W.F. (1892) "Logic," the first part of his *Encyclopaedia of the Philosophical Sciences*. Published as *The Logic of Hegel*, trans. W. Wallace, 2nd edn., revised, London: Oxford University Press.

Heidegger, M. (1959) *Introduction to Metaphysics*, trans. R. Manheim. New Haven: Yale University Press. See esp. ch. 1.

Heidegger, M. (1962) *Being and Time*, trans. J. Macquarrie and E. Robinson. New York: Harper & Row.

Heidegger, M. (1965) *The Essence of Reasons*, trans. T. Malick. Evanston: Northwestern University Press.

Heller, M. (2000) "Cosmological Singularity and the Creation of the Universe." *Zygon*, September: 665–685.

Heller, M. (2009) *Ultimate Explanations of the Universe*. Heidelberg: Springer.

Hempel, C.G. (1973) "Science Unlimited." *The Annals of the Japan Association for Philosophy of Science*, vol. 14: 187–202.

Hepburn, R.W. (1967) "Cosmological Argument for the Existence of God," pp. 232–237 of P. Edwards, ed., *The Encyclopedia of Philosophy*, vol. 2. New York: Macmillan.

Hepburn, R.W. (1988) "The Philosophy of Religion," pp. 857–877 of G.H.R. Parkinson, ed., *An Encyclopaedia of Philosophy*. London: Routledge.

Hermanni, F. (2011) *Metaphysik*. Tübingen: Mohr Siebeck. See esp. chs.1, 2, 3, and 5.

Hetherington, N.S., ed. (1993a) *Encyclopedia of Cosmology*. New York: Garland. See "Anthropic Principle," "Big Bang Cosmology," "Creation in Cosmology," "Inflationary Universe," "Islamic Cosmology," "Medieval Cosmology," "Multiple Universes," "Quantum Cosmology and the Creation of the Universe," "Religion and Cosmology," "Spontaneous Symmetry Breaking," "Steady State Theory."

Hetherington, N.S., ed. (1993b) *Cosmology: Historical, Literary, Philosophical, Religious, and Scientific Perspectives*. New York: Garland.

Hick, J. (1960) "God as Necessary Being." *Journal of Philosophy*, vol. 57 nos. 22–23, 27 October–10 November: 725–734.

Holder, R.D. (2001) "The Realization of Infinitely Many Universes in Cosmology." *Religious Studies*, September: 345–350.

Holder, R.D. (2002) "Fine-Tuning, Multiple Universes and Theism." *Noûs*, June: 295–312.

Holder, R.D. (2004) *God, the Multiverse, and Everything*. Burlington, VT: Ashgate.

Holt, J. (2012) *Why Does the World Exist?* New York: W.W. Norton.

Honderich, T., ed. (1995) *The Oxford Companion to Philosophy*. Oxford: Oxford University Press. See "Bradley, Francis Herbert," "creation," "cosmology," "existence," "Hegel, G.W.F.," "Indian philosophy," "necessary and contingent existence," "Ramanuja," "Sankara," "Spinoza, Baruch," and "Sprigge, Timothy L.S."

Hospers, J. (1956) "What is Explanation?" in A. Flew, ed., *Essays in Conceptual Analysis*, London: Macmillan.

Hoyle, F. (1955) *Frontiers of Astronomy*. New York: Harper.

Hoyle, F. (1983) *The Intelligent Universe*. London: Michael Joseph.

Hoyle, F. (1989) "Frontiers in Cosmology," pp. 97–107 of S.K. Biswas, D.C.V. Mallik, and C.V. Vishveshwara, eds., *Cosmic Perspectives*. Cambridge: Cambridge University Press.

Hughes, C. (2002) "Three Cosmological Arguments." *Ratio*, December: 213–233.

Hughes, G.J. (1995) *The Nature of God*. London and New York: Routledge.

Hume, D. (1888) *A Treatise of Human Nature*, ed. L.A. Selby-Bigge, London: Oxford University Press.

Hume, D. (1948) *Dialogues concerning Natural Religion*. In *Hume's Dialogues concerning Natural Religion*, ed. N. Kemp Smith, 2nd edn. New York: Social Sciences Publishers.

Husain, S. (1993) "Something, Nothing and Explanation." *Southwest Philosophy Review*, January: 151–161.

Hutter, A., F. Hermanni, T. Buchheim, and C. Schwöbel, eds. (2012) *Gottesbeweise als Herausforderung der modernen Vernunft*. Tübingen: Mohr Siebeck.

Iqbal, M. (1934) *The Reconstruction of Religious Thought in Islam*. Oxford: Oxford University Press.

Isham, C.J. (1988) "Creation of the Universe as a Quantum Process," pp. 375–408 of R.J. Russell et al., eds., *Physics, Philosophy and Theology*. Vatican City State: Vatican Observatory, and Notre Dame: University of Notre Dame Press.

Jacquette, D. (2002) *Ontology*. Montreal: McGill-Queens University Press. See ch. 3, "Why There Is Something rather than Nothing."

James, W. (1911) *Some Problems of Philosophy*. New York: Longmans, Green. See esp. ch. 3, "The Problem of Being."

Jeans, J. (1930) *The Mysterious Universe*. London: Macmillan.

Jubien, M. (1997) *Contemporary Metaphysics*. Oxford: Blackwell. See ch. 11.

Kane, R.H. (1976) "Nature, Plenitude and Sufficient Reason." *American Philosophical Quarterly*, January: 23–31.

Kant, I. (2003) *Critique of Pure Reason*, trans. N. Kemp Smith, 2nd edn., revised. Basingstoke: Palgrave Macmillan. See esp. part 1, ch. 3, section 5.

Kapp, R.O. (1955) "Hypotheses about the Origin and Disappearance of Matter." *British Journal for the Philosophy of Science*, November: 177–185. See also the exchanges with H. Bondi in the same issue.

Keane, K. (1975) "Why Creation? Bonaventure and Thomas Aquinas of God as Creative Good." *Downside Review*, vol. 93: 100–121.

Kenny, A. (1972) *The Five Ways: St. Thomas Aquinas' Proofs of God's Existence*. London: Routledge & Kegan Paul.

Kenny, A. (2002) *Aquinas on Being*. Oxford: Clarendon Press.

Knight, T.S. (1956) "Why Not Nothing?" *Review of Metaphysics*, September: 158–164.

Kolakowski, L. (2007) *Why Is There Something Rather Than Nothing? 23 Questions from Great Philosophers*. New York: Basic Books.

Kongtrul Lodrö Tayé, J. (1995) *Myriad Worlds: Buddhist Cosmology in Abhidharma, Kalacakra and Dzog-chen*. Ithaca: Snowdon Publications.

Koons, R. (1997) "A New Look at the Cosmological Argument." *American Philosophical Quarterly*, April: 193–211.

Kordig, C.R. (1981) "A Deontic Argument for God's Existence." *Noûs*, May: 207–208.

Kraay, K. (2010) "Theism, Possible Worlds, and the Multiverse." *Philosophical Studies*, vol. 147 no. 3: 355–368.

Krauss, L.M. (2012) *A Universe from Nothing*. New York: Free Press.

Kretzmann, N. (1997) *The Metaphysics of Theism: Aquinas's Natural Theology in Summa contra gentiles I*. Oxford: Oxford University Press.

Kretzmann, N. (1998) "A General Problem of Creation: Why Would God Create Anything at All?", pp. 208–28 of S. MacDonald, ed., *Being and Goodness*. Ithaca: Cornell University Press.

Kretzmann, N. (2002) *The Metaphysics of Creation: Aquinas's Natural Theology in Summa contra gentiles II*. Oxford: Oxford University Press.

Kuhn, R.L. (2007a) "Why This Universe? Toward a Taxonomy of Possible Explanations." *Skeptic*, vol. 13 no. 2: 30–41.

Kuhn, R.L. (2007b) "Why Ultimate Reality Works for Us: Toward a Taxonomy of Possible Explanations," pp. 235–257 of R.L. Kuhn, ed., *Closer to Truth: Science, Meaning, and the Future*, Westport and London: Praeger.

Kukkonen, T. (2000) "Plenitude, Possibility, and the Limits of Reason: A Medieval Arabic Debate on the Metaphysics of Nature." *Journal of the History of Ideas*, October: 539–560.

Küng, H. (1980) *Does God Exist?*, trans. E. Quinn. London: Collins.

Küng, H. (2007) *The Beginning of All Things: Science and Religion, trans*. J. Bowden. Grand Rapids: Eerdmans.

Kusch, M. (1990a) "On 'Why is there Something Rather Than Nothing?'" *American Philosophical Quarterly*, July: 253–257.

Kusch, M. (1990b) "Heidegger on 'Why is there Something Rather Than Nothing?'" *Acta Philosophical Fennica*, vol. 49: 144–159.

Laird, J. (1940) *Theism and Cosmology*. London: George Allen & Unwin.

Lansburg, S. E. (2009) *The Big Questions*. New York: Free Press. See esp. ch. 1.

Lao Tzu (1934) *Tao Te Ching*, trans. in A. Waley, *The Way and Its Power: A Study of the Tao Te Ching*. London: Allen & Unwin. See esp. ch. 40.

Le Poidevin, R. (1996) *Arguing for Atheism*. New York: Routledge.

Le Poidevin, R. (2011) *Agnosticism*. Oxford: Oxford University Press.

Leclerc, I. (1981) "The Metaphysics of The Good." *Review of Metaphysics*, September: 3–25.

Leclerc, I. (1984) "God and the Issue of Being." *Religious Studies*, March: 63–78.

Leftow, B. (2012) *God and Necessity*. Oxford: Oxford University Press.

Leibniz, G.W. (1898) "On the Ultimate Origination of Things," pp. 337–351 of *Leibniz: The Monadology and Other Philosophical Writings*, trans. R. Latta. London: Oxford University Press.

Leibniz, G.W. (1981) *New Essays on Human Understanding*, trans. J. Bennett and P. Remnant. Cambridge: Cambridge University Press.

Leibniz, G.W. (1988) *Discourse on Metaphysics and Related Writings*, trans. R.N.D. Martin and S.C. Brown. Manchester: Manchester University Press.

Leibniz, G.W. (1989) *Principles of Nature and Grace*, in *G.W. Leibniz: Philosophical Essays*, trans. R. Ariew and D. Garber. Indianapolis: Hackett. See esp. section 7.

Lennox, J.C. (2011) *God and Stephen Hawking*. Oxford: Lion.

Leslie, J. (1978) "Efforts to Explain all Existence." *Mind*, April: 181–194.

Leslie, J. (1979) *Value and Existence*. Oxford: Blackwell.

Leslie, J. (1989) *Universes*. London and New York: Routledge.

Leslie, J., ed. (1990) *Physical Cosmology and Philosophy*. New York: Macmillan. Expanded edn. from Prometheus Books, Amherst N.Y., as *Modern Cosmology and Philosophy* (1998): see esp. the contributions by Bondi, Bonnor, Carr, Carter, Craig, Davies, Dicke, Ellis, Gale, Gamow, Grünbaum, Leslie, Linde, McMullin, Narlikar, Rees, Swinburne, Tryon, and Wheeler.

Leslie, J. (1995) "Cosmology," "Cosmos," "Finite/Infinite," "World, "Why There Is Something," in J. Kim and E. Sosa, eds., *A Companion to Metaphysics*, Oxford: Blackwell.

Leslie, J. (1996) *The End of the World.* London and New York: Routledge. See esp. pp. 155–170.

Leslie, J. (1997) "The Anthropic Principle Today," pp. 163–187 of R. Hassing, ed., *Final Causality in Nature,* Washington: Catholic University of America Press.

Leslie, J. (1998) "Cosmology and Theology," at http://plato.stanford.edu/archives/sum2003/entries/cosmology-theology and with new Afterword as pp. 127–156 of C. Tandy, ed., *Death and Anti-Death,* vol. 6: *Thirty Years after Kurt Gödel,* Palo Alto: Ria University Press, 2009.

Leslie, J. (2001) *Infinite Minds.* Oxford: Clarendon Press; New York: Oxford University Press.

Leslie, J. (2007) *Immortality Defended.* Oxford: Blackwell.

Leslie, J. (2009) "A Cosmos Existing Through Ethical Necessity." *Philo,* vol. 12 no. 2, special issue on *Theism and Naturalism*: 172–187.

Leslie, J. (2013) "A Proof of God's Reality," in T. Goldschmidt, ed., *The Puzzle of Existence,* London and New York: Routledge.

Levine, M. (1994) *Pantheism.* London and New York: Routledge.

Lewis, D. (1983) *Philosophical Papers,* vol. 1. New York and Oxford: Oxford University Press.

Lewis, D. (1986) *On the Plurality of Worlds.* Oxford: Blackwell.

Lewis, D. (2003) "Things qua Truthmakers," pp. 25–38 of H. Lillehammer and G. Rodriguez-Pereyra, eds., *Real Metaphysics,* London: Routledge.

Linde, A.D. (1985) "The Universe: Inflation out of Chaos." *New Scientist,* 7 March: 14–18.

Linde, A.D. (1986) "Eternally Existing, Self-Reproducing, Chaotic Inflationary Universe." *Physics Letters B,* vol. 175: 395–400.

Linde, A.D. (1990) *Inflation and Quantum Cosmology.* San Diego: Academic Press.

Linde, A.D. (1994) "The Self-Reproducing Inflationary Universe." *Scientific American,* November: 48–55.

Linde, A.D. (2007) "The Inflationary Multiverse," pp. 127–149 of B. Carr, ed., *Universe or Multiverse?* Cambridge: Cambridge University Press.

Lloyd, S. (2006) *Programming the Universe: A Quantum Computer Scientist Takes On the Cosmos.* New York: Alfred A. Knopf.

Lockwood, M. (1989). *Mind, Brain and the Quantum.* Oxford: Blackwell.

Lott, E.J. (1980) *Vedantic Approaches to God.* Liverpool: Barnes & Noble.

Lotze, H. (1885) *Microcosmos.* Edinburgh: T. & T. Clark.

Lotze, H. (1887) *Metaphysic.* Oxford: Clarendon Press.

Lovejoy, A.O. (1936) *The Great Chain of Being.* Cambridge, MA: Harvard University Press.

Lowe, E.J. (1996) "Why Is There Anything At All?" *Proceedings of the Aristotelian Society,* supplementary vol. 70: 111–120.

Lowe, E.J. (1998) *The Possibility of Metaphysics.* Oxford: Oxford University Press.

Lowe, E.J. (2007) "Metaphysical Nihilism and the Subtraction Argument." *Analysis,* vol. 62 no. 1: 62–73.

Mackie, J.L. (1982) *The Miracle of Theism.* Oxford: Oxford University Press.

MacDonald, S., ed. (1991) *Being and Goodness: The Concept of the Good in Metaphysics and Philosophical Theology.* Ithaca: Cornell University Press.

Maimonides (1963) *The Guide of the Perplexed,* trans. S. Pines. Chicago: University of Chicago Press.

Maitzen, S. (2012) "Stop Asking Why There's Anything." *Erkenntnis,* July: 51–63.

Malcolm, N. (1960) "Anselm's Ontological Arguments." *Philosophical Review*, January: 41–62.

Mann, R.B. (2005) "Inconstant Multiverse." *Perspectives on Science and Christian Faith*, December: 1–9.

Mann, R.B. (2009) "The Puzzle of Existence." *Perspectives on Science and Christian Faith*, September: 139–150.

Manson, N.A., ed. (2003) *God and Design: The Teleological Argument and Modern Science*. London and New York: Routledge.

Manson, N.A., and M.J. Thrush (2003) "Fine-Tuning, Multiple Universes and the 'This Universe' Objection." *Pacific Philosophical Quarterly*, March: 67–83.

Margenau, H. (1984) *The Miracle of Existence*. Woodbridge, CT: Ox Bow Press. See ch. 10, "A Universal Mind?".

Markosian, N. (1995) "On the Argument from Quantum Cosmology Against Theism." *Analysis*, October: 247–251.

Marmura, M.E., ed. (1984) *Islamic Theology and Philosophy*. Albany: SUNY Press.

Martin, C.B. (1959) *Religious Belief*. Ithaca: Cornell University Press. See esp. ch. 9, "Why Is There Anything At All?".

Matthews, C.N., and R.A. Varghese, eds. (1995) *Cosmic Beginnings and Human Ends*. Chicago: Open Court.

Mawson, T.J. (2005) *Belief in God*. Oxford: Oxford University Press.

Mawson, T.J. (2009) "Why Is There Anything At All?," pp. 36–54 of Y. Nagasawa and E. Wielenberg, eds., *New Waves in Philosophy of Religion*. New York: Palgrave Macmillan.

McCabe, G. (2005) "The Concept of Creation in Inflation and Quantum Cosmology." *Studies in History and Philosophy of Modern Physics*, March: 67–102.

McMullin, E. (1981) "Is Philosophy Relevant to Cosmology?" *American Philosophical Quarterly*, July: 177–189.

McMullin, E., ed. (1985) *Evolution and Creation*. Notre Dame: University of Notre Dame Press.

Meynell, H. (1974) "Kant's Anaesthetic." *Philosophical Forum* (Boston), Spring: 340–352.

Meynell, H. (1982) *The Intelligible Universe*. London: Macmillan. See esp. chs. 2 and 5.

Meynell, H. (2011) *The Epistemological Argument Against Atheism*. Lewiston, N.Y.: Edwin Mellen.

Miller, B. (1992) *From Existence to God*. London: Routledge.

Miller, J.B., ed. (2003) *Cosmic Questions*. New York: New York Academy of Sciences.

Milne, E.A. (1952) *Modern Cosmology and the Christian Idea of God*. Oxford: Oxford University Press.

Morris, T.V., and C. Menzel (1986) "Absolute Creation." *American Philosophical Quarterly*, October: 353–362.

Mortensen, C. (1986) "Explaining Existence." *Canadian Journal of Philosophy*, December: 713–722.

Munitz, M.K., ed. (1957) *Theories of the Universe: from Babylonian Myth to Modern Science*. New York: The Free Press/Macmillan.

Munitz. M.K. (1965) *The Mystery of Existence*. New York: Appleton-Century-Crofts.

Munitz. M.K. (1986) *Cosmic Understanding*. Princeton: Princeton University Press.

Murphy, N., and G.F.R. Ellis (1996) *On the Moral Nature of the Universe*. Minneapolis, MN: Fortress Press.

Nagasawa, Y. (2011) *The Existence of God*. London: Routledge.

Nagasawa, Y., and E. Wielenberg, eds. (2009) *New Waves in Philosophy of Religion*, New York: Palgrave Macmillan.

Nagel, T. (2012) *Mind and Cosmos*. New York: Free Press.

Narlikar, J.V. (1988) *The Primeval Universe*. Oxford: Oxford University Press.

Narlikar, J.V. (1989) "Did the Universe Originate in a Big Bang?," pp. 109–120 of S.K. Biswas, D.C.V. Mallik, and C.V. Vishveshwara, eds., *Cosmic Perspectives*. Cambridge: Cambridge University Press.

Narlikar, J.V. (1992) "The Concepts of 'Beginning' and 'Creation' in Cosmology." *Philosophy of Science*, September: 361–371.

Nasr, S.H. (2006) *Islamic Philosophy from Its Origin to the Present*. Albany: SUNY Press. See esp. chs. 4 and 5.

Nicolaus Cusanus (1954) *Of Learned Ignorance*, trans. G. Heron. London: Routledge & Kegan Paul. See book 2, chs. 2 and 3.

Nozick, R. (1981) *Philosophical Explanations*. Cambridge, MA: Harvard University Press. See ch. 2, "Why Is There Something Rather Than Nothing?".

Nozick, R. (1989) *The Examined Life*. New York: Simon & Schuster. See chs. 5 and 19.

O'Connor, T. (2008) *Theism and Ultimate Explanation*. Malden, MA: Blackwell.

Odenwald, S.F. (1990) "A Modern Look at the Origin of the Universe." *Zygon*, March: 25–45.

O'Hear, A., ed. (2000) *Philosophy, the Good, the True and the Beautiful*. Cambridge: Cambridge University Press. See the contributions by Evans and Leslie.

Oppy, G. (1995) *Ontological Arguments and Belief in God*. Cambridge: Cambridge University Press.

Oppy, G. (1997) "On Some Alleged Consequences of the Hartle-Hawking Cosmology." *Sophia*, March/April: 84–95.

Oppy, G. (2006) *Arguing about Gods*. Cambridge: Cambridge University Press.

Ormsby, E.L. (1984) *Theodicy in Islamic Thought: The Dispute over al-Ghazali's "Best of all Possible Worlds."* Princeton: Princeton University Press.

Page, D.N. (2010) "Does God So Love the Multiverse?," pp. 396–410 of M.Y. Stewart, ed., *Science and Religion in Dialogue*, vol. 1. Chichester: Wiley-Blackwell.

Parfit, D. (1991) "Why Does the Universe Exist?" *Harvard Review of Philosophy*, Spring: 4–5.

Parfit, D. (1992) "The Puzzle of Reality." *Times Literary Supplement*, 3 July: 3–5.

Parfit, D. (1998) "Why Anything? Why This?" *London Review of Books*, 2 parts: 27 January: 24–27, and 5 February: 22–25.

Parfit, D. (1998) "The Puzzle of Reality: Why Does the Universe Exist?" pp. 418–426 of P. van Inwagen and D.W. Zimmerman, eds., *Metaphysics: The Big Questions*. Malden MA: Blackwell.

Parfit, D. (2011) *On What Matters*, 2 vols. Oxford: Oxford University Press. See esp. part 6, and appendices D and J, in vol. 2.

Paseau, A. (2006) "The Subtraction Argument(s)." *Dialectica*, vol. 60 no. 2: 143–156.

Peacocke, A.R. (1979) *Creation and the World of Science*. Oxford: Clarendon Press.

Peirce, C.S. (1965) *Collected Papers of Charles Sanders Peirce*, ed. C. Hartshorne and P. Weiss. Cambridge, MA: Harvard University Press. See esp. (cited by volume and by section) 1.175; 1.409–416; 6.13; 6.33; 6.189–220; 6.490; 7.513–515; 8.317–318.

Penelhum, T. (1960) "Divine Necessity." *Mind*. April: 175–186.

Penelhum, T. (1971) *Religion and Rationality*. New York: Random House. See esp. ch. 4.

Bibliography and Further Reading 303

Penrose, R. (1989) *The Emperor's New Mind*. Oxford: Oxford University Press.

Penrose, R. (1994) *Shadows of the Mind*. Oxford: Oxford University Press.

Penrose, R. (2005) *The Road to Reality: A Complete Guide to the Laws of the Universe*. London: Vintage Books.

Penrose, R. (2010) *Cycles of Time: An Extraordinary New View of the Universe*. London: Bodley Head.

Penrose, R., A. Shimony, N. Cartwright, S. Hawking, and N. Longair (1997) *The Large, the Small and the Human Mind*. Oxford: Blackwell.

Perenboom, R.P. (1990) "Cosmogony, the Taoist Way." *Journal of Chinese Philosophy*, July: 157–174.

Perkins, R.K. (1983) "An Atheistic Argument from the Improvability of the Universe." *Noûs*, 17: 239–250.

Pius XII (1952). "Science and the Catholic Church." *Bulletin of Atomic Scientists*, vol. 8: 142–146, 165.

Plantinga, A. (1967) *God and Other Minds*. Ithaca: Cornell University Press.

Plantinga, A. (1973) "Which World Could God Have Created?" *The Journal of Philosophy*, vol. 70: 539–552.

Plantinga, A. (1974a) *The Nature of Necessity*. Oxford: Oxford University Press.

Plantinga, A. (1974b) *God, Freedom and Evil*. Grand Rapids: Eerdmans.

Plantinga, A. (1980) *Does God Have a Nature?* Milwaukee: Marquette University Press.

Plantinga, A. (2011) *Where the Conflict Really Lies: Science, Religion, and Naturalism*. Oxford: Oxford University Press.

Plantinga, A., and N. Wolterstoff, eds. (1983) *Faith and Rationality: Reason and Belief in God*. Notre Dame: University of Notre Dame Press.

Plato (1953) *The Republic* and *Phaedo*. In *The Dialogues of Plato*, trans. B. Jowett, vol. 1, 4th, revised, edn. Oxford: Clarendon Press.

Plotinus (1956) *The Enneads*, trans. S. MacKenna, 4th edn., revised by B.S. Page. London: Faber & Faber.

Polkinghorne, J. (1986) *One World: The Interaction of Science and Theology*. Princeton: Princeton University Press.

Polkinghorne, J. (1988) *Science and Creation*. New York: Random House.

Polkinghorne, J. (1994) *The Faith of a Physicist*. Princeton: Princeton University Press.

Polkinghorne, J. (1996) *Beyond Science*. Cambridge: Cambridge University Press.

Polkinghorne, J., ed. (2001) *The Work of Love: Creation as Kenosis*. Grand Rapids: Eerdmans.

Post, J.F. (1987) *The Faces of Existence*. Ithaca: Cornell University Press.

Post, J.F. (1991) *Metaphysics: A Contemporary Introduction*. New York: Paragon House. See esp. ch. 4, "Why Does Anything At All Exist?".

Power, W.L. (1992) "Ontological Arguments for Satan and Other Sorts of Evil Beings." *Dialogue*, Fall: 667–676.

Pruss, A.R. (1988) "The Hume-Edwards Principle and the Cosmological Argument." *International Journal for Philosophy of Religion*, vol. 434: 149–165.

Pruss, A.R. (2006) *The Principle of Sufficient Reason*. Cambridge: Cambridge University Press.

Pruss, A.R. (2011) *Actuality, Possibility, and Worlds*. New York: Continuum.

Putnam, H. (1997) "Thoughts Addressed to an Analytical Thomist." *The Monist*, October: 487–499.

Quinn, P.L. (1993) "Creation, Conservation, and the Big Bang," pp. 589–612 of J. Earman, A.I. Janis, G.J. Massey, and N. Rescher, eds., *Philosophical Problems of the Internal and External Worlds*, Pittsburgh: University of Pittsburgh Press.

Quinn, P.L. (2005) "Cosmological Contingency and Theistic Explanation." *Faith and Philosophy, special issue*, vol. 22 no. 5: 581–600.

Rea, M.C. (2002) *World without Design*. Oxford: Oxford University Press.

Rea, M.C., ed. (2009) *Arguing About Metaphysics*. New York and Abingdon: Routledge. See esp. part 5, "Worlds and Worldmaking."

Redhead, M. (1998) "Other Universes," *Times Literary Supplement*, 2 January: 5.

Rees, M. (1997) *Before the Beginning: Our Universe and Others*. Reading, MA: Addison-Wesley.

Rees, M. (2000) *Just Six Numbers: The Deep Forces that Shape the Universe*. New York: Basic Books.

Rees, M. (2004) *Our Cosmic Habitat*. Princeton: Princeton University Press.

Rees, M. (2007) "Cosmology and the Multiverse," pp. 57–75 of B. Carr, ed., *Universe or Multiverse?* Cambridge: Cambridge University Press.

Rescher, N., ed. (1983) *Scientific Explanation and Understanding*. Lanham, MD and London: University Press of America.

Rescher, N. (1984) *The Riddle of Existence*. Lanham, MD and London: University Press of America.

Rescher, N., ed. (1986) *Current Issues in Teleology*. Lanham, MD and London: University Press of America.

Rescher, N. (2000a) *Nature and Understanding*. Oxford: Oxford University Press.

Rescher, N. (2000b) "Optimalism and Axiological Metaphysics." *The Review of Metaphysics*, June: 807–835.

Rescher, N. (2006) *Studies in Leibniz's Cosmology*. Heusenstamm: Ontos.

Rescher, N. (2010) *Axiogenesis: An Essay in Metaphysical Optimalism*. Lanham, MD: Lexington Books.

Rice, H. (2000) *God and Goodness*. Oxford: Oxford University Press.

Robinson, J.A.T. (1963) *Honest to God*. London: SCM Press.

Rodriguez-Pereyra, G. (1997) "There Might Be Nothing: The Subtraction Argument Improved." *Analysis*, vol. 57 no. 3: 159–66.

Rodriguez-Pereyra, G. (2000) "Lowe's Argument Against Nihilism." *Analysis*, vol. 60 no. 4: 335–340.

Rodriguez-Pereyra, G. (2004) "Modal Realism and Metaphysical Nihilism." *Mind*, October: 683–704.

Rolston, H. (1987) *Science and Religion*. New York: Random House.

Rosen, J. (1991) "Self-generating Universe and Many Worlds." *Foundations of Physics*, August: 977–981.

Rowe, W.L. (1968) "The Cosmological Argument and the Principle of Sufficient Reason." *Man and World*, vol. 1: 278–292.

Rowe, W.L. (1975) *The Cosmological Argument*. Princeton: Princeton University Press.

Rozental, I.L. (1988) *Big Bang, Big Bounce*. Berlin: Springer.

Rundle, B. (2004) *Why There Is Something Rather Than Nothing*. Oxford: Oxford University Press. See esp. section 5.2, "Whether There Might Have Been Nothing."

Russell, B. (1927) *The Analysis of Matter*. London: Kegan Paul.

Russell, B. (1945) *A History of Western Philosophy*. New York: Simon & Schuster. See book 3, ch. 3: "Leibniz."

Russell, B. (1957) *Why I Am Not a Christian, and Other Essays on Religion and Related Subjects*. London: George Allen & Unwin.

Russell, B., and F.C. Copleston (1948) "The Existence of God," a broadcast debate. Printed as pp. 524–541 of *The Collected Papers of Bertrand Russell*, McMaster University Edition, vol. 11. London: Routledge, 1997.

Russell, J.L. (1986) "Scientific Explanation and Metaphysical Explanation: Some Reflections on the Cosmological Argument." *The Heythrop Journal*, April: 163–170.

Russell, R.J., N. Murphy, and C.J. Isham, eds. (1999) *Quantum Cosmology and the Laws of Nature*, 2nd edn. Notre Dame: University of Notre Dame Press.

Russell, R.J., N. Murphy, and A. Peacocke, eds. (1997) *Chaos and Complexity: Scientific Perspectives on Divine Action*. Vatican City State: Vatican Observatory Publications.

Russell, R.J., W. Stoeger, and G. Coyne, eds. (1988) *Physics, Philosophy and Theology*. Vatican City State: Vatican Observatory Publications, and Notre Dame: University of Notre Dame Press.

Rutherford, D. (1995) *Leibniz and the Rational Order of Nature*. Cambridge: Cambridge University Press.

Santayana, G. (1923) *Scepticism and Animal Faith*. New York: Dover. See esp. ch. 7.

Santayana, G. (1927) *The Realm of Essence*. New York: Charles Scribner's Sons. See esp. ch. 4, "Pure Being."

Schelling, F.W.J. von (1936) *Of Human Freedom*, trans. J. Gutman. Chicago: Open Court.

Schelling, F.W.J. von (1984) *Bruno*, trans. M.G. Vater. Albany: SUNY Press.

Schelling, F.W.J. von (2000) *The Ages of the World*, trans. J.M. Wirth, Albany: SUNY Press.

Schlesinger, G.N. (1998) "The Enigma of Existence." *Ratio*, April: 66–77.

Schopenhauer, A. (1883) *The World as Will and Idea*, trans. R.B. Haldane and J. Kemp. London: Routledge & Kegan Paul. See esp. vol. 2, ch. 17.

Schrödinger, E. (1958) *Mind and Matter*. Cambridge: Cambridge University Press.

Schrödinger, E. (1964) *My View of the World*. Cambridge: Cambridge University Press.

Seager, W. (1999) *Theories of Consciousness*. London and New York: Routledge.

Sedley, D. (2007) *Creationism and Its Critics in Antiquity*. Berkeley: University of California Press.

Shoemaker, S. (1969) "Time without Change." *The Journal of Philosophy*, 19 June: 363–381.

Skow, B. (2010) "The Dynamics of Non-Being." *Philosophers' Imprint*, January: 1–14.

Smart, J.J.C. (1955) "The Existence of God," in A. Flew and A. MacIntyre, eds., *New Essays in Philosophical Theology*, London: SCM Press.

Smart, J.J.C. (1987) "Philosophical Problems of Cosmology." *Revue Internationale de Philosophie*, 41: 112–125.

Smart, J.J.C. (1989) *Our Place in the Universe*. Oxford: Blackwell.

Smart, J.J.C., and J.J. Haldane. (1996) *Atheism and Theism*. Oxford: Blackwell.

Smart, N. (1967) "Sankara," pp. 290–292 in P. Edwards, ed., *The Encyclopedia of Philosophy*, vol. 7. New York: Macmillan. See also other articles in the same encyclopedia, particularly "Buddhism" (vol. 1, pp. 416–420) and "Indian Philosophy" (vol. 4, pp. 155–169).

Smith, Q. (1990) "A Natural Explanation for the Existence and Laws of our Universe." *Australasian Journal of Philosophy*, March: 22–43.

Smith, Q. (1993) "The Uncaused Beginning of the Universe," pp. 108–140 of W.L. Craig and Q. Smith, *Theism, Atheism and Big Bang Cosmology*, Oxford: Oxford University Press.

Smith, Q. (1997) "Simplicity and Why the Universe Exists." *Philosophy*, January: 125–132.

Smith, Q. (1999) "The Reason the Universe Exists Is That It Caused Itself to Exist." *Philosophy*, October: 579–586.

Smolin, L. (1997) *The Life of the Cosmos*. New York: Oxford University Press.

Sobel, H. (2004) *Logic and Theism*. Cambridge: Cambridge University Press.

Sommers, F. (1966) "Why Is There Something Rather Than Nothing?" *Analysis*, June: 177–181.

Sorensen, R. (2006) "Nothingness" at http://plato.stanford.edu/entries/nothingness.

Spinoza, B. (1963) *Spinoza's Short Treatise on God, Man, and his Well-Being*, trans. A. Wolf. New York: Russell & Russell.

Spinoza, B. (1949) *Ethics*, ed. J. Gutman. New York: Hafner.

Sprigge, T.L.S. (1983) *The Vindication of Absolute Idealism*. Edinburgh: Edinburgh University Press.

Sprigge, T.L.S. (1984) *Theories of Existence*. Harmondsworth: Penguin Books.

Sprigge, T.L.S. (1997) "Pantheism." *The Monist*, April: 191–217.

Sprigge, T.L.S. (2006) *The God of Metaphysics*. Oxford: Oxford University Press.

Stannard, R. (1999) *The God Experiment*. London: Faber and Faber.

Steinhardt, P.J. (2011) "The Inflation Debate." *Scientific American*, May: 36–43.

Steinhardt, P.J., and N. Turok (2007) *Endless Universe: Beyond the Big Bang*. New York: Doubleday.

Stenger, V.J. (2007) *God: The Failed Hypothesis*. Amherst: Prometheus Books.

Stenger, V.J. (2011) *The Fallacy of Fine-Tuning: Why The Universe Is Not Designed for Us*. Amherst: Prometheus Books.

Stewart, M.Y., ed. (2010) *Science and Religion in Dialogue*, 2 vols. Oxford: Wiley-Blackwell.

Sullivan, K. (1986) "A Critical Survey of the Principle of Order in Chinese Philosophy." *De Philosophia*, vol. 6: 92–117.

Sullivan, T.D. (1990) "Coming To Be Without a Cause." *Philosophy*, July: 261–270.

Susskind, L. (2005a) *The Cosmic Landscape: String Theory and the Illusion of Intelligent Design*. New York: Little Brown.

Susskind, L. (2005b) "Because We're Here." *New Scientist*, 17 December: 48–50.

Susskind, L. (2007) "The Anthropic Landscape of String Theory," pp. 247–266 of B. Carr, ed., *Universe or Multiverse?* Cambridge: Cambridge University Press.

Swinburne, R. (1966) "The Beginning of the Universe." *Proceedings of the Aristotelian Society*, supplementary vol. 40: 125–138.

Swinburne, R. (1977) *The Coherence of Theism*. Oxford: Oxford University Press.

Swinburne, R. (1990a) "God's Necessary Being," in M.M. Olivetti, ed., *L'Argumento Ontologico*. Milan: Cedam.

Swinburne, R. (1990b) "The Limits of Explanation," in D. Knowles, ed., *Explanation and Its Limits*, Cambridge: Cambridge University Press.

Swinburne, R. (1996a) *Is There a God?* New York: Oxford University Press.

Swinburne, R. (1996b) "The Beginning of the Universe and of Time." *Canadian Journal of Philosophy*, June: 169–189.

Swinburne, R. (2004) *The Existence of God*, 2nd edn., revised. Oxford: Clarendon Press.

Swinburne, R. (2005) "Prior Probabilities in the Argument from Fine-Tuning." *Faith and Philosophy*, vol. 22 no. 5: 614–653.

Taylor, A.E. (1903) *Elements of Metaphysics*. London: Methuen.

Taylor, R. (1992) *Metaphysics*, 4th edn. Englewood Cliffs: Prentice-Hall. See esp. ch. 11.

Tegmark, M. (1998) "Is 'The Theory of Everything' Merely the Ultimate Ensemble Theory?" *Annals of Physics*, vol. 21: 1–51.

Tegmark, M. (2003) "Parallel Universes." *Scientific American*, May: 41–51.

Tegmark, M. (2007a) "Reality by Numbers." *New Scientist*, 15 September: 38–41.

Tegmark, M. (2007b) "The Multiverse Hierarchy," pp. 99–125 of B. Carr, ed., *Universe or Multiverse?* Cambridge: Cambridge University Press.

Thomas, H. (1993) "Modal Realism and Inductive Scepticism." *Noûs*, September: 331–354.

Tillich, P. (1952) *The Courage To Be*. New Haven: Yale University Press.

Tillich, P. (1953–63) *Systematic Theology*. London: Nisbet.

Tillich, P. (1962) *The Shaking of the Foundations*. New York: Charles Scribner's Sons.

Treviño, A.J. (2000) "Could the Universe Cause Itself to Exist?" *Philosophy*, October: 604–612.

Tryon, E.P. (1973) "Is the Universe a Vacuum Fluctuation?" *Nature*, 14 December: 396–397.

Tryon, E.P. (1984) "What Made The World?" *New Scientist*, 8 March: 14–16.

Turok, N. (2001) "Inflation and the Beginning of the Universe," pp. 83–96 of J.B. Miller, ed., *Cosmic Questions*. New York: New York Academy of Sciences.

Unger, P. (1984) "Minimizing Arbitrariness: Toward a Metaphysics of Infinitely Many Isolated Concrete Worlds," pp. 29–51 of P.A. French, T.E. Uehling, and H.K. Wettstein, eds., *MidWest Studies in Philosophy*, vol. 9. Minneapolis: University of Minnesota Press.

Urban, W.M. (1929) *The Intelligible World*. London: George Allen & Unwin.

Vaas, R., ed. (2007) *Beyond the Big Bang*. Heidelberg: Springer. Includes, for instance, M. Gasperini and G. Veneziano on String Theory pictures of the birth of the universe.

Vaas, R. (2008) "Ist uns das All auf den Leib geschneidert?" *Bild der Wissenschaft*, 8: 34–32, 49.

Vallicella, W.F. (2000) "Could the Universe Cause Itself to Exist?" *Philosophy*, June: 167–187.

van Inwagen, P. (1993) *Metaphysics*. Boulder, CO: Westview Press. See esp. part 2, "Why the World Is."

van Inwagen, P. (1996) "Why Is There Anything at All?" *Proceedings of the Aristotelian Society*, supplementary vol. 70: 95–110.

van Inwagen, P., and D.W. Zimmerman, eds. (1998) *Metaphysics: The Big Questions*. Oxford: Blackwell. See part 4, "Why Is There a World?," for material from James, Parfit, Swinburne, Rowe, Anselm, and Malcolm.

Varghese, R.A., ed. (1994) *Cosmic Beginnings and Human Ends*. New York: Open Court.

Veneziano, G. (2004) "The Myth of the Beginning of Time." *Scientific American*, May: 54–65.

Vilenkin, A. (1982) "Creation of Universes from Nothing," *Physics Letters B*, 4 November: 25–28.

Vilenkin, A. (1984) "Quantum Creation of Universes," *Physical Review D*, 15 July: 509–511.

Vilenkin, A. (2006) *Many Worlds in One*. New York: Hill & Wang.

Voltaire (1962) *Philosophical Dictionary*, trans. P. Gay, New York: Basic Books. See esp. the article "Why?".

Walker, M.A., and M.M. Circovik (2006) "Astrophysical Fine Tuning, Naturalism, and the Contemporary Design Argument." *International Studies in the Philosophy of Science*, vol. 20 no. 3: 285–307.

Ward, K. (1993) *Images of Eternity*. Oxford: Oneworld Publications.

Ward, K. (1996) *Religion and Creation*. Oxford: Oxford University Press. Includes chapters on the Quran and the Upanishads.

Ward, K. (2006) *Pascal's Fire*. Oxford: Oneworld Publications.

Ward, K. (2008) *The Big Questions in Science and Religion*. West Conshohoken: Templeton Foundation Press.

Ward, K. (2009) *God and the Philosophers*. Minneapolis: Fortress Press. Simultaneously published as *The God Conclusion: God and the Western Philosophical Tradition*. London: Darton, Longman & Todd.

Weinberg, S. (1977) *The First Three Minutes*. New York: Bantam Books.

Weinberg, S. (1993) *Dreams of a Final Theory*. London: Hutchinson.

Weinberg, S. (2001) "A Universe with No Designer," pp. 169–174 of J.B. Miller, ed., *Cosmic Questions*, New York: New York Academy of Sciences.

Weinberg, S. (2007) "Living in the Multiverse," pp. 29–42 of B. Carr, ed., *Universe or Multiverse?* Cambridge: Cambridge University Press.

Weinberg, S. (2011) "Can Science Explain Everything? Anything?", *New York Review of Books*, vol. 48 no. 9 (31 May): 47–50.

Wesson, P.S. (1985) "Avoiding the Big Bang: Matter Production from Minkowski Space and the Early Universe." *Astronomy and Astrophysics*, vol. 151: 276–8.

Wesson, P.S. (2011) *Weaving the Universe: Is Modern Cosmology Discovered or Invented?* Singapore: World Scientific.

Wheeler, J.A. (1977) "Genesis and Observership," pp. 3–33 of R.E. Butts and J. Hintikka, eds., *Foundational Problems in the Special Sciences*, Dordrecht: Reidel.

Wheeler, J.A. (1998) *Geons, Black Holes, and Quantum Foam*. New York: W.W. Norton. See esp. ch. 15, "It from Bit."

Whitehead, A.N. (1927) *Religion in the Making*. Cambridge: Cambridge University Press.

Whitehead, A.N. (1938) *Modes of Thought*. New York: Macmillan.

Whitehead, A.N. (1978) *Process and Reality*, corrected edn. New York: Macmillan.

Whittaker, E. (1946) *Space and Spirit: Theories of the Universe and the Arguments for the Existence of God*. London: Nelson.

Williams. P.W. (1981) "On the Abhidharma Ontology." *Journal of Indian Philosophy*, September: 227–257.

Williamson, T. (2002) "Necessary Existents," pp. 233–251 of A. O'Hear, ed., *Logic, Thought and Language*. Cambridge: Cambridge University Press.

Wilson, N.L. (1956) "Existence Assumptions and Contingent Meaningfulness." *Mind*, July: 366–345.

Wilson, N.L. (1973) "The Two Main Problems of Philosophy." *Dialogue*, vol. 12 no. 2: 199–217.

Wippel, J.F. ed. (2011) *The Ultimate Why Question*. Washington: Catholic University of America Press.

Witherall, A. (2002) *The Problem of Existence*. Aldershot: Ashgate.

Wittgenstein, L. (1922) *Tractatus Logico-Philosophicus,* trans. C.K. Ogden. London: Routledge. See section 6.44.

Wittgenstein, L. (1968) "A Lecture on Ethics," pp. 4–14 of J.H. Gill, ed., *Philosophy Today,* no. 1. New York and London: Macmillan.

Wolter, A.B. (1982) "A Scotistic Approach to the Ultimate Why-Question," pp. 109–130 of P. Morewedge, ed., *Philosophies of Existence.* New York: Fordham University Press.

Worthing, M. (1996) *God, Creation, and Contemporary Physics.* Minneapolis: Fortress Press.

Wynn, M. (1999) *God and Goodness.* London and New York: Routledge.

Zaehner, R.C., ed. and trans. (1966) *Hindu Scriptures.* London: Dent.

Index of Names

Adams, R.M., 28
Aharonov, Y., 169
Alfven, H., 60
al-Ṭūsī, Naṣīr al-Dīn, 160
Anaxagoras, 109–11
Anselm, 103–4, 113–15
Aquinas, 9, 58, 60, 112–13, 143–4, 151, 154, 157, 178, 267, 288
Aristotle, 8, 61–4, 83, 102–3, 107, 110–13, 125, 151, 203–4, 206, 239, 241, 287–8
Armstrong, D.M., 276
Ashtiyani, M., 160
Augustine, 57, 60

Baldwin, T., 276
Barbour, J., 203
Barrow, J.D., 64, 67–8, 185–6, 204, 217
Bentley, R., 84
Bergson, H., 19, 24
Besso, M., 3–4, 138
Bohm, D., 141, 145
Boltzmann, L., 84
Bondi, H., 58, 160–3
Bonnor, W.B., 42–3, 51–2, 57
Bostrom, N., 274
Bousso, R., 174, 190
Bradley, F.H., 19, 24, 46, 145

Carr, B., 207
Carter, B., 216, 248
Collins, R.A., 177, 207–10, 271
Copleston, F.C., 43–4, 53–6
Craig, W.L., 144, 155–9, 278, 287

Dalai Lama XIV, 145, 160–1
Darwin, C., 179, 194, 222
Davies, P., 65, 146–7, 163–70, 184, 251, 254, 257
de Sitter, W., 68
Democritus, 81
Descartes, R., 44, 59, 62, 98, 104, 106–7, 114–15, 141
Deutsch, D., 203
DeWitt, B., 146, 162
Dicke, R.H., 248, 264
Dingle, H., 63
Dirac, P.A.M., 179–80, 248, 264
Dyson, F., 166

Edwards, P., 264
Egan, G., 202
Eilstein, H., 282–4
Einstein, A., 3, 63, 67, 72, 84, 86, 105, 138, 180, 209, 226, 282
Ellis, G.F.R., 255, 259

The Mystery of Existence: Why Is There Anything At All?, First Edition. Edited by John Leslie and Robert Lawrence Kuhn.
© 2013 John Wiley & Sons, Inc. Published 2013 by John Wiley & Sons, Inc.

Index of Concepts

The Mystery of Existence: Why Is There Anything At All?, First Edition. Edited by John Leslie and Robert Lawrence Kuhn.
© 2013 John Wiley & Sons, Inc. Published 2013 by John Wiley & Sons, Inc.